Pliny the Elder: The Natural History Book VII

(with Book VIII 1–34)

Other titles in the series:

Pliny the Elder: The Natural History Book VII

(with Book VIII 1–34)

Edited by Tyler T. Travillian

Bloomsbury Academic
An imprint of Bloomsbury Publishing Plc

B L O O M S B U R Y
LONDON · NEW DELHI · NEW YORK · SYDNEY

Bloomsbury Academic

An imprint of Bloomsbury Publishing Plc

50 Bedford Square	1385 Broadway
London	New York
WC1B 3DP	NY 10018
UK	USA

www.bloomsbury.com

BLOOMSBURY and the Diana logo are trademarks of Bloomsbury Publishing Plc

First published 2015

© Tyler T. Travillian, 2015

British Library Cataloguing-in-Publication Data
A catalogue record for this book is available from the British Library.

ISBN: PB: 978–1–47253–566–5
 ePDF: 978–1–47252–102–6
 ePub: 978–1–47252–101–9

Library of Congress Cataloging-in-Publication Data
Pliny, the Elder, author.
[Naturalis historia. Liber 7]
The Natural history book VII (with book VIII 1–34) / Pliny the Elder; edited by Tyler T. Travillian.
pages cm
Includes bibliographical references and index.
ISBN 978-1-4725-3566-5 (pbk.)
1. Pliny, the Elder. Naturalis historia. I. Travillian, Tyler T., editor. II. Pliny, the Elder. Naturalis historia.
Liber 8. Selections. III. Title.
PA6611.B07T73 2015
508—dc23
2014046977

Typeset by RefineCatch Limited, Bungay, Suffolk
Printed and bound in India

Contents

Preface

The *Natural History* is an addictive read, the only source for much of the knowledge and many of the anecdotes we have received from the ancient world; we learn from it that the earth is a sphere, and then journey to its ends; we travel to Sri Lanka, learn the extremes of human endurance, and discuss life after death. As hard as the *Natural History* is to put down, it should not be so hard to pick up. I hope that this volume will make one of Pliny's most compelling books, his anthropology of humankind, more accessible to students and readers at all stages.

In recent years, Pliny studies have begun to recover from the pall that was first cast over them in 1509 by Leoniceno's attack on Pliny's accuracy and utility. The Budé has issued a nearly complete text and translation, and the Loeb a complete one, which, while necessarily imperfect, are both a sizeable advance over Mayhoff's Teubner. Several excellent volumes have been published meanwhile, including Beagon's *Roman Nature* and *The Elder Pliny on the Human Animal*, Marchetti's *Plinio il Vecchio e la tradizione del moralismo Romano* and *La scienza della natura per un intellettuale romano*, French and Greenway's *Science in the Early Roman Empire*, Gibson and Morello's *Pliny the Elder: Themes and Contexts*, Healy's *Pliny the Elder on Science and Technology*, and Naas's *Le Projet Encyclopédique de Pline l'Ancien*. That these are all written for the specialist is perhaps no surprise, but as there is a growing consensus that Pliny has more to offer than a mine for facts, figures, and quotations, it is appropriate to bring his text to a wider audience, who can appreciate the Roman worldview that breathes from his pages, a sense that all the world is discoverable, knowable, comprehensible— that is, conquerable—and that the Roman is the natural *telos* of humanity. But we see also in Pliny's voluminous quotations a glimpse of the sheer breadth of the intellectual activity in the ancient world of which we can so easily lose sight in the tightly intertextual and self-referential world of the Ciceros, Horaces, and Vergils.

In making this commentary, I have tried to take for granted as little contextual and historical knowledge as possible. Some readers may find the explanations of the more famous individuals, as for example Cicero, tedious, but the aim has been to be as inclusive as possible, so that all readers may find their footing more easily. To this end, I have avoided abbreviations even of common authors and works, and I have paid special attention to identifying every named person, providing help with grammatical structures and ambiguous or difficult syntactical features, and, on occasion, explaining Pliny's apparent digressions or seemingly bizarre leaps. Pliny deserves to be credited with the significant intellect he in fact possessed and to be approached charitably; we may often find in his disconcertingly rough style a conscious effect, an implication, or a commentary on the "facts" he reports and so painstakingly attributes to other authors.

I am glad to mention here my debt to my colleagues Lee Fratantuono at Ohio Wesleyan University and David O. Davies at the University of Dallas, who encouraged this project in its early stages, to Eric D. Nelson at Pacific Lutheran University, who has been free with support and kind words, and to the librarians in charge of interlibrary loan at Pacific Lutheran, who have truly gone above and beyond. Especial thanks must go to my students Molly Lindberg, for her perspective on the text and astute comments, Shiori Oki for her tireless work wrangling the glossary, and Molly Ubben for her artistic skills and attention to detail in drawing the images. All errors remain, of course, my own.

Introduction

Pliny's life and early career

Early years

Gaius Plinius Secundus, whom we know as Pliny the Elder to distinguish him from his namesake nephew, was born in 23 or 24 CE at Novum Comum (modern Como) in Transpadane Gaul to an equestrian family of means. Novum Comum had been founded in 59 BCE by Julius Caesar as a bulwark against the tribes to the North and populated with a mix of Romans, Italians, and Greeks imported for that purpose. We know little more of Pliny's parents save that his father must have possessed a fortune between 400,000 and 1,000,000 sesterces. To place this sum, by no means a large one in the Imperial period, in context, a common foot soldier in the legion at this time earned 900 sesterces per year.

As might be expected of an equestrian family with aspirations, Pliny's father sent his young son to Rome in the 30s, where Publius Pomponius Secundus, the general and tragedian, introduced him to political life, becoming his patron, his teacher, and eventually his friend. Unlike Pliny's *conterraneus*, Catullus, whose tenure under Memmius in Bithynia was more of a distraction than a calling, Pliny seems genuinely to have enjoyed military service. Equestrians at this time were encouraged to serve at least one tour in the army, but it was not an unavoidable obligation and did not necessarily involve serving in a region that would see battle: they might rather prefer administrative or bureaucratic posts. Pliny, however, served multiple tours from 46–58, each in Germany: first on the Lower Rhine in Gnaeus Domitius Corbulo's command against the Chauci in 47, then on the Upper Rhine under his friend and patron Pomponius Secundus from 49–50/51.

Figure 1.1 Pliny's phalera.

Pliny met the future emperor Titus (who was at this time around 16) on a further expedition on the Lower Rhine in 56–57/8 under Duvius Avitus, from which expedition likely dates the *phalera* found at Castra Vetera (modern Xanten) attesting to Pliny's praefecture of the alae (cavalry).

Between excursions in Germany, Pliny must have begun his earliest two works, his *De Iaculatione Equestri* (*On Fighting From Horseback*) and *Bella Germaniae* (*The Wars of Germany*). The impetus for the latter came to him in a dream in which Drusus Nero, the brother of Tiberius and father of Claudius, "prayed that he [Pliny] defend him against the wrongs of being forgotten" (Pliny Minor, *Ep.* 3.5.2). Drusus had secured several victories in Germany from 13 BCE until his death from injuries sustained in falling from his horse in 9 BCE, so he was a natural figure for Pliny, with his German service, to eulogize. It seems unlikely that Pliny, just beginning a promising career, meant the *Bella Germaniae* as an implicit criticism of Claudius's policies toward Germany, but rather saw an opportunity to engage his own personal experience while at the same time ingratiating the regime by restoring glory to Claudius's father.[1]

---

[1]   See J. Reynolds 'The Elder Pliny and his Times,' in French and Greenway (eds), *Science in the Early Empire: Pliny the Elder, his Sources and Influence*, London: Croom Helm, 1986, 5–6.

Under Nero

In 59 CE Pliny returned to Rome, but by this point his patron, Pomponius Secundus, had died, as had the emperor Claudius. While we cannot know for certain Pliny's attitudes toward Nero during Nero's lifetime, years later he held the same low opinion of Nero as did much of the upper class, calling him "the human race's firebrand" (*NH* 7.45) and "in all his principate, an enemy of the human race" (*NH* 7.46). If, as seems likely, these comments reflect Pliny's contemporary assessment of Nero, he was right to keep silent. As early as 63 CE, a conspiracy coalesced around the senator Gaius Calpurnius Piso, which aimed at assassinating Nero and replacing him with the senator. After long delays, the conspirators intended to achieve their goal at the festival of the Cerialia in mid April of 65, but the plot was uncovered, implicating some 41 men and women of all classes—senator, freedman, and slave—many of whom Nero invited to commit suicide. Among these were his tutor Lucius Annaeus Seneca the Younger, the philosopher and tragedian, and Seneca's nephew Marcus Annaeus Lucanus, author of the epic *Pharsalia* (Tacitus, *Annales* 15.48–74).

Pliny, however, seems to have taken a temporary hiatus from public life and avoided their fates. At any rate, he must not have actively suffered under Nero or we would expect to have learned of it from his nephew. As Pliny the Younger tells us instead, he focused on his literary ambitions: "*scripsit sub Nerone novissimis annis, cum omne studiorum genus paulo liberius et erectius periculosum servitus fecisset*": "In the last years of Nero's reign he wrote, when every type of pursuit, even a little freer or more assertive, had become dangerous due to the common slavery." First came his *Studiosus* in 66/67, a handbook on rhetoric in three books (later divided into six books due to their length), and then the *Dubius Sermo*, a treatise on grammar in eight books published in 67/8.

Return to politics

The year 69 CE brought a welcome turn for Pliny: Nero had committed suicide in 68, and in the chaos that followed, the general Titus Flavius

Vespasianus, father to his former comrade in arms and friend, Titus, became the emperor Vespasian. With this, Pliny's political career surged. Pliny became close to Vespasian, often attending him at home in the early hours of the morning when both liked to start their work. We know that he served multiple procuratorships, positions with financial and occasionally military responsibilities in the provinces, but the exact offices, their number, their dates, and even the provinces are uncertain. The most thorough effort at reconstruction suggests four possible procuratorships: Gallia Narbonensis in 70, the least secure; Africa from 70/71 to 71/72, likely; Hispania Tarraconensis from 72/73–74, the most secure and datable on evidence from Pliny the Younger, *Epistle* 3.5.17; and Gallia Belgica 74–6, possible but uncertain.[2] In the course of these postings, Pliny found time—largely in the evenings, at night, and on walks and marches—to write a weighty continuation of Aufidius Bassus's *History* in 31 books, covering the years 50 CE to 71 CE, the end of the reign of Claudius to the accession of Vespasian. We can expect that this work had a strong pro-Flavian bent, as we learn from the preface to Pliny's *Natural History* (pref. 20) that Pliny himself wished the work to be published posthumously in order to avoid charges of fawning or bias.

Final years

The prefecture of the imperial fleet in Campania, stationed at Misenum (*praefectus classis Misenensis*) was Pliny's final office, from 76–79. This was largely an administrative post, in charge of repairs, maintenance, overseeing safe grain trade in the Mediterranean, not one that required Pliny's constant presence and oversight. This left him time to attend Vespasian in Rome and simultaneously to assemble what would be his final work, the *Natural History*, a compendium in 37 volumes of all

---

[2] Ronald Syme, 'Pliny the Procurator,' *Harvard Studies in Classical Philology* 73 (1969), 201–236.

available scientific and natural knowledge. Pliny seems to have composed the *Natural History* beginning in 76 and to have completed his work in 78, although portions may have remained unedited at the time of his death in 79.

On August 24th, 79 CE, Pliny happened to be present at Misenum when, around 1:00 in the afternoon, a great cloud appeared in the distance rising from a mountain which he would later determine to be Vesuvius. Spurred on at first by scientific curiosity to observe the mountain, Pliny's intentions quickly changed to the humanitarian when he received a letter from his friend Rectina begging him to save her. Her villa lay along the shoreline beneath the mountain. Escape would prove impossible. The rough seas and winds prevented access to Rectina, but Pliny was able to reach his friend Pomponianus, son of his old patron Pomponius. The whole household was in disarray, unsure and frightened by the ongoing disaster. Pliny calmed their disquiet as much with his own even demeanor as with his presence of mind: he prepared their baggage for an escape by ship which would not happen, and in the middle of the night as earthquakes shook the foundations of the villa and ash and pumice fell thick enough to bury a man, they escaped by foot, with pillows tied to their heads as their only protection against the raining debris. Pliny himself did not make it. He suffered some ailment akin to asthma and the labor of clambering over pumice and ash in a cloud of sulfurous vapor overcame him. After falling several times, he found himself unable to get back up. His body was recovered two days later with a peaceful expression, as if he were sleeping.

Pliny's works

Lost

Title	Length	Date
De Iaculatione Equestri (On Fighting from Horseback)	1 volume	between 62–66

Title	Length	Date
De Vita Pomponii Secundi (On the Life of Pomponius Secundus)	2 volumes	between 62–66
Bella Germaniae (The German Wars)	20 volumes	between 62–66
Studiosus (The Student)	3 volumes (later 6)	66/67
Dubius Sermo (Uncertainties of Expression)	8 volumes	67/68
A fine Aufidi Bassi (Continuation of Aufidius Bassus)	31 volumes	70–76

Extant

Naturalis Historia (Natural History)	37 volumes	76–78

Suetonius, Life of Pliny the Elder[3]

Plinius Secundus Novecomensis equestribus militiis industrie functus procurationes quoque splendidissimas atque continuas summa integritate administravit, et tamen liberalibus studiis tantam operam dedit, ut non temere quis plura in otio scripserit. Itaque bella omnia, quae unquam cum Germanis gesta sunt, XXXVIII voluminibus comprehendit, item Naturalis Historiae XXXVII libros absolvit. Periit clade Campaniae; cum enim Misenensi classi praeesset et flagrante Vesuvio ad explorandas propius causas liburnica pertendisset, neque adversantibus ventis remeare posset, vi pulveris ac favillae oppressus est, vel ut quidam existimant a servo suo occisus, quem deficiens aestu ut necem sibi maturaret oraverat. Hic in

---

[3]　I give here the text reconstructed by Michael Reeve, 'The *Vita Plinii*,' in Roy K. Gibson and Ruth Morello (eds), *Pliny the Elder: Themes and Contexts*, Leiden: Brill, 2011, 207–222.

libris XX milia rerum dignarum ex lectione voluminum circiter duum milium complexus est; primus autem liber quasi index xxxvi librorum sequentium consummationem totius operis et species continet titulorum.

Plinius Secundus, from Novum Comum, after he had completed his equestrian service industriously, also administered the most distinguished procuratorships one after another with the most complete honesty, and nevertheless he gave so much attention to the pursuit of the liberal arts that not easily could anyone have written more, even at leisure. And so he included all the wars which have ever been waged with the Germans in 38 volumes[4]; likewise he completed 37 books of his *Natural History*. He perished in the disaster at Campania. When he was in charge of the fleet at Misenum, Vesuvius caught fire and he set forth on a galley to explore the reasons a bit more closely. But due to the adverse winds, he was not able to return, and he was overcome by the force of the dust and ash, or, as some think, he was killed by his slave when, weakening due to the heat, he had begged the slave to hasten his death. In the books here, he included 20,000 noteworthy items from his perusal of around 2,000 volumes; the first book, however, is a kind of index of the 36 books that follow and contains a summary of the whole work and the topics of its sections.

Pliny the Younger on the Elder's work ethic

Epistle 3.5.7–17[5]

7 Miraris quod tot volumina multaque in his tam scrupulosa homo occupatus absolverit? Magis miraberis si scieris illum aliquamdiu causas actitasse, decessisse anno sexto et quinquagensimo, medium tempus distentum impeditumque qua officiis maximis qua amicitia principum egisse. 8 Sed erat acre ingenium, incredibile studium, summa vigilantia.

---

4   A clear error influenced by the XXXVII of the following clause. Pliny the Younger (3.5) gives the number of books at 20.

5   I follow the text of A. N. Sherwin White, *Fifty Letters of Pliny*, 2nd ed., Oxford: Oxford University Press, 2000, 19–21, which in turn follows the OCT of R. A. B. Mynors.

Lucubrare Vulcanalibus incipiebat non auspicandi causa sed studendi statim a nocte multa, hieme vero ab hora septima vel cum tardissime octava, saepe sexta. Erat sane somni paratissimi, non numquam etiam inter ipsa studia instantis et deserentis. 9 Ante lucem ibat ad Vespasianum imperatorem (nam ille quoque noctibus utebatur), inde ad delegatum sibi officium. Reversus domum quod reliquum temporis studiis reddebat. 10 Post cibum saepe (quem interdiu levem et facilem veterum more sumebat) aestate si quid otii iacebat in sole, liber legebatur, adnotabat excerpebatque. Nihil enim legit quod non excerperet; dicere etiam solebat nullum esse librum tam malum ut non aliqua parte prodesset. 11 Post solem plerumque frigida lavabatur, deinde gustabat dormiebatque minimum; mox quasi alio die studebat in cenae tempus. Super hanc liber legebatur adnotabatur, et quidem cursim. 12 Memini quendam ex amicis, cum lector quaedam perperam pronuntiasset, revocasse et repeti coegisse; huic avunculum meum dixisse: 'Intellexeras nempe?' Cum ille adnuisset, 'Cur ergo revocabas? decem amplius versus hac tua interpellatione perdidimus.' 13 Tanta erat parsimonia temporis. Surgebat aestate a cena luce, hieme intra primam noctis et tamquam aliqua lege cogente.

14 Haec inter medios labores urbisque fremitum. In secessu solum balinei tempus studiis eximebatur (cum dico balinei, de interioribus loquor; nam dum destringitur tergiturque, audiebat aliquid aut dictabat). 15 In itinere quasi solutus ceteris curis, huic uni vacabat: ad latus notarius cum libro et pugillaribus, cuius manus hieme manicis muniebantur, ut ne caeli quidem asperitas ullum studii tempus eriperet; qua ex causa Romae quoque sella vehebatur. 16 Repeto me correptum ab eo, cur ambularem: 'poteras' inquit 'has horas non perdere'; nam perire omne tempus arbitrabatur, quod studiis non impenderetur. 17 Hac intentione tot ista volumina peregit electorumque commentarios centum sexaginta mihi reliquit, opisthographos quidem et minutissimis scriptos; qua ratione multiplicatur hic numerus.

Are you amazed that a busy man completed so many volumes, and many of them so detailed? You will be more amazed if you know that he had sometimes argued court cases, that he had died in his 56th year, and that he spent the middle of his life distracted and impeded sometimes by the highest offices and sometimes by the friendship of the princes. But his intellect was keen, his energy unbelievable, and his powers of attention of the highest caliber. He was in the habit of beginning to work at night in full dark during the festival of Vulcan, not for the good omens, but for the sake of studying; indeed, in the winter, he would start from the seventh hour, or the eighth at the latest—often from the sixth. He could fall asleep at a moment, and it often came upon him and left as suddenly in the middle of his studies. He was in the habit of going before dawn to Vespasian when he was emperor, for he too liked to use the nocturnal hours, and he would go from there to the office that had been delegated him. After he had come home, he would give what time was left to his studies. Often after his meal—which, during the day, he kept light and simple in the custom of the ancients—if he had any free time, he would lay in the sun, a book would be read, and he would make annotations and excerpts. There was no book he read which he would not take excerpts from: he was even in the habit of saying that there was no book so bad that it would not be useful in some passage. After laying in the sun, he generally took a cold bath, then ate a snack, then slept a little; soon after that, as if it were a new day, he would study until dinnertime. Over dinner, a book would be read and annotated, but in a cursory way. I recall that a certain one of his friends, when the reader had mispronounced something, called him back to it and made him repeat it; my uncle said to him, "Surely you understood?" When he agreed that he had, my uncle asked, "Why then did you call him back to it? We lost ten more verses to this interruption of yours." So carefully did he guard his time. In summer, it was his custom to rise from dinner when it was still light; in winter, before the first hour of night had elapsed, and he did this as if there were a law compelling him.

These were his way in the midst of his labors and the tumult of the city. On retreat, only the time spent on his bath was stolen from his studies, and when I say the time spent on his bath, I speak of the actual bath chambers, for when he was being scraped down and scrubbed, he was listening to something or dictating something. When he was on a journey, it was as if he had been freed from his other concerns: he had time for this one thing. A secretary was by his side with a book and tablets, whose hands in winter were fortified with gloves so that not even the harshness of heaven could snatch away any opportunity for study. It also was for this reason that he rode in a sedan at Rome. I recall that he once scolded me for walking: "You could have used these hours beneficially," he said, for he considered lost all time that was not spent on studies. With this type of exertion he completed all those volumes I mentioned, and he left me 160 commentaries on choice passages, which were indeed written on both sides of the papyrus and in very small script, and with this taken into consideration, the number is really several-fold larger.

Introduction to Book VII

The structure of Book VII

For the overarching structure of Book VII, corresponding to the Roman numerals in the table of contents, I have followed Schilling,[6] but I see a somewhat different arrangement within the larger outline than does either Schilling or Beagon (2005), which I will sketch below. The overall structure is carefully composed and transparent: (1) §§1–8, an introduction that addresses the marvelous and paradoxical nature of man, setting the stage for a deeper investigation of the unexpected, though inevitable vicissitudes of human life; (2) §§9–32, an excursus into the variation possible within the human species, which serves not just as a reflection on the inventive powers of nature but also a rumination on what being human means; (3) §§33–129, a study of mankind from birth and maturation to the limits of all its capabilities; (4) §§130–190, a sober reflection on the human condition: what it means to be happy, how long we have to live, what type of death is best,

---

[6]   Schilling (2003), pp. ix–xi.

and what comes after; and (5) §§191–215, a list of human inventions that parallels the inventions of nature and sets man-made culture opposite nature-made man.

Within these major sections, however, I see a more detailed progression. Pliny introduces his book by noting that humankind's place in the world is paradoxical: it is at once the ruler for whom nature has crafted all other things, and also the weakest and most vulnerable of nature's creations. The book proper begins with an attempt to define humanity, but by a method we will see Pliny apply again and again: he traces the extremes in an effort to encompass the whole. Human populations vary considerably from each other in both custom and appearance, and while there were once marvelous types in all regions of the world according to the sources, now they are relegated to the shifting edges. Here Pliny exposes the credulity of the geographers and ethnographers who were his sources, but also an unsurprising Romano-centric worldview in which the Mediterranean (and Rome in particular) is the center of the world, as if those at the far reaches led in fact as fog-like an existence as that perceived by Pliny. After looking at the outliers of humanity and so implicitly defining the physical and cultural characteristics of a normative humanity, Pliny considers the physical origins of the "normal" human. First, generation: a woman's experience of pregnancy and how it affects the gestating child, oddities of birth, and disorders of birth, by which he again creates a normative experience in the negative space defined by the abnormal, and finally ends with sterility, disorders of the generative organs, and menopause. This precisely mirrors the book as a whole, moving from oddities of birth then chronologically through the physical aspects of gestation, birth itself, appearance of the child, and finally into sterility (a kind of diseased relation), and menopause (procreative death). In Pliny's depiction, ontogeny recapitulates humanity. His description of the resulting child seems at first brief and capricious, focusing more on teeth and abnormally tall or short adults than on children *per se*. The teeth, however, allow a child to chew its own food, granting it a true separation from the mother, which, unlike the other animals, it did not gain at birth. It is the teeth that give a child full membership into society as an individual, and so they represent the next stage of development in a concrete way. As if by way of explanation, Pliny highlights that one cannot determine childhood and adulthood by physical maturation, as there are those who grow very rapidly, entering into puberty while still young children (as for example the son of the equestrian Tacitus at *NH* 7.76) and those who never grow beyond a couple of feet. This leads Pliny naturally into a discussion of what the normative, adult human is capable of, starting with the physical body. Self-control comes first as the fundamental quality that defines a Roman *vir*. From there, the other physical attributes: strength, stamina, vision, hearing, and endurance. This last brings Pliny to think about what happens when the body cannot endure and begins to fail. Postponing death for a later section, he notes instead the physical effects of memory loss, which serve as a segue to excellent deeds, particularly those of Julius Caesar, whose greatness was due in large part to his mental energy. Any discussion of Caesar necessarily implicates his foe and Rome's greatest general, Pompey, on whom a long digression is lavished—to the ultimate glory of Rome and Caesar. After numerous examples of bravery in battle, Pliny moves to literary genius, showing how one general after another gave way to great artists and scholars: Homer, Archilochus, Sophocles, Plato, Thucydides, Posidonius, Ennius, Varro, and of course Cicero. In this long catalogue, Cicero stands in opposition to Homer: the Roman orator and philosopher to the Greek poet, but also in opposition to Caesar: littérateur to general. Pliny makes clear which he prefers. There is, of course, excellence in all the other spheres of morality, art, and science, and these receive their mention, ending oddly with instances of extreme prices paid for slaves. Schilling considers this a digression,[7] but the implication of the placement is that these slaves were priced and purchased for their abilities: a suggestion on Pliny's part that excellence is independent of status and circumstance. Any slave could have excellences or genius despite being reduced by the vicissitudes of life.

---

[7]   Schilling (2003), p. x.

It should be less of a surprise then that Pliny transitions from here to reflections on the human condition generally. He looks at what it means to be happy and the apparently foolish ways in which many people and cultures attempt to quantify their happiness. There are many people who have possessed excellences and genius, who have achieved great deeds, earned fame, and are well remembered, but their lives were full of misfortune and unhappiness, most notably Augustus, whose sea of misfortunes nearly drowned him time and again. For Pliny, as for Herodotus's Solon, happiness is not an emotion or a feeling but a judgment about the condition of a person's *life in full*. And life, as he moves into discussion of longevity, is deeply uncertain. Astrological authorities give wildly disparate and fantastical figures for human lifespans, disagree with each other's interpretations of the stars, and are easily proved unreliable. All that can be known for certain is the certain unknowableness of the time of one's death. Coupled with the unpleasant infirmities of old age, this makes a sudden, unexpected death the happiest event of a person's life—the alternative being necessarily unpleasant. After giving examples of those who were granted this blessing and passed out of life while enjoying their final moments, or at least not ruining them, Pliny ruminates on what comes after death, concluding somewhat darkly that all thought of an afterlife is a child's fancy and necessarily demoralizing to those who hope for rest from life. We should, he tells us, expect no more after death than we had before birth.

This would seem be an appropriate place for the book to end, and yet it continues in what Schilling calls an "appendix"[8]: the list of inventions and inventors. But this is no appendix. Individual persons die, but after their deaths they live on in their contributions to society: this is the afterlife, denied to the soul but present to the intellect. The list of inventors, much like Homer's catalogue of the ships, appears dense at first, but it has a much greater significance for the work as a whole: it outlines the progress of civilization out of barbarism made by the efforts of human genius, thus opposing civilization to nature.

8   Schilling (2003), p. xi.

Civilization, that is, culture, is a man-made order imposed upon the very nature that created humankind, improving the garden by cultivation, as it were. This list also serves as a preamble to the true culmination of the book: the three great international accords: the Ionic alphabet, the barber, and clocks. Each of these is a fundamental aspect of civilization: first, the written record, which allows thoughts, ideas, personalities, and memory to be passed down accurately through the generations and across nations; second, personal grooming, which indicates self-reflection, self-improvement, self-discipline, and implies an awareness of the other as a separate self experiencing the self as an other (that is, other people see us just as we see them and so we groom for them as much as for ourselves); third, time-keeping asserts objective external control over nature: by dividing, structuring, and tracking, mankind determines the day rather than the reverse. These are not just marks of civilization, the dominance of man over nature that separates humanity from animals, but by their international quality, they transcend the local, moving culture to a broader, grander level. It is worth noting that while the vast majority of the inventors in the catalogue are Greek, the beneficiaries of the international accords are Roman. For Pliny, mankind—person and culture—culminates in the Roman.

Book 8.1–34: The elephant

It may seem counter-intuitive to include the first chapters of Book VIII in a text and commentary on Book VII, but the transition from man to animal is never so distinct as we would like it to be, and of this Pliny was no less aware than modern biologists and behaviorists. The *Natural History* has a fundamentally anthropocentric arrangement: it begins with a cosmology and geography (Books 2–6), leading up to that creature for which the universe exists, man (Book 7), chief of the animals (Books 8–11) and the plants (Books 12–27), and finally the various elements as they are useful to and used by man (Books 28–37). The most interesting transition, and the most illuminating for Pliny's discussion of mankind, is that between man and the animal kingdom of which he is an implicit part.

Pliny opens Book VIII with the animal "nearest to the human disposition",[9] the elephant, and he invests it with such emotion and inner life that it is easy to forget as one reads the Latin that he is referring to an animal and not another human tribe. The elephant serves at once as transition and as an indispensable foil for man: What separates man from an animal that thinks, feels, learns, and remembers? What does man's treatment of the elephant, its enslavement and domination, say about man's relationship to the entire kingdom and to other men? In so far as the elephant is a reflection of man in the cosmos as first among living things and yet separate even from the other sentient animals it serves, with apologies to Milton, to justify the ways of man to men.

Pliny's sources

Sources in Book VII cited by Pliny

Acta: The "acts," or public records of the state include the resolutions and records of the senate, the minutes of the senate meetings, the archives of the imperial courts, the *acta urbis* (a regular publication of public news), the *acta ordinis* (a bulletin of the *ordo decurionum*), the *acta militaria* concerning the business of the troops, the *acta triumphorum* recording imperial triumphs, and records from the provinces. (*BNP*, s.v. "Acta")

Aesculapius (school of): Aesculapius was the son of Apollo and a human woman, raised by the Centaur Cheiron to be a physician, and killed by Zeus's lightning for bringing the dead back to life. He then became the god of healing with his cult centered at Epidaurus. The Romans brought the god in the form of a snake to their city in 293 BCE in response to a plague, and his worship was established on

---

9   Proximum humanis sensibus (8.1).

Tiber Island. The cult of Aesculapius was exceedingly popular and lasted well into the Christian period.

Agatharchides: Agatharchides of Cnidos was a 2nd c. BCE historian and geographer who produced a number of works, the most well-known of which are his *History of Asia* in ten books, *History of Europe* in forty-nine books, and *About the Red Sea* in five books.

Agrippina: The mother of the emperor Nero, Julia Agrippina, known as Agrippina the Younger, was the daughter of Germanicus and Agrippina the Elder (herself the daughter of Augustus's daughter Julia and his general Agrippa). She married the emperor Claudius in 49 CE, who then adopted Nero. At some point she wrote memoirs, which both Tacitus (*Annales* 4.53.2; 13.14.3) and Pliny (*NH* 7.46) used as source material.

Alexander Polyhistor, Lucius Cornelius: Alexander (ca. 110–post 40 BCE) was the student of Crates of Mallus, but he became a slave of Cornelius Lentulus after the Mithridatic War. He was freed by Sulla and became a Roman citizen in 81. He was the teacher of Hyginus and the author of so many works that he earned the name "Polyhistor". Twenty five titles are still extant, which show that he wrote works on ethnography, philosophy, and history, as well as commentaries on Corinna and Alcman. (*BNP* s.v. "Alexander [23] Polyhistor")

Anacreon: (fl. 536/5 BCE) Born on the island Teos, Anacreon was a prolific poet whose writings survive only in fragments (the Anacreontics). He composed in a variety of lyric meters and stanzas, including elegiac couplets, iambics, glyconics, and pherecrateans. The extant fragments focus on themes of wine and love. According to tradition, he died by choking on a grape. (See Valerius Maximus 9.12.)

Annales Maximi: The Pontifex Maximus, amongst his other charges, kept a yearly record of important events. This record originally stood on a publicly posted plaque (*tabula*), but that custom was discontinued by Publius Mucius Scaevola around 130 BCE. The collected *Annales* were published possibly as early as Scaevola himself, but definitely by the imperial period.

Anticlides: Anticlides of Athens, a 3rd c. BCE historian of Alexander the Great. He also wrote a *Nostoi* (*Homecomings*) and a *Deliaca* (*On Delos*). (*BNP*, s.v. "Anticlides")

Apollonides: A geographer of the 1st c. BCE, Apollonides' only known work is a now-fragmentary *periplus* of Europe.

Archemachus: A 3rd c. BCE historian who wrote a history of Euboea, the large island off the coast of Attica.

Aristeas Proconnesius: An epic poet of the 7th c. BCE, Aristeas wrote an *Arimaspea* in three books detailing the history of the Arimaspi. He also wrote a prose *Theogony* and, according to the *Suda*, practiced astral projection (*Suda*, A3900).

Aristotle: (384–322 BCE). Aristotle was born in Stagira, a city of the Chalcidice. His father was the court physician to Amyntas II, king of Macedon, so he had close connections to the Macedonian royal family. Around 367 he joined Plato's Academy in Athens, where he stayed until Plato's death in 348/7. The rise of Philip II made Athens a difficult place for Aristotle, so he left Athens, at one point becoming the tutor to the young Alexander. He returned to Athens in 335 where he founded the Lycaeum, but again had to depart after Alexander's death in 323, dying the next year in Chalcis. Aristotle's extant works range over "(a) logic and metaphysics; (b) nature, life, and mind; (c) ethics, politics, art"; *OCD3rd*, 166.

Artemidorus: A geographer of the 1st c. BCE from Ephesus who wrote two known works: *Commentaries on Ionia* and a *Geographies* in 11 books.

Asconius Pedianus, Quintus: Asconius (3–88 CE) wrote commentaries on the speeches of Cicero, providing much historical information. His lost works included a *Life of Sallust, Against Vergil's Detractors*, and a work on longevity. (*BNP*, s.v. "Asconius Pedianus")

Baeton: An official in charge of measuring the distances on Alexander's marches. Pliny twice calls him "*itinerum eius mensor*" "measurer of his journeys", where "his" refers to Alexander the Great. See also *NH* 6.61–3, 69.

Berosus: An Alexandrian astrologer and contemporary of Alexander the Great. He wrote a history of Chaldea titled *Babylōniaka* in three books and dedicated it to Antiochus I of Syria.

Callimachus: Greek poet and scholar under Ptolemy II Philadelphus (285–246 BCE) and Ptolemy III Euergetes. Callimachus wrote over 800 books, but only a small portion of his works still survive: six hymns, sixty epigrams, a selection of his *Paradoxa*, and fragments. His most famous quotation is μέγα βιβλίον μέγα κακόν (mega biblion meka kakon), "a big book is a big evil". This is usually taken to mean that short works are to be preferred over long ones, but a more accurate reading would be that tight books are preferred to bloated ones. Shorter, refined poems with careful, conscious construction moving between genres and picking the best from each, like flowers or drops of spring water—that is the Callimachean aesthetic. The Roman poets beginning with Catullus and his circle (the so-called "neoterics") adopted the Callimachean aesthetic.

Cicero: (106–43 BCE). Marcus Tullius Cicero was a Roman orator and consul of 63 BCE during the Catilinarian conspiracy. Cicero was educated in oratory and philosophy in Rome and Greece, making a name for himself in the law courts in 80 when he successfully defended Roscius against a charge of parricide. He held the quaestorship of Sicily in 75, and after his return, he prosecuted Sicily's former governer, Gaius Verres, for corruption. That case (and the defeat of his rival Quintus Hortensius, who had defended Verres) earned Cicero the reputation of Rome's greatest orator. In 66 he won the praetorship, and as praetor, supported the Lex Manilia (see Pliny, *NH* §7.96), which gave Pompey control over the Mithridatic War. Cicero won the consulship for 63, the first *novus homo* to do so in 30 years. In the process, he defeated Lucius Sergius Catilina, an impoverished member of a noble family, who then tried to raise a slave revolt, which Cicero discovered and put down. As a consequence of his role in executing the Catilinarian conspirators, Cicero was briefly exiled from Rome in 61 and not recalled until 57, after which he largely dedicated himself to his philosophical writings. When civil war broke out between Pompey and Caesar, Cicero joined the Republican (Pompeian) faction, but he went over to Caesar after the Republican defeat at Pharsalus. Cicero played little role in politics after this, but his opposition to Marc Antony irritated the latter sufficiently that in 43, Antony, as part of a deal with Octavian, proscribed Cicero. Antony's soldiers killed Cicero on 7 December 43. Cicero was a prolific author. Of 88 known speeches, 58 survive, along with two major works on rhetoric (*De inventione; De oratore*), several minor works (*Partitiones oratoriae; Topica; De optimo genere oratorum*), poetic works (*Consulatus suus; De temporibus suis; Aratea*), letters (*Ad Atticum; Ad Quintum fratrem; Ad Brutum; Ad familiares*), and 17 philosophical works. Pliny is likely drawing from Cicero's *Memorabilia*, a now-lost work on marvels.

Claudius Caesar: (10 BCE–54 CE). The son of Antonia Minor, the younger daughter of Marc Antony and Octavia. Antonia was grandmother to Claudius's predecessor Caligula and to Claudius's last wife, Agrippina. Claudius himself had a limp and a lisp and was thought unsuited for rule until 41 CE when, immediately after the assassination of Gaius Caesar (Caligula), a soldier found him in hiding and took him to the praetorians where he was hailed as emperor. Claudius proved to be a strong emperor, overseeing numerous conquests, including that of Britain, and ruling three times longer than his predecessor. He was also a scholar and historian, writing works on Roman, Etruscan, and Carthaginian history.

Clitarchus: Clitarchus (or Cleitarchus) was the son of Dinon of Colophon, a Greek historian who wrote a history of Persia. Clitarchus met Alexander the Great in 324/3 and authored a history of Alexander ca. 280 BCE, which may have been a source for a number of later histories of Alexander, including those of Curtius Rufus and Plutarch.

Crates Pergamenus: Crates of Pergamum, originally from the city Mallus in Cilicia, was a 2nd c. BCE grammarian and textual critic. He became the head of the library at Pergamum and composed works on Homer,

Hesiod, Alcman, Pindar, Euripides, and a number of other ancient authors. Crates was also a member of a Greek embassy to Rome sent, according to Suetonius, *de Grammaticis* 2, by king Attalus II.

Critodemus: A Hellenistic astrologer who wrote a work titled *Vision*. His work seems to have dealt primarily with horoscopes. (*BNP* s.v. "Critodemus")

Ctesias: Ctesias of Cnidos was a physician to Artaxerxes II (from 405–398/7 BCE) and a historian. He wrote a *Periodos*, a *History of India*, and a *History of Persia* from the mythical founding of Assyria to 398/7.

Damastes: A geographer and historian from the 5th c. BCE. He was student of Hellanicus. His works are not extant. (*BNP*, s.v. "Damastes")

Damon: Damon was a historian who wrote on Byzantium, as we can see from Aelian, *Various Histories* 3.14 and Athenaeus 10.442c.

Duris: (340–270 BCE). Duris was a historian as well as tyrant of Samos beginning ca. 300. He wrote a number of works, among which are the now-fragmentary *Macedonica, Chronicles of the Samians*, and a biography of Agathocles, tyrant of Syracuse.

Ennius: (239–169 BCE) Called *semigraecus* (Suet. *De gramm.* 1.2) for his fluency in Greek and southern-Italian origins, Ennius was brought to Rome in 204 BCE by Cato the Elder. Once there, he taught Greek and Latin grammar. In addition to works of many other kinds, Ennius produced tragedy and comedy, and an epic, the *Annales*, on the history of Rome in originally 15 books, to which he later added three, taking the history to the 170s. He was also the first to import into Latin dactylic hexameter as the epic meter; previous epic, such as Livius Andronicus's *Odysia*, were composed in the Saturnians, the native Italian meter.

Ephorus: (ca. 400–330 BCE). A native of Cyme in Asia Minor, Ephorus wrote an *Epichorios Logos* (*History of the Homeland*), as well as the first universal history (*Historiae*) in thirty books, which were divided by topics, rather than chronology. He was a contemporary of Theopompus and is followed closely by Diodorus Siculus.

Epigenes: of Byzantium, an astrologer of the 3rd or 2nd c. BCE, educated by Babylonians. (*BNP* s.v. "Epigenes [5]")

Eudoxus: (391–338/7 BCE). Eudoxus of Cnidus was an important mathematician, astronomer, geographer, and philosopher. Eudoxus learned mathematics with Archytas, met and possibly took lectures with Plato, studied astronomy in Egypt and wrote laws for Cnidos. Among his works were *On Speeds,* describing a geocentric motion of the planets, a *Phaenomena,* based on observations of the stars, an *Eight-Year Cycle,* on the Egyptian calendar, and a *Circuit of the Earth,* in the style of Hecataeus of Miletus.

Gellius, Gnaeus: A 2nd c. BCE annalist whose massive work covered the beginning of the city of Rome through to the last half of the 2nd century. He was a source for Licinius Macer and Dionysius of Halicarnassus, but not for Livy. (*BNP* s.v. "[2] Gellius, Gnaeus")

Hegesias: A 4th and 3rd c. BCE orator and historian from Magnesia. All that remains of his works are fragments of some speeches and a history of Alexander the Great. (*BNP* s.v. "Hegesias [2]")

Hellanicus: of Lesbos (480–395 BCE). Hellanicus was a mythographer, ethnographer, and a historian standing alongside Herodotus and Thucydides, but now only fragments survive. His works arranged in monograph form the topics that Herodotus had arranged chronologically or geographically. He is also notable for using the lists of victors of games, magistrates, and priests around Greece to establish a common chronology of events in Greek history. (*BNP* s.v. "Hellanicus")

Heraclides: (ca. 390–post-322 BCE). Heraclides of Pontus was a philosopher who studied at Plato's Academy under Speusippus, Plato's nephew and successor. He studied while Plato was still alive and alongside Aristotle, whom he outlived. Heraclides wrote mainly dialogues but dealing with a wide variety of spheres of interest, including especially astronomy, where he posited the earth's revolution about its axis and around the center of the universe.

Herodotus: (ca. 484–425 BCE). Called the "Father of History" by Cicero *de Legibus* 1.5, according to the Suda (H536) Herodotus was a Dorian Greek from the city of Halicarnassus in Asia Minor. He left Halicarnassus for Samos, where he practiced the Ionian dialect and wrote his *Histories* in nine books. Before this, he had traveled widely, including some time spent in Egypt. Herodotus's opus makes up the first extant work of the genre that would come to be called "History", after Herodotus's own word, *historia* (investigation). He combined the preexisting traditions of ethnography and geography along with first-hand evidence to weave a narrative whose goal was two-fold: (1) monumental: to preserve the great deeds of past men, and (2) investigative: to understand the causes of the Persian Wars. The narrative itself is episodic and broadly chronological, but reveals qualities more associated with story-telling and entertainment than with the scientific historiography pioneered by Thucydides. See *OCD3rd*, 696–8.

Hesiod: The author of the *Theogony*, a genealogy of the gods and the universe; the *Works and Days*, an example of wisdom literature; the *Shield of Heracles*, a short epic narrative on Heracles' combat with Cycnus; and the *Catalogue of Women* (in fragments), a genealogy of heroic women. Hesiod is traditionally thought to have been a contemporary of Homer, or slightly after (fl. ca. 650 BCE). He was born in Aeolian Cyme but moved as child to Ascra in Boeotia, where he kept sheep on Mt. Helicon; he died in Epizephyrean Locri and was buried in Orchomenus.

Hippocrates: The most famous of the ancient physicians, he lived in the 5th c. BCE (possibly into the 4th) on Cos. He was well known to Plato (*Phaedrus* 270c–3, *Protagoras* 311b–c) and Aristotle (*Politics* 1326a). The Hippocratic corpus bears his name, but he cannot confidently be linked with the texts therein. In fact, Aristotle's *Historia Animalium* 512b provides the only pre-Hellenistic quotation of a Hippocratic text, the *De Natura Hominum*, but he ascribes it to Polybus. (*BNP* s.v. "[6] Hippocrates of Cos")

Homer: The traditional author of the *Iliad* and *Odyssey*, placed roughly in the middle of the 8th c. BCE and generally thought to predate

Hesiod. The authorship of the *Iliad* and the *Odyssey* faces a multitude of unanswerable questions: particularly, whether they were composed by the same person and whether each individually was the work of a single person or the cumulative composition of many rhapsodes over time. The historical Homer, if he existed, likely lived on or near Chios, and was thought from a very early period to have been blind: the word "*homēros*" in the Aeolic dialect can have that meaning, and the blind bard Demodocus in the *Odyssey* has seemed to critics the poet's self-portrait.

Isigonus Nicaeensis: Little is known about Isigonus save that he was a paradoxographer. *Aulus Gellius, NA* 9.4 names Isigonus along with Aristaeus of Proconessus, Ctesias, Oneisicritus, Philostephanus, and Hegesias as trustworthy authors of incredible tales.

Licinius Mucianus: An Iberian who became a member of the senate under Claudius, Licinius Mucianus's career reached its heights under Nero and the Flavians. He was governor of Lycia-Pamphylia in the 60s CE, suffect consul in 64, served each of the four emperors in turn in 69, secured Rome for Vespasian, and held consulships in 70 and 72. He wrote memoirs of his time in the East as well other works on which Pliny drew. (*BNP* s.v. "[II 14] Gaius Licinius Mucianus")

Masurius: Mas(s)urius Sabinus, a Roman lawyer from the 1st c. CE from Verona. He was awarded by Tiberius the *ius respondendi ex auctoritate principis*, the right of giving legal opinions in the voice of the emperor. He was the author of books on public and private law, particularly the *Ius civile*, which became the basis of the works of later jurists, among them Ulpian. Among his many other works was a *Memoralia*. (*BNP* s.v. "[II 5] Sabinus")

Megasthenes: (ca. 350–290 BCE). A Greek historian and diplomat. He spent time with the satrap in Arachosia, and king Seleucus I made him envoy to India (the Maurya empire of north India). Megasthenes wrote a three or four volume *Indica*, which was used by Arrian, Diodorus Siculus, Pliny, and Strabo.

Messala Rufus: (ca. 102–27/6 BCE). Marcus Valerius Messala Rufus was suffect consul of 53. He was brother-in-law to Sulla and later joined

Caesar's faction in the Civil Wars. He was also author of works on augury (*De auspiciis*) and the histories of noble families (*De familiis*), on which see Pliny, *NH* 35.8.

Mnesigiton: Mnesigiton, a grammarian mentioned in Plutarch's *Quaestiones Graecae* 19 and in Pliny *NH* 7.57. He likely flourished during the Hellenistic period. (*RE* 15.2 s.v. "Mnesigiton")

Necepsos: A 2nd c. BCE astrological text (*Astrologoumena*) takes as its pseudonymous authors Petosiris (d. before 350 BCE) and Nechepso, king during the 26th dynasty (663–522 BCE). The text included at least 14 books and covered all of the contemporary Hellenistic astrology. (*BNP* s.v. "Nechepso")

Nigidius Figulus: (ca. 100–45 BCE). Publius Nigidius Figulus, a Pompeian and friend of Cicero's. Nigidius Figulus was a grammarian, writing *Commentarii grammatici*, a scholar of religion, a naturalist, and a mystic. His writings included a *De hominum natura, De animalibus, De dis, De ventis, Sphaera* (on constellations), and others.

Nymphodorus: (fl. ca. 335 BCE). A Syracusan author of travel literature who wrote *On the Wonders in Sicily*, and a *Periploi of Asia*. (*BNP* s.v. "Nymphodorus [1]")

Onesicritus: A Cynic philosopher and student of Diogenes of Sinope, Onesicritus accompanied Alexander the Great on his eastern conquests where he served as helmsman on the royal ship ca. 325–324 BCE. Onesicritus wrote a life of Alexander: "*How Alexander was educated*". (*BNP* s.v. "Onesicritus")

Petosiris: See "Necepsos" above.

Philostephanus: of Cyrene. Philostephanus lived in the 3rd c. BCE under Ptolemy Philopator and was a student of Callimachus. Philostephanus's works included geographies (*On the Cities of Asia, On the Cities of Europe, On Cyllene, On Epirus, On Islands, On Peculiar Rivers, On Springs*), a book *On Inventions*, a *Hypomnemata* (*Commentaries*) as well as an elegiac poem *On Peculiar Lakes*. He may also have authored an *Aitia* (*Causes*). (*BNP* s.v. "Philostephanus [1]")

Theophrastus: of Eresus on Lesbos. Theophrastus was Aristotle's successor at the Lyceum when the latter was forced to leave Athens after the death of Alexander in 323 BCE. Among his students there was the playwright Menander. Theophrastus continued Aristotle's inquiries in every subject, and Diogenes Laertius gives us 225 titles of his works, but few remain extant. The most important include treatises on botany, human physiology, metaphysics, sense perception, and his *Characters*, on character types.

Theopompus: from Chios (378–ca. 320 BCE). Theopompus was considered a trouble maker and twice exiled from Chios due to his pro-Spartan attitudes before nearly being executed at his final refuge at the court of Ptolemy I. He was a student of Isocrates, an orator, and a Greek historian whose histories were full of careful, literary figures of speech and Gorgianic style. His works included an epitome of Herodotus, a *Hellenica* (*History of Greece*) and a *Philippica* (*History of Philip II*) in 58 books that was in fact a universal history. Theopompus was hugely influential in the Hellenistic era, but only minor fragments survive today. (*BNP* s.v. "[3] Theopompus of Chios")

Thucydides: (ca. 460–ca. 400 BCE). Thucydides, son of Olorus, the historian (not the politician Thucydides, son of Milesias). He was exiled after his failure to prevent the Spartan general Brasidas from taking the city Amphipolis. He spent his exile in Sparta and was recalled in 424. His *History of the Peloponnesian War* introduces scientific historiography to Greece. See Thucydides, 1.22.

Varro: (116–27BCE). Marcus Terentius Varro was a great Roman polymath and author, who lived for 90 years. Aulus Gellius (*NA* 3.10.17) tells us that he had written 490 books by the time he was 78, but we know of only 55 titles. His works ranged across "history (*De vita populi Romani*, on Rome's 'social history'; *De gente populi Romani*, placing Rome's remote past in a Greek context), geography, rhetoric, law, (*De iure civili lib. XV*), philosophy, music, medicine, architecture, literary history (*De poetis, De comoediis Plautinis*), religion, agriculture, and language (at least 10 works on this last alone)" *OCD3rd*, 1582. The only works extant in more than fragments are *De lingua latina* and *De re rustica*.

Verrius: (ca. 55BCE–ca. 20CE). Marcus Verrius Flaccus, a prolific polymath like Varro, was a freedman from Praeneste. He gained fame as a teacher and was summoned to Rome to become the tutor to Augustus's grandchildren Gaius and Lucius. Verrius authored a number of works (all lost): *De Orthographia; Saturnus; Res memoria dignae* (important to Pliny); *Fasti Praenestini*; and *De verborum significatu*, of which epitomes and abridgments survive.

Xenagoras: A 3rd c. BCE Greek historian who wrote *Chronicles* of the Greeks covering Greek history up to the Ionian revolt (490 BCE) or into the Hellenistic period and including Sicily and Egypt and possibly Rome. He also wrote a work *On Islands.* (*BNP* s.v. "Xenagoras [1]")

Xenophon: A geographer from Lampsacus in Asia Minor who lived at the end of the 2nd c. BCE and the beginning of the 1st. Among his writings was a *Periplus* of the north and west, including what is likely a reference to Scandinavia. He also seems to have written two works on Syria. (*BNP* s.v. "Xenophon [8]")

Sources cited but otherwise unknown

Calliphanes
Fabius Vestalis
Tauron

Pliny and Valerius Maximus[10]

An author during the reign of Tiberius, Valerius Maximus published his *Facta ac dicta memorabilia* ca. 31 CE. The book is arranged topically with no clear plan, preserving an uncritical mass of anecdotes from Roman and Greek sources. It does, however, provide frequent and uncited source material for Pliny. The following chart, taken from König and Winkler, gives major comparable passages.

---

[10] From R. König and G. Winkler, *C. Plinius der Ältere, Naturkunde VII*, Tusculum Bücherei ed., Munich, 1975, 246–247. These pages also include parallel passages from Solinus, and a chart of Pliny's references to Aristotle's *Historia Animalium, De Generatione Animalium,* and *De Partibus Animalium.*

Pliny, *NH* 7	Valerius Maximus	Pliny, *NH* 7	Valerius Maximus
§28	8.13 ext. 5	§121	5.4.7
§44	9.12 ext. 8	§122	4.6.1
§53ff.	9.14 ext. 1	§125	8.7.7
	14.1 ff		12 ext. 2
§ 61f.	8.13 ext. 1	§133	8.15 ext. 4
§69	1.8 ext. 12	§135	6.9.9
§84	5.5.3	§137	6.4.4
§85	1.8 ext. 14		9.2.1
§86	1.8.1	§141	1.4.5
§87	3.3 ext. 4	§142	7.1.1
§88	8.7 ext.16	§142	7.1.1
§89f.	1.8.ext 2	§154	8.13 ext. 5ff.
§96	8.15.8	§156ff.	8.13 ext. 1ff.
§101	3.2.24	§165	1.8 ext. 6
§104ff.	3.6.1	§168	8.13 ext. 3
§109	5.6 ext. 5	§172	1.8 ext. 16
§110	8.10 ext. 1	§180	9.2.2
§112ff.	8.14.1		12 ext. 5
§118	3.4 ext. 1	§182	9.12.3
§120	8.15.3	§184	9.12.8
	12		
	7.5.2		

Some notes on Pliny's grammar, style, and syntax

Style

Eduard Norden's condemnation of Pliny's style—and by extension, his intellect—has, since its publication in 1898, left its imprint on Pliny studies like a stamp on warm wax.

Sein Werk gehört, stilistisch betrachtet, zu den schlechtesten, die wir haben. Man darf nicht sagen, daß der Stoff daran schuld war, denn Columella hat vortrefflich, Celsus gut geschrieben, und daß gerade eine Naturgeschichte stilisiert werden kann, hat Buffon gezeigt. Plinius hat es einfach nicht besser gekonnt, so wenig wie Varro, an den es überhaupt erinnert: wer so unendlich viel las, wie diese beiden, der konnte nicht gut schreiben. Bei beiden steht die Fülle des Tatsächlichen, das sie bieten, in keinem Verhältnis zu der Art, wie sie es bieten.

(Eduard Norden, 1915, p. 314)[11]

His work, considered stylistically, belongs to the worst which we have. One should not say that the content of it was to blame, since Columella wrote admirably, Celsus well; and that a Natural History is able to be stylized, Buffon has already shown. Pliny simply was not able to do better, as little as Varro, of whom he is generally reminiscent—one who read so endlessly much, as these two, who could not write well. Among both of them stands the whole of the factual, which they provide, but in no relation to style, as they provide it.

Hardly a fair assessment. Conte, despite his equivocation, goes a long way toward rehabilitating Pliny's style in the *Natural History*, comparing him favorably to Varro (also maligned by Norden), but noting that "Pliny in fact does not always write in the same way. The scattered, muddled style that dominates entire books contrasts with true rhetorical tirades; his praises of science, nature, and Italy and his moral condemnations of luxury and the exploitation of nature are demonstrative passages in which one detects a certain literary ambition" (501). He goes on: "Like all prose writers of the Neronian and Flavian periods, Pliny tends to undo the large, balanced structure of Ciceronian periods. This new freedom in writing, which in the case of Seneca and Tacitus produces a revolution in literary art, in

---

[11]   Eduard Norden, *Die antike Kunstprosa*, Vol. 1, Leipzig: Teubner, 1915.

Pliny's case dissolves into an impersonal confusion" (501–2). One wonders if the perspective on Pliny's style may be backwards. Rather than judging that while Pliny sometimes shows real rhetorical ability but elsewhere he both abandons Ciceronian regularity and falls short of Senecan or Tacitean innovation—i.e., judging the muddled passages as the failures of a genius not sufficiently potent—, might we instead consider that in some passages and even whole books Pliny has actively abandoned rhetorical flourish *in exchange for* something else? What might motivate Pliny to follow the elder Cato's maxim, *rem tene, verba sequentur*? To what extent is Pliny's "muddle" a reflection of his genre, or even a *captatio benevolentiae*, an argument in favor of his focus on unadorned truth over painted persuasion?

Pliny has many idiosyncracies of style, some of which will seem more or less peculiar to individual readers according to their preparation and tastes. Pinkster, in his (2006) article "The Language of Pliny the Elder", is the most recent continuation of the work of cataloging Pliny's stylistic trends, but Pliny studies are still waiting for a sympathetic investigation of our author's style, not judging his successes and failures against the likes of Cicero and Livy, but against his own program. While there is insufficient space to make a thorough study of Pliny's language here, it will be worth noting some few points of special difficulty and engaging briefly with Pinkster's analysis.

Vocabulary

(1) Breadth of vocabulary

The first hurdle students of Pliny will notice is the breadth of his vocabulary, a largess due primarily to the variety of the subject matter, but partially to Pliny's own usage. He has, like his nephew, a fondness for abstract expressions, nor does he have any fear of neuter adjectives, both of which Pinkster identifies as "techniques" common among the other technical writers.[12]

---

[12]   Pinkster (2006), p. 243.

In Divo quoque Augusto, quem *universa mortalitas* in hac censura nuncupet, si diligenter aestimentur *cuncta*, magna sortis humanae reperiantur volumina.

(7.XLV.147)

Even in the case of the Divine Augustus, whom *all the living world* [lit., "universal mortality"] judges to be in this bracket [i.e., of the fortunate], if *all his accounts together* [lit. "all things"] were to be tallied carefully, great vicissitudes of human fortune would be discovered.

(2) Technical vocabulary

The subject matter also often induces Pliny to use words in very technical senses, which are not immediately obvious to non-technical readers.[13] I have tried to make notes of these where possible. For example, 7.20:

> sicut Pyrro regi pollex in dextro pede, cuius tactu *lienosis* medebatur.

> As, for example, the big toe on king Pyrrhus's right foot, whose very touch cured an *inflamed spleen*.

The adjective "*lienosus*" merely means "of the spleen" or "splenetic", but Pliny uses it as a substantive in the neuter plural for the medical condition, inflamed spleen.

Grammar and syntax

(3) Use of cases

Pinkster notes that Pliny's use of the cases "is often difficult to classify under the traditional labels",[14] particularly Pliny's ablatives, which he

---

[13]　For more, see Healy, 'The Language of Pliny the Elder,' 1988.
[14]　Pinkster (2006), p. 244.

uses much more frequently without prepositions than do those authors on whom the traditional descriptions of case usage are based. We can approach an explanation for Pliny's use of the "bare" ablative from several different angles. Pinkster attributes this both to a stylistic choice on Pliny's part and to a deficiency in our list of categories for the cases: "This is partly caused by his endeavor to be as brief as possible, [...], partly also by the fact that the situations he describes are relatively unfamiliar and the use of the cases therefore infrequent."[15] I would suggest that, to the extent that we encounter difficulty applying traditional categories to Pliny's use of the cases, Pliny's Latin unmasks the fundamental artificiality and insufficiency of our description of the case usage, particularly the ablative. We must not lose sight of the fact that the case descriptions are a method scholars have overlaid on Latin usage, and not rules to which the Latin authors must bend and by which they must be judged. For Pliny, the ablative can often more easily be understood in its basic sense: indicating the circumstance under which the rest of the sentence occurs. For example, 7.47:

> Vopiscos appellabant e geminis qui retenti utero nascerentur altero interempto *abortu.* namque maxima, etsi rara, circa hoc miracula existunt.

> It used to be the custom to call "Vopisci" those among twins who, retained in the uterus, were born when the other twin had been killed *by premature delivery.* For in fact, very extraordinary miracles of this kind do exist, even if they are rare.

We may see "*abortu*" as an ablative of means (especially if "abortion" is meant), as an ablative of cause (especially if "miscarriage" is meant), or more generally as an ablative of attendant circumstance: a child used to be named Vopiscus if it had been one of a set of twins and was born *under the circumstance of* the other twin having been killed *under the additional circumstance of* a premature delivery.

---

[15] Pinkster (2006), p. 244.

(4) Ellipse

Pliny's use of ellipse, the omission of an element that has already
occurred in a previous clause, may likewise pose a problem for readers.
Ellipse of repeated elements is a common feature of Latin, but Pliny
often takes it to what may seem to us extreme lengths, as Pinkster
observes, allowing entire clauses to intervene between the omitted
element and its earlier instance.[16] We can see two examples in 7.117,
both a traditional ellipse and the more extreme Plinian ellipse:

> salve primus omnium parens patriae appellate, primus in toga
> triumphum linguaeque lauream merite [et facundiae Latiarumque
> litterarum parens] atque (ut dictator Caesar, hostis quondam tuus,
> de te scripsit) omnium triumphorum laurea maiorem, quanto
> plus est ingenii Romani terminos in tantum promovisse quam
> imperii.

> Hail, you, of all men first called Father of the Country, first having
> deserved a triumph in the toga and laurel for your tongue [and
> father of eloquence and of Latin letters] and (as the dictator Caesar,
> once your enemy, wrote about you), *having deserved a laurel as
> much* greater than the laurel of all triumphs, as having moved the
> bounds of Roman genius so much is greater than *having moved the
> bounds of Roman* empire.

We must understand "omnium triumphorum laurea [*merite lauream
tanto*] maiorem, quanto plus est ingenii Romani terminos in tantum
promovisse quam imperii [*Romani terminos promovisse*]". The latter is
an instance of a traditional ellipse, repeating a clear and obvious element
from an adjacent clause. The earlier instance, however, is much more
complex: "*laurea*" must trigger the reader to reach back beyond the
lengthy parenthetical "*ut dictator Caesar ...*" to supply "*merite*" and a
second "*lauream*" for "*maiorem*". What we see is likely an artifact of
Pliny's style of composition: moving from highly condensed notes in

---

[16] Pinkster (2006), p. 243. Pinkster calls ellipse "zero anaphora," that is, repetition of an
omitted element.

which he was intellectually steeped to highly condensed, quick-moving prose.

(5) Word order (first position)

The topic of a sentence, especially if it is also the topic of a paragraph or section, will come first, regardless of the violence it does to the word order.[17] For example, 7.101:

> *Fortitudo* in quo maxime exstiterit immensae quaestionis est.

> In which man *bravery* has most been present is a huge question.
> Lit.: *Bravery*, in whom it has most been present, is a huge question.

(6) Participles

Pliny frequently uses participles to stand in for subordinate clauses, even when they introduce unnecessary ambiguity and as ablatives absolute even when they are not technically absolute from the rest of sentence (an extension of his use of the ablative in its sense of attendant circumstance). When doing so, participles may convey any sort of circumstantial clause and often must be translated so in English to render the sentence sensible. An example will be found in item (7) below.

(7) Verb

The verb, especially in longer sentences and in cases where it indicates indirect speech and announces the source of Pliny's information, will be withheld to the end of the sentence, as are the names of the authorities themselves. The effect is the same as footnotes in modern writing: the content comes first, followed later by the citation. We can see these last two tendencies at work in a single example, 7.10, on the tribe of the Arimaspi:

---

[17] See Pinkster (2006), p. 251 for a similar observation and further examples.

quibus adsidue bellum esse circa metalla cum grypis, ferarum volucri genere, quale vulgo traditur, eruente ex cuniculis aurum, mira cupiditate et feris custodientibus et Arimaspis rapientibus, multi, sed maxime inlustres Herodotus et Aristeas Proconnesius scribunt.

That these are constantly at war over metals with the griffins, a winged race of beasts (which is the popular story) who root up gold out of their burrows with a marvelous greediness [and the reason for the war is that] the beasts guard the gold while the Arimaspi steal it—many people record it, but especially the respectable Herodotus and Aristeas of Proconnesus.

We see here an indirect statement with the introducing verb (*scribunt*) and the authorities to whom Pliny attributes the tale (Herodotus and Aristeas) suspended to the end. Meanwhile, the ablative participle "*eruente*" agrees with "*genere*", and so actually explains "*grypis*", but it is immediately followed by two ablatives absolute "*feris custodientibus*" and "*Arimaspis rapientibus*", which explain the circumstances of the war. Neither of these can technically be absolute, since the beasts are already twice in the sentence (*grypis* and *genere*, not to mention *ferarum*) and the Arimaspi are those referred to by "*quibus*". And yet the switch from the singular "*eruente*" to the plural "*feris custodientibus*" warns us that Pliny has introduced a new construction, rendering a sentence that is largely a string of ablatives essentially clear.

(8) Nesting

As a principle of organization and clarity, Pliny will also employ frequent nesting, an effect common to Latin generally: each subordinate clause tends to end in its verb, allowing the verbs to bracket their content. The effect may be extended, for example, to noun-adjective pairs encompassing adverbs and adverbial phrases, etc. We see an especially good example at 7.82:

at Vinnius Valens meruit in praetorio Divi Augusti centurio, vehicula vini culleis onusta, donec exinanirentur, sustinere solitus,

carpenta adprehensa una manu retinere, obnixus contra nitentibus
iumentis, et alia mirifica facere, quae insculpta monumento eius
spectantur.

And a Vinnius Valens served as centurion in the Divine Augustus's
guard, who was in the habit of lifting up wagons laden with casks of
wine until they were emptied, of holding back carts which he had
caught hold of with a single hand, as he leaned on the beasts of
burden which were struggling against him, and of doing other
marvelous deeds, which are still visible carved on his tombstone.

If we follow our guideline and read the first clause to its verb "*at Vinnius
Valens meruit*", we find that the verb "*meruit*" ("served") demands a
predicate nominative for its full sense, which brings us to "*centurio*".
This then is the full clause, with "*in praetorio Divi Augusti*" nested inside
to explain "*meruit . . . centurio*". The following clause takes us to the next
major verb "*solitus*". Inside its nest we find the required infinitive
"*sustinere*", along with its object "*vehicula*". Nested within that is the
adjective phrase "*vini culleis onusta*" and the explanatory clause "*donec
exinanirentur*". Moving past "*solitus*", we are now primed to read further
infinitives as objects of the participle, and we have two more: "*retinere*",
which blocks out "*carpenta adprehensa in una manu*" and "*facere*" which
blocks out "*et alia mirifica*". This leaves "*obnixus*", a participle that
explains the "*retinere*" clause, but since "*obnixus*" takes a dative, it points
immediately to "*iumentis*", again blocking out its clause. The final
relative clause, as usual, ends in its verb, "*spectantur*".

We could chart the sentence like so:

at Vinnius Valens meruit in praetorio Divi Augusti centurio,
    solitus

        (a) vehicula vini culleis onusta sustinere,
              donec exinanirentur
        (b) carpenta adprehensa una manu retinere,
              obnixus contra nitentibus iumentis,
        (c) et alia mirifica facere,
              quae insculpta monumento eius spectantur.

What at first may seem a convoluted sentence reveals itself to be very regular and orderly, with clear sign-posts throughout. The less experienced reader would do well to look for nested phrases like these when a sentence seems especially complex or difficult; while Pliny may sometimes write at a ponderous length, he always does so in brief, digestible segments, one thought at a time.

(9) Non-periodic, but literary

To expand on item (8), Pliny's sentences, while occasionally quite long, tend not to follow the same sort of periodic structure one would see in Cicero or Livy. In these authors, one can expect the clauses to be arranged to show the chronological development of a narrative while using subordination to reflect the relative importance or immediacy of a given action. We might take, for example, Caesar, *BG* VI.29:

> *Caesar,*
>> postquam per Ubios exploratores comperit Suebos sese in silvas
>>> recepisse,
>> inopiam frumenti veritus,
>>> quod, ut supra demonstravimus, minime omnes Germani
>>> agriculturae student,
> *constituit non progredi longius;*
> *sed,*
>> ne omnino metum reditus sui barbaris tolleret
>> atque ut eorum auxilia tardaret,
>> reducto exercitu
> *partem ultimam pontis,*
>> quae ripas Ubiorum contingebat,
> *in longitudinem pedum ducentorum rescindit*
> *atque in extremo ponte turrim tabulatorum quattuor constituit*
> *praesidiumque cohortium duodecim pontis tuendi causa ponit*
> *magnisque eum locum munitionibus firmat.*

Caesar, after he discovered through Ubian spies that the Suebi had taken themselves into the woods, since he feared a dearth of grain (because, as we have shown above, all the Germans have extraordinarily little interest in agriculture), *decided not proceed further, but,* in order that he not altogether remove the fear of his return from the barbarians, and in order that he slow their auxiliary forces, after he had led his army back across, *he cuts back the last part of the bridge,* which was touching the banks of the Ubii, *to a length of 200 feet and sets up on the edge of the bridge a four-story tower and puts a guard of twelve cohorts to watch the bridge and fortifies that place with large munitions.*

The sentence reduces Caesar's motivations to subordinate clauses but arranges those clauses to clearly reflect the order of action while giving primacy to the ultimate consequences: Caesar stops his army, cuts the bridge, builds a tower, places a guard, and leaves munitions.

Pliny, on the other hand, is not usually writing narrative but technical description. His sentence structure, as a result, tends toward an accumulation of relatively short clauses that seem to reflect their origin as scholarly notes. Pinkster recognizes this aspect of Pliny's writing, and he likewise recognizes that Pliny's sentences, while not periodic, are still logically structured, but he sees the structure as resulting primarily from the dictation process.[18] While that may indeed be the origin of some of Pliny's sentences, we should also be ready to acknowledge a different kind of stylistic or literary arrangement.

To use the same example as Pinkster, let us look briefly at Agrippa's biography in 7.45–46:

In pedes procidere nascentem contra naturam est, quo argumento eos appellavere Agrippas ut aegre partos, qualiter et M. Agrippam ferunt genitum, unico prope felicitatis exemplo in omnibus ad hunc modum genitis—quamquam *is* quoque

    [a] adversa pedum valitudine,
    [b] misera iuventa,
    [c] exercito aevo inter arma mortesque
    [d] ac noxio successu,

---

[18] Pinkster (2006), pp. 248–253.

[e] infelici terris stirpe omni,

[f] sed per utrasque Agrippinas maxime,

>   quae Gaium, quae Domitium Neronem principes genuere

>> totidem faces generis humani,

[g] 46. praeterea brevitate aevi,

>   quinquagensimo uno raptus anno

>> in tormentis adulteriorum coniugis socerique praegravi servitio,

luisse augurium praeposteri natalis existimatur.

It is contrary to nature for a child to come out feet-first when it is born, and under this sign, [the ancients] named them "Agrippas", as "ill-born", and they say that Marcus Agrippa, too, was born like this, as almost the only example of happiness among all those born in this way—although *he*, too, due to the adverse health of his feet, his wretched early years, his life spent among arms and death, and due to his criminal issue, his entire posterity misfortunate for the earth, but most of all on account of each of the Agrippinas, one who bore Gaius, one who bore Domitius Nero, the princes, both conflagrations of the human race, and additionally, due to the shortness of his life, since he was stolen in his fiftieth year amidst the torments of his wife's adulteries and in the crushing burden of slavery to his father-in-law, *is thought to have paid for the augury of his inverted birth.*

For Pinkster, this is an example of "numerous details" being inserted into "a basic sentence" (in italics), which is itself simply in normal, unmarked Latin word order.[19] Referring to this passage and to *NH* 5.51, so Pinkster:

> The information in these two examples is presented in a very compact form. The building blocks for the sentences are relatively short. They could be produced (and dictated) in one breath

---

19   Pinkster (2006), p. 249.

and could probably also be interpreted without difficulty when read aloud. The noun phrases in these two examples have a straightforward constituent order, the only instance of discontinuity (unobtrusive and pragmatically motivated) being *quinquagensimo uno raptus anno* in example (30). This technique of sentence-building might be called 'cumulative sentence-building', to use a term employed by Spilman (1933).[20]

All of this is accurate, and yet the sentence *does* take the reader chronologically through Agrippa's life—his birth, feet first, then his early years, maturity, his children (i.e., his *nachleben*)—and then follows his legacy—the two Agrippinas (which occasion a digression on Gaius and Nero)—and finally brings us back to Agrippa in reverse order via his death, which Pliny had skipped over on the way to his descendants (and which occasions a digression on his personal relationships at the time of his death), and, in conclusion, his birth. Thus the sentence follows Agrippa's life and book-ends his life in references to his birth, which suggests a biographical reflection on the man's life, as the sentence in fact is. That the second reference to Agrippa's preposterous birth (and the final clause of the sentence) should be the main clause is only to be expected since the entire biography is a digression in the discussion of people who were born feet-first, and in this way Pliny brings us back to the main theme.

We can see a similar example in Pliny's recap of the life of Augustus. In a massive sentence, stretching from 7.147–150, Pliny counters the opinion of "*universa mortalitas*" that Augustus was chief among the fortunate by listing the many misfortunes he suffered throughout his life (thirty-seven items appear in the list, give or take, with several of them in the plural). It is certainly an example of cumulative sentence-building, but not because such is Pliny's default, but because such an exhaustive (and, again, chronological) list brings the reader *mimetically* through the exhausting experience of Augustus's misfortune. The entire structure

---

[20] Mignonette Spilman, *Cumulative Sentence Building in Latin Historical Narrative*, Berkeley, CA: University of California Press, 1933.

ends with a single short clause in unmarked Latin word order: *in summa deus ille caelumque nescio adeptus magis an meritus herede hostis sui filio excessit.* "In the last place,[21] that god (whether he earned heaven more or seized it for itself, I cannot say) departed life with his enemy's son his heir." The brevity of this sentence underscores the intentionality of the previous sentence's length (15 words to 185), and rounds out the depiction of Augustus's misfortune-filled life with a final and supreme punch: even though he became a god (whatever that means, digresses Pliny), his enemy's son, not his own, was his heir, and he still died.

The text

Mayhoff's Teubner edition has provided the base for this text, with occasional departures derived from comparison with Rackham's Loeb and Schilling's *Budé*. For a description of the MSS, the reader will want to consult A. Ernout's Introduction to J. Beujeau. *Pline l'Ancien: Histoire Naturelle, Livre I*, Paris: Belles Lettres, 1950. Schilling (2003, p. xxiv) gives a helpful list of the principal passages he improved from Mayhoff's text. For an overview of recent editions, translations, and commentaries, see Beagon (2005, pp, 37–38) and "Further Reading" below.

Reception

The *Natural History*, while perhaps the first of its kind, did not arise in a complete vacuum. The early empire, as if beset by a premonition of plateau and decline, sees a boom in handbooks, the collection and organization of large bodies of topical knowledge. Particularly notable are Celsus's *De Medicina*, Columella's *De Agricultura*, Pomponius Mela's *De Situ Orbis*, Vitruvius's *De Architectura*, and much of Varro's impressive output, but unlike Pliny's *Natural History*, these are topical,

---

[21] More idiomatically, we might say for "*in summa*," "The icing on the cake is that . . ."

not totalizing. We might see Pliny, then, as the natural conclusion, or *telos*, of a growing trend: a handbook of handbooks that sought to encompass not all of knowledge *in toto*, but all knowledge as it pertains to the natural world, that is, the world that impinges upon man.

The *Natural History*, because of its rational organizational scheme and table of contents, was among the most easily consultable books from antiquity, but it was so large, in 37 volumes, that, like Livy, it tended to be excerpted and epitomized. Pliny's medical information, for example, was arranged into three books in the 4th c. CE along with excerpts from Celsus and other authors into what came to be known as the *Medicina Plinii*. The author Solinus, likewise, in his *Breviarium Rerum Memorabilium*, largely lifted from Pliny directly, omitting Pliny's occasional commentary on his sources and his irony.[22] The importance of Pliny's *Natural History* and the frequency of its use, however, is shown by the fact that this work, unlike Livy's and the rest of Pliny's own *opera*, survived the epitomizing process in full. We know that he was read by Bede and Augustine, that Jerome praised him "as the Latin equivalent of Aristotle and Theophrastus",[23] that he remained in use by the scholar Alcuin at Charlemagne's court,[24] and that he was part of monastic culture, "being used for astronomy and medicine and as a source for illustrations for biblical commentaries"[25] alongside Aristotle, Seneca, and Galen. Pliny's *Natural History* continued to be consulted well into the Renaissance even as Leoniceno's *De Erroribus Plinii* in 1509 called into question his accuracy and utility as a scientific text.

Leoniceno's attack proved, however, a watershed moment for Pliny studies, affecting the way scholars have viewed Pliny until the present day. Conte illustrates the uncharitable attitude: "Unlike scholars who

---

[22] For correspondences with Book VII, see König and Winkler, *C. Plinius der Ältere, Naturkunde VII*, 246–247.
[23] Mary Beagon, *The Elder Pliny on the Human Animal*, Oxford: Clarendon Press, 2005, 35–36.
[24] Gian Biagio Conte, *Latin Literature: A History*, 2nd ed., Baltimore: Johns Hopkins University Press, 1999, 502.
[25] John Healy, *Pliny the Elder: Natural History: A Selection*, 2nd ed., New York: Penguin Books, 2004, xxxvii.

had greater intelligence, more self-confidence, or simply more time at their disposal, he preserves everything and passes it on to us."[26] The project of the *Natural History* was not to display Pliny's intelligence, self-confidence, or free time—it was no ἀπόδεξις—but to preserve in an encyclopedia the knowledge of others: passing everything on was precisely the point. It seems patently unfair to critique Pliny's intellect and confidence based on a work that was necessarily not of the same literary style and method as the works by which other authors are deemed more intelligent and confident, particularly when we know that Pliny did in fact write other works of the literary style that are now lost to us. Conte himself implicitly acknowledges the unjustness of the comparison earlier but does not continue the thought: "It is likely, moreover, that Pliny's historical work had a different style: historical works in Latin literature observe a principle of greater attention to form than do technical and natural works."[27]

The contemporary view of the *Natural History* is divided between those who, following Leoniceno, criticize Pliny for his errors, and those who take a more nuanced view, rehabilitating Pliny by noting that he does not vouch for the information, but cites his sources and often expresses skepticism. For these, Pliny remains useful for investigations into ancient worldviews and the treatment of knowledge in different periods.

Conte (1999, 502–503) provides a very brief overview of the tradition. For another good summary of the tradition along with relevant bibliography, see Beagon (2005, 35–37). See also, Beagon (1992, 22–25) and Healy (2004 [1991], xxxvi–xl). For a detailed look at Pliny's reception in medieval and Renaissance astronomy, see B. S. Eastwood, "Plinian Astronomy in the Middle Ages and Renaissance" in French and Greenway (1986, 197–251). For Pliny's reception in Renaissance medicine, see R. K. French, "Pliny and Renaissance Medicine" in French and Greenway (1986, 262–281).

---

[26] Conte, *Latin Literature*, 503.
[27] Conte, *Latin Literature*, 501

Further reading

The following bibliography aims only to be an introduction to further reading on Pliny for an English speaking audience. For an overview of the most important European language works on Pliny in general and on Book VII in specific, see Schilling (2003, 263–268). For a relatively exhaustive bibliography of the particulars in Book VII, see Beagon (2005, 473–498).

Modern Editions, Translations, and Commentaries: Books VII and VIII

(a) Edition

Mayhoff, Karl, *C. Plini Secundi Naturalis Historia*, Leipzig: Teubner, 1906.

(b) Edition and Translation

Rackham, H., *Pliny: Natural History in Ten Volumes, Volume II: Libri III–VII*, Cambridge, MA: Harvard University Press, 1969.

Rackham, H., *Pliny: Natural History: Books 8–11*, Cambridge, MA: Harvard University Press, 1983.

(c) Edition and Commentary

Ernout, Alfred, *Pliny l'Ancien: Histoire Naturelle Livre VIII*, Paris: Les Belles Lettres, 2003.

Schilling, Robert, *Pliny l'Ancien: Histoire Naturelle Livre VII*, Paris: Les Belles Lettres, 2003.

(d) Translation and Commentary

Beagon, Mary, *The Elder Pliny on the Human Animal: Natural History v.7*, Oxford: Clarendon Press, 2005.

Serbat, Guy, et al., *Historia Natural*, Madrid: Biblioteca Clásica Gredos, 1995.

(e) Edition, Translation, and Commentary

Conte, G. B., Barchiesi, A. and Ranucci, C., *Plinio: Storia Naturale*, Turin: Einaudi, 1982–1988.

König, R. and Winkler, G., *C. Plinius der Ältere, Naturkunde VII*, Tusculum Bücherei ed., Munich, 1975.

(f) Translation

Bostock, John, *The Natural History: Pliny the Elder*, London: Taylor and Francis, 1855.

Healy, John F., *Pliny. Natural History, A Selection*, 2nd ed., New York: Penguin Books, 2004.

(g) Student Reader and Grammar Instruction

Chambers, P. L. and Pliny, *The Natural Histories of Pliny the Elder: An Advanced Reader and Grammar Review*, Norman, OK: University of Oklahoma Press, 2012.

Pertinent works (primarily English language)

Beagon, Mary, *Roman Nature: The Thought of Pliny the Elder*, Oxford: Oxford University Press, 1992.

Bremmer, J., *The Early Greek Concept of the Soul*, Princeton, NJ: Princeton University Press, 1983.

Campbell, David A, *Greek Lyric Poetry: A Selection of Early Greek Lyric, Elegiac and Iambic Poetry*, London: Bristol Classical Press, 1999.

Carey, Sorcha, *Pliny's Catalogue of Culture. Art and Empire in the Natural History*, Oxford: Oxford University Press, 2003.

Doody, Aude, 'Finding Facts in Pliny's Encyclopaedia: the Summarium of the Natural History', *Ramus*, 30(1) (2001), 1–22.

Doody, Aude, 'Pliny's *Natural History: Enkuklios Paideia* and the Ancient Encyclopedia', *Journal of the History of Ideas*, 70(1) (2009), 1–21.

Doody, Aude, *Pliny's Encyclopedia: The Reception of the Natural History*, New York: Cambridge University Press, 2010.

Doody, Aude, 'The Science and Aesthetics of Naming in the *Natural History*,' in Roy Gibson and Ruth Morello, eds., *Pliny the Elder: Themes and Contexts*, Leiden: Brill, 2011.

Doody, Aude, 'Literatures of the World: Seneca's *Natural Questions* and Pliny's *Natural History*,' in Emma Buckley and Martin Dinter, eds., *A Companion to the Neronian Age* [Blackwell Companions to the Ancient World], Malden, MA: Wiley-Blackwell, 2013.

French, R. and Greenaway, F., eds., *Sciences in the Early Roman Empire: Pliny the Elder, His Sources and Influence*, London: Croom Helm, 1986.

Gibson, Roy K. and Morello, Ruth, eds., *Pliny the Elder: Themes and Contexts*, Leiden: Brill, 2011.

Healy, John F., 'The Language of Pliny the Elder', *Filologia e forme letterarie; studi offerti a Francesco Della Corte* 4 (1988), 1–24.

Healy, John F., *Pliny the Elder on Science and Technology*, Oxford: Oxford University Press, 1999.

Howe, Nicholas Phillies, 'In Defense of the Encyclopedic Mode: on Pliny's "Preface" to the "Natural History"', *Latomus* 44(3) (1985), 561–576.

Isager, Jacob, *Pliny on Art and Society: The Elder Pliny's Chapters on the History of Art*, New York: Routledge, 1991.

Marchetti, Sandra Citroni, *Plinio il Vecchio e la tradizione del moralismo romano*, Pisa: Giardini, 1991.

Marchetti, Sandra Citroni, *La scienza della natura per un intellettuale romano: studi su Plinio il Vecchio*, Pisa: F. Serra, 2011.

McHam, Sarah Blake, *Pliny and the Artistic Culture of the Italian Renaissance*, New Haven, CT: Yale University Press, 2013.

Murphy, Trevor, *Pliny the Elder's Natural History. The Empire in the Encyclopaedia*, Oxford: Oxford University Press, 2004.

Naas, Valérie, *Le projet encyclopédique de Pline l'Ancien*, Rome: École française de Rome, 2002.

Pinkster, Harm, 'The Language of Pliny the Elder', in Tobias Reinhardt, Michael Lapidge, and J. N. Adams, eds. *Aspects of the Language of Latin Prose*, Oxford: Oxford University Press, 2006.

Syme, Ronald, 'Pliny the Procurator', *Harvard Studies in Classical Philology* 73 (1969), 201–236.

Syme, Ronald, 'Carrière et amis consulaires de Pline', *Helmática* 38(115–117) (1987), 223–231. Reprinted in English: in Ronald Syme, *Roman Papers, vol. 7*, Oxford: Clarendon Press, 1991, 496–511.

Wallace-Hadrill, Andrew, 'Pliny the Elder and Man's Unnatural History', *Greece and Rome,* 1 (1990), 80–96.

Select reference works

Adkins, Lesley and Adkins, Roy A., *Handbook to Life in Ancient Rome*, New York: Oxford University Press, 1994.

Brill's New Pauly, Hubert Cancik and Helmuth Schneider, eds., Boston, MA: Boston, 2006. (abbreviated *BNP*)

Chaintraine, Pierre, *Dictionnaire étymologique de la langue grecque*, Paris: Klinksieck, 1999.

Conte, Gian Biagio, *Latin Literature: A History*, trans. Joseph B. Solodow, rev. Don Fowler and Glen W. Most., 2nd ed., Baltimore, MD: Johns Hopkins University Press, 1999.

Ernout, Alfred and Meillet, Antoine, *Dictionnaire étymologique de la langue latine*, Paris: Klinksieck, 2001.

Lesky, Albin, *A History of Greek Literature*, New York: Crowell, 1966

Lewis, Charlton T., *A Latin Dictionary*, Oxford: Clarendon Press, 2002.

Liddell and Scott: Greek-English Lexicon, Stuart Jones and Roderick McKenize, eds., Oxford: Clarendon Press, 1996.

Oxford Classical Dictionary, 3rd Edition, Simon Hornblower and Antony Spawforth, eds., New York: Oxford University Press, 1996.

Oxford Latin Dictionary, P. G. W. Glare, ed., Oxford: Clarendon Press, 2000.

Realencyclopädie der classischen Altertumswissenschaft: Neue Bearbeitung, August Pauly, Georg Wissowa, Wilhelm Kroll, Kurt Witte, Karl Mittelhaus, Konrat Ziegler, eds., Stuttgart: J. B. Metzler, 1893–1980.

Smith, William, *Classical Dictionary of Greek and Roman Biography, Mythology, and Geography*, Charles Anthon, ed., New York: Harper and Brothers, 1851.

Common abbreviations

AG	*Allen and Greenough's New Latin Grammar*
Beagon (2005)	Beagon, Mary (2005), *The Elder Pliny on the Human Animal: Natural History v.7*
BNP	*Brill's New Pauly*
OCD3rd	*Oxford Classical Dictionary, 3rd edition*
OLD	*Oxford Latin Dictionary* (2000)
RE	*Realencyclopädie der classischen Altertumswissenschaft*
Schilling	Schilling, Robert, *Pliny l'Ancien: Histoire Naturelle Livre VII*

Text

I **1.** Mundus et in eo terrae, gentes, maria, ... †insignia†, insulae, urbes ad hunc modum se habent. animantium in eodem natura nullius prope partis contemplatione minore, si quidem omnia exsequi humanus animus queat. Principium iure tribuetur homini, cuius causa videtur cuncta alia genuisse natura magna, saeva mercede contra tanta sua munera, non ut sit satis aestimare, parens melior homini an tristior noverca fuerit.

2. ante omnia unum animantium cunctorum alienis velat opibus. ceteris varie tegimenta tribuit, testas, cortices, coria, spinas, villos, saetas, pilos, plumam, pinnas, squamas, vellera; truncos etiam arboresque cortice, interdum gemino, a frigoribus et calore tutata est: hominem tantum nudum et in nuda humo natali die abicit ad vagitus statim et ploratum, nullumque tot animalium aliud ad lacrimas, et has protinus vitae principio; at Hercule risus praecox ille et celerrimus ante XL diem nulli datur.

3. ab hoc lucis rudimento quae ne feras quidem inter nos genitas vincula excipiunt et omnium membrorum nexus; itaque feliciter natus iacet manibus pedibusque devinctis, flens animal ceteris imperaturum, et a suppliciis vitam auspicatur unam tantum ob culpam, quia natum est. heu dementiam ab his initiis existimantium ad superbiam se genitos!

4. prima roboris spes primumque temporis munus quadripedi similem facit. quando homini incessus! quando vox! quando firmum cibis os! quam diu palpitans vertex, summae inter cuncta animalia inbecillitatis indicium! iam morbi totque medicinae contra mala excogitatae, et hae quoque subinde novitatibus victae! et cetera sentire naturam suam, alia pernicitatem usurpare, alia praepetes volatus, alia nare: hominem nihil scire, nisi doctrina, non fari, non ingredi, non vesci, breviterque non aliud naturae sponte quam flere! itaque multi extitere qui non nasci optimum censerent aut quam ocissime aboleri.

5. uni animantium luctus est datus, uni luxuria et quidem innumerabilibus modis ac per singula membra, uni ambitio, uni avaritia, uni inmensa vivendi cupido, uni superstitio, uni sepulturae cura atque etiam post se de futuro. nulli vita fragilior, nulli rerum omnium libido maior, nulli pavor confusior, nulli rabies acrior. denique cetera animantia in suo genere probe degunt. congregari videmus et stare contra dissimilia: leonum feritas inter se non dimicat, serpentium morsus non petit serpentes, ne maris quidem beluae ac pisces nisi in diversa genera saeviunt. at hercule homini plurima ex homine sunt mala.

6. Et de universitate quidem generis humani magna ex parte in relatione gentium diximus. neque enim ritus moresque nunc tractabimus innumeros ac totidem paene quot sunt coetus hominum, quaedam tamen haud omittenda duco, maximeque longius ab mari degentium, in quibus prodigiosa aliqua et incredibilia multis visum iri haud dubito. quis enim Aethiopas antequam cerneret credidit? aut quid non miraculo est, cum primum in notitiam venit? quam multa fieri non posse priusquam sunt facta iudicantur?

7. naturae vero rerum vis atque maiestas in omnibus momentis fide caret, si quis modo partes eius ac non totam complectatur animo. ne pavones ac tigrium pantherarumque maculas et tot animalium picturas commemorem, parvum dictu, sed inmensum aestimatione, tot gentium sermones, tot linguae, tanta loquendi varietas, ut externus alieno paene non sit hominis vice!

8. iam in facie vultuque nostro cum sint decem aut paulo plura membra, nullas duas in tot milibus hominum indiscretas effigies existere, quod ars nulla in paucis numero praestet adfectando! nec tamen ego in plerisque eorum obstringam fidem meam potiusque ad auctores relegabo, qui dubiis reddentur omnibus, modo ne sit fastidio Graecos sequi, tanto maiore eorum diligentia vel cura vetustiore.

II **9.** Esse Scytharum genera et quidem plura, quae corporibus humanis vescerentur, indicavimus. id ipsum incredibile fortasse, ni cogitemus in medio orbe terrarum ac Sicilia [et Italia] fuisse gentes huius monstri, Cyclopas et Laestrygonas, et nuperrime trans Alpis hominem immolari gentium earum more solitum, quod paulum a mandendo abest.

10. sed iuxta eos, qui sunt ad septentrionem versi, haud procul ab ipso aquilonis exortu specuque eius dicto, quem locum Ges clithron appellant, produntur Arimaspi, quos diximus, uno oculo in fronte media insignes. quibus adsidue bellum esse circa metalla cum grypis, ferarum volucri genere, quale vulgo traditur, eruente ex cuniculis aurum, mira cupiditate et feris custodientibus et Arimaspis rapientibus, multi, sed maxime inlustres Herodotus et Aristeas Proconnesius scribunt.

11. super alios autem Anthropophagos Scythas in quadam convalle magna Imavi montis regio est quae vocatur Abarimon, in qua silvestres vivunt homines aversis post crura plantis, eximiae velocitatis, passim cum feris vagantes. hos in alio non spirare caelo ideoque ad finitimos reges non pertrahi neque ad Alexandrum Magnum pertractos Baeton itinerum eius mensor prodidit.

12. priores Anthropophagos, quos ad septentrionem esse diximus, decem dierum itinere supra Borysthenen amnem ossibus humanorum capitum bibere cutibusque cum capillo pro mantelibus ante pectora uti Isigonus Nicaeensis. idem in Albania gigni quosdam glauca oculorum acie, a pueritia statim canos, qui noctu plus quam interdiu cernant. idem itinere dierum XIII supra Borysthenen Sauromatas tertio die cibum capere semper.

13. Crates Pergamenus in Hellesponto circa Parium genus hominum fuisse, quos Ophiogenes vocat, serpentium ictus contactu levare solitos et manu inposita venena extrahere corpori. Varro etiamnum esse paucos ibi, quorum salivae contra ictus serpentium medeantur.

14. similis et in Africa Psyllorum gens fuit, ut Agatharchides scribit, a Psyllo rege dicta, cuius sepulcrum in parte Syrtium Maiorum est. horum corpori ingenitum fuit virus exitiale serpentibus et cuius odore sopirent eas; mos vero liberos genitos protinus obiciendi saevissimis earum eoque genere pudicitiam coniugum experiendi, non profugientibus adulterino sanguine natos serpentibus. haec gens ipsa quidem prope internicione sublata est a Nasamonibus, qui nunc eas tenent sedes. genus tamen hominum ex iis, qui profugerant aut cum pugnatum est afuerant, hodieque remanet in paucis.

15. simile et in Italia Marsorum genus durat, quos a Circae filio ortos ferunt et ideo inesse iis vim naturalem eam. et tamen omnibus hominibus contra serpentes inest venenum: ferunt ictum salivae ut ferventis aquae contactu fugere; quod si in fauces penetraverit, etiam mori, idque maxime humani ieiuni oris. Supra Nasamonas confinesque illis Machlyas androgynos esse utriusque naturae, inter se vicibus coeuntes, Calliphanes tradit. Aristoteles adicit dextram mammam iis virilem, laevam muliebrem esse.

16. in eadem Africa familias quasdam effascinantium Isigonus et Nymphodorus, quorum laudatione intereant probata, arescant arbores, emoriantur infantes. esse eiusdem generis in Triballis et Illyris adicit Isigonus, qui visu quoque effascinent interimantque quos diutius intueantur, iratis praecipue oculis, quod eorum malum facilius sentire puberes; notabilius esse quod pupillas binas in oculis singulis habeant.

17. huius generis et feminas in Scythia, quae Bitiae vocantur, prodit Apollonides. Phylarchus et in Ponto Thibiorum genus multosque alios eiusdem naturae, quorum notas tradit in altero oculo geminam pupillam, in altero equi effigiem; eosdem praeterea non posse mergi, ne veste quidem degravatos. haud dissimile iis genus Pharmacum in Aethiopia Damon, quorum sudor tabem contactis corporibus afferat.

18. feminas quidem omnes ubique visu nocere quae duplices pupillas habeant, Cicero quoque apud nos auctor est. adeo naturae, cum ferarum morem vescendi humanis visceribus in homine genuisset, gignere etiam in toto corpore et in quorundam oculis quoque venena placuit, ne quid usquam mali esset quod in homine non esset.

19. Haud procul urbe Roma in Faliscorum agro familiae sunt paucae quae vocantur Hirpi. hae sacrificio annuo, quod fit ad montem Soractem Apollini, super ambustam ligni struem ambulantes non aduruntur et ob id perpetuo senatus consulto militiae omniumque aliorum munerum vacationem habent.

20. quorundam corpori partes nascuntur ad aliqua mirabiles, sicut Pyrro regi pollex in dextro pede, cuius tactu lienosis medebatur. hunc cremari cum reliquo corpore non potuisse tradunt conditumque loculo in templo.

21. Praecipue India Aethiopumque tractus miraculis scatent. maxima in India gignuntur animalia. indicio sunt canes grandiores ceteris. arbores quidem tantae proceritatis traduntur, ut sagittis superiaci nequeant—et facit ubertas soli, temperies caeli, aquarum abundantia, si libeat credere, ut sub una fico turmae condantur equitum—, harundines vero tantae proceritatis, ut singula internodia alveo navigabili ternos interdum homines ferant.

22. multos ibi quina cubita constat longitudine excedere, non expuere, non capitis aut dentium aut oculorum ullo dolore adfici, raro aliarum corporis partium: tam moderato solis vapore durari. philosophos eorum, quos gymnosophistas vocant, ab exortu ad occasum perstare contuentes solem inmobilibus oculis, ferventibus harenis toto die alternis pedibus insistere. in monte, cui nomen est Nulo, homines esse aversis plantis octonos digitos in singulis habentes auctor est Megasthenes;

23. in multis autem montibus genus hominum capitibus caninis ferarum pellibus velari, pro voce latratum edere, unguibus armatum venatu et aucupio vesci; horum supra centum viginti milia fuisse prodente se. Ctesias scribit, et in quadam gente Indiae feminas semel in vita parere genitosque confestim canescere. idem hominum genus, qui Monocoli vocarentur, singulis cruribus, mirae pernicitatis ad saltum; eosdem Sciapodas vocari, quod in maiore aestu humi iacentes resupini umbra se pedum protegant. non longe eos a Trogodytis abesse, rursusque ab his occidentem versus quosdam sine cervice oculos in umeris habentes.

24. sunt et satyri subsolanis Indorum montibus (Catarcludorum dicitur regio), pernicissimum animal, iam quadripedes, iam recte currentes humana effigie; propter velocitatem nisi senes aut aegri non capiuntur. Choromandarum gentem vocat Tauron silvestrem, sine voce, stridoris horrendi, hirtis corporibus, oculis glaucis, dentibus caninis. Eudoxus in meridianis Indiae viris plantas esse cubitales, feminis adeo parvas, ut Struthopodes appellentur.

25. Megasthenes gentem inter Nomadas Indos narium loco foramina tantum habentem, anguium modo loripedem, vocari Sciratas. ad extremos fines Indiae ab oriente circa fontem Gangis Astomorum gentem sine ore, corpore toto hirtam vestiri frondium lanugine, halitu tantum viventem et odore, quem naribus trahant. nullum illis cibum nullumque potum, radicum tantum florumque varios odores et silvestrium malorum, quae secum portant longiore itinere, ne desit olfactus; graviore paulo odore haud difficulter exanimari.

26. super hos extrema in parte montium Trispithami Pygmaeique narrantur, ternas spithamas longitudine, hoc est ternos dodrantes, non excedentes, salubri caelo semperque vernante montibus ab aquilone oppositis, quos a gruibus infestari Homerus quoque prodidit. fama est insidentes arietum caprarumque dorsis armatos sagittis veris tempore universo agmine ad mare descendere et ova pullosque earum alitum consumere; ternis expeditionem eam mensibus confici; aliter futuris gregibus non resisti. casas eorum luto pinnisque et ovorum putaminibus construi.

27. Aristoteles in cavernis vivere Pygmaeos tradit, cetera de iis ut reliqui. Cyrnos Indorum genus Isigonus annis centenis quadragenis vivere, item Aethiopas Macrobios et Seras existimat et qui Athon montem incolant, hos quidem, quia viperinis carnibus alantur; itaque nec capiti nec vestibus eorum noxia corpori inesse animalia.

28. Onesicritus, quibus locis Indiae umbrae non sint, corpora hominum cubitorum quinum et binorum palmorum existere, et vivere annos CXXX nec senescere, sed ut medio aevo mori. Crates Pergamenus Indos, qui centenos annos excedant, Gymnetas appellat, non pauci Macrobios. Ctesias gentem ex his, quae appelletur Pandae, in convallibus sitam annos ducenos vivere, in iuventa candido capillo, qui in senectute nigrescat,

29. contra alios quadragenos non excedere annos, iunctos Macrobiis, quorum feminae semel pariant. idque et Agatharchides tradit, praeterea locustis eos ali et esse pernices. Mandorum nomen iis dedit Clitarchus, et Megasthenes trecentos quoque eorum vicos adnumerat. feminas septimo aetatis anno parere, senectam quadragesimo accidere.

30. Artemidorus in Taprobane insula longissimam vitam sine ullo corporis languore traduci. Duris Indorum quosdam cum feris coire mixtosque et semiferos esse partus. in Calingis eiusdem Indiae gente quinquennes concipere feminas, octavum vitae annum non excedere. et alibi cauda villosa homines nasci pernicitatis eximiae, alios auribus totos contegi.

Oritas ab Indis Arabis fluvius disterminat. hi nullum alium cibum novere quam piscium, quos unguibus dissectos sole torreant atque ita panem ex iis faciant, ut refert Clitarchus.

31. Trogodytas super Aethiopiam velociores equis esse Pergamenus Crates, item Aethiopas octona cubita longitudine excedere; Syrbotas vocari gentem eam. Nomadum Aethiopum secundum flumen Astragum ad septentrionem vergentium gens Menisminorum appellata abest ab oceano dierum itinere viginti. animalium, quae cynocephalos vocamus, lacte vivit, quorum armenta pascit maribus interemptis praeterquam subolis causa.

32. in Africae solitudinibus hominum species obviae subinde fiunt momentoque evanescunt. Haec atque talia ex hominum genere ludibria sibi, nobis miracula ingeniosa fecit natura. ex singulis quidem quae facit in dies ac prope horas, quis enumerare valeat? ad detegendam eius potentiam satis sit inter prodigia posuisse gentes. hinc ad confessa in homine pauca.

III **33.** Tergeminos nasci certum est Horatiorum Curiatiorumque exemplo. super inter ostenta ducitur praeterquam in Aegypto, ubi fetifer potu Nilus amnis. proxime supremis Divi Augusti Fausta quaedam e plebe Ostiae duos mares, totidem feminas enixa famem, quae consecuta est, portendit haud dubie. reperitur et in Peloponneso quinos quater enixa, maioremque partem ex omni eius vixisse partu. et in Aegypto septenos uno utero simul gigni auctor est Trogus.

34. Gignuntur et utriusque sexus quos hermaphroditos vocamus, olim androgynos vocatos et in prodigiis habitos, nunc vero in deliciis. Pompeius Magnus in ornamentis theatri mirabiles fama posuit effigies, ob id diligentius magnorum artificum ingeniis elaboratas, inter quas legitur Eutychis a XX liberis rogo inlata Trallibus, enixa XXX partus, Alcippe elephantum. quamquam id inter ostenta est. namque et serpentem peperit inter initia Marsici belli ancilla, et multiformes pluribus modis inter monstra partus eduntur.

35. Claudius Caesar scribit hippocentaurum in Thessalia natum eodem die interisse, et nos principatu eius adlatum illi ex Aegypto in melle vidimus. est inter exempla in uterum protinus reversus infans Sagunti quo anno deleta ab Hannibale est.

IV **36.** Ex feminis mutari in mares non est fabulosum. invenimus in annalibus P. Licinio Crasso C. Cassio Longino coss. Casini puerum factum ex virgine sub parentibus iussuque haruspicum deportatum in insulam desertam. Licinius Mucianus prodidit visum a se Argis Arescontem, cui nomen Arescusae fuisse, nupsisse etiam, mox barbam et virilitatem provenisse uxoremque duxisse; eiusdem sortis et Zmyrnae puerum a se visum. ipse in Africa vidi mutatum in marem nuptiarum die L. Consitium civem Thysdritanum, <vivebatque cum proderem haec>.

37. ... editis geminis raram esse aut puerperae aut puerperio praeterquam alteri vitam; si vero utriusque sexus editi sint gemini, rariorem utrique salutem. feminas celerius gigni quam mares, sicuti celerius senescere. saepius in utero moveri mares et in dextera fere geri parte, in laeva feminas.

V **38.** Ceteris animantibus statum et pariendi et partus gerendi tempus est; homo toto anno et incerto gignitur spatio, alius septimo mense, alius octavo et usque ad initia undecimi. ante septimum mensem haud umquam vitalis est. septimo non nisi pridie posterove plenilunii die aut interlunio concepti nascuntur.

39. tralaticium in Aegypto est et octavo gigni, iam quidem et in Italia tales partus esse vitales, contra priscorum opiniones. variant haec pluribus modis. Vistilia, Gliti ac postea Pomponi atque Orfiti clarissimorum civium coniunx, ex iis quattuor partus enixa septimo semper mense, genuit Suillium Rufum undecimo, Corbulonem septimo, utrumque consulem, postea Caesoniam, Gai principis coniugem, octavo.

40. in quo mensum numero genitis intra quadragensimum diem maximus labor, gravidis autem quarto et octavo mense, letalesque in iis abortus. Masurius auctor est L. Papirium praetorem secundo herede lege agente bonorum possessionem contra eum dedisse, cum mater partum se tredecim mensibus diceret tulisse, quoniam nullum certum tempus pariendi statutum videretur.

VI **41.** A conceptu decimo die dolores capitis, oculorum vertigines tenebraeque, fastidium in cibis, redundatio stomachi indices sunt hominis inchoati. melior color marem ferenti et facilior partus, motus in utero quadragensimo die. contraria omnia in altero sexu, ingestabile onus, crurum et inguinis levis tumor, primus autem XC die motus.

42. sed plurimum languoris in utroque sexu capillum germinante partu et in plenilunio, quod tempus editos quoque infantes praecipue infestat. adeoque incessus atque omne quicquid dici potest in gravida refert, ut salsioribus cibis usae carentem unguiculis partum edant et, si respiravere, difficilius enitantur. oscitatio quidem in enixu letalis est, sicut sternuisse a coitu abortivum.

VII **43.** Miseret atque etiam pudet aestimantem quam sit frivola animalium superbissimi origo, cum plerisque abortus causa odor a lucernarum fiat extinctu. his principiis nascuntur tyranni, his carnifex animus! tu qui corporis viribus fidis, tu qui fortunae munera amplexaris et te ne alumnum quidem eius existimas, sed partum,

44. tu cuius imperatoria est mens, tu qui te deum credis aliquo successu tumens, tanti perire potuisti! atque etiam hodie minoris potes, quantulo serpentis ictus dente aut etiam, ut Anacreon poeta, acino uvae passae, ut Fabius Senator praetor, in lactis haustu uno pilo strangulatus. is demum profecto vitam aequa lance pensitabit, qui semper fragilitatis humanae memor fuerit.

VIII **45.** In pedes procidere nascentem contra naturam est, quo argumento eos appellavere Agrippas ut aegre partos, qualiter et M. Agrippam ferunt genitum, unico prope felicitatis exemplo in omnibus ad hunc modum genitis. quamquam is quoque adversa pedum valitudine, misera iuventa, exercito aevo inter arma mortesque ac noxio successu, infelici terris stirpe omni, sed per utrasque Agrippinas maxime, quae Gaium, quae Domitium Neronem principes genuere totidem faces generis humani,

46. praeterea brevitate aevi, quinquagensimo uno raptus anno in tormentis adulteriorum coniugis socerique praegravi servitio, luisse augurium praeposteri natalis existimatur. Neronem quoque, paulo ante principem et toto principatu suo hostem generis humani, pedibus genitum scribit parens eius Agrippina. ritus naturae hominem capite gigni, mos est pedibus efferri.

IX **47.** Auspicatius enecta parente gignuntur, sicut Scipio Africanus prior natus primusque Caesarum a caeso matris utero dictus, qua de causa et Caesones appellati. simili modo natus et Manilius, qui Carthaginem cum exercitu intravit.

X Vopiscos appellabant e geminis qui retenti utero nascerentur altero interempto abortu. namque maxima, etsi rara, circa hoc miracula existunt.

XI **48.** Praeter mulierem pauca animalia coitum novere gravida; unum quidem omnino aut alterum superfetat. extat in monimentis et medicorum et quibus talia consectari curae fuit uno abortu duodecim puerperia egesta. sed ubi paululum temporis inter duos conceptus intercessit, utrumque perfertur,

49. ut in Hercule et Iphicle fratre eius apparuit et in ea quae gemino partu alterum marito similem alterumque adultero genuit, item in Proconnesia ancilla, quae eiusdem diei coitu alterum domino similem, alterum procuratori eius, et in alia, quae iusto partu quinque mensum alterum edidit, rursus in alia, quae septem mensum edito puerperio insecutis in mensibus geminos enixa est.

50. Iam illa vulgata sunt: varie ex integris truncos gigni, ex truncis integros, eademque parte truncos; signa quaedam naevosque et cicatrices etiam regenerari, quarto partu Dacorum originis nota in brachio reddita

XII **51.** (in Lepidorum gente tres, intermisso ordine, obducto membrana oculo genitos accepimus); similes quidem alios avo, et ex geminis quoque alterum patri, alterum matri, annoque post genitum maiori similem fuisse ut geminum; quasdam sibi similes semper parere, quasdam viro, quasdam nulli, quasdam feminam patri, marem sibi. indubitatum exemplum est Nicaei nobilis pyctae Byzanti geniti, qui, adulterio Aethiopis nata matre nihil a ceteris colore differente, ipse avum regeneravit Aethiopem.

52. Similitudinum quidem inmensa reputatio est et in qua credantur multa fortuita pollere, visus, auditus, memoria haustaeque imagines sub ipso conceptu. cogitatio etiam utriuslibet animum subito transvolans effingere similitudinem aut miscere existimatur, ideoque plures in homine quam in ceteris omnibus animalibus differentiae, quoniam velocitas cogitationum animique celeritas et ingenii varietas multiformes notas inprimit, cum ceteris animantibus inmobiles sint animi et similes omnibus singulis in suo cuique genere.

53. Antiocho regi Syriae e plebe nomine Artemo in tantum similis fuit, ut Laodice coniunx regia necato iam Antiocho mimum per eum commendationis regnique successionis peregerit. Magno Pompeio Vibius quidam e plebe et Publicius etiam servitute liberatus indiscreta prope specie fuere similes, illud os probum reddentes ipsumque honorem eximiae frontis.

54. qualis causa patri quoque eius Menogenis coci sui cognomen inposuit, iam Strabonis a specie oculorum habenti vitium imitato etiam servo; Scipioni Serapionis indiderat suarii negotiatoris vile mancipium. eiusdem familiae Scipioni post eum nomen Salvitto mimus dedit, sicut Spinther secundarum tertiarumque Pamphilus collegio Lentuli et Metelli consulum, in quo perquam inportune fortuitum hoc quoque fuit, duorum simul consulum in scaena imagines cerni.

55. e diverso L. Plancus orator histrioni Rubrio cognomen inposuit, rursus Curioni patri Burbuleius itemque Messalae censorio Menogenes, perinde histriones. Surae quidem proconsulis etiam rictum in loquendo intractionemque linguae et sermonis tumultum, non imaginem modo, piscator quidam in Sicilia reddidit. Cassio Severo, celebri oratori, Armentari murmillonis obiecta similitudo est. [modo in Annaea domo Gallionem a Castellano liberto non discernebant, nec a Sannio mimo Paride cognominato Agrippinum senatorem.]

56. Toranius mango Antonio iam triumviro eximios forma pueros, alterum in Asia genitum, alterum trans Alpis, ut geminos vendidit: tanta unitas erat. postquam deinde sermone puerorum detecta fraude a furente increpitus Antonio est, inter alia magnitudinem preti conquerente (nam ducentis erat mercatus sestertiis), respondit versutus ingenii mango, id ipsum se tanti vendidisse, quoniam non esset mira similitudo in ullis eodem utero editis; diversarum quidem gentium natales tam concordi figura reperire super omnem esse taxationem; adeoque tempestivam admirationem intulit, ut ille proscriptor animus, modo et contumelia furens, non aliud in censu magis ex fortuna sua duceret.

XIII **57.** Est quaedam privatim dissociatio corporum, et inter se steriles, ubi cum aliis iunxere se, gignunt, sicut Augustus et Livia. item alii aliaeque feminas tantum generant aut mares, plerumque et alternant, sicut Gracchorum mater duodeciens et Agrippina Germanici noviens. aliis sterilis est iuventa, aliis semel in vita datur gignere.

58. quaedam non perferunt partus, quales, si quando medicina et cura vicere, feminam fere gignunt. Divus Augustus in reliqua exemplorum raritate neptis suae nepotem vidit genitum quo excessit anno, M. Silanum, qui, cum Asiam obtineret post consulatum Neronis principis successione, veneno eius interemptus est.

59. Q. Metellus Macedonicus, cum sex liberos relinqueret, XI nepotes reliquit, nurus vero generosque et omnes, qui se patris appellatione salutarent, XXVII.

60. in actis temporum Divi Augusti invenitur duodecimo consulatu eius L.que Sulla collega a. d. III idus Aprilis C. Crispinium Hilarum ex ingenua plebe Faesulana cum liberis VIII, in quo numero filiae duae fuere, nepotibus XXVII, pronepotibus XVIII, neptibus VIII, praelata pompa tum omnibus, in Capitolio immolasse.

XIV **61.** Mulier post quinquagensimum annum non gignit, maiorque pars XL profluvium genitale sistit. nam in viris Masinissam regem post LXXXVI annum generasse filium, quem Methimannum appellaverit, clarum est, Catonem censorium octogensimo exacto e filia Salonis clientis sui.

62. qua de causa aliorum eius liberum propago Liciniani sunt cognominati, hi Saloniani, ex quis Uticensis fuit. nuper etiam L. Volusio Saturnino in urbis praefectura extincto notum est e Cornelia Scipionum gentis Volusium Saturninum, qui fuit consul, genitum post LXII annum. et usque ad LXXV apud ignobiles vulgaris reperitur generatio.

XV **63.** Solum autem animal menstruale mulier est; inde unius utero quas appellaverunt molas. ea est caro informis, inanima, ferri ictum et aciem respuens. movetur sistitque menses, ut et partus, alias letalis, alias una senescens, aliquando alvo citatiore excidens. simile quiddam et viris in ventre gignitur, quod vocant scirron, sicut Oppio Capitoni praetorio viro.

64. sed nihil facile reperiatur mulierum profluvio magis monstrificum. acescunt superventu musta, sterilescunt tactae fruges, moriuntur insita, exuruntur hortorum germina, fructus arborum, quibus insidere, decidunt, speculorum fulgor aspectu ipso hebetatur, acies ferri praestringitur, eboris nitor, alvi apium moriuntur, aes etiam ac ferrum robigo protinus corripit odorque dirus aera, et in rabiem aguntur gustato eo canes atque insanabili veneno morsus inficitur.

65. quin et bituminum sequax alioqui ac lenta natura in lacu Iudaeae, qui vocatur Asphaltites, certo tempore anni supernatans non quit sibi avelli, ad omnem contactum adhaerens praeterquam filo quod tale virus infecerit. etiam formicis, animali minimo, inesse sensum eius ferunt abicique gustatas fruges nec postea repeti.

66. et hoc tale tantumque omnibus tricenis diebus malum in muliere existit et trimenstri spatio largius, quibusdam vero saepius mense, sicut aliquis numquam. sed tales non gignunt, quando haec est generando homini materia, germine e maribus coaguli modo hoc in sese glomerante, quod deinde tempore ipso animatur corporaturque. ergo cum gravidis fluxit, invalidi aut non vitales partus eduntur aut saniosi, ut auctor est Nigidius;—

XVI **67.** (Idem lac feminae non corrumpi alenti partum, si ex eodem viro rursus conceperit, arbitratur)—incipiente autem hoc statu aut desinente conceptus facillimi traduntur. fecunditatis in feminis praerogativum accepimus inunctis medicamine oculis salivam infici.

68. Ceterum editis primores septimo mense gigni dentes priusque in supera fere parte, haud dubium est, septimo eosdem decidere anno aliosque suffici, quosdam et cum dentibus nasci, sicut M'. Curium, qui ob id Dentatus cognominatus est, et Cn. Papirium Carbonem, praeclaros viros. in feminis ea res inauspicati fuit exempli regum temporibus.

69. cum ita nata esset Valeria, exitio civitati in quam delata esset futuram responso haruspicum vaticinante; Suessam Pometiam illa tempestate florentissimam deportata est, veridico exitu consecuto.—(Quasdam concreto genitali gigni infausto omine Cornelia Gracchorum mater indicio est)—aliqui vice dentium continuo osse gignuntur, sicuti Prusiae regis Bithyniorum filius superna parte oris.

70. dentes autem in tantum invicti sunt ignibus, ut nec crementur cum reliquo corpore, iidemque flammis indomiti cavantur tabe pituitae. candorem trahunt quodam medicamine. usu atteruntur multoque prius in aliquis deficiunt. nec cibo tantum et alimentis necessarii, quippe vocis sermonisque regimen primores tenent, concentu quodam excipientes ictum linguae serieque structurae atque magnitudine mutilantes mollientesve aut hebetantes verba et, cum defuere, explanationem omnem adimentes.

71. quin et augurium in hac esse creditur parte. triceni bini viris adtribuuntur excepta Turdulorum gente: quibus plures fuere, longiora promitti vitae putant spatia. feminis minor numerus: quibus in dextra parte gemini superne a canibus cognominati, fortunae blandimenta pollicentur, sicut in Agrippina Domiti Neronis matre; contra in laeva.— **72.** (Hominem prius quam genito dente cremari mos gentium non est)—sed mox plura de hoc, cum membratim historia decurret. Risisse eodem die quo genitus esset unum hominum accepimus Zoroastren; eidem cerebrum ita palpitasse, ut inpositam repelleret manum, futurae praesagio scientiae.

73. In trimatu suo cuique dimidiam esse mensuram futurae certum est. in plenum autem cuncto mortalium generi minorem in dies fieri propemodum observatur rarosque patribus proceriores, consumente ubertatem seminum exustione, in cuius vices nunc vergat aevum. in Creta terrae motu rupto monte inventum est corpus stans XLVI cubitorum, quod alii Orionis, alii Oti esse tradunt.

74. Orestis corpus oraculi iussu refossum VII cubitorum fuisse monumentis creditur. iam vero ante annos prope mille vates ille Homerus non cessavit minora corpora mortalium quam prisca conqueri. Naevii Pollionis amplitudinem annales non tradunt, sed quia populi concursu paene sit interemptus, vice prodigii habitum. procerissimum hominum aetas nostra Divo Claudio principe Gabbaram nomine ex Arabia advectum novem pedum et totidem unciarum vidit.

75. fuere sub Divo Augusto semipede addito, quorum corpora eius miraculi gratia in conditorio Sallustianorum adservabantur hortorum; Pusioni et Secundillae erant nomina. eodem praeside minimus homo duos pedes et palmum Conopas nomine in deliciis Iuliae neptis eius fuit, et mulier Andromeda, liberta Iuliae Augustae. Manium Maximum et M. Tullium equites Romanos binum cubitorum fuisse auctor est M. Varro, et ipsi vidimus in loculis adservatos. sesquipedales gigni, quosdam longiores, in trimatu inplentes vitae cursum, haud ignotum est.

76. Invenimus in monumentis Salamine Euthymenis filium in tria cubita triennio adcrevisse, incessu tardum, sensu hebetem, puberem etiam factum, voce robusta, absumptum contractione membrorum subita triennio circumacto. ipsi non pridem vidimus eadem ferme omnia praeter pubertatem in filio Corneli Taciti, equitis Romani Belgicae Galliae rationes procurantis. ἐκτραπέλους Graeci vocant eos; in Latio non habent nomen.

XVII **77.** Quod sit homini spatium a vestigio ad verticem, id esse pansis manibus inter longissimos digitos observatum est, sicuti vires dextra parte maiores, quibusdam aequas utraque, aliquis laeva manu praecipuas, nec id umquam in feminis; mares praestare pondere et defuncta viventibus corpora omnium animalium et dormientia vigilantibus; virorum cadavera supina fluitare, feminarum prona, velut pudori defunctarum parcente natura.

XVIII **78.** Concretis quosdam ossibus ac sine medullis vivere accepimus. signum eorum esse nec sitim sentire nec sudorem emittere, quamquam et voluntate scimus sitim victam equitemque Romanum Iulium Viatorem e Vocontiorum gente foederata in pupillaribus annis aquae subter cutem fusae morbo prohibitum umore a medicis naturam fecisse consuetudinem atque in senecta caruisse potu. nec non et alii multa sibi imperavere.

XIX **79.** Ferunt Crassum, avum Crassi in Parthis interempti, numquam risisse, ob id Agelastum vocatum, sicuti nec flesse multos. Socratem clarum sapientia eodem semper visum vultu nec aut hilaro magis aut turbato. exit hic animi tenor aliquando in rigorem quendam torvitatemque naturae duram et inflexibilem affectusque humanos adimit, quales ἀπαθεῖς Graeci vocant, multos eius generis experti,— quod mirum sit—

80. auctores maxime sapientiae, Diogenen Cynicum, Pyrrhonem, Heraclitum, Timonem, hunc quidem etiam in totius odium generis humani evectum. sed haec parva naturae insignia in multis varia cognoscuntur, ut in Antonia Drusi numquam expuisse, in Pomponio consulari poeta non ructasse.—(Quibus natura concreta sunt ossa, qui sunt rari admodum, cornei vocantur)—

XX **81.** Corpore vesco, sed eximiis viribus Tritanum, in gladiatorio ludo Samnitium armatura celebrem, filiumque eius militem Magni Pompei et rectos et traversos cancellatim toto corpore habuisse nervos, in brachiis etiam manibusque, auctor est Varro prodigiosa virium relatione atque etiam hostem ab eo ex provocatione dimicante inermi dextera superatum et postremo correptum uno digito in castra tralatum.

82. at Vinnius Valens meruit in praetorio Divi Augusti centurio, vehicula vini culleis onusta, donec exinanirentur, sustinere solitus, carpenta adprehensa una manu retinere, obnixus contra nitentibus iumentis, et alia mirifica facere, quae insculpta monumento eius spectantur.

83. idem M. Varro: Rusticelius, inquit, Hercules appellatus mulum suum tollebat, Fufius Salvius duo centenaria pondera pedibus, totidem manibus et ducenaria duo umeris contra scalas ferebat. nos quoque vidimus Athanatum nomine prodigiosae ostentationis quingenario thorace plumbeo indutum cothurnisque quingentum pondo calciatum per scaenam ingredi. Crotoniensem Milonem athletam, cum constitisset, nemo vestigio educebat, malum tenenti modo digitum corrigebat.

84. Cucurrisse MCXL stadia ab Athenis Lacedaemonem biduo Philippidem magnum erat, donec Anystis cursor Lacedaemonius et Philonides Alexandri Magni a Sicyone Elim uno die MCCCV cucurrerunt. nunc quidem in circo quosdam $\overline{CLX}$ passuum tolerare non ignoramus nuperque Fonteio et Vipstano coss. annos VIII genitum a meridie ad vesperam $\overline{LXXV}$ passuum cucurrisse. cuius rei admiratio ita demum solida perveniat, si quis cogitet nocte ac die longissimum iter vehiculis Tib. Neronem emensum festinantem ad Drusum fratrem aegrotum in Germaniam. ea fuerunt $\overline{CC}$ passuum.

XXI **85.** Oculorum acies vel maxime fidem excedentia invenit exempla. in nuce inclusam Iliadem Homeri carmen in membrana scriptum tradit Cicero. idem fuisse qui pervideret $\overline{CXXXV}$ passuum. huic et nomen M. Varro reddit: Strabonem vocatum; solitum autem Punico bello a Lilybaeo Siciliae promunturio, exeunte classe e Carthaginis portu, etiam numerum navium dicere. Callicrates ex ebore formicas et alia tam parva fecit animalia, ut partes eorum a ceteris cerni non possent. Myrmecides quidem in eodem genere inclaruit quadriga ex eadem materia, quam musca integeret alis, fabricata et nave, quam apicula pinnis absconderet.

XXII **86.** Auditus unum exemplum habet mirabile proelium, quo Sybaris deleta est, eo die quo gestum erat auditum Olympiae. nam nuntii Cimbricae victoriae Castoresque, Romam qui Persicam victoriam ipso die quo contigit nuntiavere, visus et numinum fuere praesagia.

XXIII **87.** Patientia corporis, ut est crebra sors calamitatium, innumera documenta peperit, clarissimum in feminis Leaenae meretricis, quae torta non indicavit Harmodium et Aristogitonem tyrannicidas, in viris Anaxarchi, qui, simili de causa cum torqueretur, praerosam dentibus linguam unamque spem indicii in tyranni os expuit.

XXIV **88.** Memoria necessarium maxime vitae bonum cui praecipua fuerit, haud facile dictu est, tam multis eius gloriam adeptis. Cyrus rex omnibus in exercitu suo militibus nomina reddidit, L. Scipio populo Romano, Cineas Pyrrhi regis legatus senatui et equestri ordini Romae postero die quam advenerat. Mithridates, duarum et viginti gentium rex, totidem linguis iura dixit, pro contione singulas sine interprete adfatus.

89. Charmadas quidem in Graecia quae quis exegerat volumina in bibliothecis legentis modo repraesentavit. ars postremo eius rei facta et inventa est a Simonide melico, consummata a Metrodoro Scepsio, ut nihil non isdem verbis redderetur auditum.

90. nec aliud est aeque fragile in homine: morborum et casus iniurias atque etiam metus sentit, alias particulatim, alias universa. ictus lapide oblitus est litteras tantum; ex praealto tecto lapsus matris et adfinium propinquorumque cepit oblivionem, alius aegrotus servorum, etiam sui vero nominis Messala Corvinus orator. itaque saepe deficere temptat ac meditatur vel quieto corpore et valido. somno quoque serpente amputatur, ut inanis mens quaerat ubi sit loci.

XXV **91.** Animi vigore praestantissimum arbitror genitum Caesarem dictatorem, nec virtutem constantiamque nunc commemoro nec sublimitatem omnium capacem quae caelo continentur, sed proprium vigorem celeritatemque quodam igne volucrem. scribere aut legere, simul dictare et audire solitum accepimus, epistulas vero tantarum rerum quaternas pariter dictare [librariis aut, si nihil aliud ageret, septenas].

92. idem signis conlatis bis et quinquagiens dimicavit, solus M. Marcellum transgressus, qui undequadragiens dimicavit. nam praeter civiles victorias undeciens centena et nonaginta duo milia hominum occisa proeliis ab eo non equidem in gloria posuerim, tantam etiam coactam humani generis iniuriam, quod ita esse confessus est ipse bellorum civilium stragem non prodendo.

93. Iustius Pompeio Magno tribuatur DCCCXLVI naves piratis ademisse: Caesari proprium et peculiare sit praeter supra dicta clementiae insigne, qua usque ad paenitentiam omnes superavit. idem magnanimitatis perhibuit exemplum, cui comparari non possit aliud.

94. spectacula enim edita effusasque opes aut operum magnificentiam in hac parte enumerare luxuriae faventis est: illa fuit vera et incomparabilis invicti animi sublimitas, captis apud Pharsaliam Pompei Magni scriniis epistularum iterumque apud Thapsum Scipionis concremasse ea optima fide atque non legisse.

XXVI **95.** Verum ad decus imperii Romani, non solum ad viri unius, pertinet victoriarum Pompei Magni titulos omnes triumphosque hoc in loco nuncupari, aequato non modo Alexandri Magni rerum fulgore, sed etiam Herculis prope ac Liberi patris.

96. igitur Sicilia recuperata, unde primum Sullanus in rei publicae causa exoriens auspicatus est, Africa vero tota subacta et in dicionem redacta Magnique nomine in spolium inde capto, eques Romanus, id quod antea nemo, curru triumphali revectus et statim ad solis occasum transgressus, excitatis in Pyrenaeo tropaeis, oppida DCCCLXXVI ab Alpibus ad fines Hispaniae ulterioris in dicionem redacta victoriae suae adscripsit et maiore animo Sertorium tacuit, belloque civili, quod omnia externa conciebat, extincto iterum triumphales currus eques R. induxit, totiens imperator ante quam miles.

97. postea ad tota maria et deinde solis ortus missus hos retulit patriae titulos more sacris certaminibus vincentium—neque enim ipsi coronantur, sed patrias suas coronant—, hos ergo honores urbi tribuit in delubro Minervae, quod ex manubiis dicabat:

CN·POMPEIVS MAGNVS IMPERATOR BELLO XXX ANNORVM CONFECTO FVSIS FVGATIS OCCISIS IN DEDITIONEM ACCEPTIS HOMINVM CENTIENS VICIENS SEMEL $\overline{LXXXIII}$ DEPRESSIS AVT CAPTIS NAVIBVS DCCCXLVI OPPIDIS CASTELLIS MDXXXVIII IN FIDEM RECEPTIS TERRIS A MAEOTIS AD RVBRVM MARE SVBACTIS VOTVM MERITO MINERVAE.

98. Hoc est breviarium eius ab oriente. triumphi vero, quem duxit a. d. III kal. Oct. M. Pisone M. Messala coss., praefatio haec fuit:

CVM ORAM MARITIMAM PRAEDONIBVS LIBERASSET ET IMPERIVM MARIS POPVLO ROMANO RESTITVISSET EX ASIA PONTO ARMENIA PAPHLAGONIA CAPPADOCIA CILICIA SYRIA SCYTHIS IVDAEIS ALBANIS HIBERIA INSVLA CRETA BASTERNIS ET SVPER HAEC DE REGE MITHRIDATE ATQVE TIGRANE TRIVMPHAVIT.

99. Summa summarum in illa gloria fuit (ut ipse in contione dixit, cum de rebus suis dissereret) Asiam ultimam provinciarum accepisse eandemque mediam patriae reddidisse. si quis e contrario simili modo velit percensere Caesaris res, qui maior illo apparuit, totum profecto terrarum orbem enumeret, quod infinitum esse conveniet.

XXVII **100.** Ceteris virtutum generibus varie et multi fuere praestantes. Cato primus Porciae gentis tres summas in homine res praestitisse existimatur, ut esset optimus orator, optimus imperator, optimus senator, quae mihi omnia, etiamsi non prius, attamen clarius fulsisse in Scipione Aemiliano videntur, dempto praeterea plurimorum odio, quo Cato laboravit. itaque sit proprium Catonis quater et quadragiens causam dixisse, nec quemquam saepius postulatum et semper absolutum.

XVIII **101.** Fortitudo in quo maxime exstiterit inmensae quaestionis est, utique si poetica recipiatur fabulositas. Q. Ennius T. Caecilium Teucrum fratremque eius praecipue miratus propter eos sextum decimum adiecit annalem. L. Siccius Dentatus, qui tribunus plebei fuit Sp. Tarpeio A. Aternio coss. haud multo post exactos reges, vel numerosissima suffragia habet centiens viciens proeliatus, octiens ex provocatione victor, quadraginta quinque cicatricibus adverso corpore insignis, nulla in tergo.

102. idem spolia cepit XXXIIII, donatus hastis puris duodeviginti, phaleris viginti quinque, torquibus tribus et octoginta, armillis CLX, coronis XXVI, in iis civicis XIIII, aureis octo, muralibus tribus, obsidionali una, fisco aeris, X captivis et viginti simul bubus, imperatores novem ipsius maxime opera triumphantes secutus, praeterea (quod optimum in operibus eius reor) uno ex ducibus T. Romilio ex consulatu ad populum convicto male imperatae rei militaris.

103. Haud minora forent Capitolini decora, ni perdidisset illa exitu vitae. ante decem et septem annos bina ceperat spolia. primus omnium eques muralem acceperat coronam, sex civicas, XXXVII dona, XXIII cicatrices adverso corpore exceperat, P. Servilium magistrum equitum servaverat, ipse vulneratus umerum, femur. super omnia Capitolium summamque rem in eo solus a Gallis servaverat, si non regno suo servasset.

104. Verum in his sunt quidem virtutis opera magna, sed maiora fortunae. M. Sergio, ut equidem arbitror, nemo quemquam hominum iure praetulerit, licet pronepos Catilina gratiam nomini deroget. secundo stipendio dextram manum perdidit; stipendis duobus ter et viciens vulneratus est, ob id neutra manu, neutro pede satis utilis, uno tantum servo, plurimis postea stipendiis debilis miles. bis ab Hannibale captus—neque enim cum quolibet hoste res fuit—, bis vinculorum eius profugus, in viginti mensibus nullo non die in catenis aut compedibus custoditus.

105. sinistra manu sola quater pugnavit, uno die duobus equis insidente eo suffossis. dextram sibi ferream fecit eaque religata proeliatus Cremonam obsidione exemit, Placentiam tutatus est, duodena castra hostium in Gallia cepit, quae omnia ex oratione eius apparent habita cum in praetura sacris arceretur a collegis ut debilis, quos hinc coronarum acervos constructurus hoste mutato!

106. etenim plurimum refert, in quae cuiusque virtus tempora inciderit. quas Trebia Ticinusve aut Trasimennus civicas dedere? quae Cannis corona merita, unde fugisse virtutis summum opus fuit? ceteri profecto victores hominum fuere, Sergius vicit etiam fortunam.

XXIX **107.** Ingeniorum gloriae quis possit agere dilectum per tot disciplinarum genera et tantam rerum operumque varietatem, nisi forte Homero vate Graeco nullum felicius extitisse convenit, sive operis forma sive materie aestimetur?

108. itaque Alexander Magnus—etenim insignibus iudiciis optime citraque invidiam tam superba censura peragetur—inter spolia Darii Persarum regis unguentorum scrinio capto, quod erat auro, margaritis gemmisque pretiosum, varios eius usus amicis demonstrantibus, quando taedebat unguenti bellatorem et militia sordidum: "immo Hercule," inquit, "librorum Homeri custodiae detur," ut pretiosissimum humani animi opus quam maxime diviti opere servaretur.

109. idem Pindari vatis familiae penatibusque iussit parci, cum Thebas raperet, Aristotelis philosophi patriam suam credidit tantaeque rerum claritati tam benignum testimonium miscuit. Archilochi poetae interfectores Apollo arguit Delphis. Sophoclem tragici cothurni principem defunctum sepelire Liber pater iussit, obsidentibus moenis Lacedaemoniis, Lysandro eorum rege in quiete saepius admonito ut pateretur humari delicias suas. requisivit rex, qui supremum diem Athenis obissent, nec difficulter ex his quem deus significasset intellexit pacemque funeri dedit.

XXX **110.** Platoni sapientiae antistiti Dionysius tyrannus, alias saevitiae superbiaeque natus, vittatam navem misit obviam, ipse quadrigis albis egredientem in litore excepit. viginti talentis unam orationem Isocrates vendidit. Aeschines Atheniensis summus orator, cum accusationem, qua fuerat usus, Rhodiis legisset, legit et defensionem Demosthenis, qua in illud pulsus fuerat exilium mirantibusque tum magis fuisse miraturos dixit, si ipsum orantem audivissent, calamitate testis ingens factus inimici.

111. Thucydiden imperatorem Athenienses in exilium egere, rerum conditorem revocavere, eloquentiam mirati cuius virtutem damnaverant. magnum et Menandro in comico socco testimonium regum Aegypti et Macedoniae contigit classe et per legatos petito, maius ex ipso, regiae fortunae praelata litterarum conscientia.

112. Perhibuere et Romani proceres etiam exteris testimonia. Cn. Pompeius confecto Mithridatico bello intraturus Posidonii sapientiae professione clari domum forem percuti de more a lictore vetuit et fasces litterarum ianuae summisit is cui se oriens occidensque summiserat. Cato censorius in illa nobili trium sapientiae procerum ab Athenis legatione audito Carneade quam primum legatos eos censuit dimittendos, quoniam illo viro argumentante quid veri esset haud facile discerni posset.

113. quanta morum commutatio! ille semper alioquin universos ex Italia pellendos censuit Graecos, at pronepos eius Uticensis Cato unum ex tribunatu militum philosophum, alterum ex Cypria legatione deportavit, eandemque linguam ex duobus Catonibus in illo abegisse, in hoc importasse memorabile est.

114. Sed et nostrorum gloriam percenseamus. prior Africanus Q. Ennii statuam sepulcro suo inponi iussit clarumque illud nomen, immo vero spolium ex tertia orbis parte raptum, in cinere supremo cum poetae titulo legi. Divus Augustus carmina Vergili cremari contra testamenti eius verecundiam vetuit, maiusque ita vati testimonium contigit quam si ipse sua probavisset.

115. M. Varronis in bibliotheca, quae prima in orbe ab Asinio Pollione ex manubiis publicata Romae est, unius viventis posita imago est, haud minore, ut equidem reor, gloria, principe oratore et cive ex illa ingeniorum quae tunc fuit multitudine uni hanc coronam dante quam cum eidem Magnus Pompeius piratico ex bello navalem dedit.

116. innumerabilia deinde sunt exempla Romana, si persequi libeat, cum plures una gens in quocumque genere eximios tulerit quam ceterae terrae. sed quo te, M. Tulli, piaculo taceam, quove maxime excellentem insigni praedicem? quo potius quam universi populi illius gentium amplissimi testimonio, e tota vita tua consulatus tantum operibus electis?

117. te dicente legem agrariam, hoc est alimenta sua, abdicarunt tribus; te suadente Roscio theatralis auctori legis ignoverunt notatasque se discrimine sedis aequo animo tulerunt; te orante proscriptorum liberos honores petere puduit; tuum Catilina fugit ingenium; tu M. Antonium proscripsisti. salve primus omnium parens patriae appellate, primus in toga triumphum linguaeque lauream merite [et facundiae Latiarumque litterarum parens] atque (ut dictator Caesar, hostis quondam tuus, de te scripsit) omnium triumphorum laurea maiorem, quanto plus est ingenii Romani terminos in tantum promovisse quam imperii.

XXXI **118.** Reliquis animi bonis praestitere ceteros mortales: sapientia ob id Cati, Corculi apud Romanos cognominati, apud Graecos Socrates, oraculo Apollinis Pythii praelatus cunctis.

XXXII **119.** rursus mortales oraculorum societatem dedere Chiloni Lacedaemonio tria praecepta eius Delphis consecrando aureis litteris, quae sunt haec: nosse se quemque, et nihil nimium cupere, comitemque aeris alieni atque litis esse miseriam. quin et funus eius, cum victore filio Olympiae expirasset gaudio, tota Graecia prosecuta est.

XXXIII Divinitas et quaedam caelitum societas nobilissima ex feminis in Sibylla fuit, ex viris in Melampode apud Graecos, apud Romanos in Marcio.

XXXIV **120.** Vir optimus semel a condito aevo iudicatus est Scipio Nasica ab iurato senatu, idem in toga candida bis repulsa notatus a populo. in summa ei in patria mori non licuit, non Hercule magis quam extra vincula illi sapientissimo ab Apolline iudicato Socrati.

XXXV Pudicissima femina semel matronarum sententia iudicata est Sulpicia Paterculi filia, uxor Fulvi Flacci, electa ex centum praeceptis quae simulacrum Veneris ex Sibyllinis libris dedicaret, iterum religionis experimento Claudia inducta Romam deum matre.

XXXVI **121.** Pietatis exempla infinita quidem toto orbe extitere, sed Romae unum, cui comparari cuncta non possint. humilis in plebe et ideo ignobilis puerpera, supplicii causa carcere inclusa matre cum impetrasset aditum, a ianitore semper excussa ante, ne quid inferret cibi, deprehensa est uberibus suis alens eam. quo miraculo matris salus donata pietati est, ambaeque perpetuis alimentis, et locus ille eidem consecratus deae, C. Quinctio M'. Acilio coss. templo Pietatis extructo in illius carceris sede, ubi nunc Marcelli theatrum est.

122. Gracchorum pater anguibus prehensis in domo, cum responderetur ipsum victurum alterius sexus interempto: immo vero, inquit, meum necate, Cornelia enim iuvenis est et parere adhuc potest. hoc erat uxori parcere et rei publicae consulere; idque mox consecutum est. M. Lepidus Appuleiae uxoris caritate post repudium obiit. P. Rupilius morbo levi impeditus nuntiata fratris repulsa in consulatus petitione ilico expiravit. P. Catienus Philotimus patronum adeo dilexit, ut heres omnibus bonis institutus in rogum eius se iaceret.

XXXVII **123.** Variarum artium scientia innumerabiles enituere, quos tamen attingi par sit florem hominum libantibus: astrologia Berosus, cui ob divinas praedictiones Athenienses publice in gymnasio statuam inaurata lingua statuere; grammatica Apollodorus, cui Amphictyones Graeciae honorem habuere; Hippocrates medicina, qui venientem ab Illyriis pestilentiam praedixit discipulosque ad auxiliandum circa urbes dimisit, quod ob meritum honores illi quos Herculi decrevit Graecia. eandem scientiam in Cleombroto Ceo Ptolemaeus rex Megalensibus sacris donavit centum talentis servato Antiocho rege.

124. magna et Critobulo fama est extracta Philippi regis oculo sagitta et citra deformitatem oris curata orbitate luminis, summa autem Asclepiadi Prusiensi condita nova secta, spretis legatis et pollicitationibus Mithridatis regis, reperta ratione qua vinum aegris medetur, relato e funere homine et conservato, sed maxime sponsione facta cum fortuna, ne medicus crederetur, si umquam invalidus ullo modo fuisset ipse. et vicit suprema in senecta lapsu scalarum exanimatus.

125. Grande et Archimedi geometricae ac machinalis scientiae testimonium M. Marcelli contigit interdicto, cum Syracusae caperentur, ne violaretur unus, nisi fefellisset imperium militaris inprudentia. laudatus est et Chersiphron Gnosius aede Ephesi Dianae admirabili fabricata, Philon Athenis armamentario CD navium, Ctesibius pneumatica ratione et hydraulicus organis repertis, Dinochares metatus Alexandro condente in Aegypto Alexandriam. idem hic imperator edixit ne quis ipsum alius quam Apelles pingeret, quam Pyrgoteles scalperet, quam Lysippus ex aere duceret. quae artes pluribus inclaruere exemplis.

XXXVIII **126.** Aristidis Thebani pictoris unam tabulam centum talentis rex Attalus licitus est, octoginta emit duas Caesar dictator, Mediam et Aiacem Timomachi, in templo Veneris Genetricis dicaturus. Candaules rex Bularchi picturam Magnetum exitii, haud mediocris spati, rependit auro. Rhodum non incendit rex Demetrius expugnator cognominatus, ne tabulam Protogenis cremaret a parte ea muri locatam.

127. Praxiteles marmore nobilitatus est Cnidiaque Venere praecipue vesano amore cuiusdam iuvenis insigni et Nicomedis aestimatione regis grandi Cnidiorum aere alieno permutare eam conati. Phidiae Iuppiter Olympius cotidie testimonium perhibet, Mentori Capitolinus et Diana Ephesia, quibus fuere consecrata artis eius vasa.

XXIX **128.** Pretium hominis in servitio geniti maximum ad hanc diem, quod equidem conpeperim, fuit grammaticae artis, Daphnin Attio Pisaurense vendente et M. Scauro principe civitatis IIi $\overline{DCC}$ licente. excessere hoc in nostro aevo, nec modice, histriones, sed hi libertatem suam mercati, quippe cum iam apud maiores Roscius histrio IIi $\overline{D}$ annua meritasse prodatur,

129. nisi si quis in hoc loco desiderat Armeniaci belli paulo ante propter Tiridaten gesti dispensatorem, quem Nero IIi $|\overline{CXXX}|$ manumisit. sed hoc pretium belli, non hominis, fuit tam Hercules quam libidinis, non formae, Paezontem e spadonibus Seiani IIi $|\overline{D}|$ mercante Clutorio Prisco. quam quidem iniuriam lucri fecit ille mercatus in luctu civitatis, quoniam arguere nulli vacabat.

XL **130.** Gentium in toto orbe praestantissima una omnium virtute haud dubie Romana extitit. felicitas cui praecipua fuerit homini, non est humani iudicii, cum prosperitatem ipsam alius alio modo et suopte ingenio quisque determinet. si verum facere iudicium volumus ac repudiata omni fortunae ambitione decernere, nemo mortalium est felix. abunde agitur atque indulgenter a fortuna deciditur cum eo, qui iure dici non infelix potest. quippe ut alia non sint, certe ne lassescat fortuna metus est, quo semel recepto solida felicitas non est.

131. quid, quod nemo mortalium omnibus horis sapit? utinamque falsum hoc et non ut a vate dictum quam plurimi iudicent! vana mortalitas et ad circumscribendam se ipsam ingeniosa conputat more Thraciae gentis, quae calculos colore distinctos pro experimento cuiusque diei in urnam condit ac supremo die separatos dinumerat atque ita de quoque pronuntiat.

132. quid, quod iste, calculi candore illo laudato die, originem mali habuit? quam multos accepta adflixere imperia! quam multos bona perdidere et ultimis mersere suppliciis, ista nimirum bona, cum interim illa hora in gaudio fuit! ita est profecto: alius de alio iudicat dies et tamen supremus de omnibus, ideoque nullis credendum est. quid, quod bona malis paria non sunt etiam pari numero, nec laetitia ulla minimo maerore pensanda? heu vana et inprudens diligentia! numerus dierum conparatur, ubi quaeritur pondus!

XLI **133.** Una feminarum in omni aevo Lampido Lacedaemonia reperitur, quae regis filia, regis uxor, regis mater fuerit, una Berenice, quae filia, soror, mater Olympionicarum; una familia Curionum, in qua tres continua serie oratores extiterint, una Fabiorum, in qua tres continui principes senatus, M. Fabius Ambustus, Fabius Rullianus filius, Q. Fabius Gurges nepos.

XLII **134.** Cetera exempla fortunae variantis innumera sunt. etenim quae facit magna gaudia nisi ex malis aut quae mala inmensa nisi ex ingentibus gaudiis?

XLIII servavit proscriptum a Sulla M. Fidustinum senatorem annis XXXVI, sed iterum proscriptura. superstes Sullae vixit, sed usque ad Antonium, constatque nulla alia de causa ab eo proscriptum quam quia proscriptus fuisset.

135. triumphare P. Ventidium de Parthis voluit quidem solum, sed eundem in triumpho Asculano Cn. Pompei duxit puerum, quamquam Masurius auctor est bis in triumpho ductum, Cicero mulionem castrensis furnariae fuisse, plurimi iuventam inopem in caliga militari tolerasse.

136. fuit et Balbus Cornelius maior consul, sed accusatus atque de iure virgarum in eum iudicum in consilium missus, primus externorum atque etiam in oceano genitorum usus illo honore, quem maiores Latio quoque negaverint. est et L. Fulvius inter insignia exempla, Tusculanorum rebellantium consul, eodemque honore, cum transisset, exornatus confestim a populo Romano, qui solus eodem anno, quo fuerat hostis, Romae triumphavit ex iis quorum consul fuerat.

137. unus hominum ad hoc aevi Felicis sibi cognomen adseruit L. Sulla, civili nempe sanguine ac patriae oppugnatione adoptatum. sed quibus felicitatis inductus argumentis? quod proscribere tot milia civium ac trucidare potuisset? o prava interpretatio et futuro tempore infelix! non melioris sortis tunc fuere pereuntes, quorum miseremur hodie, cum Sullam nemo non oderit?

138. age, non exitus vitae eius omnium proscriptorum ab illo calamitate crudelior fuit erodente se ipso corpore et supplicia sibi gignente? quod ut dissimulaverit et supremo somnio eius, cui inmortuus quodammodo est, credamus ab uno illo invidiam gloria victam, hoc tamen nempe felicitati suae defuisse confessus est quod Capitolium non dedicavisset.

139. Q. Metellus in ea oratione, quam habuit supremis laudibus patris sui L. Metelli pontificis, bis consulis, dictatoris, magistri equitum, XVviri agris dandis, qui primus elephantos ex primo Punico bello duxit in triumpho, scriptum reliquit decem maximas res optimasque, in quibus quaerendis sapientes aetatem exigerent, consummasse eum:

140. voluisse enim primarium bellatorem esse, optimum oratorem, fortissimum imperatorem, auspicio suo maximas res geri, maximo honore uti, summa sapientia esse, summum senatorem haberi, pecuniam magnam bono modo invenire, multos liberos relinquere et clarissimum in civitate esse; haec contigisse ei nec ulli alii post Romam conditam.

141. longum est refellere et supervacuum abunde uno casu refutante, siquidem is Metellus orbam luminibus exegit senectam, amissis incendio, cum Palladium raperet ex aede Vestae, memorabili causa, sed eventu misero. quo fit ut infelix quidem dici non debeat, felix tamen non possit. tribuit ei populus Romanus quod nulli alii ab condito aevo, ut, quotiens in senatum iret, curru veheretur ad curiam: magnum ei et sublime, sed pro oculis datum.

XLIV **142.** Huius quoque Q. Metelli, qui illa de patre dixit, filius inter rara felicitatis humanae exempla numeratur: nam praeter honores amplissimos cognomenque Macedonici a quattuor filiis inlatus rogo, uno praetorio, tribus consularibus, duobus triumphalibus, uno censorio, quae singula quoque paucis contigere.

143. in ipso tamen flore dignationis suae ab C. Atinio Labeone, cui cognomen fuit Macerioni, tribuno plebis, quem e senatu censor eiecerat, revertens e campo meridiano tempore vacuo foro et Capitolio ad Tarpeium raptus, ut praecipitaretur, convolante quidem tam numerosa illa cohorte, quae patrem eum appellabat, sed, ut necesse erat in subito, tarde et tamquam in exequias, cum resistendi sacroque sanctum repellendi ius non esset, virtutis suae opera et censurae periturus, aegre tribuno, qui intercederet, reperto a limine ipso mortis revocatus alieno beneficio postea vixit,

144. bonis inde etiam consecratis a damnato suo, tamquam parum esset faucium reste intortarum, expressi per aures sanguinis poenam exactam esse. equidem et Africani sequentis inimicum fuisse inter calamitates duxerim, ipso teste Macedonico, siquidem dixit: "Ite filii, celebrate exequias, numquam civis maioris funus videbitis." et hoc dicebat iam Baliaricis, Diadematis, iam Macedonicus ipse.

145. verum ut illa sola iniuria aestimetur, quis hunc iure felicem dixerit, periclitatum ad libidinem inimici, nec Africani saltem, perire? quos hostes vicisse tanti fuit? aut quos non honores currusque illa sua violentia fortuna retroegit, per mediam urbem censore tracto—etenim sola haec morandi ratio fuerat—, tracto in Capitolium idem, in quod triumphans ipse deorum exuviis ne captivos quidem sic traxerat?

146. maius hoc scelus felicitate consecuta factum est, periclitato Macedonico vel funus tantum [tale] perdere, in quo a triumphalibus liberis portaretur in rogum velut exequiis quoque triumphans. nulla est profecto solida felicitas, quam contumelia ulla vitae rupit, nedum tanta. quod superest, nescio morum gloriae an indignationis dolori accedat, inter tot Metellos tam sceleratam C. Atini audaciam scmper fuisse inultam.

XLV **147.** In Divo quoque Augusto, quem universa mortalitas in hac censura nuncupet, si diligenter aestimentur cuncta, magna sortis humanae reperiantur volumina: repulsa in magisterio equitum apud avunculum et contra petitionem eius praelatus Lepidus, proscriptionis invidia ob collegium in triumviratu pessimorum civium, nec aequa saltem portione, sed praegravi Antonio,

148. Philippensi proelio morbi, fuga et triduo in palude aegroti et (ut fatentur Agrippa ac Maecenas) aqua subter cutem fusa turgidi latebra, naufragia Sicula et alia ibi quoque in spelunca occultatio, iam in navali fuga urgente hostium manu preces Proculeio mortis admotae, cura Perusinae contentionis, sollicitudo Martis Actiaci, Pannonicis bellis ruina e turri,

149. tot seditiones militum, tot ancipites morbi corporis, suspecta Marcelli vota, pudenda Agrippae ablegatio, totiens petita insidiis vita, incusatae liberorum mortes luctusque non tantum orbitate tristis, adulterium filiae et consilia parricidae palam facta, contumeliosus privigni Neronis secessus, aliud in nepte adulterium; iuncta deinde tot mala: inopia stipendi, rebellio Illyrici, servitiorum dilectus iuventutis penuria, pestilentia urbis, fames Italiae, destinatio expirandi et quadridui inedia maior pars mortis in corpus recepta;

150. iuxta haec Variana clades et maiestatis eius foeda suggillatio, abdicatio Postumi Agrippae post adoptionem, desiderium post relegationem, inde suspicio in Fabium arcanorumque proditionem, hinc uxoris et Tiberii cogitationes, suprema eius cura. in summa deus ille caelumque nescio adeptus magis an meritus herede hostis sui filio excessit.

XLVI **151.** Subeunt in hac reputatione Delphica oracula velut ad castigandam hominum vanitatem ab deo emissa. duo sunt haec: Pedium felicissimum, qui pro patria proxime occubuisset; iterum a Gyge rege tunc amplissimo terrarum consulti: Aglaum Psophidium esse feliciorem. senior hic in angustissimo Arcadiae angulo parvum, sed annuis victibus large sufficiens praedium colebat, numquam ex eo egressus atque, ut e vitae genere manifestum est, minima cupidine minimum in vita mali expertus.

XLVII **152.** Consecratus est vivus sentiensque eiusdem oraculi iussu et Iovis deorum summi adstipulatu Euthymus pycta, semper Olympiae victor et semel victus. patria ei Locri in Italia; ibi imaginem eius et Olympiae alteram eodem die tactam fulmine Callimachum ut nihil aliud miratum video deumque iussisse sacrificare, quod et vivo factitatum et mortuo, nihilque de eo mirum aliud quam hoc placuisse dis.

XLVIII **153.** De spatio atque longinquitate vitae hominum non locorum modo situs, verum et tempora ac sua cuique sors nascendi incertum fecere. Hesiodus, qui primus aliqua de hoc prodidit, fabulose, ut reor, multa hominum aevo praeferens, cornici novem nostras attribuit aetates, quadruplum eius cervis, id triplicatum corvis, et reliqua fabulosius in phoenice ac Nymphis.

154. Anacreon poeta Arganthonio Tartesiorum regi CL tribuit annos, Cinyrae Cypriorum decem annis amplius, Aegimio CC, Theopompus Epimenidi Gnosio CLVII; Hellanicus quosdam in Aetolia Epiorum gentis ducentos explere, cui adstipulatur Damastes memorans Pictoreum ex his praecipuum corpore viribusque etiam CCC vixisse,

155. Ephorus Arcadum reges tricenis annis, Alexander Cornelius Dandonem quendam in Illyrico D vixisse, Xenophon in periplo Lutmiorum insulae regem DC atque, ut parce mentitus, filium eius DCCC. quae omnia inscitia temporum acciderunt. annum enim alii aestate determinabant et alterum hieme, alii quadripertitis temporibus, sicut Arcades, quorum anni trimenstres fuere, quidam lunae senio, ut Aegyptii. itaque apud eos et singula milia annorum vixisse produntur.

156. sed ut ad confessa transeamus, Arganthonium Gaditanum LXXX annis regnasse prope certum est; putant quadragensimo coepisse. Masinissam LX annis regnasse indubitatum est, Gorgian Siculum CVIII vixisse. Q. Fabius Maximus LXIII annis augur fuit. M. Perpenna et nuper L. Volusius Saturninus omnium, quos in consulatu sententiam rogaverant, superstites fuere. Perpenna septem reliquit ex iis quos censor legerat; vixit annos LXXXXVIII.

157. qua in re et illud adnotare succurrit, unum omnino quinquennium fuisse quo senator nullus moreretur, cum Flaccus et Albinus censores lustrum condidere, usque ad proximos censores, ab anno urbis DLXXVIIII. M. Valerius Corvinus centum annos inplevit, cuius inter primum et sextum consulatum XLVI anni fuere. idem sella curuli semel ac viciens sedit, quotiens nemo alius. aequavit eius vitae spatia Metellus pontifex.

158. Et ex feminis Livia Rutili LXXXXVII annos excessit, Statilia Claudio principe ex nobili domo LXXXVIIII, Terentia Ciceronis CIII, Clodia Ofili CXV, haec quidem etiam enixa quindeciens. Lucceia mima C annis in scaena pronuntiavit. Galeria Copiola emboliaria reducta est in scaenam C. Poppaeo Q. Sulpicio coss. ludis pro salute Divi Augusti votivis annum CIIII agens; producta fuerat tirocinio a M. Pomponio aedile plebis C. Mario Cn. Carbone coss. ante annos XCI, a Magno Pompeio magni theatri dedicatione anus pro miraculo reducta.

159. Samullam quoque CX vixisse auctor est Pedianus Asconius. minus miror Stephanionem, qui primus togatus saltare instituit, utrisque saecularibus ludis saltavisse, et Divi Augusti et quos Claudius Caesar consulatu suo quarto fecit, quando LXIII non amplius anni interfuere, quamquam et postea diu vixit. in Tmoli montis cacumine, quod vocant Tempsin, CL annis vivere Mucianus auctor est, totidem annorum censum Claudi Caesaris censura T. Fullonium Bononiensem, idque collatis censibus, quos ante detulerat, vitaeque argumentis—etenim curae principi id erat—verum apparuit.

XLIX **160.** Poscere videtur locus ipse sideralis scientiae sententiam. Epigenes CXII annos inpleri negavit posse, Berosus excedi CXVI. durat et ea ratio, quam Petosiris ac Necepsos tradidere (tetartemorion appellant a trium signorum portione), qua posse in Italiae tractu CXXIIII annos vitae contingere apparet. negavere illi quemquam LXXXX partium exortivam mensuram (quod anaphoras vocant) transgredi, et has ipsas incidi occursu maleficorum siderum aut etiam radiis eorum solisque. Aesculapi rursus secta, quae stata vitae spatia a stellis accipi dicit, quantum plurimum tribuat, incertum est.

161. rara autem esse dicunt longiora tempora, quandoquidem momentis horarum insignibus lunae dierum, ut VII atque XV, quae nocte ac die observantur, ingens turba nascuntur scansili annorum lege occidua, quam climacteras appellant, non fere ita genitis LIIII annum excedentibus.

162. Primum ergo ipsius artis inconstantia declarat quam incerta res sit. accedunt experimenta recentissimi census, quem intra quadriennium Imperatores Caesares Vespasiani pater filiusque censores egerunt. nec sunt omnia vasaria excutienda; mediae tantum partis inter Appenninum Padumque ponemus exempla:

163. CXX annos Parmae tres edidere, Brixilli unus, CXXV Parmae duo, CXXX Placentiae unus, Faventiae una mulier, CXXXV Bononiae L. Terentius M. filius, Arimini vero M. Aponius CXL, Tertulla CXXXVII. citra Placentiam in collibus oppidum est Veleiatium, in quo CX annos sex detulere, quattuor vero centenos vicenos, unus CXL, M. Mucius M. filius Galeria Felix.

164. ac ne pluribus moremur in re confessa, in regione Italiae octava centenum annorum censi sunt homines LIIII, centenum denum homines XIIII, centenum vicenum quinum homines duo, centenum tricenum homines quattuor, centenum tricenum quinum aut septenum totidem, centenum quadragenum homines tres.

165. Alia mortalitatis inconstantia: Homerus eadem nocte natos Hectorem et Polydamanta tradidit, tam diversae sortis viros. C. Mario Cn. Carbone III coss. a. d. V kal. Iunias M. Caelius Rufus et C. Licinius Calvus eadem die geniti sunt, oratores quidem ambo, sed tam dispari eventu. hoc etiam isdem horis nascentibus in toto mundo cotidie evenit, pariterque domini ac servi gignuntur, reges et inopes.

L **166.** P. Cornelius Rufus, qui consul M'. Curio fuit, dormiens oculorum visum amisit, cum id sibi accidere somniaret. e diverso Pheraeus Iason deploratus a medicis vomicae morbo, cum mortem in acie quaereret, vulnerato pectore medicinam invenit ex hoste. Q. Fabius Maximus consul apud flumen Isaram proelio commisso adversus Allobrogum Arvernorumque gentes a. d. VI idus Augustas, $\overline{\text{CXXX}}$ perduellium caesis, febri quartana liberatus est in acie.

167. incertum ac fragile nimirum est hoc munus naturae, quicquid datur nobis, malignum vero et breve etiam in iis quibus largissime contigit, universum utique aevi tempus intuentibus. quid, quod aestimatione nocturnae quietis dimidio quisque spatio vitae suae vivit, pars aequa morti similis exigitur aut poena est, nisi contigit quies? nec reputantur infantiae anni, qui sensu carent, non senectae in poenam vivacis, tot periculorum genera, tot morbi, tot metus, tot curae, totiens invocata morte, ut nullum frequentius sit votum.

168. natura vero nihil hominibus brevitate vitae praestitit melius. hebescunt sensus, membra torpent, praemoritur visus, auditus, incessus, dentes etiam ac ciborum instrumenta, et tamen vitae hoc tempus adnumeratur. ergo pro miraculo et id solitarium reperitur exemplum Xenophili musici, centum et quinque annis vixisse sine ullo corporis incommodo.

169. at Hercule reliquis omnibus per singulas membrorum partes, qualiter nullis aliis animalibus, certis pestifer calor remeat horis aut rigor, neque horis modo, sed et diebus noctibusque trinis quadrinisve, etiam anno toto. [atque etiam morbus est aliquantisper sapientiam mori.]

170. morbis quoque enim quasdam leges natura posuit: quadrini circuitus febrem numquam bruma, numquam hibernis mensibus incipere, quosdam post sexagensimum vitae spatium non accedere; alios pubertate deponi, feminis praecipue; senes minime sentire pestilentiam. namque et universis gentibus ingruunt morbi et generatim modo servitiis, modo procerum ordini aliosque per gradus. qua in re observatum a meridianis partibus ad occasum solis pestilentiam semper ire nec umquam aliter fere, non hieme, nec ut ternos excedat menses.

LI **171.** iam signa letalia in furoris morbo risum, sapientiae vero aegritudine fimbriarum curam et stragulae vestis plicaturas, a somno moventium neglectum, praefandi umoris e corpore effluvium, in oculorum quidem et narium aspectu indubitata maxime atque etiam supino adsidue cubitu, venarum inaequabili aut formicante percussu, quaeque alia Hippocrati principi medicinae observata sunt. et cum innumerabilia sint mortis signa, salutis securitatisque nulla sunt, quippe cum censorius Cato ad filium de validis quoque observationem ut ex oraculo aliquo prodiderit, senilem iuventam praematurae mortis esse signum.

172. morborum vero tam infinita est multitudo, ut Pherecydes Syrius serpentium multitudine ex corpore eius erumpente expiraverit. quibusdam perpetua febris est, sicut C. Maecenati; eidem triennio supremo nullo horae momento contigit somnus. Antipater Sidonius poeta omnibus annis uno die tantum natali corripiebatur febre et eo consumptus est satis longa senecta.

LII **173.** Aviola consularis in rogo revixit et, quoniam subveniri non potuerat praevalente flamma, vivus crematus est. similis causa in L. Lamia praetorio viro traditur. nam C. Aelium Tuberonem praetura functum a rogo relatum Messala Rufus et plerique tradunt. haec est condicio mortalium. ad has et eius modi occasiones fortunae gignimur, uti de homine ne morti quidem debeat credi.

174. reperimus inter exempla Hermotimi Clazomenii animam relicto corpore errare solitam vagamque e longinquo multa adnuntiare, quae nisi a praesente nosci non possent, corpore interim semianimi, donec cremato eo inimici, qui Cantharidae vocabantur, remeanti animae veluti vaginam ademerint; Aristeae etiam visam evolantem ex ore in Proconneso corvi effigie, aeque magna ac quae sequitur fabulositate.

175. quam equidem et in Gnosio Epimenide simili modo accipio, puerum aestu et itinere fessum in specu septem et quinquaginta dormisse annis, rerum faciem mutationemque mirantem velut postero die experrectum, hinc pari numero dierum senio ingruente, ut tamen in septimum et quinquagesimum atque centesimum vitae duraret annum. feminarum sexus huic malo videtur maxime opportunus conversione volvae, quae si corrigatur, spiritus restituitur, huc pertinet nobile illud apud Graecos volumen Heraclidis septem diebus feminae exanimis ad vitam revocatae.

176. Varro quoque auctor est XXviro se agros dividente Capuae quendam, qui efferretur foro, domum remeasse pedibus. hoc idem Aquini accidisse. Romae quoque Corfidium, materterae suae maritum, funere locato revixisse et locatorem funeris ab eo elatum.

177. adicit miracula, quae tota indicasse conveniat: e duobus fratribus equestris ordinis Corfidiis maiori accidisse ut videretur expirasse, apertoque testamento recitatum heredem minorem funeri institisse; interim eum, qui videbatur exstinctus, plaudendo concivisse ministeria et narrasse a fratre se venisse, commendatam sibi filiam ab eo, demonstratum praeterea quo in loco defodisset aurum nullo conscio, et rogasse ut iis funebribus, quae comparasset, efferretur. hoc eo narrante fratris domestici propere adnuntiavere exanimatum illum, et aurum ubi dixerat repertum est.

178. plena praeterea vita est his vaticiniis, sed non conferenda, cum saepius falsa sint, sicut ingenti exemplo docebimus. bello Siculo Gabienus Caesaris classium fortissimus, captus a Sexto Pompeio, iussu eius incisa cervice et vix cohaerente, iacuit in litore toto die. deinde, cum advesperavisset, gemitu precibusque congregata multitudine petiit uti Pompeius ad se veniret aut aliquem ex arcanis mitteret; se enim ab inferis remissum habere quae nuntiaret.

179. misit plures Pompeius ex amicis, quibus Gabienus dixit inferis dis placere Pompei causas et partes pias; proinde eventum futurum quem optaret: hoc se nuntiare iussum; argumentum fore veritatis quod peractis mandatis protinus expiraturus esset. idque ita evenit. post sepulturam quoque visorum exempla sunt, nisi quod naturae opera, non prodigia, consectamur.

LIII **180.** In primis autem miraculo sunt atque frequentes mortes repentinae—hoc est summa vitae felicitas—, quas esse naturales docebimus. plurimas prodidit Verrius, nos cum dilectu modum servabimus. gaudio obiere praeter Chilonem, de quo diximus, Sophocles et Dionysius Siciliae tyrannus, uterque accepto tragicae victoriae nuntio, mater illa Cannensi filio incolumi viso contra nuntium falsum; pudore Diodorus sapientiae dialecticae professor, lusoria quaestione non protinus ab interrogatione Stilponis dissoluta.

181. nullis evidentibus causis obiere, dum calciantur matutino, duo Caesares, praetor et praetura perfunctus dictatoris Caesaris pater—hic Pisis exanimatus est, ille Romae—, Q. Fabius Maximus in consulatu suo pridie kal. Ian., in cuius locum C. Rebilus paucissimarum horarum consulatum petiit, item C. Volcatius Gurges senator, omnes adeo sani atque tempestivi, ut de progrediendo cogitarent, Q. Aemilius Lepidus iam egrediens incusso pollice limini cubiculi, C. Aufustius egressus, cum in senatum iret, offenso pede in comitio.

182. legatus quoque, qui Rhodiorum causam in senatu magna cum admiratione oraverat, in limine curiae protinus expiravit progredi volens, Cn. Baebius Tamphilus, praetura et ipse functus, cum a puero quaesisset horas, Aulus Pompeius in Capitolio, cum deos salutasset, M'. Iuventius Thalna consul, cum sacrificaret, C. Servilius Pansa, cum staret in foro ad tabernam hora diei secunda in P. fratrem innixus, Baebius iudex, dum vadimonium differri iubet, M. Terentius Corax, dum tabellas scribit in foro.

183. nec non et proximo anno, dum consulari viro in aurem dicit, eques Romanus ante Apollinem eboreum qui est in foro Augusti, super omnes C. Iulius medicus, dum inunguit, specillum per oculum trahens, A. Manlius Torquatus consularis, cum in cena placentam adpeteret, L. Tuccius medicus Valla, dum mulsi potionem haurit, Appius Saufeius, e balineo reversus cum mulsum bibisset ovumque sorberet, P. Quintius Scapula, cum apud Aquilium Gallum cenaret, Decimus Saufeius scriba, cum domi suae pranderet.

184. Cornelius Gallus praetorius et T. Hetereius eques Romanus in venere obiere et, quos nostra adnotavit aetas, duo equestris ordinis in eodem pantomimo Mystico, tum forma praecellente. operosissima tamen securitas mortis in M. Ofilio Hilaro ab antiquis traditur.

185. comoediarum histrio is, cum populo admodum placuisset natali die suo conviviumque haberet, edita cena calidam potionem in pultario poposcit simulque personam eius diei acceptam intuens coronam e capite suo in eam transtulit, tali habitu rigens nullo sentiente, donec adcubantium proximus tepescere potionem admoneret.

186. Haec felicia exempla, at contra miserarum innumera: L. Domitius clarissimae gentis apud Massiliam victus, Corfinii captus ab eodem Caesare, veneno poto propter taedium vitae, postquam biberat, omni opere ut viveret adnisus est. invenitur in actis, Felice russei auriga elato, in rogum eius unum e faventibus iecisse se, frivolum dictu, ne hoc gloriae artificis daretur, adversis studiis copia odorum corruptum criminantibus. cum ante non multo M. Lepidus nobilissimae stirpis, quem diverti anxietate diximus mortuum, flammae vi e rogo eiectus recondi propter ardorem non potuisset, iuxta sarmentis aliis nudus crematus est.

LIV **187.** Ipsum cremare apud Romanos non fuit veteris instituti: terra condebantur. at postquam longinquis bellis obrutos erui cognovere, tunc institutum. et tamen multae familiae priscos servavere ritus, sicut in Cornelia nemo ante Sullam dictatorem traditur crematus, idque voluisse veritum talionem eruto C. Mari cadavere. [sepultus vero intellegatur quoquo modo conditus, humatus vero humo contectus].

LV **188.** Post sepulturam variae manium ambages, omnibus a supremo die eadem quae ante primum, nec magis a morte sensus ullus aut corpori aut animae quam ante natalem. eadem enim vanitas in futurum etiam se propagat et in mortis quoque tempora ipsa sibi vitam mentitur, alias inmortalitatem animae, alias transfigurationem, alias sensum inferis dando et manes colendo deumque faciendo qui iam etiam homo esse desierit, ceu vero ullo modo spirandi ratio ceteris animalibus distet aut non diuturniora in vita multa reperiantur, quibus nemo similem divinat inmortalitatem.

189. quod autem corpus animae per se? quae materia? ubi cogitatio illi? quo modo visus, auditus aut qui tangit? quis usus ex iis aut quod sine iis bonum? quae deinde sedes quantave multitudo tot saeculis animarum velut umbrarum? puerilium ista delenimentorum avidaeque numquam desinere mortalitatis commenta sunt. similis et de adservandis corporibus hominum ac revivescendi promisso Democriti vanitas, qui non revixit ipse.

190. quae, malum, ista dementia est iterari vitam morte? quaeve genitis quies umquam, si in sublimi sensus animae manet, inter inferos umbrae? perdit profecto ista dulcedo credulitasque praecipuum naturae bonum, mortem, ac duplicat obituri dolorem etiam post futuri aestimatione. etenim si dulce vivere est, cui potest esse vixisse? at quanto facilius certiusque sibi quemque credere, specimen securitatis antegenitali sumere experimento?

LVI **191.** Consentaneum videtur, priusquam digrediamur a natura hominum, indicare quae cuiusque inventa sint. emere ac vendere <Mercurius, vindemiare> instituit Liber pater; idem diadema, regium insigne, et triumphum invenit; Ceres frumenta, cum antea glande vescerentur, eadem molere et conficere in Attica, ut alii, et in Sicilia, ob id dea iudicata. eadem prima leges dedit, ut alii putavere, Rhadamanthus.

192. Litteras semper arbitror Assyriis fuisse, sed alii apud Aegyptios a Mercurio, ut Gellius, alii apud Syros repertas volunt, utrique in Graeciam attulisse e Phoenice Cadmum sedecim numero, quibus Troiano bello Palameden adiecisse quattuor hac figura ΗΥΦΧ, totidem post eum Simoniden melicum ΨΞΩΘ, quarum omnium vis in nostris recognoscitur. Aristoteles decem et octo priscas fuisse et duas ab Epicharmo additas ΨΖ quam a Palamede mavult.

193. Anticlides in Aegypto invenisse quendam nomine Menen tradit, $\overline{XV}$annorum ante Phoronea, antiquissimum Graeciae regem, idque monumentis adprobare conatur. e diverso Epigenes apud Babylonios $\overline{DCCXX}$ annorum observationes siderum coctilibus laterculis inscriptas docet, gravis auctor in primis; qui minimum, Berosus et Critodemus, $\overline{CCCCXC}$, ex quo apparet aeternus litterarum usus. in Latium eas attulerunt Pelasgi.

194. Laterarias ac domus constituerunt primi Euryalus et Hyperbius fratres Athenis; antea specus erant pro domibus. Gellio Toxius Caeli filius lutei aedificii inventor placet, exemplo sumpto ab hirundinum nidis. oppidum Cecrops a se appellavit Cecropiam, quae nunc est arx Athenis. aliqui Argos a Phoroneo rege ante conditum volunt, quidam et Sicyonem, Aegyptii vero multo ante apud ipsos Diospolin.

195. tegulas invenit Cinyra, Agriopae filius, et metalla aeris, utrumque in insula Cypro, item forcipem, martulum, vectem, incudem; puteos Danaus ex Aegypto advectus in Graeciam qua vocabatur Argos Dipsion; lapidicinas Cadmus Thebis aut, ut Theophrastus in Phoenice; Thrason muros; turres, ut Aristoteles, Cyclopes, Tirynthii, ut Theophrastus;

196. Aegyptii textilia, inficere lanas Sardibus Lydi, fusos in lanificio Closter, filius Arachnae, linum et retia Arachne, fulloniam artem Nicias Megarensis, sutrinam Tychius Boeotius. medicinam Aegyptii apud ipsos volunt repertam, alii per Arabum, Babylonis et Apollinis filium, herbariam et medicamentariam a Chirone, Saturni et Philyrae filio.

197. aes conflare et temperare Aristoteles Lydum Scythen monstrasse, Theophrastus Delam Phrygem putant, aerariam fabricam alii Chalybas, alii Cyclopas, ferrum Hesiodus in Creta eos qui vocati sunt Dactyli Idaei. argentum invenit Erichthonius Atheniensis, ut alii, Aeacus; auri metalla et flaturam Cadmus Phoenix ad Pangaeum montem, ut alii, Thoas aut Aeacus in Panchaia aut Sol Oceani filius, cui Gellius medicinae quoque inventionem ex metallis assignat. plumbum ex Cassiteride insula primus adportavit Midacritus.

198. fabricam ferrariam invenerunt Cyclopes, figlinas Coroebus Atheniensis, in iis orbem Anacharsis Scythes, ut alii, Hyperbius Corinthius. fabricam materiariam Daedalus et in ea serram, asciam, perpendiculum, terebram, glutinum, ichthyocollam; normam autem et libellam et tornum et clavem Theodorus Samius, mensuras et pondera Phidon Argivus aut Palamedes, ut maluit Gellius; ignem e silice Pyrodes Cilicis filius, eundem adservare ferula Prometheus;

199. vehiculum cum quattuor rotis Phryges, mercaturas Poeni, culturas vitium et arborum Eumolpus Atheniensis, vinum aquae misceri Staphylus Sileni filius, oleum et trapetas Aristaeus Atheniensis, idem mella; bovem et aratrum Buzyges Atheniensis, ut alii, Triptolemus;

200. regiam civitatem Aegyptii, popularem Attici post Theseum. tyrannus primus fuit Phalaris Agraganti. servitium invenere Lacedaemonii. iudicium capitis in Areopago primum actum est.

Proelium Afri contra Aegyptios primi fecere fustibus, quos vocant phalangas. clupeos invenerunt Proetus et Acrisius inter se bellantes sive Chalcus Athamantis filius, loricam Midias Messenius, galeam, gladium, hastam Lacedaemonii, ocreas et cristas Cares.

201. arcum et sagittam Scythen Iovis filium, alii sagittas Persen Persei filium invenisse dicunt, lanceas Aetolos, iaculum cum ammento Aetolum Martis filium, hastas velitares Tyrrenum, eundem pilum, Penthesileam Amazonem securim, Pisaeum venabula et in tormentis scorpionem, Cretas catapultam, Syros, Phoenicas ballistam et fundam, aeneam tubam Pisaeum Tyrreni, testudines Artemonem Clazomenium,

202. equum (qui nunc aries appellatur) in muralibus machinis Epium ad Troiam, equo vehi Bellerophontem, frenos et strata equorum Pelethronium, pugnare ex equo Thessalos, qui Centauri appellati sunt, habitantes secundum Pelium montem. bigas prima iunxit Phrygum natio, quadrigas Erichthonius. ordinem exercitus, signi dationem, tesseras, vigilias Palamedes invenit Troiano bello, specularum significationem eodem Sinon, indutias Lycaon, foedera Theseus.

203. Auguria ex avibus Car, a quo Caria appellata; adiecit ex ceteris animalibus Orpheus, aruspicia Delphus, ignispicia Amphiaraus, extispicia avium Tiresias Thebanus, interpretationem ostentorum et somniorum Amphictyon. astrologiam Atlans Libyae filius, ut alii, Aegyptii, ut alii, Assyrii, sphaeram in ea Milesius Anaximander, ventorum rationem Aeolus Hellenis filius.

204. musicam Amphion, fistulam et monaulum Pan Mercuri, obliquam tibiam Midas in Phrygia, geminas tibias Marsyas in eadem gente, Lydios modulos Amphion, Dorios Thamyras Thrax, Phrygios Marsyas Phryx, citharam Amphion, ut alii, Orpheus, ut alii, Linus. septem chordis primum cecinit III ad IIII primas additis Terpander, octavam Simonides addidit, nonam Timotheus. cithara sine voce cecinit Thamyris primus, cum cantu Amphion, ut alii, Linus. citharoedica carmina conposuit Terpander. cum tibiis canere voce Troezenius Ardalus instituit. saltationem armatam Curetes docuere, pyrrichen Pyrrus, utramque in Creta.

205. versum heroum Pythio oraculo debemus. de poematum origine magna quaestio; ante Troianum bellum probantur fuisse. prosam orationem condere Pherecydes Syrius instituit Cyri regis aetate, historiam Cadmus Milesius; ludos gymnicos in Arcadia Lycaon, funebres Acastus in Iolco, post eum Theseus in Isthmo, Hercules Olympiae; athleticam Pythius, pilam lusoriam Gyges Lydus; picturam Aegyptii et in Graecia Euchir, Daedali cognatus, ut Aristoteli placet, ut Theophrasto, Polygnotus Atheniensis.

206. Nave primus in Graeciam ex Aegypto Danaus advenit; antea ratibus navigabatur inventis in mari Rubro inter insulas a rege Erythra. reperiuntur qui Mysos et Troianos priores excogitasse in Hellesponto putent, cum trasirent adversus Thracas. etiam nunc in Britannico oceano vitiles corio circumsutae fiunt, in Nilo ex papyro ac scirpo et harundine.

207. longe nave Iasonem primum navigasse Philostephanus auctor est, Hegesias Parhalum, Ctesias Samiramin, Archemachus Aegaeonem, biremem Damastes Erythraeos fecisse, triremem Thucydides Aminoclen Corinthium, quadriremem Aristoteles Carthaginienses,

208. quinqueremem Mnesigiton Salaminios, sex ordinum Xenagoras Syracusios, ab ea ad decemremem Mnesigiton Alexandrum Magnum, ad duodecim ordines Philostephanus Ptolemaeum Soterem, ad quindecim Demetrium Antigoni, ad XXX Ptolemaeum Philadelphum, ad XL Ptolemaeum Philopatorem, qui Tryphon cognominatus est. onerariam Hippus Tyrius invenit, lembum Cyrenenses, cumbam Phoenices, celetem Rhodii, cercyrum Cyprii.

209. siderum observationem in navigando Phoenices, remum Copae, latitudinem eius Plataeae, vela Icarus, malum et antennam Daedalus, hippegum Samii aut Pericles Atheniensis, tectas longas Thasii; antea ex prora tantum et puppi pugnabatur. rostra addidit Pisaeus Tyrreni, ancoram Eupalamus, eandem bidentem Anacharsis, harpagones et manus Pericles Atheniensis, adminicula gubernandi Tiphys. classe princeps depugnavit Minos.—[Animal occidit primus Hyperbius Martis filius, Prometheus bovem.]—

LVII **210.** Gentium consensus tacitus primus omnium conspiravit, ut Ionum litteris uteretur.

LVIII veteres Graecas fuisse easdem paene quae nunc sint Latinae, indicio erit Delphica antiqui aeris, quae est hodie in Palatio dono principum, Minervae dicata in bibliotheca cum inscriptione tali: ΝΑΥΣΙΚΡΑΤΗΣ ΑΝΕΘΕΤΟ ΤΑΙ ΔΙΟΣ ΚΟΡΑΙ ΤΑΝ ΔΕΚΑΤΑΝ..........

LIX **211.** Sequens gentium consensus in tonsoribus fuit, sed Romanis tardior. in Italiam ex Sicilia venere post Romam conditam anno CCCCLIIII adducente P. Titinio Mena, ut auctor est Varro; antea intonsi fuere. primus omnium radi cotidie instituit Africanus sequens; Divus Augustus cultris semper usus est.

LX **212.** Tertius consensus fuit in horarum observatione, iam hic ratione accedens, quando et a quo in Graecia reperta, diximus secundo volumine. serius etiam hic Romae contigit. XII tabulis ortus tantum et occasus nominantur, post aliquot annos adiectus est et meridies, accenso consulum id pronuntiante, cum a curia inter Rostra et Graecostasin prospexisset solem; a columna Maenia ad carcerem inclinato sidere supremam pronuntiavit, sed hoc serenis tantum diebus, usque ad primum Punicum bellum.

213. princeps solarium horologium statuisse ante XI annos quam cum Pyrro bellatum est ad aedem Quirini L. Papirius Cursor, cum eam dedicaret a patre suo votam, a Fabio Vestale proditur. sed neque facti horologii rationem vel artificem significat nec unde translatum sit aut apud quem scriptum id invenerit.

214. M. Varro primum statutum in publico secundum Rostra in columna tradit bello Punico primo a M'. Valerio Messala cos. Catina capta in Sicilia, deportatum inde post XXX annos quam de Papiriano horologio traditur, anno urbis CCCCLXXXXI. nec congruebant ad horas eius lineae, paruerunt tamen ei annis undecentum, donec Q. Marcius Philippus, qui cum L. Paullo fuit censor, diligentius ordinatum iuxta posuit, idque munus inter censoria opera gratissima acceptum est.

215. etiam tum tamen nubilo incertae fuere horae usque ad proximum lustrum. tunc Scipio Nasica collega Laenati primus aqua divisit horas aeque noctium ac dierum idque horologium sub tecto dicavit anno urbis DXCV. tam diu populo Romano indiscreta lux fuit.

Nunc praevertemur ad reliqua animalia primumque terrestria.

Appendix I: Elephants (Book VIII.1–34)

I **1.** Ad reliqua transeamus animalia et primum terrestria.

Maximum est elephans proximumque humanis sensibus, quippe intellectus illis sermonis patrii et imperiorum obedientia, officiorum quae didicere memoria, amoris et gloriae voluptas, immo vero, quae etiam in homine rara, probitas, prudentia, aequitas, religio quoque siderum solisque ac lunae veneratio.

2. auctores sunt in Mauretaniae saltibus ad quendam amnem, cui nomen est Amilo, nitescente luna nova greges eorum descendere ibique se purificantes sollemniter aqua circumspergi atque ita salutato sidere in silvas reverti vitulorum fatigatos prae se ferentes.

3. alienae quoque religionis intellectu creduntur maria transituri non ante naves conscendere quam invitati rectoris iureiurando de reditu, visique sunt fessi aegritudine, quando et illas moles infestant morbi, herbas supini in caelum iacientes, veluti tellure precibus allegata. nam, quod docilitatem attinet, regem adorant, genua submittunt, coronas porrigunt. Indis arant minores, quos appellant nothos.

II **4.** Romae iuncti primum subiere currum Pompei Magni Africano triumpho, quod prius India victa triumphante Libero patre memoratur. Procilius negat potuisse Pompei triumpho iunctos egredi porta. Germanici Caesaris munere gladiatorio quosdam etiam inconditos meatus edidere saltantium modo

5. vulgare erat per auras arma iacere, non auferentibus ventis, atque inter se gladiatorios congressus edere aut lascivienti pyrriche conludere. postea et per funes incessere, lecticis etiam ferentes quaterni singulos puerperas imitantes, plenisque homine tricliniis accubitum iere per lectos ita libratis vestigiis, ne quis potantium attingeretur.

III **6.** certum est unum tardioris ingenii in accipiendis quae tradebantur, saepius castigatum verberibus, eadem illa meditantem noctu repertum. mirum et adversis quidem funibus subire, sed maxime regredi, utique pronis. Mucianus III consul auctor est aliquem ex iis et litterarum ductus Graecarum didicisse solitumque perscribere eius linguae verbis: Ipse ego haec scripsi et spolia Celtica dicavi, itemque se vidente Puteolis, cum advecti e nave egredi cogerentur, territos spatio pontis procul a continente porrecti, ut sese longinquitatis aestimatione fallerent, aversos retrorsus isse.

IV **7.** Praedam ipsi in se expetendam sciunt solam esse in armis suis, quae Iuba cornua appellat, Herodotus tanto antiquior et consuetudo melius dentes. quam ob rem deciduos casu aliquo vel senecta defodiunt. hoc solum ebur est; cetero et in his quoque, qua corpus intexit, vilitas ossea. quamquam nuper ossa etiam in laminas secari coepere paenuria: etenim rara amplitudo iam dentium praeterquam ex India reperitur; cetera in nostro orbe cessere luxuriae.

8. dentium candore intelligitur iuventa. circa hos beluis summa cura: alterius mucroni parcunt, ne sit proeliis hebes, alterius operario usu fodiunt radices, inpellunt moles; circumventique a venantibus primos constituunt quibus sint minimi, ne tanti proelium putetur, postea fessi inpactos arbori frangunt praedaque se redimunt.

V **9.** Mirum in plerisque animalium scire quare petantur, sed et fere cuncta quid caveant. elephans homine obvio forte in solitudine et simpliciter oberrante clemens placidusque etiam demonstrare viam traditur; idem vestigio hominis animadverso prius quam homine intremescere insidiarum metu, subsistere ab olfactu, circumspectare, iras proflare nec calcare, sed erutum proximo tradere, illum sequenti, simili nuntio usque ad extremum, tunc agmen circumagi et reverti aciemque dirigi. adeo omnium odori durare virus illud maiore ex parte ne nudorum quidem pedum.

10. sic et tigris, etiam feris ceteris truculenta atque ipsa elephanti quoque spernens vestigia, hominis viso transferre dicitur protinus catulos, quonam modo agnito, ubi ante conspecto illo quem timet? etenim tales silvas minime frequentari certum est. sane mirentur ipsam vestigii raritatem. sed unde sciunt timendum esse? immo vero cur vel ipsius conspectum paveant, tanto viribus, magnitudine, velocitate praestantiores? nimirum haec est natura rerum, haec potentia eius, saevissimas ferarum maximasque numquam vidisse, quod debeant timere, et statim intellegere, cum sit timendum.

11. Elephanti gregatim semper ingrediuntur. ducit agmen maximus natu, cogit aetate proximus. amnem transituri minimos praemittunt, ne maiorum ingressu atterente alveum crescat gurgiti altitudo. Antipater auctor est duos Antiocho regi in bellicis usibus celebres etiam cognominibus fuisse; etenim novere ea. certe Cato, cum imperatorum nomina Annalibus detraxerit, eum, qui fortissime proeliatus esset in Punica acie, Surum tradidit vocatum altero dente mutilato.

12. Antiocho vadum fluminis experienti renuit Aiax, alioqui dux agminis semper. tum pronuntiatum eius fore principatum qui transisset, ausumque Patroclum ob id phaleris argenteis, quo maxime gaudent, et reliquo omni primatu donavit. ille, qui notabatur, inedia mortem ignominiae praetulit. mirus namque pudor est, victusque vocem fugit victoris, terram ac verbenas porrigit. pudore numquam nisi in abdito coeunt, mas quinquennis, femina decennis.

13. initur autem biennio quinis, ut ferunt, cuiusque anni diebus, nec amplius; sexto perfunduntur amne, non ante reduces ad agmen. nec adulteria novere nullave propter feminas inter se proelia ceteris animalibus pernicialia, nec quia desit illis amoris vis, namque traditur unus amasse quandam in Aegypto corollas vendentem ac, ne quis vulgariter electam putet, mire gratam Aristophani celeberrimo in arte grammatica,

14. alius Menandrum Syracusanum incipientis iuventae in exercitu Ptolemaei, desiderium eius, quotiens non videret, inedia testatus. et unguentariam quandam dilectam Iuba tradit. omnium amoris fuere argumenta gaudium a conspectu blanditiaeque inconditae, stipes, quas populus dedisset, servatae et in sinum effusae. nec mirum esse amorem quibus sit memoria.

15. idem namque tradit agnitum in senecta multos post annos qui rector in iuventa fuisset; idem divinationem quandam iustitiae, cum Bocchus rex triginta elephantis totidem, in quos saevire instituerat, stipitibus adligatos obiecisset, procursantibus inter eos qui lacesserent, nec potuisse effici ut crudelitatis alienae ministerio fungerentur.

VI **16.** Elephantos Italia primum vidit Pyrri regis bello et boves Lucas appellavit in Lucanis visos anno urbis CCCCLXXIV, Roma autem in triumpho V annis ad superiorem numerum additis, eadem plurimos anno DIV victoria L. Metelli pontificis in Sicilia de Poenis captos. CXLII fuere aut, ut quidam, CXL, travecti ratibus quas doliorum consertis ordinibus inposuerat.

17. Verrius eos pugnasse in circo interfectosque iaculis tradit paenuria consilii, quoniam neque ali placuisset neque donari regibus; L. Piso inductos dumtaxat in circum atque, ut contemptus eorum incresceret, ab operariis hastas praepilatas habentibus per circum totum actos. nec quid deinde iis factum sit auctores explicant qui non putant interfectos.

VII **18.** Clara est unius e Romanis dimicatio adversus elephantum, cum Hannibal captivos nostros dimicare inter sese coegisset. namque unum qui supererat obiecit elephanto, et ille dimitti pactus, si interemisset, solus in harena congressus magno Poenorum dolore confecit. Hannibal, cum famam eius dimicationis contemptum adlaturam beluis intellegeret, equites misit qui abeuntem interficerent. proboscidem eorum facillime amputari Pyrri proeliorum experimentis patuit.

19. Romae pugnasse Fenestella tradit primum omnium in circo Claudi Pulchri aedilitate curuli M. Antonio A. Postumio coss. anno urbis DCLV, item post annos viginti Lucullorum aedilitate curuli adversus tauros.

20. Pompei quoque altero consulatu, dedicatione templi Veneris Victricis, viginti pugnavere in circo aut, ut quidam tradunt, XVIII, Gaetulis ex adverso iaculantibus, mirabili unius dimicatione, qui pedibus confossis repsit genibus in catervas, abrepta scuta iaciens in sublime, quae decidentia voluptati spectantibus erant in orbem circumacta, velut arte, non furore beluae, iacerentur. magnum et in altero miraculum fuit uno ictu occiso; pilum autem sub oculo adactum in vitalia capitis venerat.

21. universi eruptionem temptavere, non sine vexatione populi, circumdatis claustris ferreis. qua de causa Caesar dictator postea simile spectaculum editurus euripis harenam circumdedit, quos Nero princeps sustulit equiti loca addens. sed Pompeiani amissa fugae spe misericordiam vulgi inenarrabili habitu quaerentes supplicavere quadam sese lamentatione conplorantes, tanto populi dolore, ut oblitus imperatoris ac munificentiae honori suo exquisitae flens universus consurgeret dirasque Pompeio, quas ille mox luit, inprecaretur.

22. pugnavere et Caesari dictatori tertio consulatu eius viginti contra pedites D iterumque totidem turriti cum sexagenis propugnatoribus, eodem quo priore numero peditum et pari equitum ex adverso dimicante, postea singuli principibus Claudio et Neroni in consummatione gladiatorum.

23. Ipsius animalis tanta narratur clementia contra minus validos, ut in grege pecudum occurrentia manu dimoveat, ne quod obterat inprudens. nec nisi lacessiti nocent idque cum gregatim semper ambulent, minime ex omnibus solivagi. equitatu circumventi infirmos aut fessos vulneratosve in medium agmen recipiunt, acie velut imperio aut ratione per vices subeunte.

VIII **24.** Capti celerrime mitificantur hordei suco. capiuntur autem in India unum ex domitis agente rectore, qui deprehensum solitarium abactumve a grege verberet ferum: quo fatigato transcendit in eum nec secus ac priorem regit. Africa foveis capit, in quas deerrante aliquo protinus ceteri congerunt ramos, moles devolvunt, aggeres construunt omnique vi conantur extrahere.

25. ante domitandi gratia reges equitatu cogebant in vallem manu factam et longo tractu fallacem, cuius inclusos ripis fossisque fame domabant. argumentum erat ramus homine porrigente clementer acceptus. nunc dentium causa pedes eorum iaculantur alioqui mollissimos.

26. Trogodytae contermini Aethiopiae, qui hoc solo venatu aluntur, propinquas itineri eorum conscendunt arbores; inde totius agminis novissimum speculati extremas in clunes desiliunt. laeva adprehenditur cauda, pedes stipantur in sinistro femine: ita pendens alterum poplitem dextra caedit ac praeacuta bipenni, hoc crure tardato profugiens alterius poplitis nervos ferit, cuncta praeceleri pernicitate peragens. alii tutiore genere, sed magis fallaci, ingentes arcus intentos defigunt humi longius; hos praecipui viribus iuvenes continent, alii conixi pari conatu contendunt ac praetereuntibus sagittarum venabula infigunt, mox sanguinis vestigiis secuntur.

IX **27.** Elephantorum generis feminae multo pavidiores. domantur autem rabidi fame et verberibus, elephantis aliis admotis, qui tumultuantem catenis coerceant. et alias circa coitus maxime efferantur et stabula Indorum dentibus sternunt. quapropter arcent eos coitu feminarumque pecuaria separant, quae haud alio modo quam armentorum habent. domiti militant et turres armatorum in dorsis ferunt magnaque ex parte orientis bella conficiunt: prosternunt acies, proterunt armatos. iidem minimo suis stridore terrentur vulneratique et territi retro semper cedunt, haud minore partium suarum pernicie. Indicum Africi pavent nec contueri audent, nam et maior Indicis magnitudo est.

X   **28.** Decem annis gestare in utero vulgus existimat, Aristoteles biennio nec amplius quam [semel gignere pluresque quam] singulos, vivere ducenis annis et quosdam CCC. iuventa eorum a sexagesimo incipit. gaudent amnibus maxime et circa fluvios vagantur, cum alioqui nare propter magnitudinem corporis non possint. iidem frigoris inpatientes; maximum hoc malum inflationemque et profluvium alvi nec alia morborum genera sentiunt. olei potu tela, quae corpori eorum inhaereant, decidere invenio, a sudore autem facilius adhaerescere.

29. et terram edisse iis tabificum est, nisi saepius mandant; devorant autem et lapides; truncos quidem gratissimo in cibatu habent. palmas excelsiores fronte prosternunt atque ita iacentium absumunt fructum. mandunt ore, spirant et bibunt odoranturque haud inproprie appellata manu. animalium maxime odere murem et, si pabulum in praesepio positum attingi ab eo videre, fastidiunt. cruciatum in potu maximum sentiunt hausta hirudine, quam sanguisugam vulgo coepisse appellari adverto. haec ubi in ipso animae canali se fixit, intolerando adficit dolore.

30. durissimum dorso tergus, ventri molle, saetarum nullum tegimentum, ne in cauda quidem praesidium abigendo taedio muscarum (namque id et tanta vastitas sentit), sed cancellata cutis, et invitans id genus animalium odore. ergo cum extentis recepere examina, artatis in rugas repente cancellis comprehensas enecant. hoc iis pro cauda, iuba, villo est.

31. dentibus ingens pretium et deorum simulacris lautissima ex his materia. invenit luxuria commendationem et aliam expeti in callo manus saporis, haud alia de causa, credo, quam quia ipsum ebur sibi mandere videtur. magnitudo dentium videtur quidem in templis praecipua, sed tamen in extremis Africae, qua confinis Aethiopiae est, postium vicem in domiciliis praebere saepesque in his et pecorum stabulis pro palis elephantorum dentibus fieri Polybius tradidit auctore Gulusa regulo.

XI **32.** Elephantos fert Africa ultra Syrticas solitudines et in Mauretania, ferunt Aethiopes et Trogodytae, ut dictum est, sed maximos India bellantesque cum iis perpetua discoria dracones tantae magnitudinis et ipsos, ut circumplexu facili ambiant nexuque nodi praestringant. conmoritur ea dimicatio, victusque conruens conplexum elidit pondere.

XII **33.** Mira animalium pro se cuique sollertia est ut his. una ascendendi in tantam altitudinem difficultas draconi; itaque tritum iter ad pabula speculatus ab excelsa se arbore inicit. scit ille inparem sibi luctatum contra nexus; itaque arborum aut rupium attritum quaerit. cavent hoc dracones ob idque gressus primum alligant cauda: resolvunt illi nodos manu; at hi in ipsas nares caput condunt pariterque spiritum praecludunt et mollissimas lancinant partes. iidem obvii deprehensi in adversos erigunt se oculosque maxime petunt. ita fit ut plerumque caeci ac fame et maeroris tabe confecti reperiantur.

34. quam quis aliam tantae discordiae causam attulerit nisi naturam spectaculum sibi ac paria conponentem?

Est et alia dimicationis huius fama. elephantis frigidissimum esse sanguinem; ob id aestu torrente praecipue draconibus expeti. quam ob rem in amnes mersos insidiari bibentibus intortosque inligata manu in aurem morsum defigere, quoniam is tantum locus defendi non possit manu. dracones esse tantos, ut totum sanguinem capiant, itaque elephantos ab iis ebibi siccatosque concidere et dracones inebriatos opprimi conmorique.

Commentary

Book VII

INTRODUCTION (§§1–8). Pliny introduces his topic with a rumination on man's paradoxical condition. Nature, his loving mother, has granted him first place in her schema, and has destined him to rule all other creatures, but she is revealed to be a cruel stepmother as well by the weakness and vulnerability with which he is born and the consciousness he has of his sufferings. Man has a remarkable variety, which, while a product of geography and so a topic of the earlier books, will also be touched upon here. Pliny gives a methodological statement at the end of §7.8: he will, like Herodotus before him, record the findings of experts without in most cases making claims about their veracity.

Chapter 1

1. Mundus ... se habent: refers to Books II–VI. Book II covers the "world" (*mundus*), and Books III–VI cover the "situations, races, seas, towns, ports, mountains, rivers, dimensions, and nations which are or used to be" (situs, gentes, maria, oppida, portus, montes, flumina, mensurae populi qui sunt aut fuerunt) (pref. II–VI). **se habent:** The phrase "*se habere*" is similar to a bare *esse*, but describes a situation or manner: "to find oneself, hold oneself". (OLD s.v. *habeo* 21) **insignia:** the text here is corrupt, with some manuscripts reading *insignia*, and others reading *insignes*. Mayhoff sees a lacuna and suggests "*flumina insignia*", but Schilling notes a parallel passage in Cicero *de Natura Deorum* 1:100 "*cum ipsum mundum, cum eius membra, caelum, terras, maria, cumque horum insignia, solem, lunam, stellas, vidissent, ...*". Taking Cicero as a cue, "*insignia*" would translate "those things worth mentioning" or "the notable/remarkable aspects". Beagon (2005) omits the problem. **in eodem:** sc. "*mundo*"; this phrase simply repeats the "*in eo*" from the previous clause. **nullius prope partis:** *nullius partis* depends on *natura*, and *animalium* on *nullius partis*. *Prope* is an adverb here meaning "nearly". "*The nature of nearly no part of the animals . . .*". **nullius:** a subclass of adjectives/pronouns take their genitive singular in -ius and their dative singular in -i. These include *alius, alter, hic, ille, iste, neuter, nullus, qui, solus, totus, ullus, unus, uter.* (AG §113) **contemplatione minore:** ablative of characteristic. **si:** some mansucripts have *etsi*, a reading adopted by Mayhoff and Rackham, but this requires further changes. Mayhoff added *ne hic* so that the text would read "etsi ne hic quidem omnia exsequi humanus animus queat". The changes, however, are unnecessary, and I follow Schilling and Beagon (2005) in rejecting them. If we read "*si*" and take "*queat*" as a potential subjunctive, we have "if indeed the human intellect should prove able to follow all things to their conclusions." (AG §§445–7) **magna:** the epithet is suspect. Mayhoff and Schilling take "*magna*" and "*saeva*" together with "*mercede*", while Rackham and Beagon (2005) take it with "*natura*". Rackham suggests, probably rightly, that "*magna*" is an interpolated gloss on "*saeva*" and should be excised. **sua:** refers back to *natura*, not to man. **non ut sit:** A result clause in which *sit* is existential: "with the result that it is not possible", equivalent to "*ut liceat*". (AG §536) (OLD s.v. *sum* 9) **melior . . . tristior:** the absolute comparative: "fairly good . . . rather severe" (as opposed to the comparative use: "better . . . sadder"). For "*melior parens / melior natura*", compare Ovid, *Met* 1.21. **an:** as often with *an*, the preceding *utrum* has been omitted: *utrum parens melior homini an tristior noverca fuerit.*

2. ante omnia: "in the first place". **unum:** refers to "the animal man". **cunctorum:** Schilling reads "*cunctarum*" "which is attested in the readings of the best manuscripts", citing Cicero, *de Finibus* 4.28 as a parallel: "*Chrysippus autem exponens differentias animantium ait alias earum corpore excellere, alias autem animo*"; "*animantium*" likely disguises a hidden "*bestiarum*", as often when *animans* contrasts with humans. Compare "*nullumque tot animalium aliud*" below, and "*cetera animantia*" in §8.5. **velat:** the subject is "Nature". **truncos etiam arboresque:** hendiadys: "trunks and trees" for "trunks of trees" or "tree trunks". **gemino:** "two-fold", modifying "*cortice*". May refer to a tree's inner and outer bark or to the thickness of the bark. **hominem . . . principio:** Schilling and Beagon (2005) note the similarity to Lucretius 5.222-7. **nullumque tot animalium aliud *pronius* ad lacrimas:** "pronius" was added by the early editors of Pliny and adopted by Rackham. Mayhoff, Schilling, and Beagon reject it. With "*pronius*", "*nullum . . . principio*" is a new clause; without it, "*nullum . . . aliud*" is in apposition to "*hominem*". **Hercule:** a common exclamation: "by Hercules", "I swear". **ante XL diem:** compare Zoroaster at 7.72. **XL:** here, the ordinal "quadragesimum", not the cardinal "quadraginta". (AG §133) See Appendix I for a list of numerals.

3. quae . . . vincula excipiunt: supply "*sunt*" and note that the antecedents of "*quae*" (*vincula* and *nexus*) have been drawn into the relative clause: "*sunt vincula quae . . . excipiunt*". (AG §307b) The "vincula" and "nexus" refer to swaddling clothes, although Beagon (2005) suggests that they might also be read metaphorically for the infant's helplessness. **feliciter:** born without incident, but also a contrast with "*devinctis*" and "*flens*". **natus:** Pliny has slipped into the masculine, thinking as he is of *homo*. **imperaturum:** another paradoxical statement, contrasting the infant's presumed future with "*vincula*", "*nexus*", and "*devinctis*", which are more characteristic of a slave than a ruler. **a suppliciis:** ablative of source. (AG §403) **auspicatur:** from "*auspicor*", "to take auspices at the start of" and thus "to start, enter into". **unam:** with "*culpam*". **natum est:** neuter because the subject is still *animal*. **dementiam:** exclamatory accusative after "*heu*". Rightly printed by Rackham. Mayhoff and Schilling retain the mss. "*dementia*". **existimantium:** introduces the indirect statement *se genitos*. **ad superbiam:** *ad* here indicates purpose: "for". **se genitos:** sc. "esse".

4. spes: not "hope" but "expectation". **quadripedi similem:** compare the riddle of the Sphinx given by Apollodorus 3.5.8: "What is that which, having a single voice, becomes four-footed and two-footed and three-footed?" Oedipus answers the riddle with "man", for he is four-footed as an infant, two-footed as a man, and three-footed as an old man. **quando homini incessus:** supply "*est*". "When does walking begin for man?" **palpitans vertex:** a reference to the fontanelle, or "soft spot" on a baby's head. Again, see Zoroaster at 7.72. **indicium:** in apposition to "*palpitans vertex*". **novitatibus:** literally, "novelties", but here, "new sicknesses". **sentire ... scire:** exclamatory infinitives. Translate as if they were indirect statements: "And the fact that the rest know ... ". **praepetes volatus ... nare:** objects of "*usurpare*". **fari ... ingredi ... vesci ... flere:** depend on "*scire*" "to know how to ...". **extitere:** syncopated 3rd person plural perfect active indicative of "*exsisto*". (AG §166) **non nasci optimum ... aut ... aboleri:** that death is a blessing for men is a common theme: Sophocles *Oedipus Coloneus* 1224–7; Theognis 425–8; Plutarch, *Moralia* 115b–e; Cicero, *Tusculanae Disputationes* 1.113–15; Plato, *Apology* 40c–41e; Lactantius *Divinae Institutiones* 3.19.14; **qui non nasci optimum <esse> censerent:** in English word order: *qui censerent esse optimum non nasci*; "*censerent*" is subjunctive in a relative clause of characteristic. (AG §535) **aut quam ocissime aboleri:** supply "*natum*" after "*aut*". **ocissime:** superlative adverb from "*ocior*". (AG §130)

5. uni: see "*nullius*" above, §7.1. **luxuria:** Beagon (2005) translates *luxuria* as "self-indulgence". **superstitio:** Pliny's word for religion of any kind. **vivendi:** objective genitive with "*cupido*". (AG §§347–8) **cura:** not "care" but "concern". **de futuro:** depends on "*cura*". **probe degunt:** "*dego*", a compound of *de+ago*, frequently means "to live" or "pass one's life". Cf. Bostock's "live at peace". **congregari videmus:** The subject of the infinitive "*congregari*" is "*animalia*". **dissimilia:** refers to "*animalia*": "different kinds of animals". **leonum feritas:** for "*leones feri*". In the phrases "*leonum feritas*" and "*serpentium morsus*", the emphasis is on the characteristic actions of the animals: lions are fierce and snakes bite. This explains the genitive construction, which is absent in the case of "*maris ... beluae ac pisces*", which have no characteristic action and so must themselves be the subjects of "*saeviunt*".

6. de universitate . . . diximus: in Books III–VI. **universitate:** "totality, whole". **relatione:** account. **duco:** "consider". (OLD s.v. *duco* 30) **ab mari:** the Mediterranean. Beagon (2005) includes "the other inner seas". **degentium:** see note on "*degunt*" at §1.5 above, refers to "*hominum*". **visum iri:** the future passive infinitive in indirect statement: "are going to seem". The subject is "*aliqua;*" "*prodigiosa*" and "*incredibilia*" are the predicates. **Aethiopas:** "People of the Burnt Faces," a Greek term for black Africans. "Aethiopians" is often used hazily to describe mythically distant people with exceptional lifespans and who live in close communion with the gods. The Aethiopians occur five times in Homer: *Iliad* 1.423, 22.206; *Odyssey* 1.22–3, 4.84, 5.282–7. By Pliny's period, "Aethiopia" was a distinct region south of Egypt. **miraculo:** dative of purpose. (AG §382) **fieri:** to happen.

7. naturae vero rerum: "*Rerum natura*" is the usual phrase for the "nature of the universe". Compare Lucretius's epic poem, *de Rerum Natura*. **vero:** "indeed", "in truth". Compare the other adverbial forms of *verus*: "*verum*," "but"; and "*vere*", "in truth, truly" (opposite of "falsely"). **fide:** "good faith, trustworthiness". **modo:** "only". **ne . . . commemorem:** "and let me not mention" = "to say nothing of, not to mention". **picturas:** not "paintings", but "colorations" or "markings". **parvum dictu . . . varietas:** supply "*est*" with "*parvum*"; "*sermones*", "*linguae*", and "*varietas*" are in apposition to "*parvum*". **dictu:** the supine: "to say, mention". (AG §510) **ut . . . vice:** a result clause. (AG §536) **externus:** foreigner. **alieno:** man of another country. **hominis vice:** "*vice*" functions as a post-positive preposition with the genitive: "*hominis vice*" = "in the place of a human".

8. in facie vultuque: "*facies*" is the external surface of the face, while "*vultus*" includes its expression. **aut paulo plura:** "*paulo*" is ablative of degree of difference with "*plura*": literally "more by a little", so "a little more, a few more". (AG §414) **membra:** parts, features: the nose, eyes, ears, etc. **nullas . . . existere:** exclamatory indirect statement: "to think that . . ." (AG 397d–e) **indiscretas:** "indistinguishable, identical". Beagon

(2005) takes *indiscretas* attributively: "no two identical faces exist"; Rackham takes it predicatively to preserve the effect of the word order: "there exist no two countenances that are not distinct". **quod:** "a thing which … ", refers back to the entire previous indirect statement. **in paucis:** adv., "especially". **numero … adfectando:** the gerundive construction: "when applying that number" (i.e., "ten"). **nec tamen ego … cura vetustiore:** Pliny's statement of his historical method. Cf. the other fundamental statements of method: Herdotus 1.1, Thucydides 1.21–3, Polybius 1.1–2, Sallust *In Catilinam* 1, Dionysius of Halicarnassus *Roman Antiquities* 1.1–8, Livy *Praefatio*, Valerius Maximus *Memorabilia* 1.praef., Josephus *Antiquities of the Jews* 1.1–17, *Wars of the Jews* 1.1–3. **modo:** "only". **fastidio:** dative of purpose. (AG §382) **tanto:** ablative of degree of difference: "by so much". (AG §414) **vetustiore:** "*vetus*: "old, of long standing / still existing". (OLD s.v. *vetus* 1–3) Compare the other adjectives for "old": *antiquus*: "old, from an earlier time / no longer existing" (OLD s.v. *antiquus* 2–4); *priscus*: "old, old-fashioned" (OLD s.v. *priscus* 3); *senior*: "older in years, more aged". (OLD s.v. *senior* 1–3)

PART ONE: ODDITIES OF HUMAN APPEARANCE AMONG THE DIFFERENT POPULATIONS (§§9–32). The variation within humankind is marvelous and occasionally incredible. While remarkable oddities have existed in all places, such as the Hirpi in Italy, they are by Pliny's day concentrated in the far ends of the known world: Pliny catalogues bizarre social customs, unearthly powers, and the unlikely bodily features of the blurred edges of humanity. The tradition of ethnography goes back at least to the 6th c. BCE and Ionian periploi, accounts of sea voyages, coastlines, and the people who dwelled there, with special attention to local customs. Particularly well-known is Hecataeus of Miletus for his Periodos Ges (Circuit of the World), extant in fragments, a geographical and ethnographical work as well as precursor to Herodotus.

Chapter 2

9. Scytharum: The term "Scythian" refers to a wide variety of semi-related tribes and peoples to the North and East of the Greeks and Romans, particularly in the Danubian region. They were nomadic, horse-riding peoples and fierce warriors, characterized in the Greco-Roman sources by every kind of barbarity, but reliable sources are scarce. **quae . . . vescerentur:** relative clause of characteristic. (AG §535) **indicavimus:** *NH* 4.26; *NH* 6.20. **incredibile:** sc. *"sit"*, the apodosis of a future less vivid condition, of which *"cogitemus"* is the protasis. **ac Sicilia et Italia:** Mayhoff secluded this phrase as an interpolation. Rackham includes the phrase, but notes that some manuscripts read *"ab Sicilia et Italia."* Schilling reads *"ac Sicilia"*, secluding only *"et Italia"*, and Beagon (2005) follows, noting that *"medio orbe terrarum"* and *"Italia"* are synonymous. **Cyclopas et Laestrygonas:** Not to be confused with the Hesiodic Cyclopes (*Theogony* 139–46, 501–6), Brontes, Stereopes, and Arges, the children of Uranus and Gaia, and the forgers of Jupiter's lightning. The Homeric Cyclopes, meant here, were giants characterized by a single round eye in the center of their heads, the barbarous children of Neptune. They were also cannibals, like the Laestrygonians, who ate many of Ulysses's men. Both were thought to have lived on Sicily. See *Odyssey* 9, 10.80–132 and Thucydides 6.2.1. Cicero, however, puts the Laestrygonians in Italy at Formiae (*ad Atticum* 2.13.2), which could explain the presence of *"Italia"* above. Pliny himself places the Laestrygonians at Formiae (*NH* 3.59) but later places both the Cyclopes and the Laestrygonians in Sicily (*NH* 3.89). **Alpis:** accusative plural. (AG §§65–78) **solitum:** sc. *"esse"*, indirect statement still depending on *"cogitemus"*. **mandendo:** supply *"homines"* again: "from eating men".

10. septentrionem: more commonly plural: "septentriones", the constellations of the Greater and Lesser Bears, which signify the North. **aquilonis:** the North Wind, in Greek "Boreas". **specuque eius dicto:** either "the place called its cave" (i.e., named for it) or "the cave previously mentioned". **Ges clithron:** γῆς κλεῖθρον "earth's bar/keyhole". Beagon

(2005, citing J. D. P. Bolton, *Aristaeus of Proconnessus*, Oxford: Clarendon Press, 1962, pp. 94–96), points out that *clithron* is also the medical term for the "windpipe", which is more appropriate in the context. The end of the world. **Arimaspi quos diximus:** *NH* 4.88; 6.50. The Arimaspi, who occur in Herodotus at 4.27, were one-eyed cannibals who dwelt in the far North. Compare the ancient claim that the days were so long among the Laestrygonians that a man could earn a double wage (Crates in schol. *Od.* 10.86). **bellum esse:** indirect statement depending on "scribunt". **grypis:** griffins. **quale vulgo traditur:** "as is commonly reported". **eruente:** agrees with "*genere*" and thus also with "*grypis*". **Herodotus:** ca. 484-425 BCE, the first Greek historian, called the "Father of History" by Cicero, *de Leg.* 1.5. See *Histories* III.116 and IV.13, 27 for the Arimaspi and the griffins. **Aristeas Proconnesius:** Aristeas of Proconnesus, a poet of the 7th c. BCE. He wrote a poem about the Arimaspi, as well as paradoxagraphical works, and he was connected with a shamanic cult of Apollo. See Herodotus 4.14–15.

11. Anthropophagos: ἀνθρωπωφάγους "man-eaters, cannibals". **Imavi:** Mount Imaus—either a mountain in the Himalayas, or a portion of the range. See also *NH* 6.60, 64. Beagon (2005) identifies it with either the Karakorem or Tien Shan projections. **Abarimon:** described here and in Aulus Gellius, *Attic Nights* 9.4. **aversis post crura plantis:** "with their feet turned around behind their shins", i.e., with their feet on backwards. **eximiae velocitatis:** genitive of quality. (AG §345) **hos ... pertractos:** indirect statement depending on "*Baeton ... prodidit.*" **pertractos:** supply "esse". **Baeton:** An official in charge of measuring the distances on Alexander's marches. See also *NH* 6.61-3, 69.

12. Priores ... uti: indirect statement depending on "*Isigonus Nicaeensis*" (supply "*tradit*"). **Borysthenen:** the river Borysthenes, modern Dnieper, flowing into the Black Sea from Ukraine, Belarus, originating in Russia. The name "Borysthenes" is Scythian, meaning "Wide Land." **ossibus humanorum capitum bibere:** said of many barbarians, especially the Scythians and the Germans. Consider the modern German for head, "der Kopf," derived from Late Latin "*cuppa*", "cup" (a variation on "*cupa*", "tub"), although that derivation may also parallel the French "tête" from Latin "*testa*", "tile, sherd". **mantelibus:** handtowels, napkins. **ante pectora:** tucked into the collar, as napkins. **cutibusque:** ablative, depending on "*uti*". **Isigonus Nicaeensis:** A paradoxographer about whom little is known. Compare Aulus Gellius, *Attic Nights* 9.4, which names Isigonus along with Aristaeus of Proconessus, Ctesias, Oneisicritus, Philostephanus, and Hegesias. **idem:** Isigonus; again supply "tradit". **Albania:** not modern Albania, but a dry plain where modern Azerbaijan and Daghestan now are. See Pliny *NH* 6.29, 38–9 and Strabo 11.4.1–8. **glauca oculorum acie:** transferred epithet. The adjective "*glauca*" agrees grammatically with "*acie*" but logically with "*oculorum*". **acie:** "*acies*" = "keenness", but also "eyesight" (OLD s.v. *acies* 2). **canos:** modifies and understood "*capillos*" or "*crines*". **Sauromatas:** or Sarmatae. The Sarmatians were a group from east of the Don River, separate from but often intermingled with the Scythians. **tertio die:** "every other day"; the Romans count inclusively, so, for example, the third day from Monday is Wednesday (Monday-Tuesday-Wednesday). (AG §631)

13. Crates Pergamenus: Crates of Pergamum, head of the library there in the 2nd c. BCE. Crates was a member of the Greek embassy to Rome in 168 BCE. Supply "*tradit*". **Hellesponto:** The modern Dardanelles, between the Aegean and the Sea of Marmara. **Parium:** a Greek city on the Hellespont. Not to be confused with Paros, the island famous for its marble. **Ophiogenes:** "snake-born" or "snake-race". See Strabo 13.1.14 and Pliny *NH* 28.30. **solitos:** masculine plural agreeing with the logical, but not grammatical, gender of "*genus hominum*". We might have expected either "*solitum*" or "*solitorum*". **corpori:** dative of separation with the compound verb "*extrahere*". (AG §381) **Varro:** sc. "*tradit*". The great Roman polymath and author, Marcus Terentius Varro was born in 116 BCE and lived 90 years until his death in 27 BCE. Aulus Gellius, *Attic Nights*, 3.10.17, tells us that he had written 490 books by the time he was 78, but we know of only 55 titles. His works ranged across "history (*De* *vita populi Romani*, on Rome's 'social history'; *De gente populi Romani*, placing Rome's remote past in a Greek context), geography, rhetoric, law, (*De iure civili lib. XV*), philosophy, music, medicine, architecture, literary history (*De poetis, De comoediis Plautinis*), religion, agriculture, and language (at least 10 works on this last alone)" *OCD³ʳᵈ* 1582. The only works extant in more than fragments are *De lingua latina* and *De re rustica*.

14. Psyllorum: Psylli, a tribe of snake-charmers in North Africa. **Agatharchides:** From Cnidos. Greek historian of the 2nd c. BCE. According to *OCD³ʳᵈ*, he lived "ca. 215 to after 145 BCE", but Beagon (2005) puts him at the Ptolomaic court "ca. 116 BC". **dicta:** "so-called". **parte:** "region," not "part," as often. **Syrtium Maiorum:** the Gulf of Sidra off the northern coast of Libya. **virus:** "poison", a second declension -us, -i, neuter. **mos:** supply "*est*". **vero:** See the note at §7.7 above. **liberos genitos protinus:** "children immediately upon being born". **obiciendi . . . experiendi:** gerunds depending on "*mos*". "There is the custom of throwing . . . and of testing . . .". **saevissimis earum:** feminine because the antecedent is "*serpens*", snake. **eoque genere:** i.e., of poisonous snake. **pudicitiam:** "chastity". **adulterino sanguine:** ablative of source (AG §403). **internicione:** = *pernicione*, "destruction". **Nasamonibus:** another African tribe. For an alternate story of the destruction of the Psylli, see Herodotus 4.172–3, who claims that, according to the Libyans, the Psylli perished in the desert while making war upon the South Wind. **cum pugnatum est:** the impersonal passive: literally, "when it was fought," but better, "when the battle occurred". (AG §207d)

15. Marsorum: an Italian tribe in central Italy, who likely spoke in an Oscan dialect. They were friendly to Rome from the earliest period, aiding Rome in its wars with the Samnites and Hannibal. The Marsi, as perhaps a natural result, took a leading role against Rome in the Social War (90-88 BCE; sometimes called the "Marsic War") and were fully joined to the Roman people at its conclusion. **ortos:** supply "*esse*". **Circae filio:** Circe lived on the island Aeaea (*Odyssey* 10), which was later identified with Italian Circeii. She had three sons by Ulysses: Telegonus (*Telegonia* [lost]; Hyginus, *Fabulae* 127; etc.), and Agrius and Latinus (Hesiod, *Theogony* 1011). Agrius, the son of Circe and Ulysses, was the ancestor of the Italian Marsi. See Pliny 25.11 and Aullus Gellius *Attic Nights* 16.11.1-2. **ferunt:** the subject is the indefinite "they". **fugere:** indirect statement depending on *"ferunt"*; "snakes" are the subject. **mori:** indirect statement, still depending on *"ferunt"*. **humani ieiuni oris:** "from the lips of a fasting human". **Machlyas:** a hermaphroditic race, mentioned also at Herodotus, 4.178, 180. Beagon (2005) identifies the Machlyae with the Machroae (Pliny, *NH* 5.28). **utriusque naturae:** of either gender. **coeuntes:** having sexual intercourse. **Calliphanes:** otherwise unknown. **Aristoteles:** (384-322 BCE). Aristotle's father was a court physician at Pella in Macedonia, but at the age of 17 Aristotle joined Plato's Academy in Athens. In 342 Philip II invited Aristotle to become his son Alexander's tutor, and he returned to Pella. In 335 Aristotle returned to Athens and set up his own school, the Lyceum, teaching, among others, Theophrastus and Eudemus, but when Alexander died in 323, he was forced to leave Athens, leaving Theophrastus as his successor. Aristotle's extant works range over "(a) logic and metaphysics; (b) nature, life, and mind; (c) ethics, politics, art" *OCD*[3rd] 166.

16. Isigonus et Nymphodorus: Supply *"tradunt"*. **Isigonus:** See above at §7.12. **Nymphodorus:** fl. ca. 335 BCE. A Syracusan author of travel literature who wrote *On the Wonders in Sicily*, and a *Periploi of Asia*. (*BNP* s.v. Nymphodorus [1]) **effascinantium:** those who give the evil eye, the *"fascinum"*, against which the Mediterranean peoples have various talismans, including representations of the phallus (also called *"fascinum"*). **intereant … arescant … emoriantur:** Subjunctives because the relative clause *"quorum . . ."* is inside indirect speech, as also *"effascinent"*, *"interimant"* and *"intueantur"* below. (AG §591) **probata:** Not the participle from the verb *probo, probare*, but the Greek word πρόβατα, meaning "sheep", *"pecudes"*. **Triballis:** Thracians who lived in Lower Moesia, an area of the Balkans west of the Black Sea and including modern-day Serbia and northern Macedonia. **Illyris:** The Illyrians were Thracians who occupied the area of the Balkans roughly equivalent to modern Albania. Beagon (2005) suggests that "*et Illyris*" is a gloss on "*Triballis*". **quod ... puberes:** still in indirect statement after "*tradit*". **quod ... malum:** "an evil which ..." refers back to the entire clause "*qui ... oculis*". **notabilius esse:** still indirect statement after "*tradit*". The indirect statement here again produces a subjunctive in "*quod ... habeant*".

17. generis: here, "type". **Bitiae:** Aulus Gellius (*Attic Nights* 9.4, especially 9.4.7–8) and Solinus 1.101 (Theodor Mommsen, *C. Iulii Solini Collectanea Rerum Memorabilium*, Berolinus: Weidmann, 1895). **Apollonides:** Supply "*prodit*". Apollonides was a 1st c. BCE geographer. **Phylarchus:** 3rd c. BCE Greek historian who wrote a *History* from 272 (death of Pyrrhus of Epirus) to 220 (death of Cleomenes, king of Sparta). He was fascinated by tales of the marvelous and frequently included them in his work, making him of special interest for Pliny. **Ponto:** the region along the south coast of the Black Sea between Paphlagonia and Cappadocia. Pontus reached its height under Mithridates VI, who was later conquered by Pompey the Great. **Thibiorum:** See Plutarch, *Quaestiones Conviviales* (*Symposiacs*) 5.7, who describes the consumptive effect of the Thibians' gaze and touch and compares it to the effect of a normal human's touch on a bird's feathers. **geminam pupillam:** The so-called "*pupula duplex*" or "double pupil", likely a condition now known as a "bridge coloboma", a fissure in the iris which creates the impression of a second pupil, affects only one eye, and is hereditary. **Pharmacum:** an unknown people, whose name likely derives from Greek φαρμακεύς, pharmakeus, "poisoner, sorcerer", from the drugs they compounded. **Damon:** Supply "*prodit*". Damon was a historian from Byzantium. His name occurs once in Athenaeus 10.442.

18. feminas ... nocere: indirect statement depending on "*Cicero ... auctor est*". **quae ... habeant:** relative clause of characteristic. (AG §535) **Cicero:** Marcus Tullius Cicero (106–43 BCE) was a prolific author. Of 88 known speeches, 58 survive, along with two major works on rhetoric (*De inventione; De oratore*), several minor works (*Partitiones oratoriae; Topica; De optimo genere oratorum*), poetic works (*Consulatus suus; De temporibus suis; Aratea*), letters (*Ad Atticum; Ad Quintum fratrem; Ad Brutum; Ad familiares*), and 17 philosophical works. **naturae:** dative with "*placuit*". **cum ferarum morem vescendi humanis visceribus in homine genuisset:** a complicated structure; "*ferrarum*" is a possessive genitive governing "*morem*", and "*vescendi*" is an objective genitive depending on "*morem*". (AG §§347–8) "*Humanis visceribus*" is the ablative object of the gerund "*vescendi*". **ne quid usquam mali esset:** a negative purpose clause; "*quid*" for "*aliquid*"; "*mali*" is a partitive genitive depending on "*quid*". (AG §§529–33) **quod . . . esset:** relative clause of characteristic. (AG §535)

19. Faliscorum: The Falisci were a Bronze- and Iron-Age Latinate people dominated by the Etruscans. The Romans conquered and absorbed them by the 3rd c. BCE. They inhabited the area north of Veii in the Treia basin. **Hirpi:** or perhaps the "*Hirpini*" (Servius *In Aen.* 11.785–7), a group of priests resembling the Roman Luperci. "*Hirpus*" is Sabine for "wolf". **Soractem:** the modern mountain "Soratte", where the Hirpi worshipped Apollo Soranus. Cf. Horace, *Odes* 1.9. **senatus:** genitive depending on "*consulto*". **vacationem:** "exemption from" + genitive.

20. ad aliqua: "in some regards". **Pyrrho:** King Pyrrhus of Epirus (319–272 BCE). One of the early Hellenistic kings, Pyrrhus obtained his throne through the aid of Ptolemy I and Agathocles of Syracuse, whose daughters he married in turn. Pyrrhus extended his empire significantly, and when the citizens of Tarentum appealed to him for aid against the Romans in 279, he brought a large force of 25,000 men to Italy. After defeating the Romans repeatedly but losing large numbers of his own forces, he departed Italy in 276 with only a third of his army intact. It is from Pyrrhus that we get our phrase "Pyrrhic victory": a victory the cost of which is so great it may as well be a defeat. Pyrrhus died in Argos in 272 struck on the head by a roof tile. For the story of the toe, see Plutarch, *Life of Pyrrhus*, 3.4–5. **lienosis medebatur:** "*lienosus*" is the adjective for "spleen" ("*lien*"). Used as a substantive in the plural, it means "inflammation of the spleen". Here, "*lienosis*" is dative, with an impersonal use of "*medeor*", "to heal": "there was remedy for inflamed spleens". (AG §207d) **hunc . . . conditumque:** refers to the toe.

21. India: In the earliest sources, India was the farthest country to the East, but its people were also confused with the Aethiopians. Alexander the Great's conquests (327–325 BCE) opened up the East until the rise of the Parthian empire. Trade between Rome and India was formalized in the reign of Augustus, who received ambassadors from India (Cassius Dio, 54.9). Romans imported "perfumes, spices (especially pepper), gems, ivory, pearls, Indian textiles, and Chinese silk" *OCD*³ʳᵈ 754. **indicio:** dative of purpose. (AG §382) **tantae proceritatis:** genitive of quality (AG §345). **ut . . . condantur:** a noun clause of result depending on "*facit*". **internodia:** the distance between the joints, or knots, in a reed.

22. multos: many people of this region. **constat:** "it is agreed", introduces an indirect statement that continues through "*insistere*". **cubita:** a cubit is the length from the elbow to the tip of the middle finger. **gymnosophistas:** Indian ascetics, regarded as a type of philosopher. Strabo 15.1.63–8; Plutarch, *Life of* Alexander 64–5; Arrian, *Indica* 11.1–7; Diodorus Siculus 11.35–42; Megasthenes FGH 715, fr. 28. cf. Solinus 52.25. **in monte . . . habentes:** indirect statement depending on "*auctor est Megasthenes*". **Nulo:** a mythical mountain. Dative, with "*cui*". **octonos digitos in singulis:** "eight toes on each foot". **Megasthenes:** A Greek historian (ca. 350–290 BCE) and diplomat. He spent time with the satrap of Arachosia, and king Seleucus I made him envoy to India (the Maurya empire of north India). Megasthenes wrote a three or four volume *Indica*, which was used by Arrian, Diodorus Siculus, Pliny, and Strabo.

23. genus hominum capitibus caninis: The Greek "κυνοκέφαλος" cynocephalus, "dog-headed" refers both to violent barbarians (of any stripe) and specifically to baboons. **venatu et aucupio:** the ablative objects of *"vesci"*. (AG §410) **prodente se:** "when he [Megasthenes] was publishing his book". **Ctesias:** of Cnidus. A Greek doctor in the late 5th c. BCE who wrote a *Persica* and also an *Indica*. **canescere:** *"Canesco, canescere, canui"*, "to become gray, grow hoary", is the inchoative of *"caneo, canere, canui"*, "to be white, pale, gray." The *"-sc-"* infix indicates action which is just beginning or growing in to being. Compare *"gnosco," "cresco", "valesco"*, etc. **idem:** supply *"tradit"*. **ad saltum:** "for jumping". **Monocoli . . . Sciapodas:** Monocoli: "one-legs" from Greek Μονόκωλοι and Sciapodas: "shade-foots" from Greek Σκιάποδες. **humi:** locative case. (AG §427) **Trogodytis:** "a people of 'Ethiopia', in particular the Eastern Desert of southern Egypt and north Sudan" *OCD³ʳᵈ* 1555. See Herodotus 4.153; Strabo 16.4.17; Diodorus Siculus 3.31.4–33.7, and Pliny *NH* 5.44–5. **occidentem versus:** *"versus"* is a preposition taking the accusative: "toward the West".

24. satyri: generally identified with monkeys. **subsolanis:** "Beneath the sun", so "Eastern". **Catarcludorum:** See *"satyri"*, above. **Choromandarum:** Beagon (2005) suggests the story is also based on monkeys. **vocat:** Here, "names". **Tauron:** an otherwise unknown author. **Eudoxus:** of Cnidus (391–338/7 BCE). Supply *"tradit"*. Eudoxus was an important mathematician, astronomer, geographer, and philosopher. Eudoxus learned mathematics with Archytas, met and possibly took lectures with Plato, studied astronomy in Egypt and wrote laws for Cnidos. Among his works were Περὶ ταχῶν (*On Speeds* describing a geocentric motion of the planets), a Φαινόμενα (*Phaenomena* based on observations of the stars), an Ὀκταετηρίς (*Eight-Year Cycle* on the Egyptian calendar), and a Γῆς περίοδος (*Circuit of the Earth* in the style of Hecataeus of Miletus). **in meridianis:** "In the south". **viris:** dative of possession. (AG §373) **Struthopodes:** Sparrow-Feet, from Greek Στρουθόποδες.

25. Megasthenes: supply *"tradit"*. **Nomadas:** The term *"nomas"* applied to any non-agricultural, pastoral people who had no fixed dwelling.

Nomadism was a symbol of barbarity. **anguium modo loripedem:** "bandy-legged in the manner of snakes". **Sciratas:** The form of the name is confirmed by Aelian *de Natura Animalium* 16.22: "There is also the race of the Sciratae, beyond the Indians". The alternate reading "Sciritias" is perhaps from confusion with the Sciritae, a division of the Spartan army. **Gangis:** the river Ganges, whose source was mysterious. **Astomorum:** A Greek word, Ἄστομοι, meaning "Mouthless" or "Speechless". **malorum:** from mālum, -i, "apple", not mălum, -i, "evil".

26. Trispithami: Strabo 15.1.57. Three *spithami* in height. A *spithamos* is the distance between the thumb and little finger, or about ¾ of a foot, making a *Trispithamus* about 2¼ feet tall. **Pygmaei:** a race of dwarfs who are variously located in southern Egypt, India, Scythia, or Thrace. As early as Homer (*Iliad* 3.3–6) they are depicted in battle with cranes, called the geranomachy. **ternas spithamas:** accusative object of "*excedentes*". **dodrantes:** the Latin for "*spithamos*", that is, ¾ of a foot. **veris:** genitive of "*ver*", "Spring," not from "*verus, a, um*" "true". **resisti:** impersonal passive in indirect statement. (AG §207d)

27. reliqui: from the adjective "*reliquus*". **Cyrnos:** Schilling cites Athenaeus's account (2.47 a) of the Cyrnii: "Λύκος δὲ πολυχρονίους φησὶν εἶναι τοὺς Κυρνίους (οἰκοῦσι δ᾽ οὗτοι περὶ Σαρδόνα) διὰ τὸ μέλιτι ἀεὶ χρῆσθαι". "Lycus says that the Cyrnii are long-lived—these men dwell around Sardinia—because they are constantly consuming honey." **Macrobios:** not the author Macrobius, but the *Macrobii*, a people named after the Greek Μακρόβιοι, meaning 'long-lived'. **Seras:** See Pliny §§6.54, 88. The "Silk People": the furthest known eastern people, often identified with the Chinese (Beagon, 2005), but more likely the silk traders who acted as middle-men (*OCD³ʳᵈ* 1392). **Athon:** a mountain on the Chalcidice associated with longevity. See Pliny §29.121. **capiti … vestibus:** datives depending on the prefix "in" on "*inesse*". (AG §370) **inesse:** indirect statement depending on "*tradit*".

28. Onesicritus: A Cynic philospher and student of Diogenes of Sinope, Onesicritus accompanied Alexander the Great on his eastern conquests where he served as helmsman on the royal ship ca. 325–324 BCE. Onesicritus wrote a life of Alexander: "*How Alexander was educated*". (*BNP* s.v. Onesicritus) Suppy "*tradit*". **cubitorum ... palmorum:** genitive of quality (AG §345). **Gymnetas:** The Naked People. Cf. the Gymnosophists at §7.22 above. **Ctesias:** supply "*tradit*". **Pandae:** mentioned at Pliny §6.76, where he tells us that the Pandae are ruled by queens descended from the only daughter of Hercules.

29. contra alios: "in contrast to the others", i.e., to the *Macrobii*. **iunctos:** "next to". **Mandorum:** cf. Pliny's mention of the "Mandaei" at §6.64, who might be the same people. **Clitarchus:** an Alexandrian and author of a history of Alexander ca. 280 BCE. **aetatis:** "life" or "life-span" rather than "age".

30. Artemidorus: of Ephesus. Supply "*tradit*". Artemidorus (fl. 104-101 BCE) wrote eleven geographical works based on his voyages along the Mediterranean as well as the works of Agatharchides and Megasthenes. **Taprobane:** modern Sri Lanka (known as Ceylon until 1972). **Duris:** Supply "*tradit*". Duris (340–270 BCE) was a historian as well as tyrant of Samos beginning ca. 300. He wrote a number of works, among which are the now-fragmentary Μακεδονικά (*Macedonica*), Σαμίων ὧροι (*Chronicles of the Samians*), and a biography of Agathocles, tyrant of Syracuse. **Calingis:** cf. Pliny §6.64, where he mentions the "*Calingae*". **gente:** in apposition to "*Calingis*". **cauda villosa ... eximiae:** Likely referring again to monkeys. **Oritas:** cf. Pliny §6.95, which tells us that the Oritae did not speak an Indian language. They were fish-eaters, and Alexander, as part of his conquest, forbade them from eating fish. **Arabis:** Beagon (2005) identifies the Arabis with the Purali, citing Curtius 9.10.6. There may be some connection to the Arbii, the people whom Pliny places next to the Oritae at *NH* §6.95. **piscium:** understand "*cibum piscium*".

31. equis: ablative of comparison with "*velociores*". (AG §406) **Syrbotas:** cf. Pliny §6.190, where he tells us that the Syrbotae are twelve feet tall. **Menisminorum:** Note Beagon (2005): "In *HN* §6.190, identical characteristics are attributed to the Alabi, 'next to' the Medimni and Schwabe identifies the Menismini with the latter: Schwabe, *RE* 15.1, Menismini 895." **Menisminorum appellata:** renames "*Nomadum Aethiopum*". **cynocephalus:** baboons, see §7.23 above.

32. hominum species: Perhaps ghosts; Beagon (2005) suggests the reference is to mirages. **obviae . . . fiunt:** "arise face to face". **ludibria:** toys. **ingeniosa:** modifying "*natura*". **ex singulis:** "one by one". **in dies . . . horas:** "day-by-day" . . . "hour-by-hour". **prope:** adv. "nearly", as often. **valeat:** potential subjunctive. (AG §§ 445–7) **eius:** i.e., "*naturae*". **sit:** jussive subjunctive (also called hortatory). (AG §§ 439–40) **gentes:** i.e., "*gentes hominum*".

PART TWO: STUDY OF MAN (§§33–129). Having dealt with the outliers of humanity, Pliny embarks on a description of humankind generally, beginning appropriately enough with pregnancy and birth, and then dealing in turns with childhood and excellence in every sphere: physical, martial, literary/intellectual, and the arts.

Part 2A: Generation (§§7.33–67). The structure of this section mirrors that of the book as a whole, beginning with oddities of birth— multiple births and prodigious births—and then following gestation chronologically. Pliny describes the experience of pregnant women, types of birth, including breech birth, caesarean section, and superfetation, and a rudimentary theory of genetic resemblance. There follows a description of sterility in couples, disorders of the generative organs, menopause, and menstruation.

Chapter 3

33. tergeminos: "triplets". The adjective *"geminus"* is of uncertain origin, but it has been linked to the PIE root **yem-* for "pair", and so *"tergeminus"* is literally "a pair of three". **Horatiorum Curiatiorumque:** See Livy 1.23–5. When Alba Longa and Rome went to war with each over Latin supremacy during the reign of Tullus Hostilius, rather than devastate the youth of both cities, they put forward two sets of triplets to fight on their behalf: the Horatii for Rome, the Curiatii for Alba. In the course of the combat, all of the Curiatii were killed, but one of the Horatii survived, earning Rome its victory. **super:** an adverb. Translate "more than this", i.e., identical siblings more than three in number. **praeterquam:** "except". **Aegypto:** "Aegyptus", while strictly a name for Memphis, an important city on the Nile, was applied by Herodotus to all of what we call Egypt. The term exists in Greek as early as Homer and derives from Egyptian *"Hwt-ka-Ptah"*, "the House of the Ka (soul) of Ptah". Ptah, whose major cult center was at Memphis, was a creator and craftsman god, identified by the Greeks with Hephaestus. The Egyptians themselves called their land *Kmt*, or "Black Land" because of the fertile silt of the Nile. **Nilus:** the great river of Egypt. Until the building of the Aswan Dam in 1963, the Nile flooded reliably every year, depositing fertile silt that fed rich farms and contributed to Egypt's massive wealth. Its main tributaries are the Blue Nile and the White Nile, but many smaller sources feed it, making the search for the headwaters difficult and ongoing. As a result, Renaissance iconography often depicted the Nile's River God with his head veiled. **supremis:** here, the last rites, funeral (OLD s.v. *supremus* 5b). **Divi Augusti:** Octavian Augustus. The adjective *"divus"* is in many ways equivalent to our saying "the late Augustus"; it differs in the degree of respect and religious denotation. **Ostiae:** locative. (AG §427) Ostia lay at the mouth of the Tiber and guarded the river (and thus Rome and central Italy) against attacks by sea and pirates. In the late Republic and early Empire, it became a resort town with lavish amenities. The emperor Claudius made Ostia into a true port by building Portus, a man-made harbor two miles to the north, which Hadrian later improved and which continued to be used throughout antiquity. **Peloponneso:** The Peloponnese, "Pelops's Island" is the large peninsula of southern Greece. The major cities of the Peloponnese included Argos, Corinth, Olympia, and Sparta, among others. **quinos:** for *"quingeminos"*. **ex omni:** with *"partu"*. **eius:** referring back to the woman who gave birth. **vixisse:** indirect statement. **septenos:** for *"septengeminos"*. **Trogus:** Pompeius Trogus, an Augustan-era historian who wrote a *De animalibus* and a *Historicae Philippicae*, which began with the ancient Near East and continued through to Augustus.

34. quos: for *"ei quos"*. (AG §307) **androgynos:** ἀνδρογύνους "androgynes", or "men-women", a term meaning "hermaphrodite". **deliciis:** "delights", but also "pets" (OLD s.v. *delicia* 3). **Pompeius Magnus:** Gnaeus Pompeius Magnus, Pompey the Great (106–48 BCE). For Pliny's account of Pompey's career, see §7.95–9 below. Pompeius Magnus was the son of the general Gnaeus Pompeius Strabo. He began his career fighting under his father and then on behalf of Sulla in 83 BCE, rising quickly. The *lex Gabinia* in 67 BCE, ostensibly a charge to fight the pirates that plagued the Mediterranean, gave Pompey near-dictatorial powers over the majority of Rome's holdings. The *lex Manilia* in 66 gave him control of the Mithridatic War in the East, the settlement of which in 63 and 62 made Pompey the most influential—and thus most powerful—of the Roman politicians, which earned him the opposition of much of the senate. In response, he formed an unofficial triumvirate with the young Caesar and the wealthy Crassus, a relationship which endured until Crassus's death in 55 and Caesar's return from Gaul in 50. Civil war ensued between Pompey and Caesar, with Pompey taking the Republican side. In 48 BCE, Pompey was killed in Egypt, where he had fled for aid against Caesar. **theatri:** Rome's first permanent theater, dedicated in 55 BCE. **fama:** ablative of specification with *"mirabiles"*. (AG §418) **Trallibus:** ablative of place where (AG §429). Tralles was an important city between Lydia and Caria on the Meander, approximately modern Aydin. **Alcippe elephantum:** If there is any truth to the story that Alcippe gave birth to an elephant, it likely represents a child with severe cranial deformities. Cf. Joseph Merrick, who even in modern times has been called the "Elephant Man". **Marsici:** The Social Wars. See the note at §7.15 above. **pluribus modis:** depends on "*multiformes*".

35. Claudius Caesar: (10 BCE–54 CE) Claudius had a limp and a lisp and was thought unsuited for rule until in 41 CE when, immediately after the assassination of Gaius Caesar (Caligula), a soldier found him in hiding and took him to the praetorians where he was hailed as emperor. Claudius proved to be a strong emperor, overseeing numerous conquests, including that of Britain, and ruling three times longer than his predecessor. He was also a scholar and historian, writing works on Roman, Etruscan, and Carthaginian history. (See Suetonius, *Claudius* 41–2.) **hippocentaurum:** more commonly simply "centaur". **Thessalia:** a region of northern Greece famous for its horses and as the natural home of witches and witchcraft. **nos:** "we ourselves", "we actually". Here, the plural is, as often in Latin, the plural of modesty standing for "I". (AG §143a) **adlatum:** This seems to refer to another hippocentaur. **Saguntum:** a town on the east coast of Spain, south of the Ebro. It was a Roman ally in Carthaginian territory, and so Hannibal besieged it in 219 BCE in order to provoke Rome to the second Punic War. **deleta . . . est:** the subject is the city Saguntum; "*deleta*" is feminine because "*Saguntum urbs*" is understood. **Hannibale:** (247–183/2 BCE) The son of the Carthaginian general Hamilcar Barca (whose name means "Brother to Melqart", "Thunderer"). Hamilcar, a general of the First Punic War, had taken Hannibal with him to Spain after the war, where he had the nine-year-old Hannibal swear on an altar never to be friends with Rome. Hamilcar died in 229, leaving Hamilcar's brother-in-law Hasdrubal (I) ("the help of Ba'al/the Lord") in command. When Hasdrubal (I), too, died in 221, Hannibal ("Grace of Ba'al/the Lord") was elected general by a popular assembly in Carthage. In 219, the year the Carthaginians finished paying their tribute to Rome, he approached Saguntum, a city in Carthaginian territory according to the treaty of the

First Punic War, but also an ally of Rome. The conflict of interest gave him an opportunity to antagonize Rome into a new war, and so he besieged it and took the city. Hannibal immediately set out for Italy, leaving his brother Hasdrubal (II) in charge of Spain. He defeated Roman armies repeatedly in Italy notably at Ticinus, Trebia, Trasimene, and Cannae (see note at 7.106). The Roman general Fabius Maximus Verrucosus waged a war of attrition on Hannibal and earned the name "Cunctator" (the Delayer) for his efforts. Meanwhile in Spain, Publius Cornelius Scipio, who would be called Africanus, defeated Hasdrubal, preventing Hannibal from collecting reinforcenments. Then, instead of fighting Hannibal directly, he took his army to Africa, and with the help of Masinissa, king of Numidia, set out to attack Carthage, resulting in Hannibal's recall from Italy. In 202 BCE Scipio Africanus defeated Hannibal's forces at Zama, effectively ending the Second Punic War (also known as the Hannibalic War). After the war, Hannibal returned to Carthage and was elected to the office of Suffete (equivalent to Consul) in 196, but his political enemies sent word (falsely) to Rome that he was conspiring with Antiochus V to wage war again. Hannibal was forced to flee. In 183/2 he drank poison to avoid capture by Titus Quinctius Flamininus.

Chapter 4

36. P. Licinio Crasso C. Cassio Longino coss.: 171 BCE. **annalibus:** possibly a reference to the *Annales Maximi*, yearly records kept by the Pontifex Maximus. **Casini:** locative. (AG §427) Modern Cassino on the via Latina. **Licinius Mucianus:** suffect consul three times: 64, 70, and 72 CE. See Tacitus *Hist.* 1.10. As a historian, he wrote a *Mirabilia*. **Argis:** Ablative of place where. (AG §429) A city of the Peloponnese. Argos has Bronze Age roots and was home to a Mycenaean population, but by the 10th c. BCE it was inhabited by Dorians. Throughout the archaic and classical periods, Argos remained second to Sparta, fighting the Lacedaemonians about once a generation and always losing. Under

Roman rule, Argos gained in importance, hosting both the Heraean and Nemean games. **Arescontem . . . Arescusae:** There are a number of similar stories in antiquity, usually of women transforming to men. Cf. Teiresias and his double transformation, Iphis (Ovid, *Met.* 9.666–797), Leucipus (Hermesianx in Antonius Liberalis 39), and Caenis (Ovid, *Met.* 12.170ff, 459ff.) See Bömer, *P. Ovidius Naso* for a more complete list of other sex-changes in antiquity. **Zmyrnae:** locative. (AG §427) Also "Smyrna", the modern city of Izmir on the west coast of Turkey, south of Lesbos. The city was a center of science and medicine and would, a century after Pliny, be a major focal point for the Second Sophistic. Pliny's point is that the gender change did not happen in a backwater, but in a modern, scientific metropolis and is, therefore more trustworthy. **Thysdritanum:** The city of Thysdrus is modern El Djem in Tunisia. Thysdrus was a minor city of no significance, and so Pliny's eye-witness at Thysdrus forms a counterpoint to Mucianus's report from Smyrna. **vivebatque . . . haec:** These words are not present in Pliny's manuscripts, but have been supplied from Aulus Gellius.

37. editis . . . feminas: this section is in indirect statement due to some word like *"fertur"* that has dropped out. **puerperae . . . puerperio:** The adjective *"puerperus"* is a compound of *"puer"* (originally "child") and the verb *"pario"* "to give birth to". Hence, *"puerperus"*, "one who gives birth to children" and *"puerperium"* "birthing, newborn child". The words survive in the English adjective "puerperal", "of child-bearing" and the noun in "puerperium", the four weeks following childbirth.

Chapter 5

38. animantibus: frequently used of all living things as opposed to animals only (OLD s.v. *animans²* 3). **septimo . . . undecimi:** These figures seem at first unlikely, given that human gestation lasts 280 days, give or take another 9. The Romans counted inclusively, however, so the beginning of the eleventh month, the maximum length Pliny gives to a pregnancy, would occur at a not-impossible 300 days. The problem arises with Pliny's minimum length, but this would depend on when a woman realized and acknowledged her pregnancy.

39. tralaticium: an adjective meaning "common" (OLD s.v. *translaticius* 3). **Vistilia Gliti ac postea Pomponi atque Orfiti:** Vistilia's exact identity is unknown: she was either the sister or the daughter of Sextus Vistilius. Her first husband, Glitius, was likely Publius Glitius Gallus, father of the Glitius of the same name who was implicated in the Pisonian conspiracy of 65 CE. She then married Pomponius Secundus, father of the poet and friend of Pliny the Younger. After Pomponius came Cornelius Scipio Salvidienus Orfitus. **Suillium Rufum:** either P. Suillius Rufus (consul in the 40s CE) or his son of the same name, also consul in the 40s. **Corbulonem:** Gnaeus Domitius Corbulo, suffect consul in 39 CE. Corbulo, as propraetor in the East under Nero, reorganized the Roman army and installed Tigranes as king of Armenia. He later signed a treaty with the Parthians governing the disposition of Armenia, which would remain a buffer state between the two empires. **Caesoniam Gai principis coniugem:** Milonia Caesonia married Caligula in 39 CE when she was between the ages of 24 and 34 (Suetonius, *Gaius* 25.3; Beagon, 2005).

40. in quo mensum numero: i.e., in eight months. **genitis:** dative of reference or possession, most easily taken with "*labor*". (AG §373, 376) **labor:** "difficulty" (i.e., for the infants). **letalesque in iis abortus:** "abortions/miscarriages in these cases are lethal" i.e., to the pregnant women. **Masurius:** Mas(s)urius Sabinus, a Roman lawyer from the 1st c. CE from Verona. He was awarded by Tiberius the *ius respondendi ex auctoritate principis*, the right of giving legal opinions in the voice of the emperor. He was the author of books on public and private law, which became the basis of the works of later jurists, among them Ulpian. **L. Papirium:** Beagon (2005) suggests Lucius Papirius Maso, Praetor Urbanus in 176 BCE. Cf. Livy, 41.14.5, 15.5. **secundo herede:** the second heir, who would inherit if the first heir were unable. **lege agente:** "*lege agere*", "to bring a lawsuit, bring an action according to the law". "*Agente*" here agrees not with "*lege*" but with "*herede*": "when the second heir was bringing a lawsuit". **contra eum:** i.e., against the second heir. **mater partum se tredecim mensibus diceret tulisse:** i.e., to the first heir.

Chapter 6

41. hominis inchoati: "The formation of a human". This is the so-called "*Ab urbe condita*" construction. (AG §497) We might also translate the phrase simply as "embryo". **ferenti:** agrees with an understood "*matri*". **XC:** an ordinal number: "*nonagesimo*".

42. editos: "after they have been born". **refert:** "it matters". The subject is "*incessus et omne quidquid dici potest*". **ut ... edant:** a result clause triggered by "*adeo*". (AG §536) **salsioribus cibis:** ablative object of "*usae*". **oscitatio:** "yawning". **sternuisse:** "to have sneezed" (OLD s.v. *sternuo*). **a coitu:** "after intercourse". **abortivum:** neuter, modifying "*sternuisse*".

Chapter 7

43. miseret ... pudet: along with "*taedet*," "*paenitet*," and "*pigret*", these verbs take an accusative of person affected and a genitive of cause of emotion. "It causes pity and shames ...". (AG §354b) **viribus:** ablative object of "*fidis*". **fidis:** One of the semi-deponents. Also "*audeo*," "*gaudeo*", and sometimes "*soleo*". (AG §192)

44. tanti: genitive of (indefinite) value. (AG §417) **minoris:** like "*tanti*," a genitive of value: "for less". (AG §417) **potes:** understand "*perire potes*". **quantulo ... dente:** "struck by as little as a snake's tooth"; "*quantulo*" agrees with "*dente*", picking up the diminutive that properly describes the tooth. **Anacreon:** (fl. 536/5 BCE) Born on the island Teos, Anacreon was a prolific poet whose writings survive only in fragments (the Anacreontics). He composed in a variety of lyric meters and stanzas, including elegiac couplets, iambics, glyconics, and pherecrateans. The extant fragments focus on themes of wine and love. According to tradition, he died by choking on a grape. (See Valerius Maximus 9.12.) **uvae passae:** i.e., a raisin (OLD s.v. *uva* 1b). **Fabius Senator:** a figure otherwise unknown.

Chapter 8

45. in pedes procidere: i.e., feet-first. **Agrippas:** A so-called "Varronian" or "Stoic" etymology, which strives to explain a word's meaning through an (often superficial) relationship to similar words. Pliny takes the name "Agrippa" from "*aegri partus*" "of difficult birth", while Aulus Gellius, *Attic Nights* 16.16.1, derives it from "*aegritudo*" and "*pedes*": "quorum in nascendo non caput, sed pedes primi extiterant, qui partus difficillimus aegerrimusque habetur, 'Agrippae' appellati vocabulo ab aegritudine et pedibus conficto." But one can see the close association between "*partus*" and "*aegerrimus*" in Gellius, too, which might explain Pliny's etymology. **Marcum Agrippam:** Marcus Vipsanius Agrippa, the emperor Augustus's general and friend. Agrippa was born ca. 64 BCE in Arpinum, the birthplace of Marius and Cicero. He held the consulship in 37 and converted lake Avernus into a harbor in which he could train a fleet for Octavian. His efforts led to the naval defeat of Antony at Actium in 31. For a time, he appeared to be Augustus's choice for a successor, even wielding the tribuncian power from 18 until his death in 12 BCE, a power afterwards borne only by emperors and their heirs. Agrippa was responsible for many public works, including the Pantheon (which Hadrian would later restore) By his first wife, Caecilia Attica, he had a daughter, Vipsania Agrippina (I), who would later marry the emperor Tiberius. His third wife, Iulia, the daughter of Augustus, gave birth to (among others) Agrippa Postumus and a second Agrippina (II) Maior, who would be mother to the emperor Gaius (Caligula) and grandmother to Nero. **unico . . . exemplo:** dative of purpose. (AG §382) **terris:** depends on "*infelici*". **Agrippinas:** see the preceding note. **Gaium:** the emperor Caligula. **Domitium Neronem:** The emperor Nero was the son of Julia Agrippina, better known as Agrippina the Younger, who was sister to Caligula and daughter of Agrippina Maior.

46. socerique: the emperor Augustus. Agrippa was at this time married to Augustus's daughter, Julia, who was famous for her adultery. **praeposteri:** Here, literal: "hindquarters first". Cf. the English "preposterous." **Neronem:** (37–68 CE). Born Lucius Domitius Ahenobarbus, Nero was adopted by the emperor Claudius in 50 CE and became Tiberius Claudius Nero Caesar or Nero Claudius Caesar Drusus Germanicus, or Domitius Caesar. He became emperor at age 17 when Claudius died in 54. The first five years of his reign were seen as a golden age, but senatorial opinion of Nero quickly dropped. In 65, a conspiracy to overthrow Nero and make Gaius Calpurnius Piso emperor was uncovered, and Nero had executed or condemned to suicide a number of noble Romans, among them Petronius, his tutor Seneca and the poet Lucan. In 67 Nero deposed and executed several commanders, including Gnaeus Domitius Corbulo (see above, note §7.39). In 68, the governors Iulius Vindex, Galba, and Clodius Macer revolted, spurring Nero to commit suicide. 69 would be known as the year of the four emperors as Galba, Otho, Vitellius, and the eventual emperor, Vespasian, struggled for supremacy. **paulo ante:** i.e., shortly before Pliny's time. (AG §414) **Agrippina:** Agrippina Minor. See above, §7.45 on "Domitium Neronem". **ritus naturae:** supply "*est*". **efferri:** to be carried out for burial (OLD s.v. *effero* 3).

Chapter 9

47. Scipio Africanus: Publius Cornelius Scipio Africanus, the first so-called, general in the Second Punic War and the victor at Zama. **primusque Caesarum:** Not Julius Caesar, but the first member of the Julian gens called "Caesar". By "*a caeso matris utero dictus*", Pliny provides another Varronian etymology (see note at §7.45) for what we now call the "Caesarean section". A different etymology links "Caesar" with "*caesaries*", "mane of hair". **Manilius:** Manius Manilius consul in

149 BCE, the first year of the Third Punic War. **Carthaginem:** Founded as a trading colony by the Phoenician city Tyre in 814/3 BCE, "Carthago" in Punic means "New Town". Its influence in trade and its outposts extended from southern Spain and Morocco to Sicily. Carthage came into conflict with the Etruscans on the Italian Peninsula and the Greeks of Sicily, and after a series of wars in the 5th c. BCE, Carthage was limited to the western coast of Sicily and the western Mediterranean. Carthage had treaties with Rome as early as 508 and even aided Rome against Pyrrhus of Epirus in 280 BCE, but conflict over Sicily in 264 sparked the First Punic War. Rome and Carthage remained in conflict until the end of the Third Punic War in 146 BCE when the Romans sacked and razed the city, ending the Carthaginian state entirely. Augustus refounded Carthage as the capital of proconsular Africa. The city gradually gained in importance until it again became a threat, as the power base for the Gordians (238–244 CE) and later the capital of Gaiseric (439–477 CE).

Chapter 10

47. qui retenti utero nascerentur: refers back to "*Vopiscos*", not "*geminis*". **e geminis:** "among twins". **altero interempto abortu:** The phrase explains "*geminis*"; "*abortu*" is an ablative of means or circumstance, giving detail to the ablative absolute "*altero interempto*". **circa hoc:** "in regard to this".

Chapter 11

48. gravida: take predicatively: "when pregnant". **unum … alterum:** subjects of "*superfetat*". **superfetat:** a rare compound. "Superfetation" is to conceive while already pregnant so that embryos of different ages or of different fathers develop in the uterus simultaneously. Beagon (2005) contrasts this with "superfecundation, the conception of twins through separate acts of sexual intercourse in one menstrual cycle". Compare Hercules and Iphicles in the following section. **extat:** impersonal, taking "*puerperia*" as its object. (AG §207) **quibus:** Understand "*eorum quibus*"; "*quibus*" is a dative of reference, forming the so-called "double dative" with "*curae*", a dative of purpose. (AG §376, 382) **consectari:** "to follow up, investigate"; "*talia*" is the accusative direct object. **puerperia:** "birthings". **egesta:** from "*egero*", "to expel" (OLD s.v. *egero* 3b, 4).

49. Hercule et Iphicle: The fraternal twin sons of Alcmene. Iphicles, the son of Amphitryon, was born first, followed by Hercules, the son of Zeus. **Proconnesia ancilla:** Proconessus is the modern Marmara Island in the Sea of Marmara (ancient Propontis), which is connected to the Mediterranean by the Dardanelles and to the Black Sea by the Bosphorus. Who the "*ancilla*" is is unknown, though she may be meant merely to represent an ethnic type of Easterner. **eiusdem diei coitu:** ablative of cause. (AG §404) **procuratori:** bailiff. **quae iusto partu quinque mensum alterum edidit:** "who, in a proper birthing [i.e., a baby of nine months] produced a second child of five months".

50. truncos: "maimed, deformed". **regenerari:** Not "regenerated", but "born again in the children". **Dacorum:** The Dacians were a people closely related to the Thracians. They lived in the region west of the Black Sea and periodically threatened nearby Roman holdings. Domitian would begin a series of wars agains the Dacians in 86 CE that would culminate in Trajan's conquest of the region in 101. **originis:** Here, "generation". **nota:** A mark of any kind, possibly "birthmark", although Beagon (2005) translates it "tattoo", following Schilling's reference to *NH* 22.2, in which, speaking of plant dyes, Pliny says "*maresque etiam apud Dacos et Sarmatas corpora sua inscribunt*". "Even the men among the Dacians and the Sarmatians inscribe their bodies [with these dyes]."

Chapter 12

51. Lepidorum: Pliny describes children born with the caul, a remnant of the amniotic membrane that has adhered to an infant's head or face during the birthing process. The particular members of the Lepidi are unknown. **annoque post genitum:** "*anno*" is an ablative of degree of difference modifying the prepositional phrase "*post genitum*" "born afterwards by a year" = "born a year later". (AG §414) **quasdam . . . parere:** indirect statement still depending on "*accepimus*". **Nicaei pyctae:** "The boxer Nicaeus". The name derives from the Greek νίκη (nike), "victory". **Byzanti:** Locative. (AG §427) A Greek city on the European side of the Bosphorus. Its strategic position controlled entry to the Black Sea and so alliance with the city was much sought over, first by the Spartans and Athenians, then by Rome. Septimius Severus reduced the city substantially for supporting a rival claimant to the throne, but it gradually recovered, and in AD 330, Constantine refounded it as New Rome, later known as Constantinople, and now Istanbul (from the Greek phrase εἰς τὰν πόλιν (eis tan polin) "to the city"). **adulterio Aethiopis nata matre nihil a ceteris colore differente:** a parenthetical. The whole phrase depends on the ablative absolute "*nata matre*"; "*adulterio Aethiopis*" is an ablative of cause or means explaining "*nata*". (AG §404) "*nihil a ceteris colore differente*" extends the ablative absolute: either *differente* agrees with *matre* and *colore* is an ablative of specification (AG §418), or *colore differente* is a new ablative absolute. In either case, the point is that the mother has only her own mother's coloration, while Nicaeus has the coloration of his Aethiopian grandfather.

52. haustaeque: "derived". The verb "*haurio*" primarily means "to drink", but it has a wide variety of secondary senses based on the idea of drawing water and thus consuming it. Compare our expression "to drink [something] in". The act, when done to completion, gives us "exhaustion" i.e., "completely drained" (OLD s.v. *haurio* 5d). **sub ipso conceptu:** Beagon (2005): "at the very moment of conception". **inprimit:** the subject is "*differentiae . . . varietas*" all taken as one concept. **ceteris animantibus:** dative of possession. (AG §373) **singulis . . . cuique:** singular forms of "*quisque*" often modify plural words when the author wants to emphasize that the group is to be taken individually. Here: ". . .

since the remaining animals possess minds which are not nimble and are alike for all together and each one individually in its own species." The point is that images, whether viewed, heard, imagined, etc., leave impressions on human minds, and those impressions affect the formation of the fetus in a variety of ways, both at the moment of conception (*"sub ipso conceptu"*) and subsequently. Animals do not suffer this effect to the same degree because they do not have minds nearly as differentiated as humans do.

53. Antiocho: Antiochus II, Hellenistic king of Syria from 261 BCE to his death, age 40, in 246. Like all the Hellenistic kings, he tried to expand his empire, in this case, by putting aside his wife Laodice and marrying Berenice, daughter of Ptolemy II of Egypt. He died afterwards, whether Laodice assassinated him as Pliny records or otherwise, and a war of succession followed with Laodice and her children eventually successful. **Syriae:** Originally a Persian satrapy, Syria was conquered by Alexander the Great and after his death became one of the Hellenistic kingdoms ruled by his generals. The Seleucid dynasty claimed Syria but constantly fought for control of the land with the Ptolemies of Egypt until the victories of Antiochus III (202–198 BCE). **Artemo:** Pliny deviates from the tradition in Valerius Maximus (9.14 ext 1) by making Artemo plebian. *"Regi Antiocho unus ex aequalibus et ipse regiae stirpis nomine Artemo perquam similis fuisse traditur. quem Laodice uxor Antiochi interfecto uiro dissimulandi sceleris gratia in lectulo perinde quasi ipsum regem aegrum conlocauit admissumque uniuersum populum et sermone eius et uultu consimili fefellit, credideruntque homines ab Antiocho moriente Laodicen et natos eius sibi conmendari."* Maximus's *"ipse regiae stirpis nomine Artemo"* becomes in Pliny *"Regi Syriae e plebe nomine Artemo"*. The similarity is striking enough to suggest a question of variant readings, but see below under *"Vibius ... Publicius"*. **Laodice:** The cousin and wife of Antiochus II. Antiochus's death in 246 BCE spurred the Third Syrian War (246–241 BCE) (also known as the Laodicean War) between supporters of Laodice (the Seleucid dynasty) and supporters of Berenice (the Ptolemaic dynasty) over control of

Syria. The Seleucids won out and Laodice's son, Seleucus II, took the throne. **per eum:** "by means of him", i.e., using Artemo as mouthpiece. **commendationis regnique successionis:** depend on "*mimum*". **Vibius ... Publicius:** Unknown persons. This passage is also taken from Valerius Maximus 19.4.1: "*Magno Pompeio Vibius ingenuae stirpis et Publicius libertinus ita similes fuerunt, ut permutato statu et Pompeius in illis et illi in Pompeio salutari possent. certe, quocumque aut Vibius aut Publicius accesserant, ora hominum in se obuertebant, uno quoque speciem amplissimi ciuis in personis mediocribus adnotante.*" That Pliny has changed "*ingenuae stirpis*" to "*e plebe*" might suggest that he has adjusted the story of Artemo in order to emphasize the randomness of the similarities between unrelated persons and to create an equivalent similarity between passages. **indiscreta prope specie:** "a nearly indistinguishable appearance"

54. patri: dative with the compound verb "*inposuit*". With compound verbs, the word in the dative is the object of the prepositional prefix. So here, "*patri ... cognomen inposuit*" = "posuit cognomen *in patre*". (AG §370) **Menogenis:** from Valerius Maximus 9.14.2: "*Quod quidem fortuitum ludibrium quasi hereditarium ad eum penetrauit: nam pater quoque eius eo usque Menogenis coci sui similis esse uisus est, ut uir et armis praepotens et ferox animo sordidum eius nomen repellere a se non ualuerit.*" **cognomen:** The Roman aristocracy utilized a system of *tria nomina*: a *praenomen*, *nomen*, and *cognomen*. The *praenomen*, an informal "first" name would be used at home and among close friends, but a man was most often referred to by his *nomen* (clan name / gentilician name) and, if he had one, his *cognomen*, a descriptive nickname that might or might not be passed down to his heirs. Marcus Tullius Cicero, for example, belonged to the *gens Tullia* and had an ancestor who garnered the nickname *Cicero* ("chickpea"), perhaps for a bean-shaped wart. An additional name, nickname, or title, the *agnomen*, might occasionally be added to celebrate an individual's accomplishments or characteristics, as for example, the "Africanus" in the name "Publius Cornelius Scipio Africanus", earned for his victory over Hannibal at

Zama. Pliny will discuss the etymologies and origins of these *cognomina* throughout. Women, on the other hand, generally had only one name, taken from the *gens* of their father. They might be distinguished by numerals (*Julia Prima, Julia Tertia*, etc.), by the addition of "elder" or "younger" (*Agrippina Maior*), or by their husband's name in the genitive, as Claudia Metelli, the proposed figure behind Catullus's Lesbia. In the following passages, Pliny identifies famous Romans who were given an additional *cognomen* due to a resemblance to various base characters. In each case we might assume that the profession of the man to whom the elite figure is compared is itself significant and implies a slander. **Strabonis:** Gnaeus Pompeius Strabo, Pompey the Great's father. **Strabonis ... habenti:** "*Strabonis*" depends on an understood "*cognomen*". "*habenti*" is dative, agreeing with "*patri*". **vitium:** object of "*imitato*". **Scipioni Serapionis:** Publius Cornelius Scipio Nasica, consul of 138 BCE. "*Scipioni*" is dative depending on the "in" in the compound verb "*indiderat*" (see the note on "*patri*" above), while "*Serapionis*" depends on an understood "*cognomen*". The structure is parallel to "*patri ... inposuit*". (AG §370) **Scipioni post eum nomen Salvitto:** Cornelius Scipio Pomponianus Salvitto. **Spinther ... Metelli:** Publius Cornelius Lentulus Spinther and Quintus Caecilius Metellus Nepos Pamphilus, consuls in 57 BCE. Lentulus Spinther was a Republican, a Pompeian, and a friend to Cicero. He was executed by Caesar after the battle of Pharsalus. Quintus Metellus Nepos, also a Pompeian, died shortly after his proconsulship in Spain (56). **sicut Spinther ... consulum:** supply "*inposuerunt*" or "*indederant*". "*collegio*" is dative and governs "*Lentuli et Metelli consulum*". "*secundarum tertiarumque*" are feminine with an understood "*partium*" "roles". **duorum ... cerni:** indirect statement depending on "*fortuitum hoc quoque fuit*". Actors were considered among the lowest of professions, on par with slaves and prostitutes, so to be likened to an actor or to be forced on stage (in this case, vicariously) was a deep insult that affected one's social standing.

55. L. Plancus: Lucius Munatius Plancus Orator. Consul in 42 BCE with Lepidus, Plancus had an illustrious career, managing always to ally himself with the winning side: abandoning Brutus for Antony and Lepidus, proscribing his own brother, abandoning Lucius Antonius at Perusia, fleeing to Antony and Cleopatra, but abandoning them for Octavian shortly before the battle of Actium, and finally in 27 BCE making the motion in the senate that Octavian be named Augustus. **histrioni Rubrio:** an actor. The word "*histrio*" was the Etruscan word for "actor" or "player". Given the context (various undesirables who gave their names to members of the aristocracy), Pliny may be making a very sharp comment on Plancus: he is the only member of the aristocracy in this list who is himself so undesirable that his name degrades an actor, rather than the reverse. **Curioni:** Gaius Scribonius Curio, consul in 76 BCE. Cicero, in his *Brutus* 216, says of him: "*itaque in Curione hoc verissime iudicari potest, nulla re una magis oratorem commendari quam verborum splendore et copia. nam cum tardus in cogitando tum in struendo dissipatus fuit. reliqua duo sunt, agere et meminisse: in utroque cacinnos inridentium commovebat. motus erat is, quem et C. Iulius in perpetuum notavit, cum ex eo in utramque partem toto corpore vacillante quaesivit, quis loqueretur e luntre*". "And so in the case of Curio, this can justly be ascertained, that in nothing is an oratory more recommended than in the splendor and facility of his words. For he was both slow at thinking on his feet and distracted in his logical arrangement. As for the other two [facets of oratory], in each he stirred laugher among his detractors. His affect was precisely that which Gaius Julius remarked upon for future remembrance when he asked about Curio, who was swaying side to side with his whole body, 'Who is that speaking from a boat?'" **Burbuleius:** An actor. Sallust likely recorded the same anecdote in his *Historiae*: "*Quia corpore et lingua percitum et inquietem nomine histrionis vix sani Burbuleium appellabat*." (from Priscian, Keil's *Grammatici Latini*, vol. 2, p. 243). **Messalae:** Marcus Vallerius Messala Niger, consul in 61 BCE. **Menogenes:** Here, an actor, not Pompeius Strabo's cook. **Surae:** Publius Cornelius Lentulus Sura, consul in 71 BCE. See Cicero, *Brutus* 234–5. Sura was expelled from the Senate in 70, joined the Catilinarian conspiracy as its chief officer in Rome, was exposed by Cicero, and was among those excuted in 63. **Sicilia:** the large island off the toe of Italy. Sicily was settled in prehistoric time by the Siculi (possibly the Shekelesh, one of the Sea Peoples named in Bronze Age Egyptian stelae), but in the archaic period it became a point of contention between the western Greeks of Magna Graecia and the Carthaginians. The Greeks settled the eastern and southern coasts, with major cities including Syracuse, Acragas (Agrigento), Catana, Gela, Himera, and Messana, among others. The Carthaginians settled the western coast and northwestern coasts. Italian advances into Sicily ca. 265 BCE precipitated the First Punic War (264–241). After the war, Sicily became the first province of the Roman state, governed beginning in 227 by a new magistrate created just for the purpose: the propraetor. Sicily served as a breadbasket for the Roman Republic and Empire throughout the ancient period. **Cassio Severo:** As his name implies, he was a severe orator. See Tacitus *Dialogus* 19, *Annales* 1.72, 4.21; Seneca Maior *Controversiae* 3.pref. Exiled for *maiestas* (treason) by Augustus in 8 CE. **Armentarii:** Otherwise unknown. Either a man named Armentarius who fought as a *murmillo*, a type of gladiator, or, possibly, a man named Murmillo who was an *armentarius*, a cowherd. **modo ... senatorem:** Mommsen considered this passage an interpolation, as it is found only in the margin of a single manuscript in a corrector's hand. **Annaea domo:** So Rackham and Beagon read. Mayhoff and Schilling read "*Iunia*". See below on "*Gallionem*" for the explanation. The *gens Annaea* is the one to which the Senecas and the poet Lucan belonged. Here, it refers to Annaeus Novatus. See the following note. **Gallionem:** Annaeus Novatus, adopted and renamed Lucius Iunius Gallio Annaeanus. Gallio was brother to the philosopher Seneca and consul in 55 or 56 CE. It was to Gallio that the Corinthians brought Paul to be judged: "**12** While Gallio was proconsul of Achaia, the Jews of Corinth made a united attack on Paul and brought him to the place of judgment. **13** "This man," they charged, "is persuading the people to worship God in ways contrary to the law." **14** Just as Paul was about to speak, Gallio said to them, "If you Jews were making a complaint about some misdemeanor or serious crime, it would be reasonable for me to listen to you. **15** But since it involves questions about words and names and your own law—settle the matter yourselves.

I will not be a judge of such things." **16** So he drove them off. **17** Then the crowd there turned on Sosthenes the synagogue leader and beat him in front of the proconsul; and Gallio showed no concern whatever." (*NIV* Acts 18:12–17). **Castellano:** Otherwise unknown. **Sannio mimo Paride:** An actor, Sannius Paris. **discernebant:** The subject is the impersonal "they": translate "They could not tell apart". The imperfect can indicate a sense of failure or inability, particularly with a negative. See AG §470f. **Agrippinum:** Paconius Agrippinus, a senator and Stoic philosopher banished by Nero in 67 CE. Tacitus, *Annales* 16.28–9, calls him "*paterni in principes odii heredem*" "heir of his father's hatred toward the emperors" because his father had been executed by Tiberius as part of Sejanus's plot. Epictetus, *Discourses* 1.1.28–30 gives a compelling portrait of Agrippinus: διὰ τοῦτο γὰρ Ἀγριππῖνος τί ἔλεγεν; ὅ τι 'ἐγὼ ἐμαυτῷ ἐμπόδιος οὐ γίνομαι.' ἀπηγγέλη αὐτῷ ὅ τι κρίνη ἐν συγκλήτῳ.'—'ἀγαθῇ τύχῃ. ἀλλὰ ἦλθεν ἡ πέμπτη' (ταύτῃ δ᾽ εἰώθει γυμνασάμενος ψυχρολουτρεῖν): 'ἀπέλθωμεν καὶ γυμνασθῶμεν.' γυμνασαμένῳ λέγει τις, αὐτῷ ἐλθὼν ὅτι 'Κατακέκρισαι.'—'φυγῇ,' φησίν, 'ἢ θανάτῳ;'—'φυγῇ.'—'τὰ ὑπάρχοντα τί;'—'οὐκ ἀφῃρέθη.'—'εἰς Ἀρίκειαν οὖν ἀπελθόντες ἀριστήσωμεν.' "As to this, what did Agrippinus say? 'I don't get in my own way.' The announcement came to him: 'You are being tried in the Senate.' He responded, 'And good luck to me, but it's the fifth hour.' (That's the time when he would normally exercise and then take a bath.) 'Let's go and exercise.' After he had exercised, someone came up to him said, 'Your trial is over.' 'Have I been sentenced to exile or death?' he asked. 'To exile.' 'What about my property?' 'It hasn't been seized.' 'Then let's go to Aricia and have dinner.' "

56. Toranius mango: Toranius Flaccus (Suetonius, *Augustus* 69.2; Macrobius, *Saturnalia* 2.4.28). **Antonio:** Marc Antony. **iam triumviro:** Literally, "when he was already a triumvir", but we might say "after he had become a triumvir". **Asia:** Asia Minor, the area that is now western Turkey. **ut:** with "*geminos*", not "*vendidit*". **increpitus . . . est:** "a scene was made". **conquerente:** with "*Antonio*". **ducentis . . . sestertiis:** ablative of (definite) price. **versutus ingenii:** Compare Livius Andronicus's 3rd c.

BCE translation of Odysseus's epithet πολύτροπον (Fagles's "man of twists and turns") with "*versutum*". **tanti:** genitive of value. Compare with "*ducentis...sestertiis*".(AG §417) **proscriptor animus:** "proscriptive wrath/intent", i.e., "the mind of the proscriber". Antony, Octavian, and Lepidus, as triumvirs, reinstituted in 43 BCE the proscriptions that Sulla had used so effectively in 82. The triumvirs drew up lists of the proscribed and posted them publicly in the Forum. Anyone who informed on a proscribed man earned a reward, and anyone who killed one directly was entitled to a portion of the proscribed's estate. **modo:** "just now". **ex fortuna sua:** "in line with his wealth/station".

Chapter 13

57. privatim: "between individuals" or possibly "idiosyncratically". The "*privatus*", like the Greek ἰδιώτης (idiōtēs), refers to an individual, private citizen (OLD s.v. *privatim* 2-3). **Augustus:** Augustus was married three times: to Clodia Pulchra (42–40 BCE), Scribonia (40–38 BCE) and Livia (37 BCE–14 CE), but he had only one child, a daughter, Julia, by Scribonia. His long association with Livia was to prove fruitless. **Livia:** Livia was married twice: to Tiberius Claudius Nero (43–37 BCE) and then to Augustus. Though she and Augustus would have none, she bore three children to her first husband, including the future emperors Tiberius and Claudius. **Gracchorum mater:** Cornelia, wife of Tiberius Sempornius Gracchus, parents to the tribunes Tiberius (d. 133 BCE) and Gaius (d. 121 BCE). **Agrippina Germanici:** Agrippina the Elder, daughter of Marcus Agrippa and Augustus's daughter Julia.

58. quaedam non perferunt partus: i.e., give birth prematurely. Literally "Certain women do not carry their births to term". **quales:** "which sort", referring back to the "*quaedam*". **vicere:** = *vicerunt*. The subject is the women, and the object is an understood "this" (i.e., the tendency to give birth prematurely). **Marcum Silanum:** Marcus Iunius Silanus Torquatus (consul 19 CE) married the great-granddaughter of

Augustus, Aemilia Lepida, and their son, Marcus Iunius Silanus (here mentioned) was consul in 46 CE and poisoned by Nero in 54 at the behest of his mother Agrippina. (Tacitus, *Annales* 13.1). The exact relationship is as follows: Augustus's daughter Julia married Agrippa, producing among other offspring, Julia the Younger, Augustus's granddaughter ("*neptis*"). Julia the Younger married Lucius Aemilius Paullus, producing Aemilia Lepida, and thus Julia the Younger's grandson was M. Silanus (consul 46 CE). **Neronis principis succesione:** Nero succeeded to the empire in 54 CE.

59. Quintus Metellus Macedonicus: Quintus Caecilius Metellus Macedonicus. See Pliny §7.142–6 below. Metellus Macedonicus fought under Aemilius Paullus at Pydna in 168 BCE, but he earned his agnomen when he fought Andriskos, the pseudo-Philip, last king of Macedon in 148. He was consul in 143, opposed Tiberius Gracchus in 133, and became one member of the first pair of plebeian censors in 131. **nurus vero generosque et omnes . . . XXVII:** supply "*reliquit*". The "*et*" here indicates that there are three categories: daughters-in-law, sons-in-law, and everyone altogether (descendants and in-laws).

60. Lucioque Sulla: 5 BCE. Little else is known. **duodecimo . . . immolasse:** indirect statement after "*invenitur*". The verb is "*immolasse*". **a. d. III idus Aprilis:** "*ante diem tres idus Aprilis*": three days before the Ides of April. Pace Beagon (2005) and Rackham, this is the 11th of April. (AG §631) One can remember the dates of Nones and Ides by the following rhyme from Gildersleeve and Lodge, *Gildersleeve's Latin Grammar*, Bolchazy-Carducci, 1989, reprint of 1895 3rd ed., p. 491.

> In March, July, October, May,
> the Ides are on the fifteenth day,
> the Nones, the seventh; but all besides
> have two days less for their Nones and Ides.

The Ides of April are on the 13th. Three days prior, by Roman inclusive counting, is the 11th (13-12-11). **Gaium Crispinum Hilarum:**

unknown, but one might imagine his cognomen comes from the happiness that so large a family was supposed to bring.

Chapter 14

61. XL: supply "*anno*". **profluvium genitale:** "procreative emission", i.e., "menstruation". **Masinissam:** (238–148 BCE) King of Numidia. At first he fought on behalf of the Carthaginians in the Second Punic War, leading Numidian cavalry in Africa and then in Spain against Scipio, but after Scipio's siege of Ilipa, he pledged support to the Romans, losing his kingdom in Numidia as a result. Masinissa joined with Scipio in Africa, leading the Numidian cavalry on Scipio's right, and afterwards he was recognized as king again by the Roman Senate. Under his rule, Numidia prospered and grew. **Methimannum:** The son of Masinissa's old age. See Polybius 36.16; Valerius Maximus 18.12.ext.1. **Catonem censoruium:** Understand "*filium generasse*". (234–149 BCE) Marcus Porcius Cato the Elder. A staunch supporter of old Roman customs and morals, Cato was consul in 195 BCE and censor in 184. As censor, he severely revised the senate rolls and instituted heavy taxes on luxury items, but also built public works, including renovations to the sewers. Cato the Elder is most famous today for his strong opposition to Carthage, purportedly ending his speeches with a variation on "*ceterum censeo Carthaginem delendam esse*". (See Plutarch, *Life of Cato* 27; Pliny, *NH* 15.23; Aurelius Victor *De viris illustribus* 47.8; Livy, *periochae* 49). Cato authored at least 150 speeches, various literary works, including a *De agricultura*, the extant example of his writing, and was the first to write history in Latin. His *Origines* began with the foundation of Rome, and later books detailed Roman wars from the First Punic War up to his own time. Cato famously omitted the names of generals in order to emphasize Rome over individuals, but he did record the name of one brave elephant: Syrus (Pliny, *NH* 8.11). **Saloni:** The son that Cato the Elder had with Salonia, daughter of his client, was grandfather to Cato the Younger, called Uticensis.

62. aliorum eius liberum propago: "*eius*" refers back to Cato; "*liberum*" is genitive plural with "*aliorum*". **Liciniani:** Cato the Elder's first wife was a Licinia, by whom he had one son, thus beginning the Licinian branch of the Catones. **Saloniani:** see "Saloni" in the previous section. **ex quis:** "*quis*" is an alternative dative/ablative plural, =*quibus*. (AG §150c) **Uticensis:** (95–46 BCE), the great-grandson of Cato the Elder (Censorius). Cato the Younger, known for his uncompromising ideals. Cato argued on behalf of the execution of the Catilinarians in 63. Cato was approached by Pompey to form an alliance and repeatedly rebuffed him, forcing Pompey to ally with Caesar and Crassus in 60. His fairness and principles were so well known that when, after settling the finances of Cyprus, his ledgers were lost at sea, no charges of corruption or embezzlement were levied against him. In the Civil Wars, Cato, on the side of Republicanism, aided Pompey. As Lucan puts it in his *Pharsalia*, 1.128: "*Vixtrix causa deis placuit, sed victa Catoni.*" "The gods sided with the winning cause, but Cato with the beaten." In 46, cornered in the African city of Utica, Cato committed suicide rather than allow himself to be pardoned by Caesar and so annexed to Caesar's regime. This commitment to his Republican ideals earned Cato his place as guard of Purgatory in Dante's *Commedia*. **Lucio Volusio Saturnino:** (38 BCE–56 CE), consul in 3 CE. (See Tacitus, *Annales* 13.30.) He had two sons, Lucius Volusius Saturninus, a pontiff, and Quintus Volusius Saturninus. The latter was consul in 56, the same year that the elder Saturninus died. "*Volusio Saturnino*" is dative with "*genitum*". **Cornelia Scipionum gentis:** wife to Lucius Volusius Saturninus, consul in 3 CE. **genitum:** for "*genitum esse*": indirect statement depending on "*notum est*".

Chapter 15

63. inde . . . molas: A complicated clause. With "*unius*" supply some word such as "*huius*". The antecedent to the relative clause, "*quas . . .*" is an understood "things" or "tumors". Likely this refers to a "molar pregnancy": an inviable egg may be fertilized, implant on the uterine wall, and grow into a small, hard clump of cells. A miscarriage that is not expelled may also form a similar mole. Either type can be benign or give rise to malignant tumors. **movetur:** a middle sense: "it moves about". (AG §156a, note) **alvo citatiore:** "when the belly is rather violently moved". "*Alvus*" can refer both to the womb and to the bowels, where it is used in expressions referring to diarrhea. **scirron:** From Greek σκῖρος, a hard tumor. **Oppio Capitoni:** Beagon (2005) identifies this Oppius with "the propraetor in charge of Antony's fleet in 37–35 BCE". Unlikely is Gaius Oppius, Caesar's friend who wrote biographies and pamphlets, including for Octavian, as he never exceeded equestrian rank.

64. reperiatur: potential subjunctive. (AG §§ 445–7) **profluvio:** In addition to the negative effects mentioned here, menstruation was also thought to have beneficial magical properties, such as "averting hail or killing caterpillars and other crop pests" (*BNP*, vol. 8, p. 702). See Columella, *De Re Rustica* 10.3.57–63, 11.3.38, 64, and 11.3.50. **aera:** From "*aes*", "bronze", the material out of which mirrors were commonly made, not from "*aer*", "air".

65. quin: here, a particle of assertion: "indeed!". **sequax:** "sticky". **Iudaeae:** The Romans took an interest in Judaea first with Pompey's disposition of the East in 63 BCE, and they made it a province in 6 CE after banishing Archelaus, Herod's successor. Compare Josephus *BJ* 3.54–5 and Pliny, *NH* 5.14.70. **Asphaltites:** the Dead Sea. The term ἀσφαλτίτης (asphaltites) in Greek means "bituminous". Bitumen, or asphalt, is a form of petroleum that is sticky, black, and viscous; it is naturally occuring in the Dead Sea. **quit:** from "*queo*". **virus:** See the note above at §7.14. Here, the "poison" is menstrual blood. The Dead Sea's relationship to menstruation is not immediately apparent, but the connection can be found in Tacitus, *Hist* 5.6.9: *Certo anni bitumen egerit, cuius legendi usum, ut ceteras artis, experientia docuit. Ater suapte natura liquor et sparso aceto concretus innatat; hunc manu captum, quibus ea cura, in summa navis trahunt: inde nullo iuvante influit oneratque, donec abscindas. Nec abscindere aere ferrove possis: fugit* *cruorem vestemque infectam sanguine, quo feminae per mensis exolvuntur.* "At a certain point of the year, it [the Dead Sea] produces bitumen, and experience has taught the method of collecting it, just as it has the other arts. It floats on the surface, black and a liquid in its natural state but it congeals when sprinkled with vinegar. Those whose business it is draw it onto the top of their ship, cupped in their hands. After that, it flows onto the ship under its own power and loads it down until you cut it off. But you would not be able to cut it with bronze or iron: it shuns blood and clothing stained with the blood of which women are delivered by means of menstruation." **sensum eius:** "*eius*" refers to bitumen.

66. omnibus tricenis diebus: ablative of time within when. (AG §423) **germine . . . glomerante:** ablative absolute. **coaguli:** rennet, an enzyme in the stomachs of mammals that causes coagulation. Rennet was necessary for cheese production and would be collected from calf stomachs by soaking them overnight in mixtues of brine and wine and then straining out the clumping rennet. When added to milk, the milk coagulates. Cf. Columella, *De re rustica* 7.8 "*De caeseo faciendo*"; Pliny, 11.97 **gravidis:** dative of (dis)advantage. (AG §376) **Nigidius:** Publius Nigidius Figulus (ca. 100–45 BCE), a Pompeian and friend of Cicero's, Nigidius Figulus was a grammarian, writing *Commentarii grammatici*, a scholar of religion, a naturalist, and a mystic. His writings included a *De hominum natura, De animalibus, De dis, De ventis, Sphaera* (on constellations), and others. Aulus Gellius, *Attic Nights* 4.9.1.1 says of him, "*Nigidius Figulus, homo, ut ego arbitror, iuxta Varronem doctissimus*", and again at 4.16.1.1 "*M. Varronem et P. Nigidium, viros Romani generis doctissimos*". Their names appear together six times in Gellius.

Chapter 16

67. idem: I.e., Nigidius Figulus. **feminae:** dative with "*alenti*". **salivam infici:** indirect statement depending on "*accepimus*". See Beagon (2005) for a thorough discourse on ancient beliefs about the interconnectedness of the bodily fluids of women.

Part 2B: Children (§§68–77). The child after birth is characterized by two qualities: an early set of teeth, soon replaced, and gradual growth into an adult. Both of these receive long digressions that compose the majority of this section. The explanation for the digression on teeth (§§68–72) comes in §72: teeth are what make a child wholly human and part of society, and so their expression is properly the beginning of a life independent from the mother. Pliny's discussion of abnormal growth patterns (§§74–7) reveals that although there is a correlation between growth and maturation, the two are not always linked.

68. ceterum . . . viros: the sentence is in indirect statement depending on "*haud dubium est*". **editis:** "children" in the dative of reference. (AG §376) Literally "for those, after they have been born". **primores . . . dentes:** We call these "baby teeth" or "deciduous teeth". But "*primores*" might also refer to the "front teeth" here (as below at §7.70), and indeed these are the first teeth to appear. **in supera fere parte:** i.e., the upper gums. **Manium Curium . . . Dentatus:** Manius Curius Dentatus, consul in 290 BCE, 284, 275, and 274 and censor in 272. See Cicero, *De Republica* 3.6 and Valerius Maximus 4.3.5. **Gnaeum Papirium Carbonem:** Gnaeus Papirius Carbo, tribune in 92 BCE and a supporter of Cinna. Carbo was consul in 82 with Gaius Marius, son of the more famous general of the same name, and fought Sulla on his return from the East. Pompey caught and executed him in 81. **inauspicati . . . exempli:** genitive of characteristic.

69. Valeria . . . Suessam Pometiam: Attested only by Pliny. Suessa Pometia, perhaps to be identified with the city Satricum, was sacked by the Romans under Tarquinius Priscus in the regal period and the spoils used to build the Capitoline Temple (Livy 1.53), then sacked by Rome again in 495 BCE (Livy 2.25.4) and then, with its name changed to Satricum, was again sacked by the Volsci in 488 BCE, with Coriolanus leading them (Livy 2.39.3). **exitio . . . vaticinante:** The grammar here is difficult. The ablative absolute "*responso haruspicum vaticinante*" governs an indirect statement "*exitio civitati ... futuram [esse]*", in which "*exitio civitati*" is a double dative. "*in quam delata esset*" is a pluperfect subjunctive standing inside secondary sequence indirect speech standing in for a future perfect indicative. The main verb of the sentence is "*deportata est*". **quasdam ... omine:** The indirect statement is the subject of "*est*" and "*Cornelia, Gracchorum mater indicio*" is the predicate. "*indicio*" is a dative of purpose. (AG §382) **Prusiae regis Bithyniorum filius:** This is Pausanius, son of Prusias (II) Cynegus. For his condition, see Livy, *Periochae* 50, and Valerius Maximus, 1.8.ext.12. Beagon (2005) suggests that the child had amelogensis imperfecta, but this is very unlikely, as that condition does not result in fused teeth, but rather weakened, pitted teeth. Much more likely was an extreme case of fused teeth, which, while rare, does occur, particularly in primary teeth. Although the passage is usually read as indicating all of Pausanias's teeth were fused into a single strip, there is nothing here in Pliny that requires that reading. Pliny (or his source) may simply mean that several teeth were fused ("*continuo osse*"), possibly more than one set—a much more plausible occurrence. Valerius Maximus, 1.8.ext.12, however, does state explicitly that there was only a single, long tooth on the upper part of Pausanias's mouth: "*pro superiore ordine dentium unus os aequaliter extentum habuit, nec ad speciem deforme neque ad usum ulla ex parte incommodum*". Except for the extent, this description is consistent with fused teeth.

70. indomiti: take concessively "although ...". **tabe pituitae:** refers not to saliva but to the humour phlegm, which ancient medical authors theorized to be the cause of dental decay. **in aliquis:** "*aliquis*" here is ablative plural. (AG §150c) **primores:** the front teeth. Compare above at §7.68.

71. quin: here, a particle of assertion: "indeed". **Turdulorum:** A tribe in Lusitania. See Pliny, *NH* 3.8; Varro, 2.10.4; Livy, 28.39.8. **gemini:** "a pair". Supernumerary teeth can occur in any place in the dental arch, but they are most common above the incisors and canine teeth. **a canibus cognominati:** These teeth are still called "canines" or "cuspids". **Agrippina Domiti Neronis matre:** Agrippina the younger, mother of the emperor Nero.

72. Zoroastren: Accusative singular. The name is a Latin transcription of the Greek Ζωροάστρης (Zōroastrēs), corresponding to the Iranian Zarathustra. See Pliny, *NH* 11.242 and 30.3–4. Not much is known about Zoroaster; he is traditionally dated to the 7th or 6th centuries BCE, but there is still debate, with 11th and 10th c. BCE also in contention. Zarathustra is thought to have codified to some extent the Persian religion, and he is credited with writing the Gathas, seventeen hymns sacred to Zoroastrianism. The Zoroastrian faith envisions a dualistic universe in which Ahura Mazda, the creator god, whose name combines the transcendental qualities "Being" and "Mind", is in conflict with Angra Mainyu (Ahriman), whose name means "Destructive Spirit" or "Evil Mind". Ahura Mazda is destined to prevail over Angra Mainyu, but only with the active participation of men, whose efforts are necessary to keep back evil and chaos. **praesagio:** the dative explains the indirect statement and result clause "*cerebrum . . . manum*".

73. in trimatu suo: i.e., when three years old. **futurae:** Understand "*mensurae*". **minorem:** Understand "*mensuram*". **consumente ubertatem seminum exustione in cuius vices nunc vergat aevum:** "since desiccation is consuming the fertility of the seeds, desiccation into whose misfortune [literally, "turns"] our age is now approaching". "*exustione*" may refer to the Stoic ekpyrosis, the end of the universe in fire. "*aevum*" is "age" in the sense of "epoch, era". **in Creta:** the large island south of the Peloponnese. **terrae motu:** "earthquake". **cubitorum:** See the note at §7.22. 46 cubits equals 69 Roman feet, which is 67 English feet or about 20.4 meters. **Orionis:** The Cretan hunter and giant, son of Poseidon and Euryale (daughter of Minos). There are various stories of Orion's relationship with Artemis and his death, after which he was made a constellation. See *Iliad* 18.486, *Odyssey* 5.121–4,

11.572–5 **Oti:** another giant, brother to Ephialtes and son of Poseidon. They attempted to storm Heaven by piling the mountains Ossa on Olympus and then Pelion on Ossa, but they were shot down by Jupiter, or Apollo, or tricked into hitting each other with spears. See *Iliad* 5.385–91, *Odyssey* 11.305–20. These bones were likely those of prehistoric beasts, like the Dwarf Elephant that lived in the Aegean.

74. Orestis: The son of Agamemnon and Clytemnestra. Aeschylus's trilogy, the *Oresteia* (*Agamemnon, Choephoroi, Eumenides*) revolves around the murder of Agamemnon, Orestes's vengeance against Clytemnestra, and his final purification at Athens. See Herodotus, 1.68. **VII cubitorum:** Just over 3 meters or 10 English feet. **monumentis:** ablative of place where (or source): "in the records" or "according to the records" (i.e., "from the records"). (AG §403, 429) **minora corpora . . . conqueri:** cf. *Iliad* 5.302–4; 12.378–83, 445–50; but also *Aeneid* 12.896–902; Juvenal, *Satires* 15.62–70. **Naevii Pollionis:** Columella, *De re rustica* 3.8.2: *Nam et M. Tullius Cicero testis est Romanum fuisse civem Naevium Pollionem pede longiorem quam quemquam longissimum.* "Marcus Tullius Cicero is the source that there was a Roman citizen, 'Naevius Pollio' a foot taller than even the tallest other person." **vice:** "In the manner of". "*Vice*" is a prepositional noun in the ablative and taking the genitive, as *causā* and *gratiā* do (OLD s.v. *vicis* 9b). **habitum:** Understand "*habitum esse*", referring back to Naevius Pollio and depending on "*tradunt*": "The annals hand down that he was considered . . .". **divo Claudio principe:** the emperor Claudius. **Gabbaram:** Otherwise unknown, but the sentence in Columella immediately following his mention of Naevius Pollio mentions an exceedingly tall man of the Jewish race, and the same man may be meant. **Arabia:** a larger area than Saudi Arabia, encompassing three distinct regions: Arabia Petraea (modern Jordan, Sinai Peninsula, and Syria); Arabia Deserta (the desert interior of the Arabian Peninsula), and Arabia Felix (the fertile areas corresponding to modern Yemen). **novem pedum et totidem unciarum:** "Nine feet and nine inches". Just under nine and a half English feet or 2.9 meters. This is only slightly taller than the tallest confirmed people in the modern period. Compare Robert Wadlow, who stood 8 feet, 11.1 inches (2.72 meters) at his death by infection in 1940. He was 22 years old and still growing.

75. conditorio Sallustianorum: a tomb in Sallust's gardens (*horti Sallustiani*), which belonged to the historian Gaius Sallustius Crispus, and, on the death of his son of the same name in 20 CE, became part of the imperial properties. **Pusioni et Secundillae:** The name "Pusio" is a dimunitive of "Puer", just as "Secundilla" is of "Secunda". The diminutives are ironic, like "Little John" of Robin Hood's Merry Men. The names are dative, agreeing with an understood "*eis*", dative of possession. (AG §373) **duos pedes et palmum:** The "*palmus*", like the English "hand", was a unit of measure tied to the width of the palm. It measured about a quarter of a Roman foot. Two feet and a palm equates to just over 2 English feet, 2 inches or 0.666 meters. Compare Chandra Bahadur Dangi, born in 1939, who stands at 1 foot, 9.5 inches, or 0.546 meters. **Conopas:** Otherwise unknown. Beagon (2005) suggests that his name might derive from the Greek κώνωψ (*kōnōps*) "gnat". **in deliciis:** "among the pets". Compare §7.34 above. **Iulia:** Julia Minor, also Vipsania Iulia Agrippina, granddaughter of Augustus by his daughter Julia Maior and Agrippa. **Andromeda liberta:** unknown. **Iuliae Augustae:** Livia, wife of Augustus. She was adopted into the Julian family in Augustus's will. See Tacitus, *Annales* 1.8. **Manium Maximum:** "Maximus" is an ironic cognomen. Cf. "*Pusioni et Secundillae*" above. **Marcum Tullium:** otherwise unknown. **binum cubitorum:** Just under three English feet or 0.9 meters. **sesquipedales . . . ignotum est:** Pliny refers to children with a pituitary disorder.

76. Salamine: Likely the city Salamis on Cyprus. **Euthymenis:** Euthymenes. Otherwise unknown. **tria cubita:** Just over 4 English feet, 4 inches, or 1.333 meters. **puberem etiam factum:** i.e., already experiencing puberty. **contractione . . . circumacto:** Beagon (2005) takes this as "seizure", while Rackam translates it as "paralysis". **Corneli Taciti:** Father to the historian. **Belgicae Galliae:** The northernmost portion of Gaul, opposite Britain and separated from Germania on the east by the river Rhine. **rationes procurantis:** "who oversees the [financial] accounts". ἐκτραπέλους: ektrapelous. lit. "turning away [from the normal]" and therefore "deviant", "abnormal", but without the moral sense in the English "perverse".

Chapter 17

77. aliquis: Dative. (AG §150c) **defuncta viventibus:** Here and in the following pairs, the accusative is another subject of *"praestare pondere"* and the dative depends on the compound verb *"praestare"*: "of all the animals the dead bodies exceed in weight the living . . .". (AG §370)

Part 2C: Physical Excellence (§§78–90). Pliny segues from physical growth to the fully-grown human's physical capabilities, offering examples of control over the body's physical and emotional affects through willpower, and the positive limits of strength, stamina, vision, hearing, and endurance. Amazing feats of memory cap off the section: by concluding with the anecdote of Messala Corvinus's mental deterioration at the end of his life, Pliny houses human memory in the body, subject to the body's failings.

Chapter 18

78. Iulium Viatorem: Beagon (2005) would identify him with Tiberius Julius Viator, who lived under the emperor Tiberius and so could have been known to Pliny, but Schilling asserts that there is insufficient evidence for the identification. **Vocontiorum:** a tribe in Gallia Narbonensis, south of the Allobroges. **pupillaribus:** i.e., when he was a legal minor. **aquae subter cutem fusae morbo:** edema ("dropsy"), a condition of extreme fluid retention and swelling, associated with a number of conditions. The same is said of Octavian at §7.148. *"morbo"* is an ablative of cause. (AG §404) **nec non et alii:** the double negative is a type of litotes: the affirmation of a positive by the denial of the negative. So "*nec non et alii*" = "*et multi alii*".

Chapter 19

Sections 79 and 80 are a digression expanding on the claim that "*nec non et alii multa sibi imperavere*". Pliny gives us examples of people who did not laugh, cry, show expression, feel emotions at all, spit, or belch. He then returns abruptly at the end of 80 to his original theme of solid bones.

79. Ferunt: introduces indirect speech that continues through sentences 79–80. **Crassum:** Marcus Licinius Crassus Agelastus, i.e, "the unlaughing / mirthless". **Crassi:** The grandson, Marcus Licinius Crassus Agelastus, was one of the triumvirs with Caesar and Pompey. He died with his son at the Battle of Carrhae in 53 BCE. The standards they lost became a great shame for the Roman people until Augustus negotiated their return. **Agelastum:** The grandfather takes his agnomen from the Greek word ἀγελαστός, meaning "not able to laugh". **Socratem:** (469–399 BCE). The Athenian philosopher Socrates was a stonemason by trade. He was not particularly wealthy, but had enough property to qualify as a hoplite in the Athenian army, in which he distinguished himself at Potidaea, Amphilpolis, and Delium. Socrates was part of the sophistic tradition that grew out of Ionian natural philosophy and reached Athens in the 5th century. He left no written texts, but he was immortalized by his two followers, Plato and Xenophon, and his critic Aristophanes (in his *Clouds*), from whom we learn about Socrates' *elenchus* (his question-and-answer style of inquiry), now known as the "Socratic Method". Socrates was a "gadfly" to the Athenian people, encouraging them to question their fundamental values and received knowledge, a practice that is epistemologically sound but socially disruptive. While he seems to have avoided active politics, he was deeply influential on a number of prominent Athenian statesmen, especially Alcibiades, Charmides, and Critias, all of whom turned against the democracy and worked toward oligarchy. After Athens was defeated by Sparta in 404, the Spartan Lysander set up a regime of thirty oligarchs (called the "Thirty Tyrants") under the leadership of Critias. The Thirty were overthrown and democracy restored in 403. Socrates was put on trial in 399 for impiety and corrupting the youth. He was convicted and executed by hemlock. ἀπαθεῖς: "apatheis." Unfeeling, emotionless, agreeing with *quales*.

80. auctores . . . sapientiae: "originators of philosophy". "*Sapientia*" is the normal Latin for "*philosophia*" (OLD s.v. *sapientia* 3). **maxime:** "most of all". **Diogenes the Cynic:** 412–323 BCE, the founder of the philosophic school Cynicism, which championed "natural" behavior over conventional (i.e., societal) behavior. The school was, as a result, named for their "dog-like" behavior ("cynic", from the Greek κυνικός, "dog-like"). **Pyrrho:** 360–270 BCE, the first of the Skeptic philosophers, who argued that absolute knowledge was impossible. **Heraclitus:** 535–475 BCE, Ionian philosopher who espoused principles of change and *logos*. **Timon:** a conflation of Timon of Athens, a legendary misanthrope who lived during the Peloponnesian War (late 5th c. BCE), and Timon of Phlius (320–230 BCE), a Skeptic philosopher and student of Pyrrho. **Antonia Drusi:** Antonia Minor (36 BCE–37 CE), third daughter of Marc Antony and Octavia (Octavian's sister), married to Nero Claudius Drusus Germanicus (38–9 BCE, also called Drusus I), the brother of Tiberius. Antonia Minor was mother to the emperor Claudius. **Pomponius:** Publius Pomponius Secundus, suffect consul under Caligula in 41 CE, wrote tragedies extant now only in a few fragments. Pliny served under Pomponius, his friend and patron, in the war on the Chatti in Upper Germany in 50/51 CE. **cornei:** hard as horn, see also Pliny, *NH* 31.45 where he uses the same word to describe the bodies of fishermen, hardened by the sea-salt.

Chapter 20

81. The entire section is in indirect statement depending on "*auctor est Varro*". **Tritanum:** The identification of this Tritanus is uncertain.

Samnitium armatura: "*Armatura*" is ablative, depending on "*celebrem*". Gladiators fought in various styles. The Samnite type fought armed as a Samnite warrior with a *gladius*, rectangular *scutum*, greaves, and a helmet. **Magni Pompei:** The triumvir Pompey the Great. See below at §§7.95 ff. **cancellatim:** "In a network". The verb *cancello* means "to make a lattice", that is a structure formed from a series of overlapping crosses or x-shapes. Hence our *cancel*, "to cross out". The adverb *cancellatim*, then, literally means "in a latticed fashion" and refers to the sinews or muscles which criss-cross Tritanus's body. **nervos:** here, "sinew", not "nerve". **ex provocatione:** "In single combat". **Varro:** See note at §7.13. **superatum . . . tralatum:** Supply "*esse*".

82. Vinnius Valens: possibly the addressee (or his son) of Horace, *Epistles* 1.13. **meruit:** here, "to serve in the military". **in praetorio . . . centurio:** "a centurian in the praetorian guard", the emperor's picked bodyguard. Augustus first established the praetorians as a permanent guard in 27 BCE, and under Tiberius they established their camp in Rome. **culleis:** The "*culleus*", like the English "barrel", was both a container (in this case, a wine sack) and a unit of measure. As unit of measure, it holds 20 amphorae, or 137.5 gallons. **retinere:** depends on "*solitus*". **contra:** adverb "opposite", depending on the participle "*nitentibus*", which agrees with "*iumentis*". **iumentis:** dative, depending on "*obnixus*".

83. Rusticelius: or perhaps "Rusticellus", so either "Rusticelius, who was nicknamed 'Hercules'" or "A peasant named 'Hercules'". The name "Rusticelius" is attested in Cicero's *Brutus* 169, and "Rusticel-" in *CIL* 3.15036a. **mulum:** Mules can weigh up to about 460 kg or 1000 lbs. Incredible as it may seem, assuming a cooperative mule, this is within the bounds of what a contemporary strongman can lift. **Fufius Salvius:** Otherwise unknown. Pace Beagon (2005) and Schilling, the name "Fufius" is not particularly rare in literature or inscriptions. **duo centenaria pondera:** A Roman pound weighed 335.9 grams, so 100 Roman *pondera* equal 33 kg 590 g, or about 74 lbs, 1 oz. Salvius would then be lifting 268 kg 720 g or almost 592.5 pounds, well within the amount lifted by contemporary strong men. **prodigiosae ostentationis:** genitive of quality depending on "*Athanatum*". (AG §345) **quingenario ... quingentum:** A 500-weight lead breastplate (167 kg 950 g or 370¼ lbs) and 50-weight shoes (16 kg 795 g each or just over 37 lbs each) for a total of 201 kg 540 g or 444⅓ lbs. **Milonem:** 6th c. BCE, a wrestler from Croton and a victor in both the Olympic and Pythian games, six times each. Milo caps the list of strong men not because he is the most extreme example of strength (that goes to Fufus Salvius above), but because he shows the greatest control. No one can budge a single finger of his while he grips an apple, presumably without crushing it.

84. MCXL stadia: Assuming the Attic measure, the stadium (Greek στάδιον) is 185 meters or just over 202 yards. So, 1140 stadia are 210 k 900 m, or just over 131 miles, which is the correct distance. **Athenis:** The chief city of Attica. Athens was an important center during the Mycenaean period, as early as the 14th c. BCE. The fragmented communities that remained or arose in Attica after the collapse of the Mycenaean civilization synoicized around 900 BCE (a movement ascribed in mythology to Theseus). The lawgiver Draco instituted a severe code in the late 7th c. and Solon in the early 6th likewise attempted political reforms. Both were attempts to prevent the Athenian state from succumbing to tyranny, but they ultimately failed, as the Peisistratids took power at the end of the 6th c. BCE. The 5th c. saw the rise of democracy, along with the development of an Ionian spirit that led the Athenians to aid their fellow Ionians in Asia Minor against the Persians in the 490s—an act that effectively triggered the Persian Wars. The Persian Wars would see Athens become a major naval power and rise to a position of leadership alongside the Spartans. Their prominence inevitably led to the Peloponnesian War, a confrontation with Sparta in the second half of the 5th century. Athens lost the war and spent the first half of the 4th c. trying to regain its empire, until the rise of Philip II of Macedon. **Lacedaemonem:** Sparta, the main city of the southern Peloponnese. The Spartan people appear not to have a direct connection to the earlier Mycenaean society but to have come into the Peloponnese during the Dorian Invasion, perhaps in the 10th c. BCE. By the late 8th c. they had subjugated the native peoples of the Peloponnese, the Messenians, making them into a slave nation and Sparta into the dominant state in the region. (See §7.200.) Sparta was remodeled into a warrior-centric society, perhaps by the mythical law-giver Lycurgus in the 8th c. but definitely by the time of the Great Rhetra in the 7th: the Messenian helots worked the land to produce sustenance, while the Spartan overlords trained for combat. As a result, Sparta would maintain supremacy in southern Greece until its defeat by the Thebans at Leuctra in 371 BCE. **Philippidem:** Philippides, more famously Phidippides. In the Herodotean version of the story (6.105), Phidippides runs from Athens to Sparta to ask for help at the battle of Marathon, and on his way he meets the god Pan, who asked why the Athenians had no care for him though he came to their aid. But according to Lucian (*De Lapsu inter Salutandum* 3), Philippides ran from Marathon to Sparta to announce the Athenian victory over the Persians. The two stories grew conflated, if the latter was not outright invented. **Philonides Alexandri Magni:** *sc.* "cursor". See also Pliny, *NH* 2.181. **Sicyone Elim:** Sicyon is just to the west of Corinth, and Elis is located near Olympia in the northwest Peloponnese. **MCCCV:** 1305 stadia is about 241k 425m or just over 150 miles. $\overline{\text{CLX}}$**:** The horizontal bar over Roman numerals indicates that the number is to be multipled by 1000. **passuum:** A "*passus*" ("pace"): 1000 *passus* made a Roman mile. In standard measures, 5 *pedes* = 1 *passus*, 125 *passus* = 1 stadium, 1000 *passus* = 1 mile. A foot measure about 11.65 inches, and so a Roman mile is 1618½ yards (4855½ feet, compared to the English mile, which is 1760 yards, or 5280 feet). With "*passus*," as with currency, "*milia*" is often understood. 140,000 paces (or 140 Roman miles) is the equivalent of 207 k 200 m or 128¾ miles. **Fonteio et Vipstano:** 59 CE: Gaius Fonteius Capito and Gaius Vipstanus Apronianus. **annos VIII genitum:** "an eight-year-old boy", lit. "a boy with eight years passed since he was born". $\overline{\text{LXXV}}$ **passuum:** 75 Roman miles = 111 k or 69 miles. **Tib. Neronem ... Drusum fratrem:** Claudius Drusus Nero, the younger brother of the emperor Tiberius, died in his camp on the Elbe in 9 BCE after falling from his horse. **ea:** i.e., the stages of the journey. $\overline{CC}$ **passuum:** 200 Roman miles = 296 k or 184 miles.

Chapter 21

85. fidem: The object of "*excedentia*". Here, something like "believability". **scriptum:** Supply "*esse*". The subject is "*Homeri carmen*". **idem fuisse:** i.e., Cicero. Supply "*tradit*". **Strabo:** Not the Augustan-era geographer (64 BCE–ca. 21 CE), but a legendary figure. The agnomen "Strabo" means "squinty" and refers to anyone whose sight is abnormal, as for example, Pompey the Great's father, Pompeius Strabo. cf. Cicero's *Lucullus* (*Academica Prior*) 81 "*o praeclarum prospectum: Puteolos videmus; at familiarem nostrum P. Avianium fortasse in porticu Neptuni ambulantem non videmus. At ille nescio qui, qui in scholis nominari solet, mille et octingenta stadia quod abesset videbat.*" "O crystal-clear vista: I see Puteoli; but I do not, as it may be, see my friend Publius Avianius strolling on Neptune's portico. But that what's-his-name who tends to be mentioned in schools could see what was 1080 stades away." $\overline{CXXXV}$ **passuum:** 135 Roman miles. **Punico bello:** Probably the First Punic War (264–241 BCE). **Lilybaeum:** modern "Marsala" on the northwest tip of Sicily. Originally a Punic settlement, the Romans conqured it in 241 BCE. **Carthaginis portu:** The distance is about 133 miles (215 km). Distances aside, the curvature of the earth makes it impossible to see Carthage from Lilybaeum. **Callicrates:** 5th c. BCE. One of the architects of the Parthenon, among other buildings. He also sculpted miniatures. cf. Pliny, *NH* 36.43 "*Sunt et in parvolis marmoreis famam consecuti Myrmecides, cuius quadrigam cum agitatore operuit alis musca, et Callicrates, cuius formicarum pedes atque alia membra pervidere non est.*" "Myrmecides, whose chariot with its driver a fly covered with its wings, won fame in tiny marbles, as did Callicrates, whose ants' feet and other limbs it's not possible to see." **Myrmecides:** A sculptor famous for his miniatures. His name means "descendant of ants". cf. Cicero's

Lucullus (*Academica Prior*) 120: "*cuius quidem vos maiestatem deducitis usque ad apium formicarumque perfectionem, ut etiam inter deos Myrmecides aliquis minutorum opusculorum fabricator fuisse videatur.*" Also, Varro, *De Lingua Latina* 7.1 "*ut enim facilius obscuram operam Myrmecidum ex ebore oculi videant, extrinsecus admovent nigras setas.*" Also, Pliny, *NH* 36.43 above. **fabricata:** Use twice, with "*quadriga*" and "*nave*".

Chapter 22

86. Sybaris ... Olympiae: A city in Magna Graecia famous for its wealth. The distance is over 300 miles. There is some confusion here. Sybaris was destroyed by the Crotoniats in 510 BCE. A Sybarite, Telys, had driven out the city's oligarchs and established himself as tyrant. The oligarchs took refuge at Crotona, and when that city refused to render them to Telys, he marched on Crotona. The Crotoniats defeated the Sybarites, killed most of them, razed Sybaris to the ground, and diverted a river to wash the rest away. But Cicero, in *de Natura Deorum* 2.6, tells us that when the Crotoniats were defeated in battle at the River Sagra by the Locrians and Rhegians (sometime between 560 and 535 BCE) the sound was heard at Olympia. Sybaris lay approximately in the instep of the foot of Italy and Crotona at the ball of the foot. Olympia is in the northwest Peloponnese. **Cimbricae:** Marius defeated the Cimbri, Germanic invaders, at the Battle of Vercellae on the Po River in 101 BCE. Pliny himself tells us about this premonition (*NH* 2.148): "*Armorum crepitus et tubae sonitus auditos e caelo Cimbricis bellis accepimus, crebrosque et prius et postea.*" "We have heard that the clatter of arms and the sound of trumpets was heard from the sky in the Cymbric wars, and frequently both before and afterwards." **Castores ... Persicam victoriam:** Castor and Pollux appeared at Rome to announce Aemilius Paulus's victory over Perseus of Macedon in 168 BCE at the Battle of Pydna. This victory marked the end of the Third Macedonian War.

Chapter 23

87. clarissimum: Agreeing with an understood *"documentum"*. **Leaenae ... Harmodium et Aristogeitonem:** The legendary tyrannicides of Athens, who killed Hipparchus, the tyrant Hippias's brother and sparked the overthrow of the Peisistratean dynasty in favor of Athenian democracy. Leaena, a hetaira, was also Aristogeiton's mistress. After the death of Hipparchus, Hippias had her tortured in order to reveal what he supposed was a conspiracy, but she cut out her own tongue to keep herself from informing against her lover. (Pausanias 1.23; Pliny, *NH* 34.72) **Anaxarchi:** the happy philosopher (ὁ εὐδαιμονικός / ho eudaimonikos), a companion of Alexander the Great. According to Diogenes Laertius (*Lives* 9.58–60) Anaxarchus was put to death by the tyrant of Cyprus, Nicocreon, who ordered him to be pounded to death in a giant mortar and pestle. When Anaxarchus made light of the punishment, Nicocreon ordered his tongue to be cut out, but Anaxarchus bit it off first and spat it at Nicocreon.

Chapter 24

88. Memoria ... fuerit: indirect question governed by *"cui"*. As often in *qui/quis* clauses, the subject has been positioned outside the clause for emphasis. (AG §573) **necessarium maxime vitae bonum:** in apposition to *"memoria"*. *"Maxime"* with an adjective is an alternate way to indicate a superlative. **Cyrus:** Cyrus the Great of Persia, king from ca. 557–530 BCE. Xenophon, *Cyropaedia* 5.3.46. **L. Scipio:** Lucius Cornelius Scipio Asiagenes served under his brother Publius Cornelius Scipio (Africanus) in Spain, Sicily, and Africa (207-202 BCE), was praetor in Sicily in 193, and consul in 190, during which year he defeated Antiochus III (with his brother Scipio Africanus now serving under him) and earned the cognomen "Asiagenes". Beagon (2005) suggests that the son of this Scipio could also be meant. **populo Romano:** Beagon (2005) translates this as "every Roman citizen", which, while accurate, is impossible. It must mean in effect "all the Roman people of any note" and not every inhabitant, or even every citizen. **Cineas Pyrrhi:** Pyrrhus of Epirus (318–272 BCE), king of the Hellenistic kingdom of Epirus and Macedon, fought against the Romans from 280-275 on behalf of the Tarentines. He won most battles but at a huge loss of life, and it is from him we get the term "Pyrrhic victory". The Romans finally defeated his army at Beneventum. See note at §7.20. Cineas was a native of Thessaly and an orator; he served as Pyrrhus's diplomatic envoy to Rome in 280. **postero die quam:** "the day after", lit. "on the day later than [the one on which]". **Mithridates:** or "Mithradates", the sixth of that name, king of Pontus (120–63 BCE), defeated and triumphed over by Pompey. See Pliny, *NH* 25.6.

89. Charmadas: (168/7–107 BCE) a philosopher of the Academic school and student of Carneades. For Carneades, see §7.112 below. **quae quis:** The referent for "*quae*" is "*volumina*". "*Quis*" stands for "*aliquis*" after *si, ne nisi, num,* and other relative pronouns. (AG §310a) **eius rei:** i.e., "memory". **Simonide melico:** Simonides the lyric poet. Cf. the story in Campbell, *Greek Lyric Poetry*, p. 379: "Indeed it was said of one of his poems on victorious boxers that he had so much to say of the Dioscuri that Scopas, who had commissioned the poem, cut the fee by half: Castor and Polydeuces, he said, would pay the rest. (They did so by saving his life when the palace roof collapsed.)" While Simonides was sitting at dinner in Scopas's house, a young man came to the door asking for the poet. When Simonides came outside, the young man was gone, but the roof of the house collapsed, killing all who were still inside. Simonides was able to identify the bodies by recalling where each guest had been laying. **melico:** the adjective for "lyric poetry", here "lyric poet". **Metrodoro:** Metrodorus of Scepsis (145–70 BCE), an inhabitant of Asia Minor, likely a pupil at the Academy, famed for his memory.

90. casus: genitive. **particulatim:** "in a single sphere". **Messala Corvinus:** Marcus Valerius Messala Corvinus (ca. 64 BCE–8 CE), a general, prefect, and the patron of a literary circle that included Tibullus and Sulpicia.

Jerome's *Chronicle* (Migne, *Patrologia Latina*, vol. 27, column 442) gives a more vivid picture: "*Messala Corvinus orator, ante biennium quam moreretur, ita memoriam et sensum amisit, ut vix pauca verba coniugeret, et ad extremum ulcere sibi circa sacram spinam nato, inedia se confecit, anno aetatis LXXII.*" "Messala Corvinus, the orator, two years before he died lost his memory and sense in such a way that he was scarcely able to put even a few words together, and at the very end, when an ulcer had formed near his lower back, he finished himself off by starvation, in the 72nd year of his life." **ut . . . quaerat:** result clause. (AG §536) **ubi sit loci:** indirect question. (AG §573) "*loci*" is a partitive genitive depending on "*ubi*" as if "*ubi loci*" = "*in quo loco*". Pliny describes the sensation of waking up suddenly while still drowsy and not knowing where one is.

The Moral (Ro)Man (§§91–129). In the following excursus on Man's moral and intellectual virtues, the majority of Pliny's examples are more Roman than Man. Pliny covers martial excellence, literary genius, and artistic genius. We can understand his exempla as common stories likely to be familiar to his audience and so primarily Roman intermingled with occasional Greek exempla, such as the concession of wisdom to Socrates and the seven sages. These play into a subtle ideological statement about the centrality of Rome and the Roman race to mankind, in which the Roman encompasses and subsumes the Greek.

"Overall, Pliny's comments on the Roman achievements epitomize the two basic characteristics of the human race as a whole [. . .]: variety and universality. Rome offers many examples of every kind of excellence and outstrips in her variety and comprehensiveness the whole of the rest of the world. The Roman race is a microcosm of the human race, a fact which justifies its predominance among the examples of book 7." (Beagon, 2005, 51–2)

Part 2D: Excellent Deeds (§§91–106). The mental aspect of memory turns Pliny to the unceasing mental vigor that characterized Julius Caesar: his ability to multitask, to push himself harder than he pushed his soldiers, his victory over every enemy—even those victories deemed by Pliny immoral—and his clemency and magnanimity all make him a true example of Roman greatness. Glory in just warfare, however, must go to Caesar's foe Pompey, to whose conquests and triumphs Pliny gives an extensive digression. And yet, despite all of Pompey's accomplishments, he remains a foil to Caesar's greatness. The best statesmen were Cato the Elder and Scipio Aemilianus, as outstanding orators, generals, and senators. Bravery in battle has numerous famous examples, but these types of excellence do not always go hand in hand, as we can see from Manius Capitolinus, whose arrogance later ruined his reputation, as Catiline's ruined that of his ancestor, Marcus Sergius.

Chapter 25

91. Caesarem dictatorem: (July 100–15 March 44 BCE) The following outline sketches Caesar's career:

Career of Gaius Julius Caesar

73   Military Tribune.
69   Funeral oration for aunt Julia, wife of Marius.
        Death of Cornelia (first wife).
        Quaestor in Spain.
67   Marries Pompeia, granddaughter of Sulla.
66   Curator of the Appian Way.
63   Is elected Pontifex Maximus (for life).
62   Praetor.
        Divorce of Pompeia (second wife) over the Bona Dea scandal.
61   Propraetor in Spain, (earns title "*imperator*" from Senate in 60).
60   Creation of the "First Triumvirate" (with M. Crassus and Gn. Pompey).
59   Consul (I) (with Bibulus).
        Marries Calpurnia Pisonis.
58   Proconsul of Gaul for 5 years.

56   Conference of Luca, renews the triumvirate.

55   Pompey and Crassus consuls, both for the second time, extend
       Caesar's proconsulship for 5 years.

54   Julia (Caesar's daughter and Pompey's wife) dies in childbirth.

53   Crassus dies in Parthia, First Triumvirate ends.

50   Caesar is ordered to disband his army and return to Rome.

49   Crosses the Rubicon, bringing his army into Italy, an act of war.
       Appointed *Dictator* in Rome; Antony is *Magister Equitum*.
       Elected consul for 48, resigns the dictatorship.

48   Consul (II).
       Appointed *Dictator* again for 47.
       Defeats Pompey at Pharsalus.

47   Meets Cleopatra.

46   Consul (III).
       Caesar is appointed *Dictator* for 10 years.

45   Consul (IV).
       Caesar reforms the calendar.

44   February, Caesar is appointed *Dictator Perpetuo*.
       15 March, Caesar is assassinated in the Theater of Pompey.

nec virtutem . . . continentur: an example of a *priamel*. By passing over
Caesar's other outstanding qualities, Pliny brings them to mind and sets
the final quality, Caesar's vigor, beyond all the others. **sublimitatem
omnium capacem quae caelo continentur:** Schilling (170) sees here
an allusion to Caesar's reform of the Calendar, citing Pliny, *NH* 18.211:
"*Caesar dictator annos ad solis cursum redigens singulos*". **solitum:**
supply "*esse*". **pariter:** "at the same time". Lit., "equally".

92. signis conlatis: i.e., in pitched battles. The "*signum*" is the official
battle standard of the legion, what we might call "the eagle". **bis et
quinquagiens:** "twice and fifty times", i.e. "52 times". **Marcum Marcellum:**
In 212 BCE Marcellus conquered Syracuse. **undequadragiens:** "one less
than forty times". **civiles victorias:** victories over his own citizens. The
reference is the Civil Wars. When Caesar's proconsular office expired in

early 49 BCE, the anti-Caesarian factions in Rome refused to allow him to keep proconsular authority until the elections for the next consulship, leaving Caesar open to prosecution from actions performed in his first consulship in 59. As hostilities heated up, the senate passed the *senatus consultum ultimum* and drove out of Rome the tribunes, who fled to Caesar. On January 10th, 49 BCE, Caesar crossed the Rubicon bringing this army into Italy—an act of war against the state, although Caesar framed it as a defense of the tribunes. This began the Civil Wars, which lasted until Caesar defeated the senatorial faction, under Pompey, at Pharsalus. See "Pharsalia" below at §7.94. **undeciens centena et nonaginta duo milia:** *undeciens centena (milia)* = 1,100,000; *nonaginta duo milia* = 92,000; together: 1,192,000. **humani generis iniuriam:** "humani generis" is an objective genitive and might best be translated with "to". (AG §§347–8) **quod:** the connective relative, equivalent to "*et hoc*" or "*et id*". (AG §303.2) **prodendo:** gerund. "by publishing".

93. naves piratis ademisse: the *Lex Gabinia* of 67 BCE gave Pompey command over the entire Mediterranean in order to take care of the pirates that had proliferated there. **usque ad paenitentiam:** Since Brutus and Cassius were among those whom he had previously pardoned. **cui:** referring back to "*magnanimitatis*".

94. luxuriae faventis est: "*faventis*" is a genitive of characteristic, while "*luxuriae*" is a dative depending on "*faventis*". The subject of "*est*" is "*numerare*". **Pharsalia:** In 48 BCE, Caesar defeated Pompey's forces at the city of Pharsalus. Pompey fled to Egypt where he was killed. **captis ... non legisse:** The same anecdote is told by Seneca, *De ira* 2.23.4. **Thapsum Scipionis:** Caesar fought and defeated the forces of Quintus Caecilius Metellus Scipio in 46 BCE at the Battle of Thapsus, modern Ras Dimas in Tunisia. By burning the papers of Pompey and Scipio without first reading them, Caesar in effect declares a clean slate for all of their allies: the Romans who would have been implicated by the correspondence need not worry that Caesar will hold a grudge or later seek retribution.

95. ad viri unius: Supply "*decus*". **pertinent:** The subject is the infinitive phrase "*victoriarum ... Liberi patris*". **Liberi patris:** an Italian deity identified with Dionysus. Among his exploits, he conquered the eastern realms. See also the note at §8.4. By combining Hercules and Dionysus, Pliny calls to mind the breadth of Pompey's victories from Africa and Spain (the Pillars of Hercules / Gibraltar) to the East (Dionysus's conquests).

Chapter 26

Pliny sketches the following career for Pompey (106–48 BCE):

Career of Gnaeus Pompeius Magnus

82	As propraetor, Pompey defeats Gnaeus Papirius Carbo at Lilybaeum in Sicily.
81	Advances into Africa and defeats Gnaeus Domitius Ahenobarbus and King Iarbas.
	12 March 81 BCE, Pompey celebrates a triumph, though only an *eques*.
77	As proconsul, he assists Quintus Caecilius Metellus Pius in defeating Sertorius in Spain, and he is awarded a second triumph.
67	The *Lex Gabinia* gives Pompey dominion over the Mediterranean for three years in order to remove the threat of pirates. He finishes the job in three months.
66–63	The *Lex Manilia* gives Pompey command of the war against Mithradates in the East; upon his return in 62, he celebrates a third triumph.

96. Sullanus: As a member of Sulla's faction, an Optimate. **Pyrenaeo:** the Pyrenees Mountains, which separate Gaul from the Iberian Peninsula. **eques:** Triumphs were reserved for men of senatorial rank who had commanded an army with *imperium*. Pompey had not yet advanced to the senatorial class, a rank which was earned by election to the office of quaestor, the minimum age for which was set by Sulla at 30. Pompey was at this time only 24 and still an "*eques*". **Hispaniae:** "Hispania" refers to the entire Iberian Peninsula. During the Republic, it was divided into two provinces: Hispania Citerior (Hither/Nearer Spain) and Hispania Ulterior (Thither/Further Spain). These were originally the eastern and southern Mediterranean coasts, respectively, but they gradually extended inland across the whole of the peninsula. By Pliny's day, Hispania Citerior had extended to include the whole of northern and eastern Iberia from the city of Urci in the Southeast to Braga in the Northwest and the Pyrenees in the North, and it was renamed Tarraconensis. Hispania Ulterior included the rest of Iberia and had been split into two: Lusitania in the West and Hispania Baetica to the South. **Sertorium:** (126–72 BCE) proconsul in Spain and a Popularis. When Sulla returned from the East in 83 and retook control of Rome, he revolted. He held Spain successfully until one of his subordinates assassinated him in 72. Pompey is *maiore animo* in not including Sertorius among the conquered because triumphing over a Roman citizen would be gauche at best.

97. more sacris certaminibus vincentium: i.e., at the various sacred games, chief among which were the great four: the Isthmian, Nemean, Olympian, and Pythian. **delubro Minervae:** This temple is otherwise unknown. In 50 BCE Pompey founded another Shrine of Minerva (not the same) in the Campus Martius at the site now occupied by the church Santa Maria sopra Minerva, famous for its Bernini elephant and obelisk. **manubiis:** *Manubiae* were monies obtained from the sale of spoils taken in war. **centiens viciens semel $\overline{LXXXIII}$:** As often, "*milia*" is omitted but understood (see note at §7.84): 12,183,000. **Maeotis:** A tribe of Sarmatians who lived on the shores of Lake Maeotis. **Rubrum Mare:** Here referring to the Red Sea as we call it today, but the classical terminology is fuzzy: it may refer more generally to the Indian Ocean and all its inlets, including the modern Red Sea and the Persian Gulf. **merito:** Common in dedications: "according to what is deserved" = "in fulfillment of his debt".

98. a.d.iii kal. Oct.: *ante diem tertium kalendas octobres*, on the third day before the first of October, which in Roman inclusive counting is September 29th, Pompey's birthday. (AG §631) **Marco Pisone Marco Messala coss.:** 61 BCE. **ex Asia ... Tigrane:** the predicate following "*triumphavit*". **Asia:** Asia Minor: what is now Western Turkey. **Ponto:** The area southeast of the Black Sea. **Armenia:** The area east of Pontus, stretching to the Caspian Sea and forming a buffer between the Roman acquisitions in the East and the Parthian empire. **Paphlagonia:** The area immediately south of the Black Sea, bordered on the west by Bithyinia, on the east by Pontus. **Cappadocia:** The area south of Pontus, what is now central Turkey (and still called Cappadocia). **Cilicia:** The southern coast of what is now Turkey. **Syria:** The land along the easternmost coast of the Mediterranean, with Cilicia to its west and Palestine/Judaea to its south. **Scythis:** A barbaric tribe to the north. See note at §7.9. **Iudaeis:** The tribes living on the southeastern coast of the Mediterranean, south of Syria. **Albanis:** A tribe along the Caspian north of Armenia. **Hiberia:** A region north of Armenia and west of the Albani, between the Black Sea and the Caspian Sea. **insula Creta:** The large island south of the Peloponnese. **Basternis:** Scythian tribe to the west of the Black Sea. **Mithridate:** Mithridates VI, king of Pontus. **Tigrane:** Tigranes (II) the Great (140–55 BCE), king of Armenia. He supported Mithridates VI in his war against Rome until Pompey brought an army into Armenia in 66. See note at §7.17.

99. profecto: An adverb. **conveniet:** Impersonal verb, with "*quod*" as the subject: "will be agreed". (AG §207)

Chapter 27

100. varie: Latin uses an adverb where English would use a prepositional phrase (also adverbial): "in many ways". **Cato:** Cato the elder, also called "the censor" (234–149 BCE). **primus:** Not "Cato first ..." which would be "*primum*", but "The first Cato . . ." i.e., Cato the Elder, the first to receive "Cato" ("wise") as a cognomen. (AG §322d) **quae mihi omnia:** "*mihi*" is a dative of reference with "*videntur*". (AG §376) **plurimorum:** Subjective genitive with "*odio*": "the hatred that very many felt toward him". (AG §343 n.1) **Scipione Aemiliano:** (185/4–129 BCE), adopted by the son of Publius Cornelius Scipio Africanus. Scipio Aemilianus, elected consul in 147 defeated Carthage in the Third Punic War in 146, as consul a second time in 134, reduced Numantia in Spain, earning the agnomen Numantinus. In Rome, he was the personal friend of Polybius, and he formed the "Scipionic circle", a group of littérateurs and philosophers, who advocated philhellenism, the adoption of Greek culture, in Rome. (Cicero, *De Amicitia* 69.) **causam dixisse:** "argued in the law court", lit. "spoke a case" (OLD s.v. *dico* 6). **postulatum:** "sued" (OLD s.v. *postulo* 2–3).

Chapter 28

101. Fortitudo: The subject of the indirect question "*in quo maxime exstiterit*". **utique si:** "especially if" or "if at any rate". **fabulositas:** The quality of story-telling. **Q. Ennius:** (239–169 BCE) Called *semigraecus* (Suetonius *De illustribus grammaticis* 1.2) for his fluency in Greek and his southern-Italian origins, Ennius was brought to Rome in 204 by Cato the Elder. Once there, he taught Greek and Latin grammar. In addition to works of many other kinds, Ennius produced tragedy and comedy, and an epic, the *Annales*, on the history of Rome originally in 15 books, to which he later added three, taking the history to the 170s. He was also the first to import into Latin dactylic hexameter as the epic meter; previous epics, such as Livius Andronicus's *Odysia*, were composed in the Saturnians, the native Italian meter. **T. Caecilium Teucrum:** A junior officer. **L. Siccius Dentatus:** A celebrated early-Republican hero known for his strength and endurance and called the "Roman Achilles" (Aulus Gellius, *Attic Nights* 2.11). **Spurio Tarpeio Aulo Aternio coss.:** ca. 454 BCE. **ex provocatione:** for a duel in battle, or "in single combat". **adverso corpore:** i.e., on the front (lit., his body turned toward/facing). Scars on the front of the body, earned by facing the enemy, indicate courage, while those on the back, received during flight, show cowardice.

102. hastis puris: The *hasta pura*, a spear made without iron. This is a war decoration akin to a medal of honor. **phaleris:** The *phalerae* were round, metal ornaments fastened to the helmet or horse so that they would make noise when moved. **civicis:** A crown made of oak-leaves, given for saving a fellow citizen's life in battle. **muralibus:** A mural crown was awarded for being the first to scale the enemy's walls. **obsidionali:** Not "made of obsidian", but the adjective for "*obsidio*", a siege. The siege-crown was the highest military honor that could be awarded an officer. It was woven of the grasses from the battlefield and given for saving the entire army, perhaps by breaking a blockade around the army. See Pliny, *NH* 22.6. **fisco:** A "fiscus" was a money-chest, hence our phrase "public fisc" = "public treasury". **uno ... T. Romilio ... convicto:** An ablative absolute. **Tito Romilio:** consul of 455 BCE, who plotted to kill Dentatus but failed and was prosecuted by him in 454. **convicto:** "denounced and convicted".

103. forent ... ni perdidisset: A mixed contrafactual condition: the apodosis "*forent*" is present contrafactual, while the protasis "*ni perdisset*" is past contrafactual: "Capitolinus's honors would scarcely be less, if he had not wrecked them ...". (AG §517) **Capitolini:** Marcus Manlius, who, ca. 390 BCE (more probably 387), earned the agnomen *Capitolinus* by saving the Capitoline from an attack by Gauls after Juno's sacred geese woke him. In 385/4 BCE he was executed on the grounds of stirring a popular revolt. For the story of Capitolinus and the geese, see Livy, 5.47. **P. Servilium:** Second in command under Marcus Furius Camillus when the latter was named dictator in 387–386 BCE to fight the Gauls. **umerum, femur:** Accusatives of respect, variously called accusative of affected body part, Greek accusative, and accusative of specification. (AG §397b) This use of the accusative occurs primarily with perfect participles. **rem:** Here, the state. **si:** Here, "if only". **regno suo:** Dative of purpose, "for his own kingdom", i.e. "in order to make it his own kingdom". (AG §382)

104. Verum . . . fortunae: Pliny notes that the men he has mentioned so far exhibited their greatness not just because they were outstanding men but because chance gave them the opportunity. Truly great virtue—as in the case of Marcus Sergius who follows—overcomes even the motions of chance. **Marco Sergio:** Dative with the compound verb "*praetulerit*". Marcus Sergius Silus, who was praetor in 197 BCE. (AG §370) **praetulerit:** Perfect subjunctive. **Catilina:** Lucius Sergius Catilina was from a noble but impoverished family. He served under Pompey Strabo and Sulla, served as praetor in 68 BCE, and governor (propraetor) of Africa for two years, but on his return was prosecuted for embezzlement, winning acquittal with the efforts of Publius Clodius Pulcher. After he was defeated for the consulship of 63 by Cicero, he turned to the popular cause for support, and when he lost his bid for the consulship of 62, formed a conspiracy. Cicero drove Catiline from Rome with his Catilinarian speeches, finally proving the conspiracy to the senate when some envoys of the Allobroges provided letters the conspirators had sent seeking aid. Cicero had the conspirators arrested and executed. The other consul, Antonius, marched an army on Catiline, who was defeated and killed in January of 62. **nomini:** dative with the compound verb "*deroget*". (AG §370) **stipendio:** Here, tour of duty (OLD s.v. *stipendium* 2). **satis utilis:** Literally, "sufficiently able", but perhaps "altogether intact". **debilis miles:** Note the word order: though *debilis*, still a *miles*. **cum quolibet hoste:** "with just any enemy". **nullo non die:** Litotes. The double negative is a way of intensifying "*omni die*" in the same way that "there was no day at all on which he was not . . ." intensifies "on every day he was".

105. Cremonam . . . Placentiam: Cremona and Placentia (modern Piacenza) were both founded in 218 BCE on the Po river, as bulwarks against the Gauls to the North. Piacenza was the site for the battle of

Trebbia (named for the river that meets the Po there) in December of the same year. **oratione ... habita:** "*orationem habere*" is the normal idiom for "to give a speech" (OLD s.v. *habeo* 19, 20b). **ut debilis:** for some sacred rites, the priest was required to be whole, that is, not disabled or infirm in any way. See Seneca Maior *Contr.* 4.2: "*sacerdos integer sit*".

106: Trebia Ticinusve aut Trasimennus ... Cannis: Major Roman defeats in the Second Punic War. Ticinus: November 218 BCE; Trebbia: December 218; Lake Trasimene: June 217; Cannae: August 216. (See especially Livy, 21 and Polybius 3.) **fugisse:** "to have made it out alive".

Part 2E: Literary Genius (§§107–17). Military glory yields to literary genius, just as this section follows the previous—a conclusion Pliny is at great pains to force, with Alexander yielding to Homer, Lysander to Sophocles, Dionysius to Plato, Athens to Thucydides (after it had exiled him), Pompey to Posidonius, Scipio Africanus to Ennius, Asinius Pollio to Varro, and Rome to Cicero. The passage is divided into Greek (§§107–12) and Roman (§§113–17) genius, each of which is largely chronological. By ending with an encomium of Cicero, Pliny implicitly invites the reader to compare the Roman with Homer, and it is Cicero who (metaphorically) gets the last word. Cedant arma togae.

Chapter 29

107. dilectum: "choice, selection". Here, "list". **convenit:** "it is agreed". **operis forma:** i.e., epic poetry. **materie:** The content, i.e., the Trojan War.

108. citra: adv. + acc: on this side of, just short of, i.e., "without". **Darii Persarum regis:** Darius III, ruled from 336–330 BCE. Alexander invaded Persia in 334, defeated Darius's forces at Granicus in 334, Issus in 333, and most devastatingly, Gaugamela in 331 in which Alexander's army of 47,000 defeated Darius's army of between 100,000–1,000,000 troops, depending on the source. Darius fled, and in 330 he was killed by his cousin Bessus. Bessus subsequently made himself king, but was soon caught and executed by Alexander in the usual manner for a regicide: his nose and ears first being cut off. **taedebat:** *taedet*: to weary, takes an accusative of person wearied and a genitive of cause of weariness (i.e. of emotion). (AG §354) Supply an *"eum"* and take *"bellatorem et militia sordidum"* predicatively: *"taedebat unguenti [eum], bellatorem et militiā sordidum"*

109. Pindari ... raperet: After Alexander took Thebes, he spared the priests, the Macedonian guest-friends, the house of Pindar, and his descendants. The rest of the citizens he sold into slavery. (Plutarch, *Life of Alexander* 11.7–12; Arrian, *Anabasis Alexandri* 1.9.10). **familiae penatibusque:** *"familiae"* = all those who dwell within the house, not just those related by blood; *"penatibus"* = the house itself, by metonymy. Both are dative with *parci*. Verbs with dative direct objects, when made passive, become impersonal and still take a dative. *Parcit familiae*; he spares the family. But, *iussit familiae parci*, lit., "he orders it to be spared for the family" or better, "he orders that the family be spared". (AG §207, 369) **Aristotelis philosophi patriam suam credidit:** *"suam"* doesn't modify *"patriam"* directly but is in apposition to it: "Aristotle's country *as* his own ...". **Archilochi poetae interfectores:** We know little about Archilochus's death, except that he seems to have died in battle fighting for his native Parians against Naxos, and, according to legend, the Pythia named his slayer, Calondas, and prohibited him from the temple at Delphi. (Lesky, *History of Greek Literature*, 110) **Delphis:** A major pan-Hellenic sanctuary to Apollo and Dionysus, Delphi is located in central Greece on the slopes of Mt. Parnassus. Delphi is perhaps most famous today for its oracle, but it is uncertain precisely how the oracle operated. The oracle seems to have originated in the 9th c. BCE. A suppliant would make an offering or pay a fee, then enter the inner sanctuary and make a second offering. The Pythia (priestess) would enter into a trance and, possessed by the god, give prophesy, which interpreters (*prophetai*) would then shape into the oracle. The exact manner of the Pythia's utterance and the nature of her trance are unknown, as is the exact role of the *prophetai*. **Sophoclem . . . Lysandro:** Sophocles, one of the great Athenian tragedians, wrote more than 120 plays, of which only seven survive. He came in first place in the Greater Dionysia 18 times (the most of any Athenian playwright in the 5th c. BCE), but he also served as Treasurer of the Greeks (443–442) and as one of the ten Athenian generals alongside Pericles (441/0). He was a priest of the hero Halon and welcomed into the city Aesculapius in his guise as a snake. Sophocles died between the Greater Dionsyia of 406 (March) and the Lenaea of 405 (January). After his death, he was given hero cult under the name Dexion. The story that Lysander, a Spartan general in the Peloponnesian War, gave way for Sophocles's funeral comes from the Hellenistic *Life* of Sophocles extant in some of his manuscripts. **in quiete:** while asleep; i.e., dreaming. **ut pateretur:** indirect command relating the god's words to Lysander. (AG §588) **supremum diem:** accusative of extent of time: "during", not "on", which would be ablative.

Chapter 30

110. Platoni: (429–347 BCE). The most famous of Socrates's pupils. While Plato's stepfather was a democrat, his uncles, Critias and Charmides, also pupils of Socrates, were oligarchs and became members of the Thirty Tyrants in 404. (See the note on "*Socratem*" at §7.79 above.) Plato, however, learned from the execution of Socrates to stay clear of political involvement in Athens (although he will visit Sicily three times at the invitation of the tyrant there; see "Dionysius" below). Instead, he wrote dialogues, including as his interlocutors real men in historical settings, and giving us our clearest picture of Socrates in action. The dialogues themselves are literary as well as philosophical: the dialectical format models a process of inquiry, which invites the reader to follow new avenues and new questions with each reading. According to

Diogenes Laertius's *Life of Plato*, §4, Plato's real name was "Aristocles" ("the glory of Ariston, after his father), but his wrestling coach gave him the name "Plato" ("broad") for his build: "ἐγυμνάσατο δὲ παρὰ Ἀρίστωνι τῷ Ἀργείῳ παλαιστῇ · ἀφ' οὗ καὶ Πλάτων διὰ τὴν εὐεξίαν μετωνομάσθη, πρότερον Ἀριστοκλῆς ἀπὸ τοῦ πάππου καλούμενος [ὄνομα]" "He was trained in the gym by Ariston the Argive, from whom he got the name 'Plato' on account of his good condition, since he was previously called 'Aristocles' after his father." **antistiti:** *antistes,* "high-priest". **Platoni antistiti:** dative depending on *"obviam".* **saevitiae superbiaeque:** genitives of description (or familial relation) depending on *"natus".* (AG §345) **Dionysius:** Dionysius II, tyrant of Syracuse (367–357, 346–344 BCE). He received Plato twice, first in 366, hosting the philosopher for a year, and then again in 361, until a break resulted in Plato's departure in 360. Dionysius was driven out in 357, but he regained Syracuse in 346, holding it until 344, when he was again forced out. Dionysius died a private citizen in Corinth. **Isocrates ... Aeschines ... Demosthenis:** Isocrates (436–338 BCE), Aeschines (397–ca. 322 BCE), and Demosthenes (384–322 BCE) were the major Athenian orators and speech-writers of the 4th century. The speech Aeschines read was his *In Ctesiphontem,* while Demosthenes's speech was *De corona.* **Rhodiis:** Rhodes is a large island off the coast of Caria (southwest Turkey). Rhodes was strongly associated with rhetoric in antiquity, with Aeschines establishing a school of rhetoric there during his exile. Both Cicero and Caesar studied at Rhodes in their youth. **mirantibusque tum magis fuisse miraturos dixit, si ipsum orantem audivissent:** past contrafactual condition in indirect speech depending on *"dixit".* "He said to them then as they stood amazed that they would have been more amazed, if they had heard the man himself when he spoke it." (AG §589)

111. Thucydiden: Thucydides, son of Olorus, (ca. 460–ca. 400 BCE) the historian, not the politician Thucydides, son of Milesias. He was exiled after his failure to prevent the Spartan general Brasidas from taking the city Amphipolis. He spent his exile in Sparta and was recalled in 424. His *History of the Peloponnesian War* introduces scientific historiography to Greece. Both "*imperatorem*" and "*rerum conditorem*" are predicative: the Atheniens exiled him "when he was a general" and recalled him "after he became the founder of history". **rerum:** Here, "history". Cf. the phrase *res gestae.* **Menandro:** Menander (344/3–292/1 BCE), an Athenian New Comedy playwright. Dative object of "*contigit*". **Aegypti:** See note at §7.33. The king of Egypt at this time was Ptolemy I Soter (367–283 BCE). **Macedoniae:** The kingdom of Philip and Alexander, north of Greece, whose king was Demetrius Poliorcetes (336–283 BCE). There is no record of correspondence between Menander and either of these kings. **classe et per legatos petito:** Not an ablative absolute: "*petito*" agrees with "*Menandro*", while "*classe*" and "*per legatos*" are parallel and express means.

112. Posidonii (ca. 135–51 BCE). A famous polymath and Stoic philosopher whose work today exists only in fragments. This visit occurred in 62. Posidonius would later write an account of Pompey's wars. **Cato censorius:** Cato the Elder, who took his agnomen from holding the office of censor. See above at §7.100. **in illa nobili ... legatione:** in English word order: *in illa nobili legatione trium procerum sapientiae ab Athenis.* **Carneade:** Carneades (214/3–129/8 BCE) a Skeptic philosopher and head of the Academy at Athens. One of the three philosphers, along with Diogenes the Stoic and Critolaus the Peripatetic, sent as an embassy to Rome in 155. **illo viro argumentante:** Carneades, giving a demonstration of rhetoric, had argued both for and against justice on consecutive days. This sort of pro and con argumentation was a normal feature of Greek rhetorical training, which aimed at examining and re-examining all sides of an issue, but it also carried with it the potential to destabilize society, hence Cato's push to expel the philosophers from Rome, much like the earlier execution of Socrates in 399.

113. Cato Uticensis: Cato the Younger. He took his agnomen from his final stand against Caesar at Utica in North Africa. See above at §7.62. **ex tribunatu militum:** The military tribuneship was a military office ranking between centurian and legate, that is, the third highest ranking officer.

Cato was military tribune in Macedonia in 67 BCE and brought home Athenorodus Cordylion, a Stoic philosopher from Pergamum. **ex Cypria legatione:** Cato was sent to Cyprus in 58 BCE. Whom he brought back is unknown. **eandemque linguam ... memorabile est:** The infinitives *"abegisse"* and *"importasse"* are the subjects of *"memorabile est"*: "Of the two Catos, to have driven out the same language is memorable in the case of the former, to have imported it [is memorable] in the case of the latter".

114. prior Africanus: Publius Cornelius Scipio Africanus, the victor of Zama. **contra testamenti eius verecundiam:** Donatus's *Life of Virgil* gives us the story that in his will the poet requested that the *Aeneid* be burnt, since it was unfinished.

115. Marci Varronis: agreeing with *"unius viventis"*. The focus of the sentence has been pulled out from the beginning, despite being quite far from its referent, as happens often in Pliny's sentences. **Asinio Pollione:** Gaius Asinius Pollio (76 BCE–4 CE). Consul in 40, Pollio was a patron of the arts, saving Vergil's farm from confiscation in 41 BCE and founding the first public library in Rome and organizing the first public recitals of literature. He was friends with Catullus, Horace, and Vergil, wrote a *Historiae* of the period from 60 to 42, and critiqued Cicero, Caesar, Sallust, and Livy. The war that financed his library was against the Parthini in 39 BCE. **minore:** looks ahead to "quam". **principe oratore ... dante:** ablative absolute explaining *"haud minore gloriā"*. **quam:** *"quam"* of comparison depending on *"minore"*. **navalem:** supply *"coronam"*.

116. quo ... piaculo taceam ... quo ... insigni praedicem: deliberative or potential clauses. (AG §§443–7)

117. legem agrariam: A land distribution bill brought in 63 BCE by the tribune Publius Servilius Rullus. **suadente Roscio:** In 67 BCE, the tribune Lucius Roscius Otho passed the *Lex Roscia theatralis* restoring to the equestrians the right to sit in the first fourteen rows of the theater. Cicero later defended Roscius against the abuse of the plebs, who were unhappy with the law. **notatasque se:** feminine because *"tribus"* is the subject. **facundiae . . . parens:** Possibly an interpolation. The clause seems repetitive and out of place. **omnium . . . maiorem:** a second object of *"merite"*. **maiorem:** Supply *"lauream"*. **quam imperii:** = *quam est imperii terminos promovisse.* *"quam"* is a *quam* of comparison with *"plus"*. **promovisse:** "to have advanced".

Part 2F: Excellence in Other Spheres (§§7.118-29). There are more spheres than the martial and literary in which people can be excellent. Here Pliny covers briefly moral and artistic excellences. In the moral sphere—wisdom, divination, chastity, and piety—Romans are on equal footing with Greeks, or predominant. In the arts and sciences—astrology, philology, medicine, geometry, painting, sculpture, and bronze work—Greeks prevail. The section concludes with an apparent digression on the extreme prices paid for some slaves (§§128–9). In effect, these prices are a tribute to the slaves' special genius, an indication that Pliny, at least, recognizes that ability is not entirely dependent on circumstance.

Chapter 31

118. Reliquis . . . bonis: ablative of specification. (AG §418) **ceteros mortales:** *"Mortales"* is the nominative subject of *"praestitere"*, not in agreement with *"ceteros"*. **Cati, Corculi:** i.e., those nicknamed (or "given the cognomen") "Cati" or "Corculi". *Catus* signifies "clear-sighted, witty", while *Corculus* "sagacious" (lit. "little heart").

Chapter 32

119. Chiloni: One of the Seven Sages. Greek tradition held up seven men as specially wise and each with their own maxim or maxims. Which seven, however, varied from author to author. The earliest extant mention, from Plato's *Protagoras* (343a), has Socrates list Thales of

Miletus, Pittachus of Mytilene, Bias of Priene, Solon of Athens, Cleobolus of Lindus, Myson of Chenae, and Chilon of Sparta. See also Ausonius, *Ludus Septem Sapientium* 13.3 for a list of sages and sayings. **nosse se quemque:** γνῶθι σεαυτόν (gnōthi seauton), "know thyself". **nihil nimium cupere:** μηδὲν ἀγάν (mēden agan) "nothing in excess". **comitemque aeris alieni atque litis esse miseriam:** ἐγγύα πάρα δ᾽ἄτη (engua para d᾽ atē) The Greek reads "Make a guarantee and folly is at hand." The Latin differs. **aeris alieni:** debt (OLD s.v. *aes* 4a). **quin et:** "and furthermore" (OLD s.v. *quin* 3b).

Chapter 33

Sibylla: A number of prophetesses bore this name, most famously the Cumaean Sibyl, who sold to Tarquinius Priscus three books of prophecies, which were later kept in the temple of Capitoline Jupiter by priests established for that purpose. See below at §7.120. **Melampode:** Melampus, a mythical Greek prophet. He rescued and raised a litter of snakes, who licked his ears in gratitude, giving him the ability to understand the speech of animals. See Homer, *Od.* 11.281–97, 15.231–6; Herodotus 2.49. **Marcius:** a legendary Roman prophet who pronounced in verse. See Livy, 25.12.3–12.

Chapter 34

120. a condito aevo: = "from the time of the founding"; a variation on "*ab urbe condita*". (AG §497) **Scipio Nasica:** Publius Cornelius Scipio Nasica, consul of 191 BCE, was defeated twice in his campaign for censor, in 189 and 184. Pliny confuses him here with his grandson Publius Cornelius Scipio Nasica Serapio, the Pontifex Maximus who led the charge that killed Tiberius Gracchus in 133 BCE. He died later while in Pergamum on a commission. **in toga candida:** standing for elected office. **magis quam:** supply "*licuit mori*" again.

Chapter 35

Sulpicia Paterculi ... Fulvi Flacci: Sulpicia, the daughter of Servius Sulpicius Paterculus, Sulpicia was selected to improve female morality by dedicating a statue to Venus Verticordia, "in order that the minds of women, young and mature, might more readily be changed from lust (*libidine*) to modesty (*pudicitiam*)" (Valerius Maximus, 8.15.12). Her husband was Quintus Fulvius Flaccus, consul four times: 237, 224, 212, and 209 BCE. The dedication was made on inspection of the Sibylline books. **quae ... dedicaret:** a relative clause of purpose depending on "*ex centum praeceptis*" and referring back to Sulpicia. (AG §531.2) **ex Sibyllinis libris:** Tarquinius Priscus bought three volumes of prophecies from the Cumaean Sibyl and created a priestly college (the *quindecimviri sacris faciundis*) to oversee them. The XVviri could add books of new prophecies, and in 83 BCE, when the Capitolium (and thus the prophecies housed within it) were burnt, they reconstituted the prophecies by making a new collection. "*ex*" here means "according to" or "following". **Claudia:** Claudia Quinta. In 204 BCE, when the baetyl and statue of Cybele were being brought to Rome, they grounded in the Tiber. According to the prophecies, only a chaste woman could move the ship; Claudia Quinta, who had a dubious reputation, took hold of a rope at the front of the vessel and successfully moved it thus restoring her reputation. See Livy 29.14 and Ovid, *Fasti* 4.305–72. Supply "*pudicissima iudicata est*". **inducta:** ablative with "*matre*".

Chapter 36

121. Pietatis: There follow several anecdotes loosely aggregated under "piety". The first is true piety, i.e., filial devotion, and those that follow are variations on the power of affection attributed to close familial ties. **humilis:** "low born" (etymologically, "close to the earth"). **ignobilis:** "unknown" or "not famous", not our "ignoble". **excussa:** Nominative, introducing the purpose clause "*ne quid inferret cibi*". (AG §§529–33)

quid: For "*aliquid*" after "*ne*". (AG §310a) **ambaeque perpetuis alimentis:** Supply "*donatae sunt*". **Gaio Quinctio Manio Acilio coss.:** Either Pliny or his copyists have made an error with Quinctius's praenomen. Titus Quinctius Flamininus and Manius Acilius Balbus were consuls in 150 BCE. **templo Pietatis:** Dedicated in 181 BCE by Manius Acilius Glabrio, but destroyed in 44 BCE by Julius Caesar. The Theater of Marcellus was eventually built on the spot by Augustus and named in honor of his erstwhile heir, who had died ten years before its completion in 13 BCE. **Marcelli:** Marcus Claudius Marcellus (42–23 BCE), the son of Gaius Claudius Marcellus and Octvia, Augustus's sister. He was a rival to Agrippa for Augustus's preferred successor until his premature death in 23. See below at Pliny *NH* §7.143, and Vergil, *Aeneid* 6.860–86.

122. Gracchorum pater: Tiberius Sempronius Gracchus Maior, the consul in 177 and 163 BCE and father of the more famous Gracchi brothers. **responderetur:** Impersonal passive, introducing indirect statement. Literally, "when it was responded that that one would live . . .", but better "when the response was given . . .". (AG §207d) **ipsum victurum:** Supply "*esse*": "that one would live". The masculine gender here is generic, referring to either Tiberius Gracchus Maior or his wife Cornelia. **alterius sexus interempto:** ablative absolute with an understood "*angue*". **consecutum est:** i.e., the natural outcome, the death of Gracchus. **Marcus Lepidus:** Marcus Aemilius Lepidus (II) consul of 78 BCE and father of the triumvir of the same name. He was a member of Sulla's Optimate faction until his proconsulship. See Pliny *NH* 36.49, 109 for his villa, and *NH* 35.13 for the Basilica Aemiliana. **Appueleiae:** Appuleia, a relative of the Marian Lucius Appueleius Saturninus, had been divorced by Lepidus for political reasons. **uxoris caritate:** i.e., of a broken heart. **Publius Rupilius:** In the MSS "Rutilius". Rather, Publius Rupilius Lupus, consul of 132 BCE. **Publius Catienus Philotimus:** 1st c. BCE. A Greek freedman, possibly of Publius Catienus Sabinus. **heres omnibus bonis institutus:** take concessively: "although . . .".

Chapter 37

123. Variarum artium scientiā: As often, Pliny puts the conceptual subject at the beginning of the paragraph, regardless of its case or more natural position within the sentence. The various arts—*astrologia, grammatica, medicina*—are, like *scientia*, in the ablative. **par sit:** the expression "*par est*" means "it is right". Compare the English "It's par for the course". **florem hominum libantibus:** "*Libantibus*" is an ablative absolute or dative with an understood "*nobis*" and taking "*florem hominum*" as its object: "as we gather the flower of mankind". **Berosus:** An Alexandrian astrologer and contemporary of Alexander the Great. He wrote a history of Chaldea titled Βαβυλωνιακά (*Babylōniaka*) in three books and dedicated it to Antiochus I of Syria. **Apollodorus:** Athenian grammarian and philologue (ca. 180–ca. 120 BCE). He wrote several works, including a Χρονικά (*Chronicle*) from the Fall of Troy (traditionally 1184 BCE) to after the death of Alexander the Great; a commentary in twelve books on Homer's *Catalogue of the Ships*; and an account of Greek religion Περὶ θεῶν (*On the Gods*). **Amphictyones:** The word refers to a league of cities formed to support a cult site around which they are all situated. The most famous of these (likely meant here) was the Delphic Amphictyon, which supported the cult of Apollo and Dionysus at Delphi. **Hippocrates:** The most famous of the ancient physicians, he lived in the 5th c. BCE (possibly into the 4th) on Cos. The Hippocratic corpus bears his name, but he cannot confidently be linked with the texts therein. See below at *NH* §7.171. **Illyriis:** a group of Indo-European tribes who lived on the western side of the Balkans, particularly in what is now Albania. **pestilentiam:** Despite the claims of some ancient sources, not the plague at Athens in 430 BCE, which came from the South. **quod ob meritum:** "for which deserving deed". Compare the structure with "*quam ob rem*" and "*quem ad modum*", etc. The connective relative must come first in its clause, even when it belongs to a prepositional phrase. (AG §303.2) **Cleombroto Ceo:** Cleombrotus was the personal physician of Seleucus I Nicator (ca. 354–280 BCE), father of Antiochus I Soter of Syria. **Ptolomaeus:** Probably

Ptolemy I Soter (367–283 BCE), but possibly Ptolemy II Philadelphus (308–246 BCE). The story here is confused because Pliny at *NH* 29.5 makes Ptolemy (falsely) the son of Seleucus I. **Megalensibus sacris:** The normal Roman name for a festival of Cybele, the Magna Mater. "Megalenses" comes from Greek "megalē" (μεγάλη) "great".

124. Critobulo ... Philippi: Philip II (382–336 BCE), the father of Alexander the Great, lost his eye to an arrow in the siege of Methone in 354. **summa:** Supply "*fama*". **Asclepiadi Prusiensi:** Asclepiades of Prusa, a philosopher and physician of the 1st c. BCE, was originally from Bithynia. **condita ... facta:** A series of ablatives absolute. **ne medicus crederetur si ... fuisset ipse:** Many ancient physicians based their philosophies on the regimen of one's life: eating the right kinds of foods at the right times, exercising in the proper amount, remaining chaste at the appropriate times, and so on. Not only was health fostered by a good (and sometimes personalized) regimen, illness could be cured by altering any parts of the regimen that were out of balance. **fuisset:** A pluperfect subjunctive standing for a future perfect indicative in secondary sequence implied indirect speech depending on "*sponsione facta*". The direct statement would be a future more vivid condition: "Let me not be believed a doctor if I ever will have been ill." The sequence of changes is as follows:

	Ne credar	*si fuero*	
	medicus,	*invalidus*	Direct
Facit sponsionem	*ne credatur*	*si fuerit*	Indirect 1st
	medicus,	*invalidus*	
Fecit sponsionem	*ne crederetur*	*si fuisset*	Indirect 2nd
	medicus,	*invalidus*	
Sponsione facta	*ne crederetur*	*si fuisset*	Implied indirect
	medicus,	*invalidus*	

(AG §589.3)

125. Archimedi: dative depending on "*contigit*". (ca. 287–211/10 BCE).

A mathematician and inventor famous for inventing a "screw" to pump water, for his work with levers, and for devising various engines with which the Syracusans resisted siege. See especially Livy 25.31.9-10, Cicero *In Verrem* 4.131, and Plutarch, *Life of Marcellus* 14–19. **Marcus Marcellus:** Marcus Claudius Marcellus, consul of 222 BCE, the Roman general who captured Syracuse in 212. **ne violaretur unus:** indirect command depending on "*interdicto*". (AG §588) **militaris inprudentia:** A soldier, not recognizing Archimedes, killed him. **Chersiphron Gnosius:** (d. ca. 546 BCE) Designed the temple of Diana at Ephesus. See *NH* 36.95–7. **aede Ephesi Dianae:** The great temple of Diana in Ephesus was one of the seven wonders of the ancient world. **Philon:** of Eleusis. An Athenian architect from the second half of the 4th c. BCE, who designed the arsenal for the Athenian fleet at the Piraeus. **Ctesibius:** (fl. 270 BCE) of Alexandria, worked for Ptolemy II Philadelphus. **ratione:** Something like "theory" or "blueprints" here (cf. OLD s.v. *ratio* 4). **Dionchares:** or possibly "Dinocrates". See Valerius Maximus 1.4.ext 1 and Vitruvius 2.pref.1. **Apelles:** The most famous painter in antiquity. See *NH* 35.79–97. **Pyrgoteles:** An engraver from the time of Alexander the Great, see Pliny *NH* 37.8. **Lysippus:** of Sicyon. Maker of bronze statues. See Pliny *NH* 34.61–5 **Apelles . . . Lysippus:** For the sentiment, see Horace, *Epistles* 2.1.237–41 and Cicero *ad Familiares* 5.12.7. **ex aere duceret:** The Latin idiom is "draw out of bronze" where the English idiom is "cast in bronze"; "*ex aere*" is an ablative of material. (AG §403.2)

Chapter 38

126. Aristidis Thebani . . . Attalus: Aristides was a contemporary of Apelles. See Pliny, *NH* 35.98, 100. Pliny *NH* 35.24 and Strabo 8.381 give a story in which Lucius Mummius (who had sacked Corinth in 146 BCE) prevented Attalus from selling the painting and instead dedicated it in the temple of Ceres at Rome. **centum talentis:** Ablative of price. (AG §§416–17) The talent, usually of silver unless otherwise specified, was primarily a unit of weight. There were sixty *minae* in a talent, and 100 *drachmae* in a *mina*. In 5th and 4th c. BCE Athens, one talent could pay the wages of all the sailors on a trireme for a year. Put in another perspective, the indemnity the Romans imposed on Carthage after the First Punic War was 220 talents a year for ten years. **licitus est:** "was sold": the other sense of "*liceo*". **octoginta:** Supply "*talentis*". **Mediam et Aiacem:** Pliny mentions these two paintings againt at *NH* 35.26: "*sed praecipuam auctoritatem publice tabulis fecit Caesar dictator Aiace et Media ante Veneris Genetricis aedem dicatis*." "But the dictator Caesar made the authority [of paintings] outstanding before the public when he dedicated his *Medea* and *Ajax* in front of the temple of Venus Genetrix." See also Cicero, *In Verrem* 4.135 for a reference to the priceless nature of these two paintings. **Timomachi:** of Byzantium. See Pliny, *NH* 35.136. **templo Veneris Genetricis:** Caesar dedicated this temple in September 46 BCE. Venus, as mother of Aeneas and grandmother of Iulus, was the origin (*genetrix*) of the Julian family. The temple stood as centerpiece to the new Forum Julium. **Candaules:** King of Lydia, d. 680 BCE. See Herodotus, 1.8–14, but also Pliny *NH* 35.55, who moves Candaules's death earlier so that it will coincide with the death of Romulus. See below at §7.205 under "Gyges". **Bularchi:** an Ionian painter from the 8th c. BCE. Possessive (or subjective) genitive depending on "*picturam*". **Magnetum:** The people of Magnesia, a city on the river Meander on the coast of Anatolia (modern Turkey). Objective genitive depending on "*exitii*". **exitii:** Objective genitive depending on "*picturam*". (AG §§347–8) **haud mediocris spati:** Genitive of quality. (AG §345) **rependit:** Verbs of "weighing" often indicate payment, as the value of precious metals (gold in this case) was fixed based on weight. So here, "paid its weight in gold". **Rhodum ... Demetrius expugnator ... Protogenis:** Protogenes of Caunos, a city in Caria and subject to Rhodes. See Cicero, *Orator* 5; Pliny, *NH* 35.81–3, 102. His major painting was the Iasylos, a depiction of a hero of Rhodes. It was this painting, according to Pliny, *NH* 35.104, for which Demetrius Πολιορκητής (Poliorcētēs, Sieger of Cities) (337–283 BCE), King of Macedon, stopped his siege of Rhodes in 304. Demetrius left in situ the massive siege engine (the "Helepolis" or "City-taker") he had built to attack Rhodes, and the Rhodians, removing the bronze, fashioned from it their famous Colossus.

127. Praxiteles . . . Gnidiaque Venere: Praxiteles (fl. 375–330 BCE) was an Athenian sculptor most famous for his Aphrodite of Cnidus, the first full nude of the goddess. See Pliny *NH* 35.133, 36.20. **Gnidia Venere . . . insigni:** ablative in apposition to "*marmore*". The phrase "*vesano amore*", also ablative, depends on "*insigni*": ". . . famous for the unhealthy love . . .". The subjective genitive "*cuiusdam iuvenis*" depends on "*amore*". (AG §343 n.1) **Nicomedis:** Schilling identifies this Nicomedes with Nicomedes III Euergetes, King of Bithynia 127–94 BCE. Beagon (2005) identifies him with Nicomedes IV Philopater, King of Bithynia from 95–75/4 BCE. Her argument hinges on the Cnidians' debt having arisen in the First Mithridatic War. **grandi . . . aere alieno:** "*aes alienum*" "someone else's money" is the Latin way of saying "debt". **conati:** genitive, depending on "*Nicomedis*". **Phidiae . . . Iuppiter Olympius:** Phidias (fl. 465–425 BCE) was an Athenian sculptor, considered the greatest of the Greek sculptors and most famous for the Chryselphantine Athena in the Parthenon at Athens and for the Zeus at Olympia. See Pausanias 1.24, Pliny *NH* 36.18, Quintilian 12.10.9. He may also have directed the exterior sculpture of the Parthenon. We can see from "*Mentori*" that "*Phidiae*" is dative. **Mentori:** The most famous of engravers, active in the early 4th c. BCE. See Pliny, *NH* 33.147, 154. **Capitolinus et Diana Ephesia:** Both the temples of Capitoline Jupiter and Diana at Ephesus had works by Mentor, but by Pliny's day they had perished in fires, the former in 83 BCE and the latter in 356 BCE.

Chapter 39

128. quod . . . conpeperim: "*quod*" = "in so far as". **Daphnin:** Lutatius Daphnis, the grammarian, bought and later freed by Quintus Lutatius Catulus, consul of 102 BCE. **Attio Pisaurense:** Unknown, but possibly

Lucius Accius of Pisaurum (170–86 BCE). Accius wrote tragedies, of which we have fragments from around 50, among many other no longer extant works, including a history of Rome, titled *Annales*. **Marco Scauro:** Marcus Aemilius Scaurus, consul of 115 BCE. **IIi $\overline{DCC}$:** Ablative of price. (AG §§416–17) **IIi** is the abbreviation for "sestertii" (literally "two-and-half"). The abbreviation is often rendered in print as "H". In the Roman coinage system, the smallest unit was the bronze *as*. Two *asses* made a *dupondius* (two-weight); four *asses* made a *sestertius*, and four *sestertii* a *denarius* (a silver coin); one hundred *sestertii* made an *aureus* (a gold coin). The bar over a Roman numeral indicates that the number is to be multiplied by 1000. So **IIi $\overline{DCC}$** indicates 700,000 *sestertii*. See the appendix on weights and measures for a more detailed explanation of Roman coinage. **Roscius:** Quintus Roscius Gallus, made a knight by Sulla. See Cicero, *Pro Roscio Comoedo*.

129. Armeniaci belli . . . Tiridaten . . . Nero: After Pompey's conquests in the East, Armenia became a protectorate of Rome and a buffer state between Rome and Parthia, with each empire vying to set up a favorable king. In 54 CE, the Parthian king set up Tiridates, his brother, which act precipitated war with Rome. The matter was solved by a compromise requiring Tiridates to receive the crown from Nero. **dispensator:** "Treasurer," but literally "one who weighs out". Compare the note on "*rependit*" at §7.126 above. **IIi $|\overline{CXXX}|$:** Bars on the top and both sides of a Roman numeral indicate to multiply the number by 100,000. So, "13,000,000 *sestertii*". **tam Hercules quam:** Tmesis. "*Hercules*" is an interjection, while "*tamquam*" = "just as" and introduces the ablative absolute "*mercante Clutorio Prisco*". **Paezontem:** The slave's name (Greek: παίζων) signifies "play", "player", or possibly here "plaything". **Seiani:** Lucius Aelius Sejanus. Prefect of the Praetorian Guard under Tiberius, he moved the barracks into Rome. His power increased until he shared the consulship with Tiberius in 31 CE and was given proconsular imperium. Tiberius, growing suspicious, denounced him to the senate and had him tried and executed. **Clutorio Prisco:** Clutorius wrote a poetic lament at the death of Tiberius's nephew

Germanicus and received a reward from the emperor. When Tiberius's son Drusus fell ill, Clutorius wrote another lament in anticipation of Drusus's death, going so far as to read it in public. Tiberius rewarded the presumption and bad taste with execution in 21 CE. See Tacitus, *Annals* 3.49–51. **lucri:** Genitive of specification with "*iniuriam*". (AG §349d) **nulli vacabat:** "*Vacabat*" here is impersonal, and it takes the dative "*nulli*": "There was leisure for no one". The state of public mourning referred to here may be the death of Germanicus in 20 CE, or the execution of Sejanus in 31. If the latter, then this Clutorius is not to be identified with the poet.

PART THREE: REFLECTIONS ON THE HUMAN CONDITION (§§130–90). Having addressed the physical, moral, and intellectual qualities of Man, Pliny turns to the state or condition in which mankind lives its life. He looks first at what it means to be happy, the state toward which all people aim, which leads him directly into consideration of the human lifespan and all the vicissitudes to which it is subject. The section concludes with contemplation on the nature of life, death, and the existence of an afterlife, which Pliny himself vehemently denies.

Part 3A: On Happiness (§§130–52). In the Greco-Roman tradition, "happiness" is not an emotion or feeling, but a condition and judgment about a person's life in toto. Here, Pliny addresses the nature of happiness, asking first (§§130–2) what happiness is and how it can be measured. There are those who are accounted happy because of their achievements (§133), but all fortune is subject to vicissitudes, which fundamentally undermine the possibility of true happiness (§§134–6). Those who are generally accounted as happy in fact experienced many wretched moments, including especially Augustus (§§137–50). The list of Augustus's misfortunes is a tour de force arranged most effectively to counterbalance the highest achievements with an overwhelming unhappiness. Pliny concludes the section with an oracular and divine explanation of happiness reminiscent of Solon's treatment of the matter in Herodotus.

Chapter 40

130. felicitas cui praecipua fuerit homini: Pliny's usual trick of beginning a sentence with a word that indicates the "topic" regardless of the clause's grammar. English word order would be: *cui homini felicitas fuerit praecipua.* **humani iudicii:** genitive of characteristic. (AG §343c) **non infelix:** Note the effect of the litotes. (Compare the note on "*nec non et alii*" at §7.78). **ut alia non sint:** Literally, "Let things not be different", equivalent to "granted that this be the case".

131. quid quod: "What of the fact that …". Pliny begins a series of rhetorical examples meant to prove the ultimate inability of man to have and to know a "happy" life.

132. calculi candore illo laudato die: "What of the fact that he, on a day praised by that whiteness of the stone, had the beginning of evil?": this assumes that the color the Thracians chose for a "good" day was white, and it points out that while we might consider a day good at the time, we might find out later (if we ever realize the truth at all) that future evils derived from that day. The manuscripts are challenging here, and the text might read "*calculi candore illo laudatus dies*": "What of the fact that that very day, praised by that whiteness of the stone, held the beginning of evil". The sense is close, but first reading suggests that a man will eventually realize that the seemingly good day was the source of his misfortune, while the latter reading merely places the misfortune in the seemingly good without bringing conscious awareness into the mix. **de alio . . . de omnibus:** Supply "*homine . . . hominibus*" or perhaps "*die . . . diebus*". The sense is clear. **nullis:** Supply "*diebus*". Not the so-called "dative of agent" with a passive periphrastic, but the object of "*credendum*". Verbs that take dative direct objects, when made passive still take the dative. Compare the note on "*parci*" at §7.109. **quid quod bona malis . . . pondus:** An argument in favor of a qualitative approach to happiness rather than a quantitative one. One might compare Bentham's application of the "hedon" to measure degrees of happiness.

Chapter 41

133. una feminarum in omni aevo: an exaggeration. **in omni aevo:** "in all time", not "in every age". **Lampido Lacedaemonia:** "Lampido, the daughter of Leotychides, the wife of Archidamus, the mother of Agis, who were all kings" Plato, *Alcibiades* 1.123e–4a. Beagon (2005): "She was not unique, however. In the 4th cent. BC, Olympias was daughter of Neoptolemus of Molossia, wife of Philip II of Macedon, and mother of Alexander the Great. Others included, in the 3rd cent. BC, Berenice II and several queens of the Ptolomaic dynasty." (331). **Berenice ... Olympionicarum:** (5th c. BCE) Pausanias, Philostratus, and Aelian give her name as "Pherenike", which, if not a pun, is exceedingly fortuitous ("Pherenike" = bringer of victory). She was the daughter of Diagoras of Rhodes, a victor in boxing, and sister to three victors: Damagetos in the pankration, Akousilaos in boxing, and Dorieus in the pankration. Her son and nephew Peisirrhodos and Eucles, were victors in boxing, the former in the boys' competition. Pliny's treatment of women in this section is revealing: the greatest happiness for a woman is to have excellent male relatives. **Curionum:** Gaius Scribonius Curio, praetor of 121 BCE; Gaius Scribonius Curio, consul of 76 BCE; Gaius Scribonius Curio, tribune of 50 BCE. **Fabiorum ... Marcus Fabius Ambustus ... Fabius Rullianus ... Quintus Fabius Gurges:** Marcus Fabius Ambustus was consul in 360, 356, and 354 BCE. Quintus Fabius Maximus Rullianus was consul in 322, 310, 308, 297, 295, and dictator in 315 BCE. Quintus Fabius Maximus Gurges was consul in 292, 276, and 265 BCE.

Chapter 42

134. etenim quae facit ... gaudiis: a statement of the Wheel of Fortune, an idea that man's fortune was fit to an ever-turning wheel, destined one day to descend if now ascending, and vice versa. The image is ancient, deriving originally from Babylonian astrology. Compare Cicero, *In Pisonem* 22.8; Tacitus *De oratoribus* 23.1.1. **quae facit magna gaudia**

nisi ex malis: "*quae*" is the relative adjective agreeing with "*magna gaudia*", not referring back to "*fortuna*", which is the subject of "*facit*"; "*ex*" here has the sense "when following on". Literally, "coming out of".
quae mala . . . gaudiis: Parallel to the previous relative clause. Supply "*facit natura*".

Chapter 43

servavit: the subject is "*Fortuna*". **Marcum Fidustium:** Cassius Dio 47.11.4 gives the name as Lucius Philuscius. Sulla's proscriptions were in 81 BCE and Antony's in 43 BCE, which (pace Beagon, 2005, and Schilling) does not equal 36 years. Pliny is not counting from the initial date of Sulla's proscription, but from Sulla's death in 78 BCE when the first proscription lapsed. **constat:** impersonal verb, "it is agreed". (AG §207d) **proscriptum:** Supply "*esse*".

135. Publium Ventidium . . . Parthis . . . Asculano: Publius Ventidius Bassus. He was either a child or infant when Gnaeus Pompeius Strabo captured Asculum in 89 BCE as part of the Social Wars. In his early career, he was a foot soldier, rising to praetor and consul in 43 and winning victories over the Parthians in 39 and 38. **solum:** Note the position in the clause: the effect is one of emphasis: "him and him alone". **voluit . . . duxit:** The subject is still "*Fortuna*". **Masurius:** Masurius Sabinus. See note at §7.40. **Cicero:** Supply "*auctor est*". **plurimi:** Supply "*auctores sunt*".

136. Balbus Cornelius Maior: Originally from Spain, he was given citizenship by Pompey in 72 BCE and defended by Cicero when this was challenged in 56. In 40, he became consul, the first to be born abroad. **de iure virgarum:** A Roman citizen could not be beaten to death. Protection from this means of punishment was at stake in Balbus's trial. **iudicum in consilium:** i.e., to court. Literally, "to the consultation of judges". **illo honore:** ie., being consul. **maiores:** here, "ancestors", as often when used substantively. **Lucius Fulvius ... Tusculanorum:** Consul of 322 BCE. The story is otherwise unattested.

137. Felicis ... Lucius Sulla: Sulla took the cognomen "*Felix*" after defeating the Marians at the Colline gate in 82 BCE. The agnomen, which appealed to Sulla's superstitious belief in his own good luck, perhaps arose from his personal devotion to Aphrodite. In Greek, in fact, the epithet is translated as *Epaphroditus* "Beloved of Aphrodite". **ad hoc aevi:** "to this point in time" (lit., "to this point of time"). In English, we express the partitive of time with the preposition "in", but compare our expression "o'clock" (= of the clock). **quorum miseremur:** "*misereor*" and other verbs of strong emotion take a genitive object. See §7.43, 108 above. (AG §354) **nemo non oderit:** litotes. Cf. §7.78, 130.

138. erodente ... gignente: See the note on Pherecydes at §7.172. Beagon (2005) describes the case for taking lice to be the culprit. **ut dissimulaverit et ... credamus:** concessive subjunctive: "although ..." **supremo somnio:** ablative of cause. (AG §404) **cui inmortuus ... est:** "*cui*" is dative with the compound verb "*immortuus est*". (AG §370) **victam:** Supply "*esse*". **felicitati suae:** dative object of "*defuisse*". **quod Capitolium non dedicavisset:** the antecedent of this clause is "*hoc*".

139. Quintus Metellus: Quintus Caecilius Metellus, consul of 206 BCE and dictator of 205. **Luci Metelli:** Lucius Caecilius Metellus, consul in 251 BCE, 247, pontifex maximus in 243, dictator in 224, Master of the Horse to Atilius's dictator in 249. **primus:** as often, "*primus*" can best be translated as "who was the first to". **scriptum:** here, a neuter noun: "a piece of writing". **decem ... conditam:** All an indirect statement depending on "*scriptum*": "he left behind an account that ...". **aetatem exigerent:** "*ago*" and its compounds with words of time mean "spend".

140. uti: Possibly "enjoy" (OLD s.v. *utor* 11). **haberi:** As often, "*habeo*" in the passive means "to be considered" (OLD s.v. *habeo* 24–5).

141. is Metellus: Lucius Caecilius Metellus. **Palladium . . . Vestae:** The Palladium was a small statue of Pallas Athena that fell from the sky and was brought to Dardanus of Troy. It became a symbol of Troy's divine protection. There are two divergent myths: in the *Ilias parva*, Odysseus and Diomedes steal the Palladium. In this tradition, Diomedes keeps it, and eventually, plagued by misfortunes, gives it to Aeneas, who brings it with him to Italy. In the *Iliupersis*, the Palladium is still in Troy at the time of its sacking. In this tradition also, Diomedes or Aeneas brings it to Italy. See, especially, Servius, *Commentary on the Aeneid*, 2.166; 3.407; 5.81, but also Servius *Comm. Aen.* 2.162, 172, 175, 227, 241; 3.545, 550, 704; 7.188. The fire occurred in 241 BCE. **quo fit:** "*quo*" is an ablative of cause. (AG §404) **fit ut:** introducing subjunctive noun clauses of result. **ab condito aevo:** See the note on "*a condito aevo*" at §7.120. The variation between "*a*" and "*ab*", if not an artifact of the manuscript tradition, is a stylistic variation. **ut . . . veheretur:** The subjunctive noun clause is the normal construction for a senatorial decree, which would have begun "*senatui placuit ut . . .*".

Chapter 44

142. Quinti Metelli . . . filius: Quintus Caecilius Metellus Macedonicus, who defeated Andriscus, the pseudo-Philip in 146 BCE. See the note at §7.59 above. **a quattuor filiis:** Gaius Metellus Caprarius, consul of 113 BCE; Quintus Metellus Baliaricus, consul of 123, censor of 120; Lucius Metellus Diadematus, consul of 117; and Marcus Metellus, consul of 115. **singula:** "by themselves" or "individually".

143. Gaio Atinio Labeone . . . Macerioni: Tribune in 131 BCE. The name "*Macerio*" may derive from "*macero*" (1), "to torment, tenderize". **Tarpeium:** Named for the eponymous Tarpeia, the Tarpeium was a cliff on the Capitoline Hill from which traitors were hurled to their deaths. Livy (1.11) gives three variations on how the cliff took its name. All three stories have in common the young Tarpeia inviting the besieging

Sabines into Rome in exchange for a bribe. When the soldiers enter, they reward her with death. **in ipso tamen flore . . . poenam exactam esse:** The main clause is "*alieno beneficio postea vixit*". The sentence structure, a *tour de force* of subordinate participial clauses, is mimetic of the sudden terror and swiftness with which Metellus found himself: each succeeding clause introducing a new event or parenthetical comment, culminating in Metellus's survival. The sentence continues after the main verb with a brief coda that reflects the remaining years of Metellus's life. **sacroque sanctum:** The tribunes had the right of *sacrosanctitas*: the plebeians as a whole took an oath to kill without penalty anyone who laid hands on a tribune's person. As a result, the crowd that had gathered was unable to step in and help Metellus: only another tribune could interfere. **qui intercederet:** relative clause of purpose. (AG §531.2)

144. Africani sequentis: Publius Cornelius Scipio Aemilianus Africanus. Consul in 147 BCE, he destroyed Corinth in 146 and approved Tiberius Gracchus's death in 133. **duxerim:** Potential subjunctive due to the uncertainty in the following *siquidem* clause. (AG §§ 445–7) **Macedonico:** Quintus Caecilius Metellus Macedonicus. **siquidem:** "if in fact". **Baliaricis . . . Diadematis:** The plural is generic, agreeing with an understood "*filiis*". **Baliaricis:** Quintus Caecilius Metellus Baliaricus, who gained his cognomen from a victory over the Balearic islands in 121 BCE. **Diadematis:** Lucius Caecilius Metellus Diadematus. Plutarch, *Life of Coriolanus* 11.3 says "ἐπὶ πλέον δὲ τῷ γένει τούτῳ καὶ Ῥωμαῖοι κέχρηνται, Διαδήματόν τινα τῶν Μετέλλων καλέσαντες, ὅτι πολὺν χρόνον ἕλκος ἔχων περιενόστει διαδεδεμένος τὸ μέτωπον." "The Romans use this type [i.e., mocking surnames] even more: they called one of the Metelli 'Diadematus' because he had a wound for a long time and went around diademed ['bound'] about his forehead."

145. ut . . . aestimetur: a concessive subjunctive: "although . . .". **quis . . . dixerit:** potential subjunctive. (AG §§ 445–7) **periclitatum:** governing "*perire*". **nec Africani saltem:** Pliny counts it a mark of ignominy that, when Metellus had enemies as noble as Scipio Africanus the Younger, he was nearly killed by someone as low as the tribune Atinius Labeo. **tanti fuit:** "*tanti*" is a genitive of value. (AG §417) **haec morandi ratio:** i.e., of not killing Metellus immediately but instead dragging him through the Capitol first.

146. nescio: Introduces an indirect question (*accedat*) (AG §573), which then takes two alternatives: (1) *morum gloriae an* (or) (2) *indignationis dolori*. A fuller expression in English word order would be: *nescio [utrum] accedat gloriae morum an dolori indignationis*. **inultam:** after Atinius's tenure as Tribune elapsed, he would no longer have possessed *sacrosanctitas*. The subject of "*accedat*" is the entire indirect statement "*inter tot . . . inultam*".

Chapter 45

Note that the following list of Augustus's misfortunes, from "*In divo quoque Augusto*" to "*suprema eius cura*" in 7.150 is all a single sentence. The effect is a mimetic reflection of the exhaustion Augustus himself must have felt at the series of personal disasters, and so the syntax should, if possible, be reproduced in English.

147. universa mortalitas: A poetic expression meaning simply "*omnes mortales*". **in hac censura:** "in this assessment", i.e., of the fortunate. **si diligenter . . . volumina:** future less vivid condition. **repulsa:** The first in a series of nominatives, all in apposition to "*volumina*". **in magisterio equitum:** The "*magisterium*" is the office of the *magister equitum*, second in command to the dicator. **Lepidus:** Marcus Aemilius Lepidus. Lepidus was Caesar's magister equitum before he was a triumvir with Antony and Octavian. He served as praetor in 49 BCE, supporting Caesar and making consul in 46 and magister equitum from 46–44. After Caesar's death he sided with Antony and so won election to Pontifex Maximus, a position that he would keep until his death. With

Antony and Octavian, he formed the Second Triumvirate, taking as his share both Spains and Gallia Narbonensis (Gallia Narbonensis and Hispania Citerior having already been assigned him by Caesar before his death). In 42 he was again consul, adding Italy to his charge while Octavian and Antony fought at Philippi. Upon their return, he gradually fell from power, being ignored when they renewed in the triumvirate in 37 and defeated by Octavian in Sicily. He was banished to Circeii until his death in 13 or 12 BCE.

148. Philippensi proelio: The battle of Philippi in 42 BCE at which Octavian's and Antony's forces battled those of Cassius and Brutus, respectively. **aegroti:** genitive agreeing with an understood "*eius*" (=*Octaviani*) and depending on "*fuga*". **Agrippa ac Maecenas:** Agrippa and Maecenas were Octavian's close friends and allies, Agrippa leading Octavian's armies, and Maecenas his propaganda and literary scene. For Agrippa, see the note at §7.45. Gaius Maecenas came from an old Etruscan family, the Clinii, was extraordinarily wealthy, and known for his love of luxury. (See also Pliny, *NH* 8.170.) He was the literary patron of Vergil and Horace, amongst several others. **turgidi:** A subjective genitive depending on "*latebra*" and introducing the ablative phrase "*aqua subter cutem fusa*". (AG §343 n.1) See note at §7.78. **naufragia Sicula:** Octavian suffered several shipwrecks in his war against Sextus Pompey in Sicily from 38–36 BCE, any (or multiple) of which could be meant here. **Proculeio:** A friend of Octavian's. Cf. Horace, *Odes* 2.2.5. **urgente hostium manu:** Ablative absolute. "*manu*" here is "band," not "hand". **Perusinae contentionis:** 41–40 BCE, the war fought by Octavian against Lucius Antonius (brother to Marc Antony) and Fulvia (Antony's wife), who raised a rebellion on Antony's behalf at Perusia while he was in Egypt. **sollicitudo Martis Actiaci:** 31 BCE, the naval battle at which Octavian's forces, commanded by Agrippa, finally defeated those of Antony and Cleopatra. Suetonius, *Life of Augustus* 17, tells us that Actium was followed by mutinies, storms, shipwrecks, and delays before Octavian was able to reach Egypt. **Pannonicis bellis:** The siege of Metelum in 35 BCE. **ruina e turri:** Either the fall of a tower, or the fall from a tower. Schilling takes the first reading: "Octavian was wounded in the leg and in both arms by the fall of a wooden walkway which was intended to give the Romans access to the town's battlements" (209). Rackham takes the second: "his fall from a tower in the Pannonian Wars" (605). Beagon (2005) follows Rackham, p. 95 verbatim. Appian, *Bellum Illyricum* 4.20 has Octavian injured when the bridge he is crossing between siege towers collapses. Cassius Dio 49.35 gives a similar, but less detailed story.

149. suspecta Marcelli vota: See the note at §7.121. An ambiguous phrase. Augustus was gravely ill in 23 BCE, and this may refer to a suspicion that Marcellus's prayers on his behalf hid a secret hope for a quick succession. See Schilling, p. 209. **Agrippae:** Agrippa's delegation to the East in 23 BCE was read by later historians through the lense of Tiberius's self-imposed exile (mentioned below). That Agrippa was still on good terms with Augustus we can see when Augustus, fearing his own death, has his signet ring sent to Agrippa, implicity naming him his heir. **incusatae liberorum mortes:** Gaius and Lucius Caesar, the sons of Julia and Agrippa, adopted by Augustus, they died in 4 CE and 2 CE, respectively, with rumors that Livia, Tiberius's mother, had poisoned them to ensure the succession of her son. **contumeliosus privigni Neronis secessus:** The future emperor Tiberius. Tiberius removed himself to Rhodes in 6 BCE, likely due to Augustus's interest in Gaius and Lucius Caesar, and he stayed there until Gaius's death in 2 CE. **rebellio Illyrici:** 6–9 CE. **pestilentia urbis, fames Italiae:** There was a plague in 22 BCE, and the war in Illyricus caused a famine from 5–9 CE.

150. Variana clades: Publius Quinctilius Varus and his legions were ambushed and slaughtered by Arminius (Hermann the German) and his German forces at the Battle of Teutoberg Forest in 9 CE. Augustus lost three legions, the 17th, 18th, and 19th, which were not afterwards reconstituted. See Suetonius, *Life of Augustus* 23.49 for Augustus's tortured utterance, "*Quinctili Vare, legiones redde!*". **maiestatis:** A technical term for Augustus's authority: he held "*imperium maius*", that is the same power as a consul or proconsul, but superceding theirs when both were present (OLD s.v. *maiestas* 1c, 2–3). **abdicatio Postumi Agrippae:** Postumus Agrippa was adopted by Augustus as a possible successor, but disowned in 6 CE and exiled to Planasia in 7. The reasons for the exile are unknown, although Livia's involvement on behalf of Tiberius is suspected. **suspicio in Fabium:** Fabius Maximus Paulus. See Tacitus, *Annales* 1.5. Augustus reportedly made a secret visit to Agrippa Postumus shortly before his (Augustus's) death, accompanied only by Fabius. Fabius mentioned the visit to his wife Marcia, and she to Livia. Augustus was displeased, and Fabius shortly killed himself. **uxoris et Tiberii cogitationes:** There were rumors that Livia engineered Augustus's death, spurred on by his visit to Agrippa and her desire to see her son Tiberius succeed to the principate. **caelumque nescio adeptus magis an meritus:** In English word order: "*nescio [utrum] adeptus [sit] caelum an meritus [sit] [id] magis*". "*Nescio*" introduces an indirect question with two alternatives: "*adeptus sit caelum*" and "*meritus sit caelum*". (AG §573) The first alternative refers to gaining through one's own means, while the second is gaining through desert. **filio:** in apposition to "*herede hostis sui*". Tiberius was the son of Livia and Tiberius Nero, who had supported Antony. The grandfather, Drusus Nero, had served under Pompey. Likewise, the emperors Caligula, Claudius, and Nero were all descendants of Antony by Octavia (Augustus's sister).

Chapter 46

151. Delphica oracula: See note at §7.109. **Pedium … Gyge … Aglaum Psophidium:** Compare Solon's discussion of happiness with Croesus of Lydia in Herodotus 1.29–33. There, Solon tells the story first of Tellus, who died fighting for his city earning a public burial and with children and grandchildren still alive. Then he tells the story of Cleobis and Biton, the two sons of the Cydippe, priestess of Hera. They pull her in an oxcart to the festival of Argive Hera, earning much acclaim for their piety. Their mother prays to Hera that they might have the best thing a god can give a mortal. That night, they both die in their sleep. The lesson of both tales is that the accrual of possessions does not in itself yield happiness, and true happiness cannot be measured until after one's death, since the living always have the threat of misfortune. For the Greeks, happiness is to be judged from the expriences of a life, whereas in the modern West, it tends to be viewed as an attitude or feeling. **occubuisset:** Subjunctive in a subordinate clause in indirect speech. (AG §583) **Aglaum Psophidium:** *cum enim Gyges regno Lydiae armis et diuitiis abundantissimo inflatus animo Apollinem Pythium sciscitatum uenisset an aliquis mortalium se esset felicior, deus ex abdito sacrarii specu uoce missa Aglaum Psophidium ei praetulit. is erat Arcadum pauperrimus, sed aetate iam senior terminos agelli sui numquam excesserat, paruuli ruris fructibus [uoluptatibus] contentus. uerum profecto beatae uitae finem Apollo non adumbratum oraculi sagacitate conplexus est.* "When Gyges, swollen in pride since the kingdom of Lydia was overflowing with arms and riches, had gone to Pythian Apollo to find out whether there was any mortal happier than he, the god, by emiting his voice from the inner room of his shrine, reported to him that Aglaus of Psophis was. He was the poorest man among the Arcadians, but, although he was already fairly old, he had never left the bounds of his little farm, content with the fruits of a tiny plot of land. But in truth, Apollo concluded with the wisdom of the oracle, that the end of his blessed life was unclouded." Valerius Maximus, 7.1.2. **Arcadiae:** A mountainous and isolated region in the central Peloponnese. Arcadia was so remote that it, along with the island Cyprus, preserved a distinct degree of the old Mycenaean form of Greek, coming to be called the "Arcado-Cypriot" group. In literature, Arcadia became the icon for the pristine pastoral life, idealized, giving rise to the Renaissance phrase *"Et in Arcadio Ego"* (most famously Nicolas Poussin and Guercino). The "ego" is usually taken to refer to death, and the paintings to remind the viewer that death exists even in the most ideal of places. **victibus:** From the fourth declension noun *"victus"*, food, the stuff by which one lives, which gives English its words "victuals" and "vittles". **minima ... expertus:** The implicit question—how much enjoyment in contrast could Aglaus have experienced—could not have escaped Pliny.

Chapter 47

152. consecratus est: i.e., made into a hero and received cult. **Euthymus ... Locri:** Euthymus of (Epizephyrean) Locri won in boxing at the Olympic games in 484 BCE, 476, and 472, but he was beaten in 480. He was from Italian Locri, called "Epizephyrean Locri" by the Greeks because of its position to the West. His cult is only attested here, but he likely earned hero status by removing the hero of Temesa, a ghost that required tribute from the city. (For the story of the ghost, see Pausanias 6.6.4–11). **Callimachum:** Greek poet and scholar under Ptolemy II Philadelphus (285-246 BCE) and Ptolemy III Euergetes. Callimachus wrote over 800 books, but only a small portion of his works still survive: six hymns, sixty epigrams, a selection of his *Paradoxa*, and fragments. His most famous quotation is μέγα βιβλίον μέγα κακόν (mega biblion meka kakon), "a big book is a big evil". This is usually taken to mean that short works are to be preferred over long ones, but a more accurate reading would be that tight books are preferred to bloated ones. Shorter, refined poems with careful, conscious construction moving between genres and picking the best from each like flowers or drops of spring water—that is the Callimachean aesthetic. The Roman poets beginning with Catullus and his circle (the so-called "neoterics") adopt the Callimachean aesthetic. **Callimachum ut nihil aliud miratum:** Supply "*esse*". The clause "*Callimachum miratum esse*" depends on "*video*" and takes "*ut nihil aliud*" as its second object: "as at nothing else"; its first object is "*imaginem ... fulmine*". **de eo:** "*eo*" likely refers not to Euthymus himself but to the act of sacrificing to him. **hoc placuisse dis:** Literally "this pleased the gods", but better "the gods decided this". The placement of "*dis*" indicates that the emphasis is on the gods, so we might go so far as to render the phrase "... than that it was the *gods* who decided this".

Part 3B: On Human Longevity (§§153–65). The human lifespan is an uncertain affair. Many authorities give fantastically long lifespans for individual men and women (§§153–5), but in factual cases, people rarely live more than one hundred years (§§156–60). There are, Pliny tells us, developed astrological methods for determining in advance an individual's likely lifespan (§§160–1), but even the authorities versed in these disagree with each other, and a quick look at the census archives for Italy disproves their calculations (§§162–4). Besides that, we see from both history and daily life that people born at precisely the same moment have radically different destinies, proof of the falsehood of astrology and ultimate unknowability of the human lifespan (§165).

Chapter 48

153. Hesiodus: The author of the *Theogony*, a genealogy of the gods and the universe; the *Works and Days*, an example of wisdom literature; the *Shield of Heracles*, a short epic narrative on Heracles' combat with Cycnus; and the *Catalogue of Women* (in fragments), a genealogy of heroic women. Hesiod is traditionally thought to have been a contemporary of Homer, or slightly after (fl. ca. 650 BCE). He was born in Cyme in Aeolia but moved as child to Ascra in Boeotia, where he kept sheep on Mt. Helicon; he died in Epizephyrean Locri and was buried in Orchomenus. The anecdote about the crow is not in Hesiod's extant works. **aevo:** Here, probably "lifespan" (OLD s.v. *aevum* 5). **quadruplum eius cervis:** "*eius*" refers back to the *cornix*'s lifespan. The crow, and its close relative the raven, have lifespans around 20 years in the wild. The oldest known crow in captivity lived to the age of 59, while ravens at the Tower of London may live in excess of 40 years. **id triplicatum corvis:** "*id*" refers back to the *cervus*'s lifespan. It is worth noting the similarity of the group's names: *cornix, cervus, corvus.* **phoenice:** Herodotus 2.73 gives the phoenix a 500-year lifespan.

154. Anacreon poeta: See note at §7.44. **Arganthonio Tartesiorum regi:** Tartessus (Biblical Tarshish), a Phoenician colony in southern Spain before 1150 BCE, had Arganthonius for its king for 80 years. See Herodotus 1.163, who gave Arganthonius only 120 years of life. **Cinyrae:** Priest-king of Cyprus associated with the cult of Aphrodite at Paphos. See Homer, *Il.* 11.19–23. See also Ovid, *Metamorphoses* 10.294–739. **decem annis:** Not an ablative of comparison, but an ablative of degree of difference with "*amplius*": literally "more by ten years", but better "ten years more". (AG §414) **Aegimius:** A legendary king of Oete or Thessaly, he was the father or son of Dorus, after whom the Dorian peoples are named. He adopted Hercules's son Hyllus in gratitude after Hercules saved him from centaurs. (*BNP* s.v. Aegimius [1], *RE* s.v. Aigimios 1). **Theopompus:** (378–ca. 320 BCE) from Chios. Theopompus was a student of Isocrates, an orator, and a Greek historian whose histories were full of careful, literary figures of speech and Gorgianic style. He was hugely influential in the Hellenistic era, but only minor fragments survive today. **Epimenidi Gnosio:** A thaumaturge (miracle worker) and theologian of the 6th c. BCE on Crete. He gained the gift of prophecy after falling asleep in a cave for 57 years. See Aristotle, *Ath. Pol.* 1; Diogenes Laertius 1.109–15; Plutarch, *Life of Solon* 12. **Hellanicus:** Of Lesbos (480–395 BCE). He was a mythographer, ethnographer, and a historian standing alongside Herodotus and Thucydides, but now only fragments survive. He used the lists of victors of games, magistrates, and priests around Greece to establish a common chronology of events in Greek history. **Aetolia ... Epiorum:** The Epeans were from Elis originally, but they were driven out, establishing themselves in a new land that they named for their king Aetolus. Aetolia was located just north of the Gulf of Corinth, west of the Epizephyrean Locri. The Epeans would later return to Elis. See Homer, *Iliad* 6.19–24. **Damastes:** A geographer and historian of the 5th c. BCE, from Sigeum. **Pictoreum:** Unknown. Valerius Maximus (8.13.ext.6) calls him Litorius, and Schilling refers to Hardouin's suggestion that Pliny has merely translitered the Greek πυκτωραῖον (pyktōraion), meaning "unequaled fighter/boxer".

155. Ephorus: Of Cyme (ca. 400–330 BCE), the first universal historian, with each book devoted to a specific topic. He was followed closely by Diodorus Siculus. **Arcadum:** See note at §7.151 above. **Alexander Cornelius:** Alexander Cornelius Polyhistor, from Miletus. He was brought to Rome in the Mithridatic wars but Sulla made him a citizen in 81 BCE. He was a prolific historian and also the teacher of Hyginus. **Dandonem:** Otherwise unknown. **Xenophon:** A geographer from Lampsacus in Asia Minor who lived at the end of the 2nd c. BCE and the beginning of the 1st. Among his writings was a *Periplus* of the North and West, including what is likely a reference to Scandinavia. He also seems to have written two works on Syria. (*BNP* s.v. Xenophon [8]). **Lutmiorum:** Unknown and possibly corrupt. **milia annorum:** Following the equation 1 Egyptian year = 1 lunar month, a person would reach 1000 Egyptian years after 80 solar years and 311 days.

156. Arganthonium Gaditanum: Possibly identical with Arganthonius of Tartessus, above at §7.154. Gades was the port for Tartessus. **Masinissam:** See note at §7.61. **Gorgian Siculum:** (ca. 485–ca. 380 BCE) originally from Leontini, Gorgias studied under Empedocles in Sicily and became one of the most influential rhetoricians and sophists. In 427 he visited Athens, bringing with him a huge stylistic influence. Gorgias's major stylistic feature was balance and contrast, pairing clauses with antitheses, rhymes, assonance, even equal numbers of syllables in the more extreme cases, all of which became known as "Gorgianic figures". **Quintus Fabius Maximus:** Quintus Fabius Maximus Verrucosus Cunctator. Consul in 233 BCE, 228, 215, 214, 209; dicator 221, 217. He was given the name "Cunctator" ironically due to his policy of non-engagement with Hannibal in Italy. In actuality, it was a policy of attrition, which worked quite well to minimize Hannibal's effect and prevent a total Roman defeat. See note §7.35 under "Hannibale". **Marcus Perpenna:** (b. 148 BCE) consul 92, censor 86. His most notable achievement was enrolling the first of the newly-enfranchised Italians on the citizen lists after the Social Wars. **Lucius**

Volusius Saturninus: See note at §7.62. **quos . . . rogaverant:** i.e., those who were senators when they were consuls.

157. Flaccus et Albinus censores: Quintus Fulvius Flaccus and Aulus Postumius Albinus, censors in 174 BCE. Beagon (2005, 361–2) offers a convincing argument that the five-year period meant is from lustrum to lustrum, and that, since the lustrum was held at end of the censors' 18-month term, the span meant must be 173–168. **ab anno urbis DLXXVIIII:** 175 BCE. **Marcus Valerius Corvinus:** Also called "Corvus". Consul of 348, 346, 343, and 335 BCE. The M. Valerius Corvus/Corvinus who was consul in 300 and 299 was likely the same one who was consul in 312 and 289. **Metellus:** Lucius Caecilius Metellus. See the note at §7.139.

158. Livia Rutili: Sister of Marcus Livius Drusus, consul of 112 BCE, wife of Publius Rutilius Rufus, consul of 105 and historian. **Statilia:** Possibly a female relation of Titus Statilius Taurus, Augustus's second most prominent general after Agrippa. **Claudio:** The emperor Claudius. **Terentia Ciceronis:** Cicero's first wife and the mother of the younger Cicero and Tullia. Cicero divorced her for some undisclosed financial irregularity. She went on to marry Sallust and later Marcus Valerius Messala Corvinus. **Clodia Ofili:** Clodia was the wife of Aulus Ofilius (variously given Aufilius, Ofellius). She outlived her 15 children, dying at the age of 115. (*RE* s.v. Clodia 68, Ofellius 4). **Lucceia mima:** A Late-Republican comedian. **Galeria Copiola:** (95 BCE–after 9 CE) An "*embolaria*", one of the actresses who entertained the crowd between acts. She took to the stage during Marius and Carbo's consulshp in 82 BCE and was brought back to the stage 91 years later at the age of 104 in 9 CE. **magni theatri:** The Theater of Pompey. See the note at §7.20. **Gaio Poppaeo . . . Quinto Sulpicio:** consuls of 9 CE. **Marco Pomponio:** the aedile of 82 BCE. **Gaio Mario . . . Gnaeo Carbone:** 82 BCE. Gaius Marius is the son of the more famous Marius, who was by this time deceased. Gnaeus Papirius Carbo: See the note at §7.68.

159. Samullam: Otherwise unknown. **Pedianus Asconius:** Quintus Asconius Pedanius (ca. 3 CE–88), a writer of commentaries and other lost works. **Stephanionem:** There is much controversy over what it means that Stephanio was "*togatus*" and what sort of dancing is meant by "*saltare*". Possibilities for "*togatus*" include a revival of comedies with Roman settings, work in the mime, work in the pantomime, or wearing an actual toga. Possibilities for "*saltare*" include dancing or portraying through dance (à la pantomime). See Beagon (2005, 364–5) for a full discussion. **Tmoli montis cacumine:** The Tmolus was a chain of mountains in Lydia south of Sardis. See Pliny, *NH* 5.110; Herodotus 5.101; Strabo 13.625. **Tempsin:** Tempsis was the name of the peak of the Tmolus range. **quod vocant Tempsin CL annis vivere Mucianus auctor est:** The subject of "*vivere*" is missing. Either it has dropped out, or the verb should be translated impersonally: "it is lived = people live"). **Mucianus:** Gaius Lucinius Mucianus (d. ca. 76 CE) legate to Lydia under Nero and consul three times: 64, 70, 72. **Claudi Caesaris censura:** 47 CE. "*censura*" is ablative. **Titum Fullonium Bononiensem:** otherwise unknown. Subject of an indirect statement with the verb "*censum esse*" depending on "*Mucianus auctor est*".

Chapter 49

160. Epigenes: Of Byzantium, an astrologer of the 3rd or 2nd c. BCE. **negavit:** "said that . . . not". **Berosus:** See the note at §7.123. **Petosiris ac Necepsos:** A 2nd c. BCE astrological text (*Astrologoumena*) takes as its pseudonymous authors Petosiris (d. before 350 BCE) and Nechepso, king during the 26th dynasty (663–522 BCE). The text included at least 14 books and covered all of contemporary Hellenistic astrology. (*BNP* s.v. Nechepso). **tetartemorion:** Greek for "in four parts" or "four-partite". **partium:** "degrees". **anaphoras:** "rising" or "ascent". In astronomy, the rising of a sign from the equator. Translate as "anaphoras". **has ipsas:** Supply "*mensuras*". **Aesculapi:** Associated with astrology in the 3rd c. BCE, Aesculapius was a son of Apollo and god of healing. In 291 BCE his cult was transferred from Epidaurus to Rome, where it took root on Tiber Island, to date still the site of a hospital.

161. lunae dierum: The lunar day is the length of time between two successive moonrises, about 24 hours and 50 minutes. The language is that of astrology in which the movements of the moon were of extraordinary importance. See Beagon (2005) for the many issues surrounding the "lunar day". **ingens turba nascuntur:** The verb "*nascuntur*" agrees with the notional, not grammatical number of "*ingens turba*". **scansili annorum lege:** Ablative of cause: "the increasing/ climbing law of years", i.e., each succeeding year is more likely to contain a climacteric. (AG §404) **occidua:** With "*turba*" not "*lege*"; "liable to die". **climacteras:** The climacterics are crucial years that bring major life changes, beginning with the seventh year and proceeding according to multiples of seven, although others calculate climacterics based on multiples of nine. The most dangerous climacterics are said to be 63 and 81. Pliny, giving 54 as the most dangerous year, is followed by Censorinus, a 3rd c. CE grammarian in *De Die Natali* 14.12 (238 CE). Pliny's manuscripts, however give both LIIII and LIII, so either Pliny's 54 is correct and he is following a climacteric of multiples of nine, or the number should be emended either from LIIII (LIV) to LVI (56) or from LIII to LXIII (63). The last is the most attractive because of the prominence of 63, but we would have to posit the corruption before Censorinus.

162. quam: "*quam*" here introduces an indirect question and takes the subjunctive. (AG §573) **Caesares Vespasiani pater filiusque:** Vespasian and Titus. Pliny refers to the census of 74 CE. He also dates this portion of the work to 77, two years before he died investigating the eruption at Vesuvius. **Apenninum Padumque:** The eighth of the Augustan "regions" into which Italy had been divided for administrative purposes. This region contains each of the following cities: Parma, Brixellum, Placentia, Faventia, Bononia, and Ariminium.

163. Parmae . . . Brixilli . . . Placentiae . . . Faventiae . . . Bononiae . . . Arimini: Locative case. (AG §427) **Parmae:** the city Parma, famous in antiquity for its sheep and today for its cheese (Parmesan). **Brixilli:** The modern city Brescello (locally "Barsèl" or "Bersèl"). **Placentiae:** The modern city Piacenza. **Faventiae:** The modern Faenza. **Bononiae:** The modern Bologna. **Lucius Terrentius Marci filius:** Mentioned by Phlegon at *de Macrobiis* 96, which only notes his age. **Arimini:** The modern city Rimini. **Marcus Aponius:** Otherwise unknown. **Tertulla:** Otherwise unknown. **Marcus Mucius Marci filius Galeria Felix:** Marcus Mucius Felix, son of Marcus, from the Galerian gens. Otherwise unknown. **Galeria:** Supply "*gente*".

164. ne . . . moremur: A purpose clause. (AG §§529–33) **homines:** People of either gender.

165. Hectorem: Polydamanta: τοῖσι δὲ Πουλυδάμας πεπνυμένος ἦρχ᾽ ἀγορεύειν / Πανθοΐδης· ὃ γὰρ οἶος ὅρα πρόσσω καὶ ὀπίσσω· Ἕκτορι δ᾽ ἦεν ἑταῖρος, ἰῇ δ᾽ ἐν νυκτὶ γένοντο, / ἀλλ᾽ ὃ μὲν ἂρ μύθοισιν, ὃ δ᾽ ἔγχεϊ πολλὸν ἐνίκα "Polydamas, son of Panthous, a wise man, began to address them, for he alone saw in front and behind: he was a companion to Hector, and they were born on the same night, but Polydamas conquered more with words, and Hector more with his spear." Homer, *Iliad* 18.249–52. **Gaio Mario Gnaeo Carbone III coss:** 82 BCE. See the notes above at §7.68, 158. **a. d. V. kal. Iunias:** "*ante diem V kalendas Iunias*": five days before the first day of June = 28 May. (AG §631) **Marcus Caelius Rufus:** the Praetor of 48 BCE, Caelius was defended in trial by Cicero (giving the speech *Pro Caelio*) in 56. **Gaius Licinius Calvus:** (82–47 BCE) Calvus, in addition to being a first rate orator, was a poet and friends with Catullus. **tam dispari eventu:** Caelius was killed in a rebellion against Julius Caesar ca. 48 BCE. Calvus, who had written some damaging poems against Caesar, was reconciled with him and died ca. 47. Both were orators and politicians, with Caelius sporting a lively, witty style and Calvus a dry, severe style, but Calvus is primarily remembered as a poet.

Part 3C: On Life and Death (§§166–90). Pliny segues from his discussion of the human lifespan to one on life and death by noting that the inexplicable occurs not infrequently, taking or restoring life unexpectedly (§166). Life, Pliny tells us, is short compared to the full extent of time, and all the more so when one factors in time spent in infancy or asleep, and even so, an early death is a great blessing, because it cuts short the rigors of failing old age (§§167–70). There are signs and diseases which indicate the approach of death (§§171–2), but death is ultimately just as uncertain as life (§§173–9). The best thing for a person is a sudden and unexpected death, which can be painless and even happy (§§180–5), but can also be unpleasant (§186). After treating death, Pliny treats burial, both cremation and inhumation (§187), and he concludes the section with a rumination on the afterlife, the existence of which he denies entirely (§§188–90).

Chapter 50

166. Lucius Publius Cornelius Rufus: Or Rufinus. The consul of 290 BCE was removed due to extravagance and went blind in his sleep. See also Pliny *NH* 18.39, 33.142. **Manio Curio:** Colleague of L. P. Cornelius Rufus in 290 BCE. See the note at §7.68. **Pheraeus Iason:** 4th c. BCE tyrant of Pherae in Thessaly and assassinated in 370. For the story about the "*vomica*" (an abscess or cyst), see Cicero *De natura deorum* 3.70; Valerius Maximus 1.8.ext.6. **vomicae morbo:** A *vomica* is any cyst-like structure: abscess, boil, cyst, certain tumors, etc. (OLD s.v. *vomica*). The term is especially frequent in Celsus, *De Medicina* 2.7–8, and in Pliny, *NH* 20. **Quintus Fabius Maximus:** Consul 121 BCE. **flumen Isaram:** The modern Isère, a tributary of the Rhone, flowing into that river just north of Valence. **Allobrogum Arvernorumque gentes:** Two Gallic tribes dwelling near the Rhone. **a. d. VI idus Augustas:** "*ante diem VI idus Augustas*". Six days before the Ides of August: 8 August. (AG §631) **febri quartana:** "quartan fever", a fever that recurs every three days (every four days in the Roman inclusive counting). The protozoum Plasmodium malariae does in fact cause a quartan fever, which is based on the organism's life cycle. See Beagon (2005, 378–83) for a detailed explanation of the types of protozoa that cause malaria and their respective fevers.

167. universum ... intuentibus: Ablative absolute. For the ablative subject of "*intuentibus*", supply "*nobis*". **quid quod:** "What of the fact that ...". **dimidio ... pars aequa:** An obvious exaggeration. **tot curae:** Here, "*cura*" is "anxiety" or "worry". **nullum ... sit votum:** "*nullum*" instead of "*nihil*" because it modifies an understood "*votum*" (prayer) that Pliny leaves unexpressed due to its implicit presence in the verb "*sit votum*". Cf. Pliny the Younger, *Epist.* 6.20.14 on the behavior of those at Misenum during the eruption of Vesuvius: "*erant qui metu mortis mortem precarentur*" "There were those who, from fear of death, prayed for death".

168. natura ... melius: See the note at §7.151 on Pedius and Aglaus. **praemoritur:** The "*prae-*" signifies "in advance of the whole person". **ciborum instrumenta:** the organs of digestion. **Xenophili:** Xenophilus was a Pythagorean philosopher and musician from Chalcis in the 4th c. BCE. He taught the musician Aristoxenus.

169. morbus est ... sapientiam mori: "*sapientiam mori*" is an indirect statement and the subject of "*est*"; "*morbus*" is the predicate.

170. quadrini circuitus: Genitive. **febrem ... incipere:** Indirect statement depending on "*leges natura imposuit*". **bruma:** "midwinter". "*Bruma*" is an abbreviation of "*brevissima [dies]*", which occurs on the Winter Solstice (Varro, *Lingua Latina* 6.8). From there it generalizes to mid-winter, winter, and the weather characteristic of winter, i.e., storms. **quadrini ... incipere:** If the quartan fever was in fact malarial, then Pliny's statement makes sense in light of the life cycles of the mosquitoes that carry the disease and the protozoa that cause it. **generatim:** By "*genus*", that is, by social class. **a meridianis partibus:** "from the southern regions".

Chapter 51

171. sapientiae vero aegritudine: Literally, "in an illness of the intellect". Both Rackham and Beagon (2005) give this phrase as "delirium". **a somno moventium:** "of those shaking [the sick person] out of sleep". **praefandi umoris e corpore effluvium:** "incontinence". The verb "*praefor*" means "to say in advance", and so it usually means, "preface, aforemention", but it can refer to anything that must be spoken of (and so excused) beforehand. This phrase, "flow from the body of the moisture that needs to be excused", is a periphrastic euphemism for urinary incontinence. **Hippocrati:** See note at §7.123. **censorius Cato:** See note at §7.61. **indubitata:** with "*signa letalia*". **venarum ... percussu:** "pulse, heartbeat". **formicante:** Though normally associated with the motion of ants, the meaning here must be "fluttering". One imagines the sensation of a line of ants crawling across the skin. The metaphor has a long life in ancient medicine, for which, see Beagon (2005).

172. Pherecydes Syrius: (fl. 544 BCE) The first writer of Greek prose (§7.205) and the author of a Cosmogony, the fragments of which are strikingly different from Hesiod's *Theogony*. He is said to have died due to *phthiriasis*, the louse disease, in which lice consumed his body while he was still living. (Aristotle, *History of Animals* 557a1–2; Aelian, *Varia Historia* 4.28, 5.2; Pausanias 1.20.7, who attributes the same disease to Sulla). See §7.138. **Gaio Maecenati:** See the note above at §7.148. **Antipater Sidonius:** A 2nd c. BCE Greek epigrammatist, whose funerary and ecphrastic epigrams are preserved in the Greek Anthology. **triennio supremo nullo horae momento:** The first ablative phrase, "*triennio supremo*", expresses time within when, while the second phrase expresses time when. (AG §§423–4) That is, "for no revolution of an hour in a three-year period", meaning for three years he slept always less than an hour at at time.

Chapter 52

173. Aviola: Acilius Aviola. See Valerius Maximus 1.8.12. The exact identity of the man is in question, with different theories proposed by Schilling and Syme. See Beagon (2005, 391–2) for relevant bibliography and a summary of the discussion. **Lucio Lamia:** Schilling (p. 227) identifies him with Lucius Aelius Lamia, praetor of 42 BCE. **Gaium Aelium Tuberonem:** Otherwise unknown. **praetura functum:** An instance of *variatio* to avoid repetition after "*praetorio viro*" above. We might achieve the same effect by "over translating" these as "Lucius Lamia, a man who achieved the rank of praetor ... Gaius Aelius Tubero, who also served in the praetorship". **Messala Rufus:** Marcus Valerius Messala Rufus (ca. 102–27/6 BCE), suffect consul of 53. He was brother-in-law to Sulla and later joined Caesar's faction in the Civil Wars. He was also author of works on augury (*De auspiciis*) and the histories of noble families (*De familiis*), on which see Pliny, *NH* 35.8. **ne morti quidem debeat credi:** Cf. the notes at §7.109 and 132. Verbs with dative direct objects still take the dative when made passive. Lit., "It ought to be trusted not even in regard to death", but better, "Not even death ought to be believed".

174. Hermotimi Clazomenii: A 6th c. BCE philosopher who claimed to be the reincarnation of Pythagoras. He would enter trances the nature of which was a subject of much debate in antiquity: did his soul leave his body and if so, all or part of the soul, and which parts? **semianimi:** Probably not "half-consious", but "half-dead", i.e., apparently unconscious in a trance-state. **Cantharidae:** It is unknown to whom this name refers. The Greek word κάνθαρος (kantharos) means "cup", and so the Cantharidae may have been members of a rival Dionysiac club (Bremmer, *The Early Greek Concept of the Soul*, 1983, 42); but it also signifies the scarab, which had strong associations with the soul in Egypt and so may refer to an Egyptian cult. **veluti vaginam:** "*vaginam*" is the object of "*ademerint*"; "*veluti*", like "*quasi*" can indicate that the following words are a metaphor; translate it here "so to speak". **Aristeae ... in Proconneso:** See the note above at §7.10. **visam:** Suppy "*animam*".

aeque magna ac quae sequitur fabulositate: A difficult phrase: "with equally great an inventiveness as that which follows". Pliny expresses his disbelief.

175. Gnosio Epimenide: See note at §7.154 above. **pari numero dierum:** Equal to what? The usual reading is that he grew old in a number of days equal to the number of years he had slept, but his eventual age would suggest that the years asleep did not count against his lifespan. So we might read this as saying "with old age coming upon him in the usual number of days" (i.e., equal to everyone else), as if the years in the cave were years in suspended animation. This crux is "*tamen*": the first reading takes it as "nevertheless" (... although nevertheless he endured for 157 years) and the second reading as "still" (... with the result that he still endured for 157 years). **huic malo:** i.e., apparent but not actual death. **Heraclidis:** Heraclides of Pontus was a 4th c. BCE philosopher who studied at Plato's Academy under Speusippus, Plato's nephew and successor. He studied while Plato was still alive and alongside Aristotle, whom he outlived. Heraclides wrote mainly dialogues but dealing with a wide variety of spheres of interest, including especially astronomy. **feminae ... revocatae:** depends on "*volumen*."

176. XXviro: The XXviri (vigintiviri) were a board of twenty men assigned to redistribute land in accord with Caesar's bill of 59 BCE. **Capuae:** Originally an Etruscan city, Capua (modern Santa Maria Capua Vetere) was located in Campania north of Naples. The city was taken by the Samnites in the 5th c. BCE and gradually by the Romans starting toward the end of the 4th century. The land distribution took place as a result of Caesar's second distribution bill in 59 BCE. Varro was one of twenty men on the board. **efferretur.** The verb "*efferre*" is the usual verb for carrying out a body to its burial. See above at §46. **hoc idem:** "*idem*" here is likely neuter, not masculine: "this same thing", but if masculine: "the same [i.e., Varro] [reports] that this happened ...". The sense is the same. **Aquini:** Aquinum (modern Aquino) was a small town in Latium, birthplace of the poet Juvenal and later the theologian Thomas Aquinas. **Corfidium:** Identity unknown. **elatum:** Again in the sense of carrying out to burial.

177. quae tota indicasse conveniat: Pliny is reluctant to accuse as trustworthy a source as Varro of fabrication, but he hints at his disbelief. **indicasse:** The syncopated infinitive for "*indicavisse*". **conveniat:** An impersonal verb. (AG §207d) **Corfidiis:** Identities unknown. **recitatum heredem minorem:** "*heredem*" is in apposition to "*minorem*": the *minorem rectitatum* as *heredem*. **interim … repertum est:** While the elder brother is in a state of apparent death, the younger brother makes funeral arrangements for the elder. The younger must then be imagined to fall ill and die rather quickly, with the two brothers meeting and conversing immediately in the land of the dead or in some halfway realm. The elder brother then recovers and conveys the conversation just before the younger brother's servants arrive to report his death. The details of the gold are included to give the story factuality beyond coincidence. For similar anecdotes, see Beagon (2005, 397–8).

178. bello Siculo: The war between Sextus Pompey and Octavian. See also §7.148 "*naufragia sicula*". **Gabienus:** Unknown. **Sexto Pompeio:** Pompey's younger son (67-36 BCE). His fortunes wavered throughout the Civil Wars. He was with his father when Pompey was killed in Egypt, and then he raised an army in Africa, took it to Spain, and negotiated a settlement with Lepidus. Afterwards, he was made the Senate's naval commander in 43, but was outlawed just four months later. He usurped power in Sicily, repelling the triumvirs until they granted him official governorship there in 39. Octavian attacked in 38, and over the course of two years, with Octavian and Lepidus attacking, Sextus Pompey won victories and suffered defeats until his final defeat at Naulochus in 36. He fled to Asia but was captured and put to death. His defeat reveals Gabienus's prophecy to be false. **se enim … habere:** Implied indirect speech depending on "*petiit*". **quae nuntiaret:** Relative clause of purpose. (AG §531.2)

179. hoc se nuntiare iussum: Still in indirect statement. One must supply *"esse"* with *"iussum"*. *"hoc"* is the object of *"nuntiare"*. English word order would give: [*dixit*] *se iussum esse nuntiare hoc.* **post sepulturam ... consectamur:** An entirely new idea transitioning from the previous anecdote. "There are examples of apparitions after burial as well ...".

Chapter 53

180. summa vitae felicitas: A dark, but sincere statement. Compare §7.151 above. §§7.180–5 are a series of sudden, unexpected (and therefore happy) deaths, capped in §7.185 by the most fortuitous, that of Marcus Ofilius Hilarus. **Verrius:** Marcus Verrius Flaccus. (ca. 55 BCE–ca. 20 CE) A prolific polymath like Varro, Verrius was a freedman from Praeneste. He gained fame as a teacher and was summoned to Rome to become the tutor to Augustus's grandchildren Gaius and Lucius. Verrius authored a number of works (all lost): *De Orthographia; Saturnus; Res Memoria Dignae* (important to Pliny); *Fasti Praenestini;* and *De verborum significatu,* of which epitomes and abridgments survive. **Chilonem:** See the note at §7.119. **Sophocles:** See the note at §7.109 above. **Dionysius Siciliae tyrannus:** See the note above at §7.110. **Cannensi:** See the notes at §7.18, 35, 106. There are several stories around this theme, for example, Livy 22.7.13: "*Feminarum praecipue et gaudia insignia erant et luctus. Unam in ipsa porta sospiti filio repente oblatam in complexu eius exspirasse ferunt; alteram, cui mors filii falso nuntiata erat, maestam sedentem domi, ad primum conspectum redeuntis filii gaudio nimio exanimatam.*" "Especially remarkable were the joys and griefs of the women. They say that one, when her son suddenly showed up safe, expired at her very door in his embrace; another, to whom the death of her son had been falsely reported, while she was sitting in grief at home, died from excessive joy at the first sight of her son when he returned." **Diodorus:** Diodorus Cronus of Iasus (d. 284 BCE), a master logician. He taught, among others, Philon and the Zeno who founded Stoicism. **Stilponis:** Stilpon of Megara, head of the Megarian school, was an ethicist and writer of dialogues. Both Diodorus Cronus and Stilpon resided in Athens, Stilpon also teaching the Zeno who founded Stoicism.

181. duo Caesares: L. Julius Caesar, praetor, d. 166 BCE and Gaius Julius Caesar, d. 85 BCE, the father of the famous Julius Caesar. **praetura perfunctus:** See §7.173. **pridie kal. Ian.:** *pridie Kalendas Ianuarias:* on the day before the Kalends (first day) of January: 31 December. (AG §631) **Rebilus:** Gaius Caninius Rebilus was one of Caesar's trustworthy legates. Caesar had him elected consul to fill out the last few hours of December 31st, 45 BCE since the consul Quintus Fabius Maximus had just died. Normally, the post would have been left vacant for the few hours remaining in the year. We see here an example of Caesar's control of the highest office and one of his dubious means of ensuring the loyalty of his partisans. **Gaius Volcatius Gurges:** Unknown. **progrediendo:** Going for a stroll, or a march. **Quintus Aemilius Lepidus:** The consul of 21 BCE. **pollice:** Here, the big toe, not the thumb. **Gaius Aufustius:** Unknown.

182. Gnaeus Baebius Tamphilus: Beagon (2005) identifies him with the praetor of 168 BCE. **a puero:** From his slave, not from a child. Compare the French "garçon", used for "waiter" but meaning "boy". **Aulus Pompeius:** It is uncertain which man of this name Pliny means. **Manius Iuventius Thalna:** Consul of 163 BCE. **Gaius Servilius Pansa:** Unknown. **hora diei secunda:** About 7:00 or 7:30 am. The hours of the day start at dawn. **Publius Servilius Pansa:** Unknown. **Marcus Terentius Corax:** Unknown. "Corax" is Greek for "raven".

183. Gaius Iulius medicus: Unknown. **Aulus Manlius Torquatus:** Consul of 164 BCE. **Lucius Tuccius medicus Valla:** Lucius Tuccius Valla, unknown. **Appius Saufeius:** Unknown, but from an important family of Praeneste. **Publius Quintius Scapula:** Unknown. **Aquilium Gallum:** Gaius Aquillius Gallus, a lawyer and praetor in 66 BCE with

Cicero. He added to the law "acting in bad faith" as grounds for a suit. **Decimus Saufeius:** Unknown, but from an important family of Praeneste.

184. Cornelius Gallus: Possibly the father of the elegist and governor of Egypt whom Augustus compelled to commit suicide in 27 BCE. **Titus Hetereius:** Unknown. **in venere:** "*In Venus*", a euphemism for sexual intercourse. **in … Mystico:** An unknown actor. English uses the preposition "with" for the same idiom. **Marco Ofilio Hilaro:** A comic actor (marked by his cognomen "Hilarus"). Like the preceding examples, Hilarus dies suddenly, painlessly, and unexpectedly (a good end), and by doing so at the height of his achievements, he caps his life as a happy one. Compare Solon's statement not to count any man happy until he is dead. See §7.151.

186. miserarum: Feminine modifying an understood "*mortium*". **Lucius Domitius … Massiliam … Corfinii:** Lucius Domitius Ahenobarbus, consul of 54 BCE. He opposed Caesar throughout his career. He was to replace Caesar as governor of Gaul in 49, but instead began raising an army in Italy to meet Caesar. Caesar met him, without reinforcements, at his estate in Corfinium, where Domitius Ahenobarbus promptly surrendered to Caesar. He later tried to defend Massilia against Caesar, but failed to do so and escaped, dying after the battle at Pharsalus in 48. **eodem Caesare:** Julius Caesar. **in actis:** i.e., the *acta diurna* and *acta senatus*. See Introduction, §III. **Felice:** Schilling, 232 dates Felix to the reign of Tiberius. **russei:** i.e. of the red *team*. In this period, the chariot races were divided into two teams: the reds and the whites. **frivolum dictu:** "*dictu*" is a supine with the adjective "*frivolum*"; the phrase refers to what follows. **ne … criminantibus:** These clauses relate the reaction of the opposing chariot team's fans. "*hoc*" refers to the act of the Felix's fan throwing himself on to the pyre; "*correptum*" refers to the fan. Pliny says that the opposing team's fans, wanting to minimize the glory of the dead charioteer, claimed that the self-imolating fan had really only fainted from the fumes and not

willfully thrown himself on the pyre. **Marcus Lepidus:** Marcus Aemilius
Lepidus, cos. 78 BCE. See the note at §7.122. **iuxta:** Next to it, i.e., next to
his original pyre.

Chapter 54

187. ipsum: modifies *"cremare"*. **veteris instituti:** genitive of
characteristic. **in Cornelia:** supply *"gente"*. **Gaii Mari:** (ca. 157–86 BCE).
A native of Aquinum, Marius began his career under Scipio at Numantia,
and through subsequent commissions proved himself adept at warfare.
He served under Quintus Caecilius Metellus Numidicus in the war
against Jugurtha, but when Metellus refused to support his bid for the
consulship, Marius returned to Rome, secured the consulship on his
own, and took command of the war on Jugurtha by special election,
swiftly concluding the war. In 104 he was elected to deal with the threat
of a German invasion, which he successfully did. Marius also reorganized
the army significantly, expanding its size by admitting the unpropertied
classes, standardizing and providing the arms, and increasing discipline
by compelling the troops to carry their own packs. (Marius's soldiers
came to be called "Marius's Mules.") He was continually re-elected
consul year after year through 100, driving back a series of Germanic
incursions. In the following decade he lost his support among the
nobles and saw his power increasingly erode, a process made more
gradual by the interlude of the Social Wars. When Rome finally went to
war with Mithridates VI in Pontus, Marius engineered to have the plebs
overturn the Senate's choice of Sulla for commander and give the
command to him. Sulla, in retaliation, marched on Rome with his army.
Marius fled; Sulla regained his command and went east. After Sulla's
departure, Marius returned to Rome in force, gained the consulship for
86 (his seventh consulship), and died only a few days into the year. Sulla
later had Marius's ashes exhumed and thrown into the River Anio.
Cicero, *de Leg* 2.56: "... *gentemque Corneliam usque ad memoriam
nostram hac sepultura scimus esse usam. C. Mari sitas reliquias apud*

Anienem dissipari iussit Sulla victor, acerbiore odio incitatus, quam si tam sapiens fuisset quam fuit vehemens." "… and we know that the Cornelian clan all the way to our own time used this kind of burial. Sulla, when he had conquered, ordered that the remains of Gaius Marius be scattered in the Anio, spurred on as he was by a hatred more bitter than it would have been if he had been as wise as he was violent." See also Valerius Maximus 9.2.1. **sepultus … contectus:** Certainly a marginal note explaining the meaning of *"condebantur"*, which a scribe later inserted into the text.

Chapter 55

In the following three sections, Pliny makes a definitive statement of his beliefs of the (lack of an) afterlife.

188. vanitas: Here, "vanity".

189. quod autem corpus: Pliny takes a materialist view of the soul. For a very similar but much more expansive argument, see Lucretius, *de Rerum Natura* book 3, especially lines 180–893. **animae:** Dative of possession. (AG §373) **delenimentorum:** "soothings". Rackham prints *"deliramentorum,"* "foolishnesses, vanities" (hence our English word "delirium"). **numquam desinere:** Depends on *"avidae"*. **commenta sunt:** From *"comminiscor"* "to contrive", but may be more easily translated if *"commenta"* is taken separately from *"sunt"*. Thus, *"ista … commenta sunt"* = "those are contrivances". **Democriti vanitas:** Democritus of Abdera (b. 460–457 BCE). A Greek philosopher who is most well known for his theory of atomism, that matter can be divided down to infinitesimal, indivisible units ("atomos" = uncuttable), and that through their movement and recombination, these atoms create all the substances of the world, each with its individual properties and characteristics resulting from the shapes and characteristics of its component atoms. The theory goes on to postulate that, because of the randomness of the atomic motion, there is not one world, but infinitely many worlds in an infinitely large universe. For Democritus, the soul was a compound like any other and thus perishable. Democritus's theories as we know them precluded the possibility that he believed in the immortality of the soul, but there seems to have been an ancient anecdote to that effect nonetheless. One possible explanation is that in an infinite universe, all possible combinations of atoms will recur an infinite number of times, no matter how long between them, and since Democritus viewed the soul as composed of atoms, every soul would necessarily be recomposed over time.

190. malum: an expletive thrown in as an exclamation. "Alas!" **etiam post:** "*post*" is an adverb here: "afterwards". **potest esse:** Supply "*dulce*". **vixisse:** To have lived is to live no longer, i.e., to be dead.

PART FOUR: INVENTIONS (§§191–215). "What we have here is an extensive and varied enumeration of the productions of mankind. It is conducted in a non-moralizing tone, even when it comes to the discussion of arms. Here the list serves as a supplement to an earlier list in the same Book (§§7.123–9) in which Pliny discourses on Man's effort in the sciences of astronomy, grammar (philology), medicine, geometry, architecture, and art." (Jacob Isager, Pliny on Art and Society, *New York: Routledge, 1991, pp. 36–7).*

Part 4A: List of Inventors (§§191–209). The list of inventors is a natural conclusion to Pliny's excursus on the physical, moral, and intellectual variation in Man. It forms a Euhemeristic and naturalizing summary of human achievement, and sketches a presumed historical motion from barbarism to civilization. It also stands in ring structure with the list of human oddities in §§9–33, opposing human invention (the tools of progress toward civilization) to nature's invention (barbarians and semi-human regression). The list serves as preamble to §§210–15: the first international accords, a new kind of invention that moves culture beyond the local to the regional.

Chapter 56

191. Mercurius ... Rhadamanthus: Pliny takes a Euhemeristic approach to the gods. Euhemerus, a 4th c. mythographer, treated myth as a reflection of historical deeds and figures that has become exaggerated and warped by time. The Euhemeristic approach, therefore, rationalizes myth in an attempt to recover some historical truth. **Mercurius:** The Roman god associated with the Greek Hermes, god of travel and merchantry, hence his name from "*merx*" for "merchandise". Our "mercurial" derives from the god's association with movement. **Liber pater:** An Italian deity associated with Dionysus, and so god of wine. The name "Liber" derives not from the adjective "*liber, a, um*, free" but from the Proto-Indo-European root *LEIB, meaning "pour" and from which we get "libation". See the notes at §7.95 and §8.4. **Ceres:** The Roman goddess associated with the Greek Demeter, goddess of grains, hence our word "cereal". **Attica:** The region around Athens and under that city's control. Demeter/Ceres had a major cult center at Eleusis in Attica. **Sicilia:** Another site (at the city (H)enna) of a major cult of Demeter/Ceres. **Rhadamanthus:** Rhadamanthys, a son of Zeus and Europa, was well known for his justice and so after his death became a judge in the underworld, along with Minos and Aeacus. See Pindar, *Olympian* 2.75; Plato, *Gorgias* 524a; Homer, *Odyssey* 4.564.

192. litteras: It is still not known whether writing arose first in Sumeria and then spread to Egypt, or if both cultures developed writing independently. **Assyriis:** The Assyrians were a Semitic people in the Bronze and Iron Ages (ca. 2500–605 BCE) and taking their name from their capital at Aššur (in what is now Iraq). The Assyrians were one of many Akkadian peoples who wrote in cuneiform on clay tablets, a system which superseded the older Sumerian cuneiform around 2000 BCE becoming the common mode for written communication in the Near East. Akkadian survived in writing until around the 1st c. CE but began to be replaced in spoken language by Aramaic as early as 800 BCE. **Mercurio:** Identified with the Egyptian god Thoth, who according to Egyptian mythology, invented writing and acted as the scribe of the gods. The god was depicted with the attributes of an ibis or a baboon. See Cicero, *Natura deorum* 3.56, where Cicero gives the god's parentage and associations. **Gellius:** Gnaeus Gellius. A 2nd c. BCE Roman historian who wrote *Annales* of Rome from its beginning through the Third Punic War (146 BCE) at least. **Syros:** Syria should not be confused with Assyria, of which it was at one time a part when the Akkadian empire conquered it ca. 2330 BCE. Whereas Assyria is centered in what is now northern Iraq, Syria lay on the east coast of the Mediterranean south of Asia Minor and north of the Arabian peninsula. The distinction is made more difficult by a tendency among later writers to use "Assyria" as an elegant synonym for "Syria". **utrique:** Supply "*arbitrantur*". **e Phoenice Cadmum:** Cadmus was the son of Agenor, king of Phoenicia, and he was sent by his father to recover his sister Europa, who had been stolen by Zeus in the shape of a bull. Cadmus failed to find Europa, but at the command of the Delphic oracle, he founded Thebes in Boeotia, bringing with him the Phoenician writing system from which Greek letters are derived. **Troiano bello:** Traditionally 1186 BCE. **Palameden:** Palamedes, son of Nauplius, was known for his cleverness among the Greeks. It was he who tricked Odysseus into joining the war when the latter was feigning madness, and this earned him Odysseus's enmity. Palamedes is stoned to death by the Greeks after Odysseus frames him for plotting with Priam against the Greek army. **Simonidem melicum:** See the note at §7.89. **Aristoteles:** The verb is "*mavult*". **Epicharmo:** A 5th c. BCE comic poet from Sicily. Epicharmus was thought to excel in a variety of fields both philosophical and scientific, and a corpus (called the *Pseudepicharmeia*) grew up around this conception of him, although these works were considered fakes as early as the 4th c. BCE. **quam:** The "*quam*" of comparison, with "*mavult*"; translate it as "rather than".

193. Anticlides: Anticleides of Athens, a 3rd c. BCE historian of Alexander the Great. He also wrote a *Nostoi* (*Homecomings*) and a *Deliaca* (*On Delos*). **invenisse:** Supply "*litteras*". **Menen:** Unknown. The manuscripts give conflicting forms of the name, which may be corrupt.

Phoronea: Phoroneus, in the Argive legends, was king of the Peloponnese, created the first cities, and discovered fire. **Epigenes:** see the note at §7.160. **Babylonios:** The Sumerian speaking people of southern Iraq. The Babylonians had highly developed astronomy and mathematics, and they were seen by the Greeks and Romans as the source of astronomical and astrological knowledge. **Berosus:** See the note at §7.123. **Critodemus:** A Hellenistic astrologer, whose work *Vision* (*Horasis*) included discussion of climacterics, lifespans, violent death, and the planets. See *RE* s.v. Kritodamus 4, *BNP* s.v. Critodemus. **eas attulerunt:** Supply "*litteras*". **Pelasgi:** The "sea-peoples", a term used by ancient writers to denote the earliest inhabitants of the Aegean. The Latin alphabet derives from the Greek but through the intermediary of the Etruscans who came into contact with it through the first Greek settlements in Italy: the trading post at Pithecusae (now Ischia) and the town at Cumae, both from the 8th c. BCE.

194. Euryalus et Hyperbius: Legendary architect and brothers. *RE* suppl. 6 sv. Euryalos, 56. The Athenian Hyperbius (whose name means "Lofty" or "Proud") is not the same as the Corinthian Hyperbius at §7.198. This Hyperbius appears also in Pausanias 1.28.3 as a Pelasgian from Sicily who, along with Agrolas, built the walls on the Acropolis. **Gellio:** Gnaeus Gellius, the 2nd c. BCE historian. See the note at §7.192. **Gellio . . . placet:** i.e., Gellius accepts. **Toxius Caeli filius:** Both Toxius and Caelus are unknown. Rackham would identify Caelus with the Latin translation of the Greek Uranus, god of the sky, but Schilling and Beagon (2005) disagree. The name "Toxius" derives from Greek τόξον (toxon) meaning "bow" or "arch". "Caelus" could be, as Rackham takes it, the name of the Sky god (or someone named for him), or it might derive from *caelare*, to emboss, engrave. **Cecrops:** An autochthonous early king of Athens whose body was half man and half snake (reflecting Athens' close association with the sea). **Argos:** The city Argos in the north-eastern Peloponnese was occupied in the early Bronze Age, predating even the Mycenaean settlement. It was founded by King Phoroneus (see the note at §7.193), and in mythology was variously the home of Diomedes, Agamemnon, and Menelaus. The city remained important throughout the Classical and Hellenistic periods. **Sicyonem:** A city of the northern Peloponnese, just northwest of Corinth. See §7.84. **Diospolin:** Lit., the "city of Zeus", the name for Egyptian Thebes (modern Luxor) in the Roman period, so called because Egyptians referred to the city (whose name was Waset) as "The City of Amun", after a particularly prominent cult featuring Amun-Ra. Thebes has been continually inhabited since ca. 3200 BCE.

195. Cinyra Agriopae filius: Both Cinyra and Agriopas or Agriopa are unknown. Cinyra seems to be different from Cinyras, the king of Cyprus mentioned at §7.154. Beagon (2005) would identify the two since copper-mining was important on Cyprus. **Danaus:** The son of Belus and brother of Aegyptus, Danaus is the eponymous progenitor of the Danaans, a name which Homer uses to mean simply "Greeks". Danaus had fifty daughters (the Danaids), who were betrothed to the fifty sons of Danaus's brother Aegyptos. At Danaus's command, the daughters killed their husbands on their wedding night, all except for Hypermnestra, who spared her husband and became the origin of the kings of Argos. Danaus and his daughters were credited with bringing irrigation to Argos (Strabo 1.2.23), and so it is appropriate that by Roman times, their myths included a punishment in Hades in which the daughters had to carry water in leaking buckets. The name "Danaus" is likely connected to the Proto-Indo-European root *danu, for river. Compare the rivers Danube, Don, Dnieper, and Dniester. **in Graeciam:** Meaning "into the *part of* Greece". **Argos Dipsion:** "*Dipsion*" is Greek for "thirsty" and is the epithet given to Argos in Homer, *Iliad* 4.171 and elsewhere. The rivers there dried up during the summer. **Cadmus Thebis:** The Phoenician Cadmus at the Boeotian Thebes. See the note at §7.192 above. Beagon (2005, 427), however, suggests that the alabaster quarries at Egyptian Thebes may be meant. She goes on to discuss the relevant evidence. **Theophrastus:** Cited below also at §7.197 and 205. (ca. 371–ca. 287 BCE). Theophrastus was the successor of Aristotle at the Lyceum. Theophrastus continued Aristotle's inquiries in every subject, but little of his work survives. See also the note on "Aristotle" at 7.15. **Phoenice:** See Cadmus at §7.192. **Thrason:** unknown. **Cyclopes:** The name Κύκλωψ pl. Κύκλωπες (kyklōps, pl. kyklōpes) means "round eye". In Homer's *Odyssey*, they are savage shepherds, and the one whom Odyssues meets, Polyphemus, is a son of Poseidon. In Hesiod's *Theogony*, however, the forgers of Zeus's lightning bolt, Brontes, Steropes, and Arges (whose names mean Thunder, Lightning, and Bright/Fire, respectively), are Cyclopes and the sons of Uranus and Gaia. The walls at Tiryns, Argos, Mycenae were called "Cyclopean" because the component blocks were so large only a Cyclops was thought able to have moved them. (See Pausanias, 2.25.8.) **Tirynthii:** Tiryns was a major city in the Mycenaean period, but during the Dark Ages (ca. 1100–800 BCE) it was gradually subordinated to Argos and finally ca. 470 BCE was completely destroyed by Argos.

196. Sardibus Lydi: Sardis was the capital city of Lydia in Asia Minor. **fusos:** From *fusus, -i*, "spindle". **Closter filius Arachnae:** Unknown, but the name "Closter" is Greek for "Spinner", and his mother Arachne (Greek for "spider") was the archetypal weaver, turned into a spider after a weaving contest with Minerva. **fulloniam artem:** Ancient dry cleaners used water, urine (for the ammonia), and fuller's earth to launder woolen cloth. The fuller's earth, a type of clay, absorbs the oils from the wool and whitens it. **Nicias Megarensis:** Nicias of Megara, otherwise unknown. **Tychius Boeotius:** Tychius of Boeotia was from the subregion Hyle. See Homer, *Iliad* 7.219–223, which identifies Tychius as the best worker of leather in the region and the maker of Ajax's seven-layered shield. **Arabum Babylonis et Apollinis filium:** Otherwise unattested. **Chirone Saturni et Philyrae filio:** Chiron was the centaur who fostered many heroes, most notably Achilles, Asclepius, and Jason. He was wise, self-controlled, a healer, and an oracle, gifts that reflect his parentage. He was the son of Cronus/Saturn in the shape of a horse and the nymph Philyra, whereas the other centaurs were the children of the Lapith king Ixion and the cloud Nephele, which Ixion had mistaken for Hera. The dual nature of these centaurs reflects the violence and bestiality inside man, whereas Chiron's dual nature reflects more the wise savage in touch with and in control over his animal roots. Compare also the wise centaur Pholus (Apollodorus 2.5.4).

197. aes conflare et temperare: Bronze working differs substantially from iron working. Iron is heated first to soften the metal and allow it to be worked. It is then hardened by the rapid cooling effected by quenching, but this makes the metal brittle. Subsequent tempering (heating at a low temperature) allows carbon to suffuse in the metal's crystalline structure, giving it greater resistance to shock. Bronze, on the other hand, is malleable enough to be hammered into shape directly, but this hammering renders the metal brittle. It must as a result periodically be heated until the metal glows, which allows the crystalline structure to reform and the metal to be worked further. This process is called "annealing". Unlike iron, bronze does not need to be quenched to regain hardness. The term *aes*, like "bronze" originally, refers to any copper alloy. In contemporary usage, "bronze" signifies copper and tin, while "brass" is the softer copper and zinc. Ancient varieties of bronze included the famous Corinthian bronze, of which Pliny identifies three types (*NH* 34.1–3), alloys of gold, silver, and both, as well as a fourth type called *hepatizon* ("livered"), thought to be similar to the purpled Japanese bronze, *shakudō*. **Lydum Scythen:** Lydian Scythes. Unknown. **Delam Phrygem:** Unknown. **Chalybas:** Tribes on the southeastern coast of the Black Sea in what is now the country Georgia. **Dactyli Idaei:** Like the Telchines of Rhodes, the Idaean Dactyli were legendary, magical metalworkers. Their name derives from the dexterity of their fingers (δάκτυλοι). They were attendants of the Mother Goddess on Mt. Ida, either Cretan Ida or Phrygian Ida. **Erichthonius Atheniensis:** Like Cecrops (see the note at §7.194), Erichthonius (also "Erectheus" in the Archaic period) was an early, autochthonus king of Athens. He was the son of Hephaestus, whose seed fell on the earth when he tried unsuccessfully to rape Athena. The child was raised by Athena or by the daughters of Cecrops. The title or name "Erechtheus" ("Shaker") may indicate associations with Poseidon in his capacity as god of earthquakes.

Aeacus: The son of Zeus and the nymph Aegina. Aeacus was the father of Peleus and Telamon, and grandfather of Achilles. After his death, he became a judge in the underworld. See the note on "Rhadamanthus" at §7.191. **Pangaeum:** Pangaeus, a mountain of northern Thrace. **Thoas:** King of the island Lemnos, and the son of Dionysus and Ariadne. **Panchaia:** A mythical island in the Indian ocean. **Sol Oceani filius:** The Sun is usually the child of the Titans Hyperion and Theia (Lofty and Divine, respectively). Beagon (2005, 433) notes that the sun, moon, and stars are received into and spring from the Ocean every night and morning, but the genealogy may also reflect a lost Orphic or Near-Eastern tradition. Compare Homer, *Iliad* 14.201, where Hera calls Ocean the "genesis of the gods" and Tethys their "mother". **Gellius:** Gnaeus Gellius. See the note at §7.192. **plumbum:** Likely "*plumbum album*", i.e., tin. **Cassiteride:** Cassiterides: The word seems to mean "Tin-Isles" and refers to the tin-producing islands in the far west of the world: possibly islands to the northwest of Spain and the Scilly Islands off Cornwall (Britain). See Herodotus 3.115, and Diodorus Siculus 5.22.5, 5.38.4. *RE* s.v. Kassiterides. **Midacritus:** Otherwise unknown, but generally thought to refer to King Midas of Phrygia. See §7.204 below.

198. figlinas: Pottery is one of the few material remains from very early Greek culture. After the Mycenaean collapse in the 12th c. BCE, pottery returns first with the Protogeometric style (ca. 1050–900), then the Geometric style (9th and 8th c.) characterized by lines and abstract figures. In the 8th and 7th c. BCE we see Orientalizing art, with mythological representations and stylized figures showing contact with the near East. This is followed by Black Figure vases (ca. 620–480), in which figures were painted in black silhouette and then had details etched out of the paint. Red Figure pottery, in which figures were painted directly on the vases with greater detail, was pioneered shortly thereafter but flourished in the 5th century. **Coroebus:** Unknown. **orbem:** The potter's wheel. **Anacharsis Scythes:** A Scythian prince who traveled through Greece in the 6th c. BCE. (Herodotus 4.76.1–4.78.1) He was known for his wisdom and later was placed among the Seven

Sages. **Hyperbius Corinthius:** Not the same as the Athenian Hyperbius at §7.194. This Hyperbius is mentioned by a scholiast on Pindar, *O.* 13.27, who quotes Theophrastus's *On Discoveries.* **fabricam materiariam:** i.e. a worker in wood, from *materia,* "wood" (OLD s.v. *materia*). **Daedalus:** The mythical inventor. See below at §7.209. **terebram:** A gimlet: a small, screw-like handtool used to drill holes. **ichthyocollam:** Isinglass, a kind of glue made from the swim-bladders of sturgeon. **Theodorus Samius:** Theodorus of Samos was a mid 6th c. BCE sculptor and metalworker responsible for the Scias (an assembly hall in Sparta) and contributed to the Heraion at Samos and the temple of Artemis at Ephesus. **Phidon Argivus:** A king of Argos of uncertain date, but most likely the early to mid 7th c. BCE. He reigned over the height of Argos's power in the Peloponnese, reformed weights and measures, and possibly pioneered the phalanx battle formation. **Pyrodes Cilicis filius:** Pyrodes is unknown, but his name means "Appearance of Fire". Cilix, the eponymous founder of the Cilicians, was the son of Agenor and brother of Cadmus and Phoenix. Schilling (243) suggests another play on words between "Cilicis" and "*silice*" (flint). **Prometheus:** The Titan and son of Iapetus who stole fire from the gods by hiding it in a fennel stalk and gave it to mankind. Zeus chained him to the Caucasus mountains where a vulture daily ate out his liver. All of humankind's arts derive from Prometheus's gift of fire, and in one tradition, it was Prometheus who crafted man from clay and it is Prometheus's son Deucalion who repopulates the earth after the flood. See Hesiod, *Theogony* 506–616; *Works and Days* 51; Aeschylus, *Prometheus.*

199. vehiculum cum quattuor rotis Phryges: The Phrygians were an Indo-European people who inhabited the western coast of Anatolia in Asia Minor. Four-wheeled vehicles seem to have been invented first in Mesopotamia rather than Phrygia but were quickly wide-spread throughout the region. **Poeni:** The Phoenicians (not the Carthaginians, pace Beagon) were a merchant people who inhabited primarily the coast of the Levant with major cities at Tyre, Sidon, and Byblos. They founded trading posts and colonies throughout the Mediterranean, including most notably Carthage, whose people were therefore also known in Latin as "Poeni" (noun) and "Punicus" (adjective), hence the "Punic Wars". **Eumolpus Atheniensis:** The son of Poseidon, Eumolpus founded the sacred mysteries at Eleusis after being taught them directly by Demeter. He became the hierophant (chief priest) at Eleusis and is said also to have been taught agriculture by Demeter, which he then shared with the world. See the *Homeric Hymn to Demeter* and Apollodorus 3.201. **vinum aquae misceri:** "*misceo*" can take both an accusative and a dative of things mixed. **Staphylus Sileni filius:** Staphylus is the personification of the grape-cluster (σταφυλή, staphylē). He appears variously as the son of Dionysus, the son Dionsysus's attendant Silenus, an Assyrian king, and the discoverer of the vine. **Aristaeus Atheniensis:** A demigod and the son of Apollo, Aristaeus is connected with beekeeping, honey, olive oil, and cooling winds. For his association with the *bougonia* and with Orpheus and Eurydice, see book four of Vergil's *Georgics*. **Buzyges Atheniensis:** The name Βουζύγης (Buzyges) means "ox-yoker" in Greek. See Aristophaes, frag. 386. **Triptolemus:** Alongside Eumolpus, Triptolemus was a prince of Eleusis and learned the sacred mysteries directly from Demeter. His role is essentially identical to that of Eumolpus above.

200. Theseum: Son of Aegeus, for whom the Aegean sea is named and legendary king of Athens responsible for the synoecism of Attica. Theseus cleared Attica of bandits and monsters, freed Athens from Cretan rule by killing the Minotaur, united the local towns of Attica under the political authority of Athens, and undertook various other quests, including the kidnapping of a young Helen and the attempted rape of Persephone. This last quest ended with Theseus trapped on a bench in the underworld, from which he was eventually rescued by Hercules. **Phalaris Agraganti:** Phalaris of Acragas was tyrant of that city from 570–554 BCE, during which time he acquired an empire across the northern coast of Sicily and became renowned for his cruelty, going so far as to roast enemies alive in a bronze bull. **servitium invenere Lacedaemonii:** A reference to the Spartan helots. The Spartans reduced the native peoples of Laconia and Messenia into slavery sometime between the 10th and 7th centuries BCE. Afterwards, the helots were treated as a nation of slaves whom the Spartans suppressed by brutal means. These included the *krupteia*, an initiation rite in which Spartan ephebes were sent out at night to terrorize helot populations and kill prominent members. **iudicium capitis:** "capital trial". **Areopago:** The Hill of Ares where a council of the same name sat. The Areopagus council originally advised the king and later the archons, Athens' chief magistrates. By the 6th c. BCE, membership consisted of ex-archons and was for life. The Areopagus's decline begins when Solon's reforms (early 6th c. BCE) create a council specifically to prepare business for the assembly, and they continue with Ephialtes's reforms in 462/1 BCE in which the Areopagus's sphere is reduced to trials for murder, arson, and wounding. See Aeschylus's *Eumenides* for an account of the mythic creation of the Areopagus. **Afri:** The people of Africa, possibly the Numidians or the Aethiopians. **Proetus et Acrisius:** Twin brothers who quarreled even in their mother's womb. Proetus became king of Tiryns, while Acrisius became king of Argos. Proetus's daughters, the Proetides, after offending a god—either Hera or Dionysus—were stricken with madness and wandered about thinking themselves cows until they were cured by Melampus. Acrisius was father of Danae, mother of Perseus. **Chalcus Athamantis filius:** Otherwise unattested, but the names seem to be personifications: "Bronze, son of Unbreakable", if "Athamas" is a variation of "Adamas". **Midias Messenius:** Otherwise unattested. Messenia was dominated by Sparta (see above under "*servitium invenere Lacedaemonii*") and so this reference may reflect a lost myth, a myth invented after the end of Spartan overlordship, or may reflect the Spartans themselves. **Cares:** The Carians were a thoroughly Hellenized Indo-European people who inhabited Southwest Asia Minor and were known for serving as mercenaries, particularly on behalf of Ionian Greeks and the Egyptian Pharaohs.

201. Scythem Iovis filium: Scythes is the son of Hercules or Zeus. He becomes the eponymous founder of the Scythians (Scythae). Compare

Herodotus 4.8–10. See also "*Scytharum*" above at §7.9. **Persen Persei filium:** The son of Perseus and Andromeda. He became king after Andromeda's father Cepheus and gave his name to the Persians. The Persians were famous for shooting arrows from horseback. **Aetolos . . . Aetolum Martis filium:** The genealogy comes from this passage in Pliny. Aetolus is normally grandson of Deucalion or son of Endymion of Elis. He is the eponymous founder of the Aetolians, who inhabited the area north of Achaea across the gulf of Patrai. Beagon (2005) notes: "The wild and rugged terrain of Aetolia in central west Greece encouraged the deployment of lightly armed and mobile troops who made much use of throwing spears, cf. Thucydides 3.94–8, describing their defeat of the Athenian general Demosthenes in 427/6 BC." **Tyrrenum:** Tyrrhenus was the legendary son of king Atys of Lydia. According to Herodotus 1.94, in response to a famine Tyrrhenus led half the population of Lydia to Italy, where they founded the Tyrrhenian (Etruscan) race. **Penthesileam Amazonem:** The daughter of Ares and Otrere, who fights in the Trojan War on the side of the Trojans after Hector is killed. Achilles defeats and kills her but falls in love with her as she is dying. **Pisaeum:** Perhaps to be identified with "*Pisaeum Tyrenni*" below, Pisaeus was a son of Tyrrhenus. We may see a connection with the city Pisae, which lies on the Tyrrhenian sea in northern Italy. **venabula:** An all-encompassing term for the machines that threw bolts. **scorpionem:** The "scorpion" was a one-man catapult rather like a very large crossbow, although the size could vary. Tension was created by twisted springs ("*tormenta*"). It was so-named because the throwing arm sat at the back of a wagon-like contraption, and when the tension in the ropes was released, struck forward like a scorpion's tail. **Cretas:** Crete, the large island south of the Peloponnese, was the important center of the Minoan civilization in the Bronze Age (ca. 27th–15th c. BCE). The Minoans were a seafaring empire, exporting their wares to Greece, Egypt, the Levant, and Anatolia and placing colonies in the Cyclades. A large natural disaster in the 15th c., likely the eruption at Thera, disrupted their civilization, allowing the Mycenaeans to gain prominence. **catapultam:** The generic term for bolt or stone-throwinig machine. The name derives from Greek κατὰ πελταστάς (kata peltastas) meaning "against the peltasts". "Peltasts" were light-armed, shield-bearing troops. **Syros:** See above at §7.192. **Phoenicas:** The Phoenicians. See above at §7.199 under "Poeni". **ballistam:** Another catapult type, which usually threw stones or flaming projectiles. Its name derives from the Greek verb βάλλω (ballō), to throw. **Pisaeum Tyrenni:** See "*Pisaeum*" above. **testudines:** A type of covered siege engine. See Caesar *de Bello Gallico* 5.42.5. **Artemonem Clazomenium:** An engineer who aided Pericles at the siege of Samos in 440/39 BCE. (*RE* s.v. Artemon [1])

202. equum . . . aries: Pliny rationalizes the Trojan Horse into a battering ram. **Epium ad Troiam:** Epius was the Greek artisan who built the wooden horse that Odysseus had devised. See *Odyssey* 8.493, and Vergil, *Aeneid* 2.264. **Bellerophontem:** Bellerophon or Bellerophontes was a grandson of Sisyphus or son of Poseidon, giving him a direct connection to horses. He tamed the winged horse Pegasus with the help of Poseidon and Athena, using it to slay the Chimaera and a boar and to defeat the Amazons and Solymi. Later he attempted to fly on Pegasus to Olympus, but he was thrown from the horse and died. (*BNP* s.v. Bellerophontes) **Pelethronium:** Pelethronius is the eponymous hero after whom was named the valley on the west slope of Pelium, where Chiron was said to make his home. The valley produces an herb used against snake bites, the "chironion" or "centaurion". (*BNP* s.v. Pelethronium) **Thessalos:** Thessaly, the area of northeastern Greece north of Boeotia, was famous for its horses. See also §7.35 above. **Centauri:** Another example of Pliny's rationalization of myth. See §7.198 above. **Pelium:** A mountain range in Thessaly, as well as its highest peak. Pelium was home to the centaur Chiron. **eodem:** i.e., "*Troiano bello*". **Sinon:** Greek for "pest", a cousin of Odysseus and fighter in the Trojan War. After the Greeks leave the wooden horse and sail their fleet behind Tenedos, Sinon stays behind, allows himself to be captured, and convinces Priam that he is an enemy of Odysseus and to make a breach in the walls in order to bring the horse into the city. (*BNP* s.v. Sinon) **indutias . . . foedera:** The first is a truce or cease-fire, and the second a treaty. **Lycaon:** Possibly the son of Priam first sold and then killed by Achilles, but more likely the mythical king of Arcadia. His cult, founded in the Lycaeum mountains, was associated with lycanthropy, and Lycaon himself is transformed into a wolf by Zeus for sacrificing his son Nyctimus.

203. auguria . . . aruspicia . . . ignispicia . . . extispicia: "Augury" is the generic term for divination by omens. "*Haruspicium*" refers specifically to the augury practiced by Etruscan *haruspices*, which entailed the inspection of entrails. "*Ignispicium*" occurs only here, but is divination by fire. "*Extispicium*" is the generic term for divination by the inspection of entrails. **Car:** The eponymous founder of the Carian peoples. See above at §7.200. Car was the son of Zeus and the brother to Lydos and Mysos (eponymous founders of Lydia and Mysia). **Orpheus:** The Thracian son of Apollo and a muse, usually Calliope, Orpheus was a mythical singer whose song had power over all who heard it, including animals and inanimate objects. He is best known for descending into the underworld and charming Hades and Persephone in order to get his recently deceased wife, Eurydice, returned to the living. Orpheus fails when he violates Hades' only condition: that he not look back to see if Eurydice is following as he returns to the upper world. Orpheus is credited with authorship of "Orphic poetry" and mysteries with close ties to the Bacchic cult, which may account for Pliny's statement here. **Delphus:** The eponymous hero of Delphi, who was king there when Apollo arrived. **Amphiaraus:** A prophet from Argos who was one of the Seven Against Thebes. He participated in the attack knowing in advance that he would die there. Amphiaraus also founded the Nemean Games. **Tiresias Thebanus:** A blind Theban seer whose shade Odysseus consulted in his trip to the underworld. There are two stories of how Tiresias lost his vision: either he saw Athena bathing naked (Callimachus, *Hymn* 5) or he intervened in a quarrel between Zeus and Hera (Hesiod, fr. 275 M-W). For his connection to augury, Beagon (2005) notes that he "observed birds by listening to their cries and having their appearance described by his daughter (Sophocles, *Ant.* 1000ff.), who is also depicted aiding his interpretation of pyromantic signs and perhaps entrails in Statius, *Theb.* 10.667." **Amphictyon:** The son of Deucalian and Pyrrha, and the eponymous founder of the Amphictyony in central Greece, a group of allied towns living around and protecting the cult at Delphi. **Atlans Libyae filius:** Atlas is usually the son of the Titan Iapetus and Clymene (daughter of Ocean), or of Asia. From his parentage he knew the seas and from his station holding up the heavens, he knew the stars, several of whom he fathered, including the Pleiades. We can see why in some versions, as Pliny tells us here, he is the creator of astronomy. (*BNP* s.v. Atlas [2]) **Assyrii:** See the note at §7.192. **Milesius Anaximander:** Anaximander of Miletus, a 6th c. BCE philosopher wrote a περὶ φύσεως (*On Nature*). He studied astronomy and invented the sundial. Anaximander's first principle (ἀρχή) is the *apeiron*, the "infinite" (or better, "indefinite") out of which the distinct elements of the universe emerge and to which they eventually return. (*BNP* s.v. Anaximander) **Aeolus Hellenis filius:** A mythological king of Thessaly, son of Hellen (note: not Helen of Troy, but Hellen, son of Deucalion, who gave his name to the Greeks as a whole: Hellenes). Aeolus is the eponymous founder of the Aeolian tribes. He is not the same as Aeolus, king of the winds.

204. Lydios modulos: The Lydian, Dorian, Phrygian, Iastian, Mixolydian, and Tense Lydian are the six musical modes reportedly in use in antiquity according to Aristides Quintilianus (18.5–19.10), a late (possibly 3rd c. CE) musical theorist. **Amphion:** The son of Zeus and Antiope. Amphion built the walls at Thebes with his lyre playing. He also married Niobe, whose fourteen children by him were killed by the arrows of Artemis and Apollo. Amphion variously either goes insane, commits suicide, or is killed by Apollo for attacking his temple. (*BNP* s.v. Amphion) **Pan Mercuri:** Pan is the god of shepherds, with the head and feet of a goat. He is variously fathered, sometimes as here by Hermes, elsewhere by Zeus, Apollo, or even Kronos. In addition to inventing the pan-pipes (*syrinx*) from the reeds into which a nymph he was chasing turned (Ovid, *Met.* 1.689 ff.), Pan is associated with *panic*, a sudden sense of strong agitation. (*BNP* s.v. Pan) **Midas in Phrygia:** The king of Phrygia, Midas captured the satyr Silenus by spiking a pool with wine. In return for his freedom, Silenus gave Midas the golden touch, with disastrous consequences for Midas. The river Pactolus removed the affliction. Later, Midas was called on to judge a musical contest between Apollo and Pan. When he decided for Pan, Apollo gave him a donkey's ears. He likely corresponds with the historical king Mita (738–696/5 BCE). Suda, ε 774 associates Midas with the *aulos* (pipe / flute / double oboe). **Marsyas:** The inventor of the *aulos* (usually translated "flute", but closer to what would now be called a double oboe), Marsyas was a satyr who challenged Apollo to a musical duel. Apollo defeated him and in punishment skinned him alive. **Lydios modos . . . Dorios:** As early as the 7th c. BCE, *harmonies* (also called "nomes") were distinguished with ethnic names by the musician Terpander (see below). Over time, these were systematized into the Lydian, Dorian, Phrygian, Iastian, Mixolydian and Tense Lydian mentioned above. See *OCD*[3rd] 1009–10. **Thamyras Thrax:** See *Iliad* 2.594–600: ". . . and Dorium, where the Muses, meeting Thamyris the Thracian stopped his singing as he came from Oichalia from the house of Oichalian Eurytus: for he promised, boasting, that he would win even if the Muses themselves, daughters of aegis-bearing Zeus, should sing against him; and they, in their wrath, maimed him, yes, they took away his divine song and made him forget his skill at the cithara." **Phrygios Marsyas Phryx:** See "*Marsyas*" and "*Lydios modos . . . Dorios*" above. **Linus:** A mythical figure with a number of associations. He was the son of Apollo and therefore closely connected with music. He died variously: exposed and consumed by dogs, killed by Apollo for challenging the god in a musical context, or bashed over the head by Heracles, his student. **III ad IV primas additis:** "*tribus ad quattuor primas additis*". Ablative absolute. **Terpander:** A 7th c. BCE musician who instituted the first contest of cithara players at the Spartan festival of the Carnea in 676/3. He is credited with inventing the ethnic nomes. See above at "*Lydios modos . . . Dorios*". **Simonides:** See the note at §7.89. **Timotheus:** A cithara player and musician (ca. 450–360 BCE). Pherecrates names him as the best innovator of the 5th c. **Troezenius Ardalus:** Ardalus was a cultname of the Muses and seems to be related to the verb ἀρδεύεω (*ardeuō*) "to give drink to" and the noun ἀρδάλιον (*ardalion*) "waterpot", recalling the Muses's origins as spring nymphs. The figure is mentioned in Pseudo-Plutarch, *De Musica* 5. **Curetes:** Young Cretan divinities, the male equivalents of nymphs, who protected the infant Zeus in a cave on Mt. Dicte by striking their bronze shields to drown out his cries. **pyrrichen:** Greek πυρρίχη, a war dance which Caesar brought to Rome when he made the children of the princes of Asia and Bithynia dance it. See Pliny, *NH* 8.5, and Suetonius, *Caesar*, 39. The pyrrhic dance supposedly originated in Crete and formed a part of Greek military training, especially at Sparta. **Pyrrus:** The eponymous inventor of the pyrrhic dance. Unrelated to Pyrrhus of Epirus, from whom we get the phrase "Pyrrhic victory", but possibly derived from Pyrrhus (also called "Neoptolemus"), the son of Achilles.

205. Pythio oraculo: See the note at §7.109 on "Delphi". **Pherecydes Syrius:** See the note above at §7.172. **Cyri regis aetate:** Cyrus the Great, king from ca. 557–530 BCE. **Cadmus Milesius:** Son of Pandion. According to the Suda, he wrote a history of Miletus and Ionia (*The Founding of Miletus and all of Ionia*) in four books. He was one of the first historians and perhaps the first to write in prose. (See Pliny *NH* 5.112). (*RE* s.v. Kadmos [6]). **Arcadia Lycaon:** See above at §7.202. **Acastus in Iolco:** The son of Pelias and Anaxibia and originally one of the Argonauts with Jason, Acastus becomes king of Iolcus and expels Jason and Medea. He was eventually killed by Jason. **Theseus in Isthmo:** Theseus founded the Isthmian games, dedicated to Poseidon, after he defeated the brigand Sinis. They were held at Corinth every other year in April or May. See *OCD³ʳᵈ* 772. **Hercules Olympiae:** Founded by Hercules at Olympia (in the Peloponnese), the Olympian games honored Zeus every four years. Records of victors go back to 776 BCE. The Emperor Theodosius I abolished the games in 393 CE. See *OCD³ʳᵈ* 1066. **Gyges Lydus:** King Candaules of Lydia hides with his friend Gyges in his wife's chambers in order to show Gyges her beauty as she undresses. She notices them and tells Gyges on the following day that he must rescue her modesty by killing either Candaules or himself. Gyges kills Candaules, becomes king of Lydia, and fathers the line of kings that will end with Croesus. See Herodotus 1.8–14 and above at §7.151. **Graecia Euchir Daedali cognatus:** As Beagon (2005) notes, εὐχεῖρ means "skilled hand". *RE* s.v. Eucheir (1) identifies him with Eucheir of Corinth, citing Pausanias 6.4.4 and calls him the "cousin" of Daedalus ("Vetter", a rough translation for Pliny's "*cognatus* = relative", *pace* Beagon's, 2005, "son".) For Daedalus, see below at §7.209. **Theophrasto:** See above at §7.195. **Polygnotus Atheniensis:** fl. ca. 480–440 BCE. Polygnotus was an Athenian painter and sculptor who painted the Stoa Poikile, amongst many other still-famous works. See *OCD*[3rd] 1212–13.

206. Danaus: See above at §7.195. **mari Rubro . . . Erythra:** Erythras ("Red") was a legendary king of Persia for whom is named all the water of the Indian Ocean, including the modern Red Sea and the Persian Gulf. See above at §7.97 and also *NH* 6.107 and 6.153. **Mysos et Troianos:** The Trojans inhabited the land just south of the Hellespont, while the Mysians controlled the area to the East along the south coast of Propontis (the sea of Marmara). **Hellesponto:** The modern Dardanelles. See below at §7.207 under "*Iasonem*". **Britannico oceano vitilis:** The *vitilis* is a structure woven from wicker. Here, the word significes a "coracle," that is, a wicker-boat which in this case is water-proofed with hides. Compare Caesar, *Bellum Civilem* 1.54. **Nilo:** Pliny also mentions reed boats on the Nile at *NH* 13.72. For more on the Nile, see above at §7.33.

207. Iasonem: Jason of Iolcus in Thessaly sailed to Colchis (on the eastern edge of the Black Sea) in the Argo, the first ship. He went at the bidding of the king of Iolcus in search of the Golden Fleece, which was the fleece of the ram that had carried off Phrixus and Helle, the children of a past king of Thessaly. Helle fell into the sea and drowned (giving her name to the Hellespont, the modern Dardanelles), but Phrixus made it to Colchis where he sacrificed the ram, which became the constellation Aries. **Philostephanus:** Of Cyrene. He lived in the 3rd c. BCE under Ptolemy Philopator and was a student of Callimachus. Philostephanus wrote geographies, *commentarii*, and a book on discoveries, as well as an elegiac poem *On Peculiar Lakes*. **Hegesias:** A 4th and 3rd c. BCE orator and historian from Magnesia. All that remain of his works are fragments of some speeches and a history of Alexander the Great. **Parhalum:** Athenian hero. Parhalus was the son of Poseidon (his name signifies "from the sea"), and the Athenian State trireme was named for him. See Pliny, *NH* 35.101 for a painting of Parhalus in Athens by Protogenes. **Ctesias:** See the note at §7.23. **Samiramin:** Samiramis or Semiramus (in Assyrian, Sammu-ramat) was a powerful queen and regent of Assyria in the late 9th c. BCE. A number of legends of varying degrees of impossibility surround her including that she conquered Bactra and Armenia, built Babylon (i.e., restored it), and was the first to castrate boys. **Archemachus:** A 3rd c. BCE historian who wrote a history of Euboea, the large island off the coast of Attica. **Aegaeonem:** Along with Cottos and Gyges, Aegaeon (also known as Briareus) was one of the three Hecatonchires, the hundred-handed monsters born of Uranus and Gaia. Aegaeon had a cult on the east coast of Euboea at Carystos. Both Aegaeon and Theseus's father Aegeus gave their name to the Aegean sea. See Hesiod, *Theogony* 147–163, 502–6. **Damastes:** See the note at §7.154. **Erythraeos:** See the note at §7.206 on "Erythra". **Thucydides:** See the note at §7.111. **Aminoclen Corinthium:** The details and dating are unknown, but Aminocles would have been responsible for triremes in Greece sometime between 721 BCE and the middle of the 6th c. BCE. See Beagon (2005, 456–7) for a full discussion.

208. quinqueremem: A warship with three banks of oars that sat rowers in groups of five. The exact arrangement of the rowers is unknown, but various combinations have been suggestsed, the most likely being one rower in the lowest bank and two each in the banks above. The ship type first appears at Athens in 325/4 BCE and was the main type of warship for the Romans from the Punic Wars until after Actium (31 BCE).

Mnesigiton: Mnesigeiton, a grammarian mentioned in Plutarch's *Quaestiones Graecae* 19 and above at §7.57. He likely flourished during the Hellenistic period. **Salaminios:** The citizens of the city Salamis on Cyprus. Cyprus had been a major sea-power in the eastern Mediterranean during the reign of Euagoras (b. 435–d. 374/3 BCE). **Xenagoras:** a 3rd c. BCE Greek historian who wrote χρόνοι (*Chronicles*) of the Greeks covering Greek history up to the Ionian revolt (490 BCE) or into the Hellenistic period and including Sicily and Egypt and possibly Rome. He also wrote a work περὶ νήσων (*On Islands*). (*BNP* s.v. Xenagoras [1]) **Syracusios:** Dionysius II, the Tyrant of Syracuse (367–44 BCE) had ships with six banks of oars. **Ptolemaeum Soterem:** Ptolemy I Sōter ("Savior") (367/6–282 BCE). Ptolemy I was the childhood friend of Alexander the Great and later one of his generals. After Alexander's death in 323, Ptolemy took possession of Alexander's corpse and brought it to Memphis in Egypt because Macedonian kings established their legitimacy by burying their predecessor. This prevented Alexander's other successors from staking a stronger claim to the empire and allowed Ptolemy to establish himself as satrap of Egypt, eventually taking the title "King" (βασιλεύς) in 305 BCE. Ptolemy is likely responsible for the cult of Serapis (an amalgam of Osiris and Apis). **Demetrium Antigoni:** Demetrius Poliorcetes, son of Antigonus I Monophthalamus ("One-Eyed"). See §7.126. Antigonus and Demetrius, like all of the post-Alexandrian dynasts, attempted to recreate Alexander's empire. Antigonus had some brief success in 316 BCE, but that was short-lived, as the other dynasts formed a coalition against him and his son Demetrius. The two took to Athens and were proclaimed kings, but they were again defeated in 304, the same year that Demetrius aborted his attack on Rhodes. Demetrius was able to make himself king of Macedon in 294 by murdering Alexander V, but Ptolemy I of Egypt, Lysimachus of Macedon, and Seleucus of Syria allied against him. He then tried to attack Asia Minor (with Ptolemy I's encouragement), but he was captured by Seleucus and subsequently drank himself to death. **Ptolemaeum Philodelphum:** Ptolemy II Philodelphus ("Sister-Lover") (308–246 BCE). Ptolemy II was the son of

Ptolemy I and this third wife, Berenice. He expanded the Ptolomaic empire, fighting a number of battles with Antiochus I of Syria. His daughter, Berenice II, married Antiochus II, a union which would precipitate the Laodicean War (the Third Syrian War) when Antiochus died in 246. (See the note on "Antiochus" at §7.53.) He married Arsinoë I, daughter of Lysimachus the king of Macedon and Alexander's direct successor, and she gave birth to his children. Lysimachus in turn married Ptolemy II's sister Arsinoë II. After Lysimachus died, Ptolemy II married his sister, the widowed Arsinoë II, who brought with her some holding in the Aegean. In addition to expanding his empire, marrying the widowed sister was an Egyptian custom and so good policy for the ruler of Egypt. **Ptolemaeum Philopator Tryphon:** Ptolemy IV Philopator ("Father-Loving") (244–205 BCE). Ptolemy IV warred successfully against Antiochus III in the Fourth Syrian War (219–217). He also constructed the *Sema* in Alexandria, a tomb for Alexander and the Ptolemies. He was killed in a coup in 205. **Hippus Tyrius:** Hippus of Tyre. Unknown. Tyre was a major city of Phoenicia, famous for sending out colonies in the West, particularly Carthage. **lembum ... cumbam ... celetem ... cercyrum:** The *lembus* was a small, swift vessel with a sharp prow developed by pirates and used in navies. The *cumba* was very small, and could be rowed by a single man. The *celes* was used for sending messages quickly. The *cercyrus* was a large cargo vessel. **Cyrenenses:** The Greek city Cyrene in Africa was founded by Dorian colonists from Thera in 630 BCE. See Herodotus 4.150–8. It became a major city of North Africa, first as its own kingdom, then as a Ptolemaic possession, and finally as part of the Roman empire.

209. Copae: A town in Boeotia. The story that the town Copae was the source of the oar likely comes from the similarity of the town's name Κῶπαι (Kōpai) to the plural of the word for oar-handle: sing. κώπη (kōpē), pl. κῶπαι (kōpai). **Plataeae:** Another Boeotian town, Plataia's name, Πλαταῖα, is similar to the word for "oar blade": πλάτη (platē). **Icarus ... Daedalus:** After Daedalus, the famous inventor, built the Labyrinth in which Minos could imprison the Minotaur, Minos imprisoned Daeadalus as well with his son Icarus in a tower so that Daedalus could never share the secret of the Labyrinth. In the most well-known version of the myth, Daedalus fashions wings out of feathers and wax, so that he and Icarus can fly away. The wings work, but Icarus flies too close to the sun, melts his wax, and falls to his death in the sea that afterwards will bear his name: Icarian. A different version, however, has Daedalus and Icarus escape by ship (Diodorus 4.77). Icarus, unfortunately, fares no better in this version, falling into the sea as he disembarks the boat. **Pericles Atheniensis:** (495-429 BCE) the Athenian statesman. The reference here is to Pericles's building up of the Athenian fleet. Pericles came from a wealthy and aristocratic family, descended on his mother's side from the Alcmaeonids. Among his early civic duties, he was the choregos for Aeschylus's *Persae* in 472, but he didn't become politically prominent until the late 460s. In the 450s he focused on Athens' foreign policy and expanding its power, trying even to create a league of all Greeks, although he failed due to Spartan opposition. In the 440s and 430s he supported and guided Athens' building program. After having his rival, Thucydides son of Milesias (not the historian) ostracized in 443, he was elected *strategos* (one of the 10 chief magistrates of Athens) every year until his death by the plague in 429. Both Aristophanes and Thucydides the historian depict the Peloponnesian War (431–404 BCE) between Athens and Sparta as breaking out in no small part because of Pericles's policies. The Periclean strategy was to defeat Sparta through a war of attrition, relying on Athens' Long Walls and sea power to outlast the Spartan war effort. Pericles's early death in 429, however, prevented him from seeing the war through. **tectas longas:** Supply "*naves*". The ships are "*tectas*" in the sense that they had decks. **Thasii:** Thasos is an island in the northern Aegean just south of Thrace, which made it an excellent source for timber and particularly important to Athenian naval efforts. **Eupalamus:** The father of Daedalus. His name means "He with a skilled hand". **Anacharsis:** See the note at §7.198. **adminicula gubernandi:** The tiller. **Tiphys:** The steersman of the Argo on Jason's voyage for the Golden Fleece. **Minos:** King of Crete and son of Zeus and Europa. Like his brother Rhadamanthys, he became a judge in the underworld after his death. He was remembered by the Greeks as king of a major naval power (Herodotus1.171; Thucydides 1.41). We now call the pre-Mycenaean peoples of Crete "Minoans" after him. **Hyperbius Martis filius:** See the note at §7.194.

Chapter 57

210. Ionum: Different Greek city-states employed the alphabet differently, with states variously adding and substracting letters, sometimes even changing the value of the letter. The alphabet used by the eastern Ionians, which, among its many peculiarities, employed "H" for the vowel eta (a long "e" sound, like the "ai" in "wait") and introduced the new symbol Ω for long "o", began to spread. It was adopted at Athens in 403/2 and across the Greek world by about 370 BCE.

Part 4B: International Accords (§§210–15). Pliny ends Book VII with three brief cultural studies: the origin of writing, hair-cutting, and time-keeping as agreements between the nations of men. These three studies are not to be taken literally as the first consensus of all among nations ("Gentium consensus tacitus primus omnium" §210) but as analogues for civilization: the coming together of disparate peoples (gentium) in common feeling and understanding (consensus) despite the difference of language that comes between them (tacitus). Writing represents the preservation of thoughts (and thus of personalities) and their projection into the future; hair-cutting represents reflective self-improvement; and time-keeping is the bounding and control of nature. These are aspects of civilization, the greatest achievement and the signal characteristic of Man, and it is this that divides Man (Book VII) from Animal (Book VIII). This final section grows seamlessly from the list of inventors and mirrors the Introduction (§§1–8), opposing the salutary structure of human civilization to the natural misery into which Man is born. It is worth noting that while the list of inventors is primarily Greek, the international accords conclude with Romans. For Pliny, Man is the measure of all things, but the Roman is the measure of Man.

Chapter 58

210. veteres . . . Latinae: This indirect statement is the predicate of the main sentence "*Delphica [tabella] indicio erit*". **Graecas . . . Latinae:** Supply "*litteras/ae*". **Delphica antiqui aeris:** Supply "*tabella*" *vel sim.* "*Antiqui aeris*" is a genitive of material or quality. (AG §344–5) **Palatio:** Augustus's residence on the Palatine hill, which was enlarged and aggrandized by subsequent emperors, gives us our word "palace". **Minervae:** The goddess Athena mentioned in the inscription as the daughter of Zeus. **ΝΑΥΣΙΚΡΑΤΗΣ ΑΝΕΘΕΤΟ ΤΑΙ ΔΙΟΣ ΚΟΡΑΙ ΤΑΝ ΔΕΚΑΤΑΝ:** (Nausikratēs anetheto tāi dios korāi tān dekatān) "Nausicrates dedicated to the daughter of Zeus a tithe." The text is corrupt here and terribly confused, with different editors preferring different emendations. Scaliger read Ναυσικράτης Τισαμένου Ἀθηναῖος ἀνέθηκεν (Nausikratēs Tisamenou Athēnaios anethēken) "Nausicrates the Athenian, son of Tisamenos, dedicated [this]."

Chapter 59

211. anno CCCCLIIII: The date 454 AUC corresponds to 300 BCE. (AG §630) **Publio Titinio Mena:** Cf. Varro, *De re rustica* 2.11.10. Otherwise unknown. **Africanus sequens:** Publius Cornelius Scipio Aemilianus Africanus. See the note at §7.100.

Chapter 60

212. hic ratione accedens: "This one (i.e., the *tertius consensus*) happening by means of logic/science". A reliable means of telling the hour of the day objectively is difficult: the melting of notched candles and similar devices can show the uniform passage of time, but these are dependent on their operators. Sundials have the virtue (on a sunny day) of showing an objective time: all sundials in a given region will show the same time. They must, however, be calibrated to their latitude, so the lines on the sundial that Valerius Maximus Messala dedicated in Rome in 263 BCE (see below, §7.214) did not match the hours since it was calibrated for Catania in Sicily. **a quo . . . diximus secundo volumine:** Anaximenes of Miletus (ca. 585–ca. 528 BCE), the student of Anaximander of Miletus. See above §7.203 and Pliny, *NH* 2.187. Where Anaximander made the *apeiron* the first principle of nature, Anaximenes made air the first principle. (For more detailed discussion of Anaximenes, see Kirk, G. S., Raven, J. E., and Schofield, M., *The Presocratic Philosophers*, 2nd ed., Cambridge: Cambridge University Press, 2007, pp. 158–162.) **XII tabulis:** Rome's first written law code, written by a board of ten men ca. 450 BCE. **Rostra:** Lit., "beaks" referring to the battering rams fixed on the prows of ships. The *Rostra* was the speaker's platform on the south side of the *Comitium* in the Forum Romanum. In 338 BCE, the consul Gaius Maenius won a naval victory at Antium and adorned (what would now be called) the *Rostra* with the rams from the ships' prows. It was rebuilt several times in the succeeding centuries on the spot, until Julius Caesar moved it in 44 BCE. **Graecostasin:** Lit., "Greek stands". The Graecostasis was a platform on the southwest side of the *Comitium* in the Forum Romanum. It was built as an area where ambassadors from Greece (eventually from any foreign locale) could wait to meet with senators (since they were not allowed in the *Curia*) or listen to speeches from the *Rostra*. The *Curia Hostilia* was at the north of the *Comitium*, so when the consuls' attendant looked out from the *Curia*, the sun was between the *Rostra* and the *Graecostasis* at noon. **columna Maenia:** Erected in honor of Gaius Maenius, consul of 338 BCE. See the preceding note on "*Rostra*". It was located on the western side of the *Comitium*, just south of the *Carcer*. **carcerem:** The prison, or holding cell, in the Republic, located on the northwestern side of the *Comitium*. The underground portion, called the Tullianum (named either for the king Servius Tullius, or for the spring, *tullus*, that wells up there), was used to detain state prisoners who were awaiting execution. **primum Punicum bellum:** 264–241 BCE. Rome's first major conflict with Carthage, which (along with the Pyrrhic War below) in effect transformed a local Italian power into a regional Mediterranean force.

213. Pyrrho: Pyrrhus of Epirus. See the note at §7.20. The Pyrrhic War began in 281 BCE. **aedem Quirini:** A temple to Quirinus built on the site of a shrine to the same god. Papirius Cursor adorned it with spoils from the Samnite War, in which both he and his father had fought. The nature and attributes of Quirinus are unknown, but he seems to have been a god of the people gathered together as one unit; Kretschmer (*Glotta* 1920 pp. 147ff.) derives his name from *co-viri-um*. At some point he was also assimilated to Romulus as a founder and Romulus's wife, Hersilia, became assimilated with Quirinus's consort Hora. **Lucius Papirius Cursor:** Lucius Papirius Cursor, consul of 293 BCE. He defeated the Samnites in 293 and the Lucani in 272. The sundial he erected in 293 was the first in Rome. **Fabio Vestale:** Otherwise unknown.

214. Manio Valerio Messala: Manius Valerius Maximus Messala. Consul of 263 BCE and censor in 252. He conquered several towns in eastern Sicily and compelled Hieron II, tyrant of Syracuse, to make a truce with Rome, for which he celebrated a triumph. The sundial he dedicated in Rome came from Catania. **Catina:** Catania, a city on the eastern coast of Sicily at the foot of Mount Etna. **Papiriano:** Lucius Papirius Cursor. See the note at §7.213. **anno urbis CCCCLXXXXI:** The year 491 AUC, which corresponds to 263 BCE. (AG §630) **nec congruebant ad horas eius lineae:** See the note above at §7.212 on "*hic ratione accedens*". **Quintus Marcius Philippus:** Consul of 186 and 169 BCE, censor in 164. In 186, Marcius presided over the *Senatus Consultum de Bacchanalibus*, which prohibited Bacchanalia throughout Italy. In 169, he began the war with King Perseus of Macedon, which Lucius

Aemilius Paullus would finish, defeating him at the Battle of Pydna. **Lucio Paullo:** Lucius Aemilius Paullus, consul of 182 and 168 BCE, censor in 164. Paullus defeated King Perseus of Macedon at Pydna in 168 and he was responsible for bringing Greek hostages back to Rome, most notably the historian Polybius. (See the note on Polybius at §7.31.)

215. Scipio Nasica: Publius Cornelius Scipio Nasica Corculum, consul briefly in 162 BCE and again in 155, censor in 159. Scipio Nasica Corculum served at Pydna under Lucius Aemilius Paullus, prevented a permanent theater being built in Rome (the first one would be Pompey's—see the note at §7.20 "templi Veneris victricis"), and opposed Cato the Elder's call for war on Carthage. **Laenati:** Marcus Popillius Laenas, censor in 159. **aqua divisit horas:** A clepsydra, or water-clock. The water-clock varied in complexity from a simple pot with a hole in the bottom to a much more complex machine with gears, a dial, and a pointer to mark the passing hours. The clepsydra could even be rigged to bells or a gong to create an alarm clock. **anno urbis DXCV:** The year 595 AUC corresponds to 159 BCE. (AG §630)

Book VIII (1–34)

As the animal that opens Book VIII, it is only natural that the elephant is, according to Pliny, the "nearest to the human disposition" (proximum humanis sensibus [8.1]). Pliny invests the elephant with such emotion and inner life that it is easy to forget as one reads the Latin that he is referring to an animal and not another human tribe. That said, the structure of the passage is quite distinct from that of Book VII. Pliny begins with the ways in which the elephant is like mankind: he is impressed by its human-like senses (§1), and that it seems to understand human religion and engage in its own (§§2–3). The Roman reader, it is implied, may have noticed these qualities in elephants when it has seen them domesticated in triumphs or shows. Pliny then adds several anecdotes in which elephants practiced their tricks by night, learned to write in Greek, or actively deceived themselves, presumably in case the reader had missed seeing the earlier evidence in person (§§4–6). Humans exploit elephants for their ivory, but the elephants know this and will bury any tusks that break off in order to avoid rousing the interests of hunters (§§7–10). They have a complex inner life, too, traveling in communities, showing a sense of honor and shame, and feeling strong emotions like love (§§11–15).

After describing the elephant's human-like inner life, Pliny reverts to a naturalist's tone, describing how the Romans first experienced elephants. Here, he shows an evolution of Roman attitudes toward the animal (§§16–22). Pyrrhus first brought them to Italy, and when the Romans encountered them at Luca, they were so bewildered they named the animals "Lucan cows". Hannibal, too, brought elephants to Italy, where he compelled Roman captives to fight them for their freedom. A successful

Roman soldier had to be killed in secret lest contempt for the elephants spread among the army, which it inevitably did. By Pliny's day, elephants were an occasional sight in the circus, and they were so successful that the crowd at times sided with the elephants, as happened in a set of games sponsored by Pompey.

Their appearance in the circus naturally segues to a discussion of the means for trapping and taming elephants (§§23–6) and how they behave (and may be calmed) when upset (§27). From here, Pliny discusses the elephant's physiology: its gestation, diseases, and significant body parts— the trunk, hide, and ivory (§§28–31). The section concludes with the elephant's natural habitat: where it can be found and a detailed anecdote about its one predator, the giant snake (§32).

Chapter 1

1. ad reliqua . . . animalia: i.e., after leaving behind Man in Book VII. **Maximum ... proximumque:** Neuter because they agree with an understood "*animal*", rather than the predicate "*elephans*". **elephans:** The word is heteroclite, having both the forms "elephans, elephantis" and "elphantus, -i" (more common, including hereafter). It derives from the Greek ἐλέφας (elephas) meaning both "elephant" and, in Homer, ivory (*Iliad* 5.583). The Gate of Ivory ἐλέφας (elephas) in Hades sends forth false dreams ἐλεφαίρομαι (elephairomai) "to deceive, cheat with empty hopes," just as the Gate of Horn κέρας (keras) sends forth true dreams κραίνω (krainō), "to fulfill". (*Odyssey* 19.560–9; *Aeneid* 6.893–8). **sensibus:** here, something like "intelligence". **intellectus ... veneratio:** A list of nominative nouns governing objective genitives. (AG §§347–8) Supply an "*est*". **intellectus:** A noun, meaning "understanding". **illis:** Dative of possession. (AG §373)

2. auctores sunt: As often in Pliny, this clause introduces an indirect statement. **Mauretaniae:** Mauretania was the land of the Berber Moors

(Mauri) in northwest Africa where Morocco is today. Moors inhabited Mauretania as early as the 8th c. BCE, but did not assemble a well-defined kingdom until the 3rd century. Their kings played roles in the Hannibalic and Jugurthine Wars, and Mauretania was finally incorporated into the empire by Claudius in 44 CE. **Amilo:** The name of the river is uncertain, with possibilities including Amilo, Amilus, Audus, and Melillo; its modern counterpart is likewise obscure.

3. ante … quam: Take together. **naves conscendere:** Depends on "*creduntur*". **quod docilitatem attinet:** Literally, "a thing which pertains to their mildness", so "as far as their mildness is concerned". **regem adorant:** Meaning their human king. Aelian, *de Natura Animalium* 13.22 gives us this anecdote of Pyrrhus, and Martial, *de Spectaculis* 17 of the emperor. **Indis:** See the note at §7.21. **nothos:** Greek νόθος, for bastard, mixed-breed, or cross-breed.

Chapter 2

4. Romae: Locative. (AG §427) **iuncti:** In its etymological sense, "yoked". **Pompei Magni:** See the note at §7.34. See also Pliny, *NH* 7.95ff. **Africano triumpho:** 12 March, 81 BCE. The triumph was granted by Sulla after he defeated and killed Gnaeus Domitius Ahenobarus, a Marian partisan, and King Iarba of Numidia, who was harboring him. **India victa triumphante Libero patre:** The first ablative absolute depends upon the second: "When Liber Pater was celebrating a triumph after India had been conquered". **Libero patre:** An Italian fertility god identified with Dionysus. For Dionysus and elephants, see Diodorus Siculus 4.3.1: "He made war against India, making his return to Boeotia in the third year, bringing with him a noteworthy abundance of spoils, and he was the first to celebrate a triumph atop an Indian elephant." See §7.191 above.

Procilius: An antiquarian of the late Republic. **negat:** "says that … not", rather than "denies". Introduces indirect statement with "*potuisse …*

egredi", the subject of which is "*iunctos*". **Germanici Caesaris:** Germanicus Julius Caesar, son of the Drusus at §7.84. **inconditos meatus:** "confused gyrations".

5. non auferentibus ventis: A testament to the elephants' strength. **pyrriche:** Greek πυρρίχη, a war dance which Caesar brought to Rome when he made the children of the princes of Asia and Bithynia dance it. See §7.204, and Suetonius, *Caesar*, 39. "*pyrriche*" is ablative with "*lascivienti*". **puerperas:** The object of "*imitantes*", which agrees with "*singulos*". **homine:** Generic: "people", "mankind". **accubitum:** Supine with a verb of motion, "*iere*": "they went to to to dine". **quis:** For "aliquis". (AG §310a)

Chapter 3

6. certum est: Introduces indirect speech. **tardioris ingenii:** Genitive of quality. (AG §345) **in accipiendis:** Supply "*eis*": "in learning the things . . .". **repertum:** Supply "*esse*". The same story appears in Pseudo-Plutarch, *De Sollertia Animalium* §12. **adversis . . . funibus:** A rope ladder is probably meant here, but possibly a rope net or "rigging". **Mucianus:** Gaius Licinius Mucianus. See the note at §7.36. **ductus:** "the shapes". **Celtica:** Aelian 2.11 gives a similar story but has the elephant writing in Latin. The identification of an elephant's scratching with a foreign language might put one in mind of Poe's "Murders in the Rue Morgue" in which each of several characters identifies an ape's calls definitively with different languages they do not personally speak. "Celt" was a term originally employed by the Greeks and adopted by the Romans for a series of peoples that extended north of the Mediterranean from Spain to Turkey. They shared a common culture and art, similar languages, and a shared religion with a priesthood of druids. Despite all this, they were fiercely individualistic and did not unite into lasting kingdoms. **se vidente:** Referring to Mucianus. **Puteolis:** Ablative of place where. (AG §429) Modern Pozzuoli. Puteoli lies on the coast between Cumae and Naples, and by the end of the Republic, it had become a thriving resort town as well as a major port for trade with the East. **pontis:** A gangplank. **continente:** The land.

Chapter 4

7. expetendam: Does not go with "*esse*," but is a gerundive modifying "*praedam*": "the loot to be sought in them". **Iuba:** Raised as a Roman hostage after Caesar triumphed over Numidia in 46 BCE, Iuba was eventually instated as king there in 25 BCE and also granted Mauretania. In addition to a king, he was also scholar and author, although all of his works are now lost. **Herodotus:** (See the note at §7.10.) *Histories* 3.97. **tanto:** Ablative of degree of difference. (AG §414) **dentes:** Elephant tusks are in fact teeth. The whiteness ("*candore*") of a young elephant's tusks (mentioned at *NH* §8.8) is the tusk's enamel. As the elephant ages and the enamel wears away, the dentin beneath gives the tusk its characteristic ivory color. **quam ob rem:** I.e., because they are sought as *praeda*. **vilitas ossea:** Pliny says "bony worthlessness" instead of "worthless bone". **cessere luxuriae:** i.e., over-hunting.

8. dentium candore: See above at §8.7, "*dentes*". **circa hos:** The tusks. **quibus:** For "*eos quibus*". **minimi:** Supply "*dentes*". **tanti:** Genitive of value. Literally, "of so much worth", or in contemporary English "worth it". (AG §417) **fessi:** Wearied by the hunt. **inpactos:** From "*impingo*" and said of the "*dentes*". **arbori:** Dative with the compound "*inpactos*". **praeda:** Ablative of price (referring to the tusks) with "*se redimunt*" "redeem themselves, save themselves". (AG §§416–7)

Chapter 5

9. simpliciter: In the fashion of "*simplex*", i.e., by himself. **intremescere . . . dirigi:** This series of infinitives depends on an understood "*traditur*".

homine: Parallel in structure to "*vestigio*" in the ablative absolute "*vestigio hominis animadverso*". **erutum:** Supply "*vestigium*". **proximo:** Supply "*elephanto*". **omnium odori:** Literally, "for the scenting of all", i.e., "for all to sniff". **virus:** Second declension neuter. Supply "*traditur*" again.

10. hominis viso: Supply "*vestigio*". **ubi ante:** Depends on "*conspecto illo*"; "*illo*" here is "man". **elephanti:** Genitive, from "*elephantus*", not dative from "*elephans*". **mirentur:** potential subjunctive: "To be sure, they may marvel at the very rarity of the track . . .". (AG §§ 445–7)

11. elephanti: As in section 10, from "*elephantus*" (as also "*elephantum*" below), but here nominative. **cogit:** drives (*agit*) the herd from behind in concert with (*co-*) the leader, hence Rackham's "brings up the rear". **Antipater:** Antipater of Tarsus, the Stoic philosopher (d. 130/129 BCE). Ps.-Plutarch, *De sollertia animalium* refers to him and his comments on animals at 4.10 and also discusses elephants in section 12 of the same work. **Antiocho regi:** dative of possession. (AG §373) Antiochus III "the Great", grandson to Antiochus II (note at §7.53). He was king of Seleucid Syria from 222–187 BCE, restoring a kingdom in turmoil to stability and regaining control over a number of cities in revolt or under the rule of usurpers. His success was great enough that he expanded into Ptolemaic territory as far as Thrace, where he met the Romans. After some failed diplomatic exchanges, Antiochus III invaded Greece. The Romans defeated him in two battles: Thermopylae and Magnesia, both in 190. As a result, he ceded northern Anatolia to Rome. Antiochus died on campaign in 187. **Cato:** Cato the Elder, the censor. See the note at §7.61. **annalibus:** Dative with the compound verb "detraxerit". (AG §370) Cato the Elder's history of Roman war. See the note at §7.61. **detraxerit:** Literally, "drew out", but perhaps better "effaced" or "elided". **Punica acie:** Likely the Second Punic War. **Surum:** (See §7.61.) Most likely "the Syrian", from Greek Σῦρος (Sȳros, or Sūrus in Latin) but Pliny is making a pun on the Latin sūrus, stake, referring to his single tusk.

12. Aiax . . . Patroclum: Named for the Homeric hero Telamonian Ajax, "the Greater Ajax" and Patroclus, companion to Achilles. While "Ajax" is a suitable name for an elephant due to the former's size and strength, the story in question also plays on the death of Ajax. When Odysseus wins the contest for Achilles's armor, Ajax commits suicide, just as this elephant does when he loses the favorite position. Patroclus, likewise, boldly rallied the Argive warriors in battle against the Trojans, just as his namesake elephant boldly forded the river. **pronuntiatum:** Supply "*est*". **Patroclum:** object of "*donavit*". **ignominiae:** dative with the compound verb "*praetulit*". (AG §370) **verbenas:** Any of a number of kinds of foliage used in suppliant rituals, including bay, olive, and verbena.

13. biennio quinis, ut ferunt, cuiusque anni diebus: In English word order, "*biennio, ut ferunt, quinis diebus cuiusque anni*". **sexto:** Supply "*die*". **Aristophanes:** Aristophanes of Byzantium, the scholar, not the playwright. Aristophanes lived from 257-180 BCE and became the head of the library at Alexandria ca. 194. To him we owe critical editions of Alcaeus, Alcman, the *Iliad* and *Odyssey*, the *Theogony*, a complete edition of Pindar, and many other important works.

14. Menandrum Syracusanum: Unknown. **incipientis iuventae:** Genitive of quality: "of youthfulness, at the beginning", so "at the beginning of his youth". (AG §345) This is the so-called "*Ab urbe condita*" construction: "from the city, when it was founded" = "from the founding of the city". So too "of youth, when it begins" = "of the beginning of youth". (AG §497) **Ptolemaei:** This could refer to any of the Ptolemaic line. **Iuba:** See above at §8.7. **dilectam:** Supply "*ab elephanto*". **fuere argumenta:** The subject of "*fuere*" is "*argumenta*", while "*gaudium*", "*blanditiae*", and "*stipes*" are the predicates. **in sinum:** The lap of the beloved. **nec mirum:** Supply "*est*". This phrase introduces the indirect statement "*esse amorem*".

15. agnitum: Understand "*virum*". **Bocchus:** Bocchus I, king of Mauretania from ca. 110 BCE until his death in 49 BCE. **elephantis:**

Dative with the compound verb "*obiecisset*". (AG §370) **procursantibus:** Supply "*viris*". **ut ... fungerentur:** A noun clause of result depending on "*potuisse effici*": "it was not able to be brought about that ...". *Fungor*, along with *potior, utor, fruor*, and *vescor*, takes an ablative object.

Chapter 6

16. Pyrri regis bello: 280 BCE. See the note at §7.20 **Lucas ... Lucanis:** See Varro, *Lingua Latina*, 7.39. Lucania was a region of southern Italy corresponding roughly to the instep of the boot. It was colonized by Greeks beginning about 700 BCE as well as Italians (Oscans) about 400 BCE. All of these were hostile to the Romans during the Pyrrhic wars, and it was the Spartan colony Tarentum in this region that first sought aid from Pyrrhus in 281. **anno Urbis CCCCLXXIV:** If we count from 753 BCE, the traditional founding date of Rome as established by Varro, then AUC (ab urbe condita) 474 gives us 280 BCE. (AG §§630–1) **V annis ... additis:** i.e., AUC 479, or 275 BCE. **Luci Metelli:** Lucius Caecilius Metellus. Consul of 251 and 247 BCE, dictator in 224, and pontifex maximus from 243-221. **DIV:** AUC 504 = 250 BCE. **in Sicilia de Poenis captos:** In 250 BCE Lucius Caecilius Metellus captured elephants from the Carthaginians when he defeated them at Panormus. **ut quidam:** Conflicting accounts.

17. Verrius: Marcus Verrius Flaccus. (See note at §7.180.) **circo:** The Circus Maximus. *Circi* were used for chariot racing, and the Circus Maximus, meant here, dates all the way back to the kings. See §7.186. **placuisset:** the impersonal use of "*placet*" is the normal way to say "it is decided". So, "senatui placet," "it pleased the senate" = "the senate decided", much like the Greek construction with δοκεῖ (dokei). See also §7.141, 152. (AG §§207–8) **Lucius Piso:** Lucius Calpurnius Piso Censorius Frugi, consul of 133 BCE, censor in 120 BCE. He wrote an *Annales* down to his own time, which both Aulus Gellius and Pliny made use of. **ut ... incresceret:** Purpose clause. (AG §§529–33) **praepilatas:** Literally, "ball-tipped", so we might say "foiled".

Chapter 7

18. Hannibal: See note at §7.35. For the full story, which happened after the battle of Cannae, see Valerius Maximus 9.2 (ext.1–2). **pactus:** From "*pango*" or "*paciscor*". The participle introduces an indirect statement: "*dimitti . . . si interemisset*". **si interemisset:** A pluperfect subjunctive in indirect statement after a secondary sequence verb (*pactus*) standing in for a future perfect indicative. The original statement would have been: I promise that you will be dismissed if you will have killed the elephant. (AG §589) **qui abeuntem interficerent:** A relative clause of purpose. (AG §531.2) **proboscidem:** The Greek term προβοσκίς (proboscis). Literally, "means for food", but used of the elephant's trunk, just as it is now more commonly used for the similar appendage on some insects, such as the fly and butterfly.

19. Romae: Locative. (AG §427) **pugnasse:** The subject of the indirect statement is an understood "*elephantos*". **Fenestella:** (52 BCE–19 CE). Fenestella was an antiquarian and an annalist. His *Annales* ran at least to 57 BCE. **Claudi Pulchri:** Gaius Claudius Pulcher, aedile 99, cons. 92 BCE. **Marco Antonio Aulo Postumio coss.:** Consuls in 99 BCE. Marcus Antonius was also censor in 97 and a friend of Gaius Marius, and so a popularis, until he reversed allegiances and was killed in 87. **anno urbis DCLV:** AUC 655 = 99 BCE. (AG §§630–1) **Lucullorum:** Marcus Terentius Varro Lucullus and Lucius Licinius Lucullus Ponticus The two Luculli were brothers and aediles in 79 BCE. Licinius Lucullus was Sulla's literary executor in 78 and in 73 drove Mithridates out of Pontus and into Armenia, earning his cognomen "Ponticus". He achieved several more significant victories in the East, but fell prey to political forces back in Rome. At the passage of the *lex Manilia* in 67, Pompey took over command in the East. He triumphed in 63 but was no longer a political player, dying insane in 57/6. His brother, Terentius Varro Lucullus, was consul in 73, won victories in Danube region, and triumphed in 71. He died ca. 56.

20. templi Veneris Victricis: Dedicated in 55 BCE, the temple structure included what would be known as the Theater of Pompey, the first permanent theater built in Rome. It would also be the scene of Caesar's assassination in 44 BCE. **Gaetulis:** A nomadic Berber people of North Africa. **voluptati spectantibus:** The so-called double dative: "*voluptati*" is a dative of purpose; "*spectantibus*" is a dative of reference. (AG §376, 382) **in orbem:** "in arcs". **velut arte, non furore beluae, iacerentur:** The comparison to jugglers at once makes the elephants more human and draws attention to the equivalence, in the Roman mind, of their slaughter in the circus with simple entertainment.

21. Caesar dictator: 49 BCE. See the note at §7.91. **euripis:** Canals, from the Greek word εὔριπος (euripus), but here, perhaps, "a moat". **Nero princeps:** See Suetonius, *Life of Nero*, 11.2, and Tacitus, *Annales* 15.32. **equiti loca addens:** i.e., making a designated seating area for the Knighthood. The *Lex Roscia* in 67 BCE had established designated seats for the equites, but only at the theater, not the Circus. (See §7.117.) **Pompeiani:** Again, supply "*elephanti*". **dirasque:** curses. **quas . . . mox luit:** referring perhaps to Pompey's death in 48 BCE.

22. Caesari dictatori tertio consulatu: 46 BCE. **eodem . . . dimicante:** ablative absolute. **in consummatione gladiatorum:** Rackham: "the crowning exploit of the gladiators' careers"; Ernout: "at the end of their [i.e., the gladiators'] career".

23. manu: i.e., its trunk. **quod:** For "*aliquod*". (AG §310a) **idque cum:** "and this, even though . . .". **per vices:** "in turns".

Chapter 8

24. India: See note at §7.21.

26. Trogodytae: See the note at §7.23. **Aethiopiae:** See the note at §7.6. **novissimum:** "last part". **laeva:** Supply "*manu*". **humi longius:** "deep in the ground." **sagittarum venabula:** Literally, "spears of arrows": "*sagittarum*" is a genitive of description: spears-as-arrows. The passage describes a makeshift scorpion. See §7.201. **secuntur:** A later spelling of "*sequuntur*".

Chapter 9

27. multo: Ablative of degree of difference. (AG §414) **qui . . . coerceant:** Relative clause of purpose. (AG §531.2) **alias:** The adverb. **circa coitus:** i.e., when in heat. **efferantur:** From *effero* (1), not from *effero, efferre*. **magnaque ex parte:** "in large part". **iidem minimo suis stridore terrentur:** "*suis*" is from "*sus*", not "*suus*". For elephants' reaction to the squealing of pigs, see ps.-Plutarch, *Sollertia animalium* 32.8; Seneca, *De ira* 2.11.5; Aelian, *de Natural Animalium* 1.38, 16.36; *Geoponica* 15.1. **Indicum . . . magnitudo est:** This is generally held to be inaccurate, but there are three major species of elephant: the African bush elephant, the African forest elephant, and the Asian elephant (here called "Indian"). Of the three, the African forest elephant is in fact the smallest. The forest elephant, however, is sub-Saharan, so contact with Rome would have been limited.

Chapter 10

28. decem annis . . . Aristoteles biennio: See note at §7.15. Aristotle is correct: the gestation period of an elephant is about 22 months. **nec amplius quam [semel gignere pluresque quam] singulos:** some manuscripts read "give birth not more than once," while others read "give birth not more than one at a time". The latter is correct: twins do occur, but rarely. The idea that elephants give birth only once in their life may come from the long infancy of the elephant calf, which feeds from its mother's milk for five years. **ducenis annis . . . CCC:** Elephant lifespans mirror those of humans: they tend to live only up to about 70 years. **nare . . . non possint:** An inaccuracy. Elephants are excellent swimmers. **a sudore:** "due to sweat".

29. maxime odere murem: This is the first record of elephants' fear of mice. The fear, while counterintuitive, has proven to be real. **videre:** The syncopated form of "*viderunt*", not the infinitive. **sanguisugam:** The term "blood-sucker" stuck, as it is the source of the words for leech in French (*sangsue*), Italian (*sanguisuga*), Portuguese (*sanguessuga*), and Spanish (*sanguijuela*). **animae:** here, "breath".

30. id et tanta vastitas: "*id*" refers back to "*taedio muscarum*"; "*et*" = "*etiam*". **extentis:** Supply "*cancellis*".

31. sibi . . . videtur: Probably the personal construction "he seems to himself". Cf. "mihi videor". We might say, "He likes to think . . .". **Polybius:** (ca. 200–ca. 118 BCE) From an important Achaean family, after the Battle of Pydna in 168, Polybius was taken as a hostage to live in Rome. He quickly became friends with Scipio Aemilianus, becoming a member of the so-called "Scipionic Circle". (See §7.100.) Polybius wrote, among other things, a history whose purpose was to explain the rise of Rome from a tiny city to ruler of the Mediterreanean. Only books 1–5 survive in full of the original 40. The rest, where they exist, are in summary. This passage occurs at 34.16.1. **Gulusa:** A son of Masinissa, king of Numidia. See Livy, 42.23. The diminutive "*regulo*" might be rendered "chieftain".

Chapter 11

32. Syrticas solitudines: The Gulf of Sidra on the coast of Libya. See also Pliny, §7.14. **Aethiopes et Trogodytae:** See notes at §7.6 and §7.23, respectively. **dracones:** Rackham suggests "pythons", while Ernout suggests either "lions" or an indeterminate snake. **et ipsos:** "*et*" = "*etiam*".

"*ipsos*" = "*elephantos*". **ut . . . ambiant . . . praestringant:** A result clause. (AG §536) **nexuque:** "twist, coil".

Chapter 12

33. una . . . difficultas: Supply "*est*". **ascendendi:** The gerund depends on "*difficultas*". **ille:** i.e, the elephant. **attritum:** An abstract noun from "*attritus, -us*", not a participle. **fit ut . . . reperiantur:** "*ut*" introduces a subjunctive noun clause that serves as the subject of "*fit*". **caeca ac fame et maeroris tabe confecti:** The conjunction "*ac*" joins two broader concepts, and "*et*" two nearer concepts. We might rewrite it this way:

(1) *caeci*
ac
(2) *confecti*

    (a) *fame*
    et
    (b) *maeroris tabe*

34. quam . . . attulerit: In English word order: "*quam aliam causam tantae discordiae aliquis attulerit*," but "*aliquis*" as usual is drawn into the second position after the introductory "*quam*", and "*causa*" almost always follows its genitive, giving us "*quam quis aliam tantae discordiae causam attulerit*". **spectaculum sibi ac paria:** the two nouns are in apposition to each other. Either "nature, making the pair a spectacle for herself" or "nature, making a spectacle for herself, and that, a pair of them! [i.e., elephant and snake]". The latter is more appealing, as it makes sense of the "*ac*". **elephantis frigidissimum . . . conmorique:** Indirect statement depending on "*fama*".

Appendix I:
Numerals, Measures and Abbreviations

Numerals

Numeral	Cardinals	Ordinals	Adverbs	Distributives
I	unus	primus, -a, -um	semel	singuli, -ae, -a
II	duo	secundus	bis	bini
III	tres	tertius	ter	terni
IV	quattuor	quartus	quater	quaterni
V	quinque	quintus	quinquiens	quini
VI	sex	sextus	sexiens	seni
VII	septem	septimus	septiens	septeni
VIII	octo	octavus	octiens	octoni
IX	novem	nonus	noviens	noveni
X	decem	decimus	deciens	deni
XI	undecim	undecimus	undeciens	uneni
XII	duodecim	duodecimus	duodeciens	duodeni
XIII	tredecim	tredecimus	terdeciens	terni deni
XIV	quattuordecim	decimus et quartus	quattuordeciens	quaterni deni
XV	quindecim	quindecimus	quindeciens	quini deni
XVI	sedecim	decimus et sextus	sedeciens	seni deni
XVII	septendecim	decimus et septimus	septiens deciens	septeni deni
XVIII	duodeviginti	duodevicesimus	duodeviciens octiens deciens	duodeviceni octoni deni

Numeral	Cardinals	Ordinals	Adverbs	Distributives
XIX	undeviginti	undevicesimus	undeviciens noviens deciens	undeviceni noveni diceni
XX	viginti	vicesimus	viciens	viceni
XXX	triginta	tricesimus	triciens	triceni
XL	quadraginta	quadragesimus	quadragies	quadrageni
L	quinquaginta	quinquagesimus	quinquagies	quinquageni
LX	sexaginta	sexagesimus	sexagies	sexageni
LXX	septuaginta	septuagesimus	septuagies	septuageni
LXXX	octoginta	octogesimus	octogiens	octogeni
XC	nonaginta	nonagesimus	nonagiens	nonageni
C	centum	centesimus	centiens	centeni
CC	ducenti	ducentesimus	ducentiens	duceni
CCC	trecenti	trecentesimus	trecentiens	treceni
CD	quadringenti	quadringentesimus	quadrincentiens	quadrigeni
D	quingenti	quingentesimus	quingentiens	quingeni
DC	sescenti	sescentesimus	sescenties	sesceni
DCC	septingenti	septingentesimus	septingenties	septingeni
DCCC	octingenti	octingentesimus	octingenties	octingeni
CM	nongenti	nongentesimus	nongenties noningenties	nongeni
M	mille	millensimus	miliens	milleni
1	one	first	once	one at a time
10	ten	tenth	ten times	ten at a time
100	one hundred	one hundredth	one hundred times	one hundred at a time

Common Roman Praenomina (by abbreviation)

A	Aulus	L	Lucius	Ser	Servius
Ap(p)	Appius	M	Marcus	Sex	Sextus
C	Gaius	M'	Manius	S(p)	Spurius
Cn	Gnaeus	N	Numerius	T	Titus
D	Decimus	P	Publius	Ti(b)	Tiberius
F	Faustus	Post	Postumus	V	Vibius
K	Caeso	Q	Quintus	Vop	Vopiscus

Weights and Measures

See Smith, William, *Classical Dictionary of Greek and Roman Biography, Mythology, and Geography*, ed. Charles Anthon, New York: Harper and Brothers, 1851, pp. 1023–1039.

1. Distance and Length

Latin name	Conversion (pes as base)	English	Metric	English Imperial
mille passuum	5000 (1000 *passus*)	mile	1.48 km	4854 ft
stadium	625	stade/furlong	185 m	607.14 ft
passus	5 (double pace)	double pace	1.48 m	4.854 ft
gradus	2½	pace	740 mm	2.427 ft
pes	1	foot	296 mm	0.971 ft
uncia	⅟₁₂	inch/thumb	24.6 mm	0.971 in

Latin name	Conversion (uncia as base)	English	Metric	English Imperial
cubitus	18	cubit	444 mm	1.456 ft
palmus	3	palm	74 mm	0.243 ft
uncia	1	inch/thumb	24.6 mm	0.971 in
digitus	¾	finger	18.5 mm	0.728 in

2. Weights

Latin name	Conversion		English	Metric	English Avoirdupois
	(uncia)	(libra)			
as / libra / pondus	12	1	pound	328.9g	11.60 oz
dodrans	9	¾	pound	246.7g	8.70 oz
semis	6	½	pound	164.5g	5.80 oz
quadrans	3	¼	pound	82.2g	2.90 oz
uncia	1	$\frac{1}{12}$	ounce	27.4g	0.967 oz
semuncia	½	$\frac{1}{24}$	ounce	13.7g	0.483 oz

3. Coinage in the Time of Pliny

Name	Value (Aureus = 1)	Value (As = 1)
aureus	1	400
denarius	25	16
sestertius	100	4
dupondius	200	2
as	400	1
semis	800	½
quadrans	1600	¼

Appendix II:
Images

Maps of the Roman Forum are patterned after Samuel Ball Platner, *Topography and Monuments of Ancient Rome* (Boston, MA: Allyn and Bacon, 1904), p. 165.

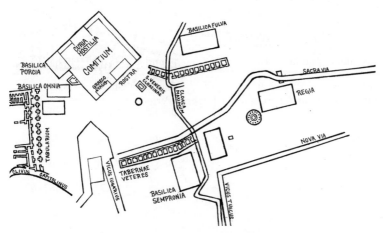

Figure A1 Roman Forum in the Republican Period.

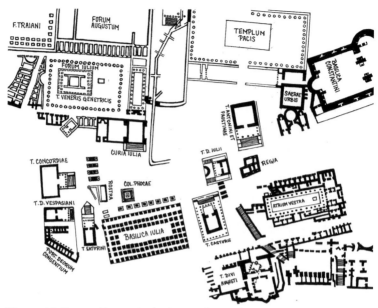

Figure A2 Roman Forum in the Imperial Period.

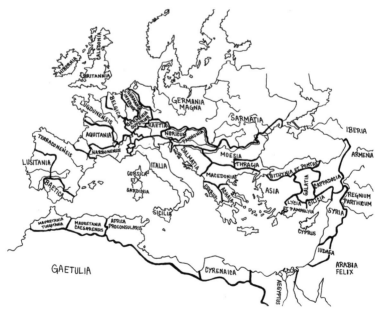

Figure A3 Roman Empire, 69 CE.

Glossary

abdicatio, -ionis, *n*. f. a disavowal

abdico (1), *v*. to announce, renounce

abdo, abdere, abdidi, abditum, *v*. to hide, conceal, remove

abeo, abire, abivi, abitum, *v*. to go away, depart, pass away

abicio, abicere, abieci, abiectum, *v*. to throw away, cast down

abigo, abigere, abegi, abactum, *v*. to drive away

ablegatio, -ionis, *n*. f. a sending away, exile

aboleo, abolere, abolevi, abolitum, *v*. to abolish, destroy

aborior, aboriri, abortus, *v*. to disappear, fail

abortivus, a, um, *adj*. abortive, causing an abortion, pertaining to premature birth

abripio, abripere, abripui, abreptum, *v*. to tear away, drag away, squander

abscondo, abscondere, abscondidi, absconditum, *v*. to hide away, make disappear

absolvo, absolvere, absolvi, absolutum, *v*. to absolve, dismiss, complete

absum, abesse, afui, afuturum, *v*. to be away, be absent

absumo, absumere, absumpsi, absumptum, *v*. to take away, consume

abundo (1), *v*. to overflow, be abundant

abundus, -a, -um, *adj*. copious

ac, *conj*. and also (variant *atque*)

accedo, accedere, accessi, accessum, *v*. to approach, add

accensus, -i, *n*. the attendant of a magistrate (from *accenseo*)

accido, accidere, accidi, *v*. to happen, fall

accipio, accipere, accepi, acceptum, *v*. to receive, accept, hear

accumbo, accumbere, accubui, accubitum, *v*. to lie down, go to table

accusatio, -ionis, *n*. f. accusation, indictment

accuso (1), *v*. to blame, call to account, indict

acer, acris, acre, *adj*. sharp, stinging

acervus, -i, *n*. m. heap

acesco, acescere, acui, *v*. to grow sour

acies, -iei, *n*. f. keenness, pupil, battle line

acinus, -i, *n*. m. (pl. *acina, -orum*), a berry, grape, seed

Actiacus, -a, -um, *adj.* pertaining to the city Actium

adcresco, adcrescere, adcrevi, adcretum, *v.* to grow, increase

adcubo, adcubare, *v.* to lie next to

addo, addere, addidi, additum, *v.* to add, bring to

adduco, adducere, adduxi, adductum, *v.* to adduce, convey to a place

adeo, *adv.* so far, to such an extent, very

adeo, adire, adivi, aditum, *v.* to approach

adficio, adficere, adfeci, adfectum, *v.* to influence, affect

adimo, adimere, ademi, ademptum, *v.* to take away, destroy

adfero, adferre, adtuli, adlatum, see "*affero*"

adfinis, -is, *n.* mf, neighboring, related by marriage

adfligo, adfligere, adflixi, adflictum, *v.* to beat, ruin, cast down

adfor, adfari, adfatus, *v.* to speak to, address

adhaereo, adhaerere, adhaesi, adhaesum, *v.* to cleave to, stick to

adhaeresco, adhaerescere, adhaesi, adhaesum, *v.* to stick to, cling to, suit

adhuc, *adv.* still, yet, to this point

adicio, adicere, adieci, adiectum, *v.* to throw toward, apply, add

adigo, adigere, adegi, adactum, *v.* to drive (to), bring to

adimo, adimere, ademi, ademptum, *v.* to take away, deprive

adipiscor, adipisci, adeptus, *v.* to attain, achieve, arrive at

adligo (1), *v.* to bind, hold fast to

adminiculum, -i, *n.* n. prop, stay, support

admirabilis, -is, -e, *adj.* wonderful, marvelous, astonishing

admiratio, -ionis, *n.* f. admiration, surprise, wonder

admodum, *adv.* very, much, to a high degree

admoneo, admonere, admonui, admonitum, *v.* to admonish, warn, bring to mind

admoveo, admovere, admovi, admotum, *v.* to move toward

adnitor, adniti, adnisus, *v.* to lean on, strive for

adnoto (1), *v.* to put a note, register, remark

adnumero (1), *v.* to count to, give the number of

adnuntio (1), *v.* to announce, proclaim

adoptio, -ionis, *n.* f. adoption

adopto (1), *v.* to choose, select

adoro (1), *v.* to pray to

adpeto, adpetere, adpetivi, adpetitum, *v.* to strive after, grasp after, attack

adporto (1), *v.* to carry to, bring

adprehendo, adprehendere, adprehendi, adprehensus, *v.* to lay hold of, seize

adpropo (1), *v.* to assent to, approve

adscribo, adscribere, adscripsi, adscriptum, *v.* to ascribe, attribute

adsero, adserere, adserui, adsertum, *v.* to declare, assert

adservo (1), *v.* to watch over, guard

adsiduus, -a, -um, *adj.* constant, continuous

adstipulatus, -us, *n.* m. assent

adstipulor (1), *v.* to agree with

adtribuo, adtribuere, adtribui, adtributum, *v.* to bestow, add to

adulterinus, -a, -um, *adj.* adulterous, false

adulterium, -i, *n.* n. adultery

aduro, adurere, adussi, adustum, *v.* to set fire to

adveho, advehere, advexi, advectum, *v.* to carry to, convey to, bring

advenio, advenire, adveni, adventus, *v.* to arrive at

adversus, -a, -um, *adj.* turned toward; *prep.* (+ acc) opposite, against, facing

adverto, advertere, adverti, adversum, *v.* to turn toward, steer toward a place

advespero (1), to be evening, grow dark

aedes, aedis, *n.* f. building, shrine, temple

aedificium, -i, *n.* n. building, edifice

aedilis, -is, -e, *adj.* an aedile

aedilitas, -tatis, *n.* f. the office of aedile

aeger, aegra, aegrum, *adj.* ill, diseased

aegritudo, aegritudinis, *n.* f. illness, sickness

aegrotus, -a, -um, *adj.* ill, sick

Aegyptus, -i, *n.* m. Egypt

aeneus, -a, -um, *adj.* made of bronze

aequitas, -tatis, *n.* f. equity, fairness, equalness

aequo (1), *v.* to make equal

aequus, -a, -um, *adj.* equal, fair, level; "*ex aequo*": in like manner, equally

aer, aeris, *n.* m. air

aerarius, -a, -um, *adj.* made of copper or its alloys, pertaining to a coppersmith

aes, aeris, *n.* bronze, money

aes alienum, aeris alieni, *n.* n. debt

aestas, aestatis, *n.* f. Summer

aestimatio, -ionis, *n.* f. estimation, valuation

aestimo (1), *v.* to estimate, value, rate

aestus, -us, *n.* m. heat

aetas, aetatis, *n.* f. age, time of life

aeternus, -a, -um, *adj.* eternal

Aethiopia, -ae, *n.* an ill-defined country in Africa

Aethiops, Aethiopis, *n.* m. a person from Aethiopia

aevum, -i, *n.* n. a lifetime, age, eternity

affectus, -us, *n.* m. affect, affection, state of mind, state of body

affero, afferre, attuli, allatum, *v.* to carry to, bring upon, produce

Africa, -ae, *n.* f. the area south of the Mediterranean, modern North Africa

Africanus, -a, -um, *adj.* pertaining to Africa

agelastus, -a, -um, *adj.* "not laughing"

ager, agri, *n.* m. field, territory

agger, aggeris, *n.* m. a pile, mound of rubbish

agmen, agminis, *n.* n. battleline, procession

agnosco, agnoscere, agnovi, agnitum, *v.* to know a person well, to acknowledge

ago, agere, egi, actum, *v.* to do

agrarius, -a, -um, *adj.* pertaining to land, agrarian

ala, -ae, *n.* wing

Albani, -orum, *n.* m. pl. the people of Albania

albus, -a, -um, *adj.* white

ales, alitis, *adj.* swift, winged; *n.* mf. a large bird

alias, *adv.* at another time

alibi, *adv.* elsewhere

alienus, -a, -um, *adj.* pertaining/belonging to someone else

alimentum, -i, *n.* food, nourishment

alioqui, *adv.* in other respects (also *alioquin*)

aliquando, *adv.* at some time, at any time

aliquantisper, *adv.* for some period of time

aliquis, aliquid, *pron.* someone, something (feminine occasionally *aliqua*)

aliquot, some number, several

alius, -a, -ud, *pron., adj.* another (of any number)

allego (1), *v.* to send on a commission, dispatch

alligo (1), *v.* to bind, hold fast

alo, alere, alui, altum, *v.* to feed, nourish

Alpes, Alpium, *n.* f.pl. the Alps

alter, altera, alterum, *pron.* the other of two

alterno (1), *v.* to do in turns

alternus, -a, -um, *adj.* by turns, alternate

altitudo, altitudinis, *n.* f. altitude, height, depth

alumnus, a, um, *adj*. nourished, nursed; *n*. mf. a charge, pupil

alveus, -i, *n*. m. a hollow, cavity, riverbed

alvus, -i, *n*. m. belly, paunch

ambages, -is, *n*. f. roundabout, digression

ambio, ambire, ambivi, ambitum, *v*. to go around, encompass

ambitio, -tionis, *n*. f. ambition

ambo, ambae, ambo, *adj*. both

ambulo (1), *v*. to walk, stroll

amburo, amburere, ambussi, ambustum, *v*. to scorch, consume by fire

Amilo, -onis, *n*. m. a river in Mauretania

amitto, amittere, amisi, amissum, *v*. to lose, send away

ammentum, -i, *n*. n. a strap, thong

amnis, amnis, *n*. m. river

amo (1), *v*. to love

amor, amoris, *n*. f. love

amplexor (1), *v*. to esteem, love, embrace repeatedly

amplitudo, amplitudinis, *n*. f. breadth, extent, bulk

amplus, -a, -um, *adj*. full, ample, abundant

amputo (1), *v*. to cut off, prune

anaphora, -ae, *n*. f. the rising of the stars

anceps, ancipitis, *adj*. two-sided, double-headed

ancilla, -ae, *n*. f. handmaid

ancora, -ae, *n*. f. anchor

androgynus, -i, *n*. m. hermaphrodite

anguis, -is, *n*. mf. snake, serpent

angulus, -i, *n*. m. angle, corner

angustus, -a, -um, *adj*. narrow, small, unspacious

animadverto, animadvertere, animadverti, animadversum, *v*. to turn one's mind to, pay attention

animal, animalis, *n*. n. animal

animator, -oris, *n*. one who animates

animo (1), *v*. to fill with breath, animate

animus, -i, *n*. m. mind, soul, intellect

annalis, annalis, *n*. annal, account of a year's events

annus, -i, *n*. m. year

annuus, -a, -um, *adj*. yearly, year-long

ante, *prep*. (+ acc), before

antea, *adv*. before, formerly

antegenitalis, -is, -e, *adj.* before birth

antenna, -ae, *n.* f. the horizontal yard attached to a mast

antequam, *conj.* before

Anthropophagus, -i, *n.* m. a member of a tribe of human-eaters

antiquus, -a, -um, *adj.* old, belonging to prior time

antistes, antistitis, *n.* m./f. high-priest/ess

anxietas, -tatis, *n.* f. the state of being anxious

aperio, aperire, aperui, apertum, *v.* to expose, uncover, open

apicula, -ae, *n.* f. little bee

apis, -is, *n.* f. bee

appareo, apparere, apparui, apparitum, *v.* to appear, become visible

appellatio, -tionis, *n.* f. an address, appeal, naming

appello (1), *v.* to call, appeal

Appenninus, -i, *n.* m. Apennine Mountains

apud, *prep.* (+ acc.) with, at, by, near (much like French *chez*)

aqua, -ae, *n.* f. water

Aquilo, Aquilonis, *n.* m. the North Wind

Arabia, -ae, *n.* f. the country Arabia

Arabs, Arabis, *adj.* from Arabia

aratrum, -i, *n.* n. plow

arbitror, arbitrari, arbitratus, *v.* to credit, believe, adjudge

arbor, arboris, *n.* f. tree

arcanus, -a, -um, *adj.* secret

Arcas, Arcadis, *n.* m. Arcadian

arceo, arcere, arcui, arctum, *v.* to keep off, enclose, shut up

arcus, -us, *n.* m. bow, arch

adoro (1), *v.* to speak to, beseech

aresco, arescere, *v.* to grow dry

argenteus, -a, -um, *adj.* made of silver

argentum, -i, *n.* n. silver

argumentor, -ari, -atus, *v.* to prove, adduce argument

argumentum, -i, *n.* n. argument, evidence, proof

arguo, arguere, argui, argutum, *v.* to prove, assert, censure

aries, arietis, *n.* m. a ram, battering, the Ram of the Zodiac

Arimaspus, -i, *n.* m. an Arimaspus

arma, -orum, *n.* n. pl. arms, weapons

armamentarium, -i, *n.* n. armory, arsenal

armatura, -ae, *n.* f. equipment, armor, arms

armentum, -i, *n*. n. cattle used for plowing
armilla, -ae, *n*. f. armband, bracelet
armo (1), *v*. to arm, equip with weapons
armum, -i, *n*. n. arm, weapon, armor
aro (1), *v*. to plow
ars, artis, *n*. f. art, skill
artifex, artificis, *n*. m. craftsman, artisan
arto (1), *v*. to contract, draw together
aruspicium, -i, *n*. n. divination; (also *haruspicium*)
arx, arcis, *n*. f. citadel
ascendo, ascendere, ascendi, ascensum, *v*. to climb, go up
ascia, -ae, *n*. f. mattock, carpenter's axe
Asia, -ae, *n*. f. Asia, Asia Minor
aspectus, -us, *n*. m. sight, appearance, aspect, a looking at
assigno (1), *v*. to mark out, assign, appoint
astrologia, ae, *n*. f. astrology, astronomy, study of the stars
at, *conj*. but, but yet
Athenae, -arum, *n*. f. pl. the city Athens, in Attica
Atheniensis, -is, -e, *adj*. Athenian, of Athens
athleta, -ae, *n*. m. athlete, prize-fighter
athleticus, -a, -um, *adj*. pertaining to an athlete
atque, *conj*. and also (variant *ac*)
attamen, *adv*. = *tamen*
attero, atterere, attrivi, attritum, *v*. to rub away, diminish
attineo, attinere, attinui, attentum, *v*. to attain, detain
attingo, attingere, attigi, attactum, *v*. to touch
attribuo, attribuere, attribui, attributum, *v*. to annex, assign to, attribute to
attritus, -us, *n*. m. rubbing on, rubbing against
auctor, auctoris, *n*. m. author
aucupium, -i, *n*. n. bird-catching
audacia, -ae, *n*. f. daring, boldness
audeo, audere, ausus, *v. semi-deponent*, to dare.
audio, audire, audivi, auditum, *v*. to hear
auditus, -us, *n*. m. hearing
aufero, auferre, abstuli, ablatum, *v*. to take away, bear off, withdraw
augur, auguris, *n*. mf. an augur, diviner
augurium, -i, *n*. n. augury, divination
aura, -ae, *n*. f. breeze, air

aureus, -a, -um, *adj.* golden
auriga, -ae, *n.* f. charioteer
auris, -is, *n.* f. ear
aurum, -i, *n.* n. gold
auspicium, -i, *n.* n. auspicy, divination by birds
auspicor, auspicari, auspicatus, *v.* to take auspices
autem, *adv.* moreover, however
auxilior (1), *v.* to bring help to
avaritia, -ae, *n.* f. greed
avello, avellere, avelli/avulsi, avulsum, *v.* to tear away
averto, avertere, averti, aversum, *v.* to turn away
avidus, -a, -um, *adj.* greedy
avis, avis, *n.* f. bird
avunculus, -i, *n.* m. uncle on the mother's side
avus, -i, *n.* m. grandfather

babylonius, -a, -um, *adj.* of Babylon, a Babylonian
balineum, -i, *n.* n. bath
ballista, ae, *n.* f. a type of large catapult
barba, -ae, *n.* f. beard
Basterni, -orum, *n.* m. pl. a people conquered by Pompey the Great
bellator, -oris, *n.* m. warrior
bellicus, -a, -um, *adj.* pertaining to war, military
bello (1), *v.* to wage war
bellum, -i, *n.* n. war
belua, -ae, *n.* f. beast, monster, elephant
beneficium, -i, *n.* n. kindness, benefit
benignus, -a, -um, *adj.* kindly
bibliotheca, -ae, *n.* f. library
bibo, bibere, bibi, bibitum, *v.* to drink
biduus, -a, -um, *adj.* two days long
biennium, -i, *adj.* two-year period
bigae, -arum, *n.* f. pl. two-horse chariot
bini, -ae, -a, *adj.* two by two
bipennis, -is, -e, *adj.* having two wings
biremis, -is, -e, *adj.* bireme, having two banks of oars
bis, *adv.* twice
bitumen, -minis, *n.* n. bitumen, pitch

blandimentum, -i, *n*. n. flattery, a charm
blanditiae, -arum, *n*. f. pl. flattery
bonus, -a, -um, *adj*. good, noble
Borysthenes, -is, *n*. m. a river in Sarmatia
bos, bovis, *n*. m. (dative/ablative plural: *bubus*) cow, ox
brachium, -i, *n*. n. arm
breviarium, -i, *n*. n. summary
brevis, -is, -e, *adj*. brief, short, little, small
brevitas, -tatis, *n*. f. shortness
bruma, -ae, *n*. f. the shortest day of the year (cf. brevissima), winter

cacumen, -minis, *n*. n. peak, utmost point
cadaver, cadaveris, *n*. n. dead body, corpse
caecus, -a, um, *adj*. blind, invisible
caedo, caedere, cecidi, caesum, *v*. to cut, hew, lop, slaughter
caeles, caelitis, *adj*. heavenly
caelum, -i, *n*. n. sky
calamitas, -tatis, *n*. f. misfortune, mishap
calcio (1) = calceo (1), *v*. to shoe, put on shoes
calco (1), *v*. to tread upon
calculus, -i, *n*. small stone
calidus, -a, -um, *adj*. hot, warm, fiery
caliga, ae, *n*. f. soldier's boot
callum, -i, *n*. n. hardened, thick skin
calor, caloris, *n*. m. heat
campus, i, *n*. m. field, plain
canalis, -is, *n*. m. channel, groove, pipe
cancellatim, *adv*. in the shape of a lattice
cancelli, -orum, *n*. m. lattice
cancello (1), *v*. to make a lattice
candidus, -a, -um, *adj*. white, shining, bright
candor, candoris, *n*. m. brightness, splendor
canesco, canescere, *v*. to grow white, grow old
caninus, -a, -um, *adj*. pertaining to a dog
canis, canis, *n*. m./f. dog, Dog Star
Cannae, -arum, *n*. f. pl. a town in southeastern Italy, site of a battle with
　　Hannibal in August 216 BCE
cano, canere, cecini, cantum, *v*. to sing

cantus, -us, *n.* m. song

capax, capacis, *adj.* (+ gen.) capacious, spacious

capillus, -i, *n.* m. hair of the head

capio, capere, cepi, captum, *v.* to catch, grab

Cappadocia, -ae, *n.* f. Cappadocia, modern Anatolia in central Turkey

capra, -ae, f. she-goat

captivus, -a, -um, *adj.* pertaining to a prisoner, captive

caput, capitis, *n.* n. head

carcer, carceris, *n.* jail

careo, carere, carui, caritum, *v.* (+ abl., gen.) to lack, be in need of

caritas, -tatis, *n.* f. dearness, affection, love

carmen, carminis, *n.* n. song, poem

carnifex, carnificis, *n.* m. executioner

caro, carnis, *n.* m. flesh

carpentum, -i, *n.* n. wagon

casa, -ae, *n.* f. hut

castellum, -i, *n.* n. fort, stronghold

castigo (1), *v.* to chastise, punish, reprove

castra, -orum, *n.* n. pl. military camp

castrensis, -is, -e, *adj.* pertaining to a military camp

casus, -us, *n.* m. vicissitude

catapulta, -ae, *n.* f. catapult

catena, -ae, *n.* f. chain

caterva, -ae, *n.* f. crowd, troop

catulus, -i, *n.* m. cub, whelp

cauda, -ae, *n.* f. tail

causa, -ae, *n.* f. cause, case

caveo, cavere, cavi, cautum, *v.* to take care, guard against

caverna, -ae, *n.* f. cavern, cave, hollow

cavo (1), *v.* to hollow out, excavate

cedo, cedere, cessi, cessum, *v.* to go, advance, yield

celeber, celebris, celebre, *adj.* famous

celebro (1), *v.* to frequent, visit a place in numbers, celebrate

celer, celeris, celere, *adj.* swift

celeritas, -tatis, *n.* f. swiftness

celes, celetis, *n.* m. yacht

Celticus, -a, -um, *adj.* pertaining to Celts

ceno (1), *v.* to dine

censeo, censere, censui, censum, *v.* to assess, value, think

censor, censoris, *n.* m. censor

censorius, -a, -um, *adj.* pertaining to a censor (a Roman office responsible for assessing property qualifications and membership in the equestrian and senatorial orders)

censura, -ae, *n.* f. censorship (the office of the censor), opinion, judgment

census, -us, *n.* m. census

centenarius, -a, -um, *adj.* pertaining to a hundred, a hundred

centeni, -ae, -a, *adj.* a hundred each

centesimus, -a, -um, *adj.* one hundredth

centiens, *adv.* one hundred times

centum, *n. indeclinable* one hundred

centurio, -onis, *n.* m. centurion

cercyrus, -i, *n.* m. a small boat among the Cyrpiots

cerebrum, -i, *n.* n. brain

cerno, cernere, crevi, cretum, *v.* to discern, separate, distinguish

certamen, -minis, *n.* n. struggle, contest

certus, -a, -um, *adj.* sure, certain

cervix, cervicis, *n.* f. neck (esp. the nape)

cervus, -i, *n.* m. deer

cesso (1), *v.* to delay, be at leisure, cease

ceteri, -ae, -a, *adj.* the rest

ceu, *adv.* just as

chorda, -ae, *n.* f. string

cibatus, -us, *n.* m. food, nourishment

cibus, -i, *n.* m. food

cicatrix, cicatricis, *n.* f. scar

Cilicia, -ae, *n.* f. Cilicia, the region of southern Turkey to the northeast of Cyprus

Cimbricus, -a, -um, *adj.* pertaining to the German tribe of the Cimbri

cinis, cineris, *m.* ash

circa, *adv. prep.* (+ acc.) around, about

circuitus, -us, *n.* m. circuit

circum, *adv. prep.* (+ acc.) around, about

circumago, circumagere, circumegi, circumactus, *v.* to drive in a circle, wheel around

circumdo, circumdare, circumdedi, circumdatum, *v.* to place around, surround

circumplexus, -us, *n.* m. embracing

circumscribo, circumscribere, circumscripsi, circumscriptum, *v.* to circumscribe

circumspecto (1), *v.* to look around attentively

circumspergo, circumspergere, circumspersi, circumspersum, *v.* to scatter around

circumsutus, -a, -um, *adj.* sewn-around, sewn together

circumvenio, circumvenire, circumveni, circumventum, *v.* to encircle

circus, -i, *n.* m. the Circus

cithara, -ae, *n.* f. the cithara

citharoedicus, -a, -um, *adj.* pertaining to *cithara* players

citra, *adv.* on this side, on the hither side, on the near side

citus, -a, -um, *adj.* swift

civicus, -a, -um, *adj.* civic

civilis, -is, -e, *adj.* pertaining to citizens, civic

civis, civis, *n.* m./f. citizen

civitas, -tatis, *n.* f. city, citizenry

clades, cladis, *n.* f. destruction, slaughter

claritas, -tatis, *n.* clarity, brightness, clearness, splendor

clarus, -a, -um, *adj.* distinguished, clear, shining

classis, -is, *n.* f. class, fleet, army

claustra, -orum, *n.* n. pl. bar, bolt, lock

clavo (1), *v.* to nail, furnish with nails, stripe

clemens, clementis, *adj.* mild, gentle

clementia, -ae, *n.* f. clemency, mercy, sympathy

cliens, clientis, *n.* mf. client

climacter, climacteris, *n.* m. climacteric (acc. pl. *climacteras*)

clithron, -i, *n.* n. bolt-hole, windpipe

clunis, -is, *n.* m./f. buttock

clupeus, -i, *n.* m. shield

coagulum, -i, *n.* n. a bond, tie

coctilis, -is, -e, *adj.* burned, cooked

cocus, -i, *n.* m. cook

coeo, coire, coii, coitum, *v.* to assemble, go together

coepi, coepisse, coeptum, *v.* to begin

coerceo, coercere, coercui, coercitum, *v.* to enclose, surround, hold together

coetus, -us, *n.* m. assembly, gathering

cogitatio, -ionis, *n.* f. deliberation, consideration, reflecting

cogito (1), *v.* to consider thoroughly, ponder, mull over, reflect

cognomen, -minis, *n.* n. surname

cognomino (1), *v.* to furnish with a surname

cognosco, cognoscere, cognovi, cognitum, *v.* to become acquainted with

cogo, cogere, coegi, coactum, *v.* to drive together, compel, collect

cohaereo, cohaerere, cohaesi, cohaesum, *v.* to cling together

cohors, cohortis, *n.* f. crowd, cohort

coitus = *coetus*

collatus, -a, -um, *adj.* (see *confero*)

collega, -ae, *n.* m. colleague

collegium, -i, *n.* a guild, college

collis, collis, *n.* m. hill

colo, colere, colui, cultum, *v.* to cherish, cultivate, pay respect

color = **colos, coloris**, *n.* m. color

columna, -ae, *n.* f. column

comes, comitis, *n.* m. companion, comrade, one who goes with (*cum* + *eo*)

comicus, -a, -um, *adj.* pertaining to comedy

comitium, -i, *n.* n. sg. assembly place; pl. assembly

commemoro (1), to recall to memory

commendatio, -ionis, *n.* f. commendation, recommendation

commentor, commentari, commentatus, *v.* to consider, meditate, think on

comminiscor, comminisci, commentum, *v.* to think up, devise, falsify

committo, committere, commisi, commisum, *v.* to commit, bring together, commit a crime

commutatio, -ionis, *n.* f. change, exchange, upheaval

comoedia, -ae, *n.* f. comedy

comparo (1), *v.* to match in pairs

compes, compedis, *n.* f. fetter, shackle

complector, complecti, complexum, *v.* to entwine, embrace

comprehendo, comprehendere, comprehendi, comprehensum, *v.* to grasp, comprehend

conatus, -us, *n.* m. trying, attempt

concentus, -us, *n.* m. harmony

conceptus, -us, *n.* gathering, conception, pregnancy

concido, concidere, concidi, *v.* to fall down together, fall in heap

concieo, conciere, concivi, concitum, *v.* to excite, rouse, collect

concipio, concipere, concepi, conceptum, *v.* to conceive, take hold of, receive

concors, concordis, *adj.* agreeing, of like heart

concremo (1), *v.* to burn up

concresco, concrescere, concrevi, concretum, *v.* to grow together, stiffen, congeal

concursus, -us, *n.* m. concourse, assembly, running together

condicio, -ionis, *n.* f. agreement, terms, demand

conditor, -toris, *n.* m. founder

conditorium, -i, *n.* n. repository, tomb

condo, condere, condidi, conditum, *v.* to found, plant, establish

confero, conferre, contuli, conlatus, *v.* to collect, gather, bring together

confestim, *adv.* immediately

conficio, conficere, confeci, confectum, *v.* to finish, complete

confinis, -is, -e, *adj.* bordering, contiguous

confiteor, confiteri, confessus, *v.* to confess, admit

conflo (1), *v.* to blow together, kindle, melt

confodio, confodere, confodi, confossum, *v.* to dig around, stab

confusus, -a, -um, *adj.* "confused" (from *confundo*).

congero, congerere, congessi, congestum, *v.* to heap up, bring together

congrego (1), *v.* to assemble, flock

congressus, -us, *n.* m. congress, assembly, meeting

congruo, congruere, congrui, *v.* to come together, meet, be suited for, agree with

conitor, coniti, conixus/conisus, *v.* to struggle with all one's strength

coniugium, -i, *n.* n. union, marriage

coniunx, coniugis, *n.* m./f. spouse.

conludo, conludere, conlusi, conlusum, *v.* to play together

conmorior, conmori, conmortuus, *v.* to die with, die together

conor, conari, conatus, *v.* to try, attempt

conpario, conparere, conpeperi, conpartum, *v.* to produce, bear, beget

conparo (1), *v.* to compare, match in pairs

conplector, conplecti, conplexus, *v.* to embrace, entwine

conplexus, -us, *n.* m. embrace

conploro (1), *v.* lament, weep loudly

conpono, conponere, conposui, conpositum, *v.* to compose, put together

conputo (1), *v.* to compute, reckon up

conqueror, conqueri, conquestum, *v.* to complain

conruo, conruere, conrui, *v.* to fall together, sink together, rush down

conscendo, conscendere, conscendi, conscensum, *v.* to climb, mount, embark

conscientia, -ae, *n.* f. conscience, joint knowledge

conscius, -a, -um, *adj.* privy to, aware of

consecro (1), *v.* to consecrate, make holy

consector (1), *v.* to follow after eagerly

consensus, -us, *n.* m. consensus, agreement, common feeling

consentaneus, -a, -um, *adj.* in agreement with

consequor, consequi, consecutus, *v.* to follow after

consero, conserere, conserui, consertum, *v.* to entwine, bind, join together

conservo (1), *v.* to conserve, preserve

consilium, -i, *n.* plan, counsel, deliberation

consisto, consistere, constiti, constitum, *v.* to stand still, halt

conspectus, -us, *n.* m. seeing, view, attention

conspicio, conspicere, conspexi, conspectum, *v.* to look at, catch sight of

conspiro (1), *v.* to breathe together, unite together, conspire

constantia, -ae, *n.* f. firmness, unchangeability, constancy

constituo, constituere, constitui, constitutum, *v.* to put down, set down, deposit

consto, constare, constiti, constatum, *v.* to stand together; *impersonal*: it is agreed

construo, construere, construxi, constructum, *v.* to heap up, build up, construct

consuetudo, consuetudinis, *n.* f. habit, custom

consul, consulis, *n.* m. consul

consularis, -is, -e, *adj.* consular, pertaining to a consul or ex-consul

consulatus, -us, *n.* m. consulship

consulo, consulere, consului, consultum, *v.* to take counsel, reflect

consummatio, -ionis, *n.* f. a reckoning up, summary

consummo (1), *v.* to sum up

consumo, consumere, consumpsi, consumptum, *v.* to consume, devour, destroy

consurgo, consurgere, consurrexi, consurrectum, *v.* to raise onself up, rise

contactus, -us, *n.* m. contact, touch

contego, contegere, contexi, contectum, *v.* to cover over, conceal

contemno, contemnere, contempsi, contemptum, *v.* to scorn, despise, disdain

contemplatio, -ionis, *n.* f. consideration, contemplation

contendo, contendere, contendi, contentum, *v.* to stretch, train, journey, contend

contentio, -ionis, *adj.* stretching, struggling

conterminus, -a, -um, *adj.* neighboring, bordering

contineo, continere, continui, contentum, *v.* to contain, hold together, be limited

contingo, contingere, contigi, contactum, *v.* to touch, *v. impersonal* (+ dat.) to befall

continuus, -a, -um, *adj.* uninterrupted, continuous

contio, contionis, *n.* f. meeting, assembly

contra, *adv. prep.* (+ acc) in turn, opposite, facing

contractio, -ionis, *n.* f. contraction, abridgement

contrarius, -a, -um, *adj.* lying opposite, contrary, opposed

contueor, contueri, contuitus, *v.* to look upon, survey

contumelia, -ae, *n.* abuse, insult, reproach

contumeliosus, -a, -um, *adj.* full of abuse, reproach

convallis, -is, *n.* f. a valley

convenio, convenire, conveni, conventum, *v.* to come together; *impersonal*: it is agreed

conversio, -ionis, *n.* f. revolution, conversion

convinco, convincere, convici, convictum, *v.* to overcome, convict

convivium, -i, *n.* n. banquet, dinner party

convolo (1), *v.* to flock together

copia, -ae, *n.* f. abundance, supply, opportunity

corium, -i, *n.* n. hide, leather

corneus, -a, -um, *adj.* made of horn

cornix, cornicis, *n.* f. crow, raven

cornu, -us, *n.* n. horn

corolla, -ae, *n.* f. small crown, garland

corona, -ae, *n.* f. a crown, wreath

corono (1), *v.* to crown, wreathe

corporo (1), *v.* to embody

corpus, corporis, *n.* n. body

corrigo, corrigere, correxi, correctus, *v.* to make straight, amend

corripio, corripere, corripui, correptus, *v.* to snatch up, seize

corrumpo, corrumpere, corrupi, corruptum, *v.* to corrupt, break apart

corvus, -i, *n.* raven

cothurnus, -i, *n.* a high shoe worn by actors of tragedy

cotidie, *adv.* daily

creber, crebra, crebrum, *adj.* frequent, thick

credo, credere, credidi, creditum, *v.* to trust, believe, credit

credulitas, -tatis, *n.* f. belief, easiness of belief

cremo (1), *v.* to burn, burn up

Cremona, -ae, *n.* f. the city Cremona

cresco, crescere, crevi, cretum, *v.* to grow

Creta, -ae, *n.* f. the island Crete

criminor (1), *v.* to accuse of a crime

crista, -ae, *n.* f. crest, cock's comb

cruciatus, -us, *n.* m. torture, execution

crucio (1), *v.* to torture, crucify

crudelis, -is, -e, *adj.* cruel

crudelitas, -tatis, *n.* f. cruelty, harshness, severity

crus, cruris, *n.* n. shin, thigh, leg

cubiculum, -i, *n.* n. bedroom

cubitalis, -is, -e, *adj.* pertaining to the elbow, a cubit long

cubitum, -i, *n.* n. elbow, cubit

culleus, -i, *n.* m. wine-sack

culpa, -ae, *n.* f. fault, blame

culter, cultri, *n.* m. a knife

cultura, -ae, *n.* f. culture, cultivation, growing

cumba, -ae, *n.* f. skiff

cunctus, -a, -um, *adj.* all, whole, entire

cuniculus, -i, *n.* m. a rabbit, rabbit's burrow, underground-tunnel, mine

cupiditas, cupiditatis, *n.* f. longing, passion

cupido, cupidinis, *n.* f. desire

cupio, cupere, cupivi, cupitum, *v.* to desire

cura, -ae, *n.* f. care, concern

curia, -ae, *n.* f. court, senate-house

curo (1), *v.* to care, take care

curro, currere, cucurri, cursum, *v.* to run

currus, -us, *n.* m. chariot

cursor, -oris, *n.* m. a runner, racer

cursus, -us, *n.* m. running, course, journey

curulis, -is, -e, *adj.* pertaining to the curule chair (indicates a higher-ranked magistrate)

custodia, -ae, *n.* f. guardianship

custodio, custodire, custodivi, custoditum, *v.* to guard, defend

cutis, -is, *n.* f. skin

Cyclops, Cyclopis, *n.* m. any of a race of one-eyed giants
cynocephalus, -i, *n.* dog-head, (usually "baboon").
Cyrenensis, -is, -e, *adj.* pertaining to Cyrene

damno (1), *v.* to damage, condemn, doom, sentence to punishment
datio, -ionis, *n.* f. allotment, distribution
dea, -ae, *n.* f. goddess
debeo, debere, debui, debitum, *v.* to owe, ought
debilis, -is, -e, *adj.* weak, lame, crippled
decem, *n. indeclinable.* Ten
decemremis, -is, -e, *adj.* having ten banks of oars
decennis, -is, -e, *adj.* of ten years
decerno, decernere, decrevi, decretum, *v.* to decide, decree, determine
decido, decidere, decidi, *v.* to fall off, fall down
deciduus, -a, -um, *adj.* falling down, deciduous
decimus, -a, -um, *adj.* tenth
declaro (1), *v.* to make clear, make evident
decurro, decurrere, decurri, decursum, *v.* to run down, over
decus, decoris, *n.* n. glory, honor, dignity
dedicatio, -ionis, *n.* f. dedication
dedico (1), to dedicate
deditio, -ionis, *n.* f. surrender
deerro (1), *v.* to wander astray
defendo, defendere, defendi, defensum, *v.* to defend, allege in defense, support
defensio, -ionis, *n.* f. defense
defero, deferre, detuli, delatum, *v.* to bring down, carry down
deficio, deficere, defeci, defectus, *v.* to fail, forsake, be deficient
defigo, defigere, defixi, defixum, *v.* to fasten down, fix
defodio, defodere, defodi, defossum, *v.* to dig up, dig down, bury
deformitas, -tatis, *n.* f. ugliness
defungor, defungi, defunctum, *v.* to do one's duty, complete one's duty
dego, degere, degi, *v.* to spend or pass time, carry on
degravo (1), *v.* to weigh down, drag down
deinde, *adv.* thereupon, after that
delenimentum, -i, *n.* n. charm, blandishment
deleo, delere, delevi, deletus, *v.* to destroy
deliciae, -arum, *n.* f. pl. delight, darling

Delphi, -orum, *n.* m. pl. the city in central Greece, site of Apollo's sanctuary

delubrum, -i, *n.* n. shrine, temple

dementia, -ae, *n.* f. madness

demo, demere, dempsi, demptum, *v.* to take away, withdraw, subtract

demonstro (1), *v.* to point out, indicate, demonstrate

demum, *adv.* at last, at length

denique, *adv.* at last, thereupon

dens, dentis, *n.* m. tooth

deploro (1), *v.* to weep

depono, depondere, deposui, depositum, *v.* to deposit, set down

deporto (1), *v.* to carry away, transport

deprehendo, deprehendere, deprehendi, deprehensum, *v.* to catch, apprehend

deprimo, deprimere, depressi, depressum, *v.* to depress

depugno (1), *v.* to fight out, contend

derigo = dirigo, -rigere, -rexi, -rectum, *v.* to lay out in lines, straighten, cleave

derogo (1), *v.* to repeal, dishonor

descendo, descendere, descendi, descensum, *v.* to climb down, descend

desero, deserere, deserui, desertum, *v.* to desert, abandon

desideo, desidere, desedi, *v.* to sit, remain inactive

desiderium, -i, *n.* n. desire

desidero (1), *v.* to desire

desilio, desilire, desilui, *v.* to leap down

desino, desinere, desii, *v.* to cease, desist

destinatio, -ionis, *n.* f. determination, purpose

desum, deesse, defui, defuturum, *v.* to be absent, fail, be wanting

detego, detegere, detexi, detectum, *v.* to uncover

determino (1), *v.* to delimit, enclose

detraho, detrahere, detraxi, detractum, *v.* to pull down, withdraw

deus, -i, *n.* m. (deus, dei, deo, deum, deo; di, deorum/deum, dis, deos, dis; voc. deus), god

devincio, devincire, devinxi, devinctum, *v.* to bind together, tie down

devolvo, devolvere, devolvi, devolutum, *v.* to roll down

devoro (1), *v.* to swallow, gulp down, devour

dexterus, -a, -um, *adj.* right, righthand, on the right side

diadema, diadematis, *n.* n. royal head-dress, diadem

dialecticus, -a, -um, *adj.* pertaining to dialectic, discussion; *n.* m.: a dialectician, logician

dicio, -ionis, *n.* f. authority, power, sovereignty
dico (1), *v.* to dedicate
dico, dicere, dixi, dictum, *v.* to say, speak
dictator, -oris, *n.* m. dictator
dicto (1), v. to dictate, say repeatedly
dictus, -us, *n.* m. a saying
dies, diei, *n.* m. day
differentia, -ae, *n.* f. difference, diversity
differo, differre, distuli, dilatum, *v.* to scatter, distract, spread
difficilis -is, -e, *adj.* difficult
difficultas, -tatis, *n.* f. difficulty
difficulter, *adv.* with difficulty
digitus, -i, *n.* m. finger
dignatio, -tionis, *n.* f. respect, esteem
digredior, digredi, digressus, *v.* to digress, depart, go astray
dilectus, -us, *n.* m. choice, choosing
diligens, diligentis, *adj.* diligent, careful
diligo, diligere, dilexi, dilectum, *v.* to value, love, cherish
dimicatio, -ionis, *n.* f. combat, struggle
dimico (1), *v.* to fight, struggle, contend
dimidius, -a, -um, *adj.* half
dimitto, dimittere, dimisi, dimissum, *v.* to send away, dismiss
dimoveo, dimovere, dimovi, dimotum, *v.* to separate, divide
dinumero (1), *v.* to count up
dirus, -a, -um, *adj.* dire, awful, fearful
discerno, discernere, discrevi, discretum, *v.* to separate, set apart
disciplina, -ae, *n.* f. discipline, teaching
discipulus, -i, *n.* m. student
disco, discere, didici, *v.* to learn
discordia, -ae, *n.* f. discord, strife, disagreement
discrimen, -minis, *n.* difference, distinction, crisis
dispar, disparis, *adj.* unequal
dispensator, -oris, *n.* m. steward, treasurer
disseco, dissecare, dissecui, dissectum, *v.* to cut up
dissero, disserere, disserui, dissertum, *v.* to discuss, discourse
dissimilis, -is, -e, *adj.* unalike
dissimulo (1), *v.* to conceal, keep secret, feign
dissociatio, -ionis, *n.* f. separation

dissolvo, dissolvere, dissolvi, dissolutum, *v.* to dissolve, loosen

distermino (1), *v.* to separate, divide

distinguo, distinguere, distinxi, distinctum, *v.* to distinguish, separate, divide

disto, distare, *v.* to differ, stand apart

diu, *adv.* a long time

diuturnus, -a, -um, *adj.* long-lasting

diversus, -a, -um, *adj.* different, separate, in different directions

diverto, divertere, diverti, diversum, *v.* to turn in different directions

divido, dividere, divisi, divisum, *v.* to separate, divide

divino (1), *v.* to divine, foresee, foretell

divinatio, -ionis, *n.* f. divination, foreseeing

divinitas, -tatis, *n.* f. divinity

divinus, -a, -um, *adj.* divine

dives, ditis, *adj.* rich

divus, -a, -um, *adj.* divine

do, dare, dedi, datum, *v.* to give

doceo, docere, docui, doctum, *v.* to teach

docilitas, -tatis, *n.* f. ability to be taught

doctrina, -ae, *n.* f. teaching

documentum, -i, *n.* n. proof

dodrans, dodrantis, *n.* m. three-quarters

dolium, -i, *n.* n. a large wine jar

dolor, doloris, *n.* m. grief, sadness, hurt

domesticus, -a, -um, *adj.* pertaining to the house

domicilium, -i, *n.* n. domicile, dwelling

dominus, -i, *n.* m. master, lord

domito, domitare, *v.* to tame, break down

domo, domare, domui, domitum, *v.* to tame, break

domus, -us and **domus, -i**, *n.* f. house

donec, *conj.* as long as, until

dono (1), *v.* to give as a gift

donum, -i, *n.* n. gift

dormio, dormire, dormivi, dormitum, *v.* to sleep

dorsum, -i, *n.* n. back

draco, draconis, *n.* m. large snake, dragon

dubito (1), to waver, doubt

dubius, -a, -um, *adj.* vacillating, uncertain, dubious

ducenarius, -a, -um, *adj.* pertaining to two hundred
duceni, -ae, -a, *adj.* by two hundreds
ducenti, -ae, -a, *adj.* two-hundred
duco, ducere, duxi, ductum, *v.* to lead, bring, consider
ductus, -us, *n.* m. strokes, drawing
dulcedo, dulcedinis, *n.* f. sweetness
dulcis, -is, -e, *adj.* sweet
dum, *conj.* while
dumtaxat, *adv.* in so far as this is concerned, only, merely
duo, -ae, -o, *adj.* two
duodecim, *n.* twelve
duodeni, -ae, -a, *adj.* twelve by twelve
duodeviginti, *n.* n. eighteen
duplex, duplicis, *adj.* double
duplico (1), *v.* to double
duro (1), *v.* to harden
durus, -a, -um, *adj.* harsh, rough
dux, ducis, *n.* m. leader

ebibo, ebibere, ebibi, ebibitum, *v.* to drink up, drain
eboreus, -a, -um, *adj.* made of ivory
ebur, eboris, *n.* n. ivory
edico, edicere, edixi, edictum, *v.* to speak out
edo, edere, edidi, editum, *v.* to produce, publish
educo, educere, eduxi, eductus, *v.* to draw forth, lead out
effascino (1), *v.* to bewitch, charm
effero, efferre, extuli, elatum, *v.* to bring out, carry forth
efficio, efficere, effeci, effectum, *v.* to bring about
effigies, -ei, *n.* f. a likeness, portrait
effingo, effingere, effinxi, effictum, *v.* to fashion, portray
effluvium, -i, *n.* n. outflow
effundo, effundere, effudi, effusum, *v.* to pour out
egeo, egere, egui, *v.* (+ abl.) to need, want
egero, egerere, egessi, egestum, *v.* to carry out, bring out
egredior, egredi, egressus, *v.* to go out
eicio, eicere, eieci, eiectum, *v.* to throw out, expel
elaboro (1), *v.* to labor over, take pains
elephans, elephantis, *n.* m. see "elephantus"

elephantus, -i, *n.* m. (also *elephans, elephantis*) elephant
elido, elidere, elisi, elisum, *v.* to strike, dash out, knock out
eligo, eligere, elegi, electum, *v.* to choose
eloquentia, -ae, *n.* f. eloquence
emboliaria, -ae, *n.* f. an entr'acte actress
emetior, emeti, emensus, *v.* to measure out
emitto, emittere, emisi, emissum, *v.* to emit, send out
emo, emere, emi, emptum, *v.* to buy
emorior, emori, emortuus, *v.* to die off
eneco, enecare, enecui, enectum, *v.* to utterly exhaust, plague to death
enim, *conj.* (post-positive, explanatory) for, because
eniteo, enitere, enitui, *v.* to shine forth
enitor, enti, enisus/enixus, *v.* to struggle, strive
enixus, -a, -um, *adj.* strenuous, zealous
enumero (1), *v.* to reckon up, count up
eo, ire, ivi, itum, *v.* to go
epistula, -ae, *n.* f. letter, epistle
eques, equitis, *n.* m. knight, equestrian
equester, equestris, equestre, *adj.* pertaining to the equestrian order
equitatus, -us, *n.* m. cavalry
equus, -i, *n.* m. horse
ergo, *adv.* therefore
erigo, erigere, erexi, erectum, *v.* to raise up, set up
erodo, erodere, –, erosum, to erode, wear away
erro (1), *v.* to wander, err
erumpo, erumpere, erupi, eruptum, *v.* to burst forth, break out
eruo, eruere, erui, erutum, *v.* to draw out, throw out, pluck out
eruptio, -ionis, *n.* f. bursting forth
etenim, *conj.* and indeed (a stronger version of *enim*)
etiam, *adv.* even, also
etiamnum, *conj.* even yet, even now, still
etiamsi, *conj.* even if, although
etsi, *conj.* even if, although
euripus, -i, *n.* m. strait, channel
Europa, -ae, *n.* f. Europe
evanesco, evanescere, evanui, *v.* to vanish away
eveho, evehere, evexi, evectum, *v.* to carry out, convey, elevate, spread
evenio, evenire, eveni, eventum, *v.* to turn out, come out

eventus, -us, m. out come, event

evidens, evidentis, *adj.* visible, evident

evolo (1), *v.* to fly away

examen, examinis, *n.* n. swarm, hive

exanimo (1), *v.* to kill, deprive of life, breath, air

exanimus, -a, -um, *adj.* (=*exanimis*) lifeless

excedo, excedere, excessi, excessum, *v.* to go out, retire, withdraw

excello, excellere, excellui, excelsum, *v.* to raise up, elevate

excelsus, -a, um, *adj.* high, lofty

excido, excidere, excidi, *v.* to fall out

excipio, excipere, excepi, exceptum, *v.* to draw out, except, take up

excito (1), *v.* to excite, stir up

excogito (1), *v.* to find out, devise

excutio, excutere, excussi, excussum, *v.* to shake out, drive out

exemplum, -i, *n.* n. example, precedent

exeo, -ire, -ivi, -itum, *v.* to go out, depart, result (cf. "outcome"), proceed

exequiae, -arum, *n.* f. pl. funeral procession

exerceo, exercere, exercui, exercitum, *v.* to work, busy, exercise

exercitus, -us, *n.* m. army

exigo, exigere, exegi, exactum, *v.* to drive out, drive off

exilium, -i, *n.* n. exile

eximius, -a, -um, *adj.* extraordinary, uncommon

eximo, eximere, exemi, exemptum, *v.* to remove, take away

exinanio, -ire, -ivi, -itum, *v.* to make empty

existimo (1), *v.* to deem, think

ex(s)isto, ex(s)istere, ex(s)titi, ex(s)titum, to step forth, emerge, appear, be manifest, exist

exitialis, -is, -e, *adj.* deadly

exitium, -i, *n.* n. death, egress

exitus, -us, *n.* m. end, exit, death

exorior, exoriri, exortus, *v.* to arise

exorno (1), *v.* to furnish, fit out

exortivus, -a, -um, *adj.* pertaining to dawn, eastern, ascendant

exortus, -us, *n.* m. rising

expeditio, -ionis, *n.* f. expedition, campaign

expergiscor, expergisci, experrectum, *v.* to wake up, rouse

experimentum, -i, *n.* n. proof, trial, experiment

experior, experiri, expertum, *v.* to try, put to the test

expers, expertis, *adj.* (+ gen.) having no share in

expeto, expetere, expetivi, expetitum, to desire, long for, covet, aspire to

expiro (1), *v.* to expire, breathe out

explanatio, -ionis, *n.* f. explanation, pronunciation

expleo, explere, explevi, expletum, *v.* to fill up

explico (1), *v.* to unfold, develop, disentangle

exprimo, exprimere, expressi, expressum, *v.* to press out

expugnator, -oris, *n.* m. besieger

expuo, expuere, expui, exputum, *v.* to spit out, eject

exquiro, exquirere, exquisivi, exquisitum, *v.* to seek out diligently, *participle*: accurate, excellent

exequor, exsequi, exsecutum, *v.* to follow to the end

exsisto, exsistere, exstiti, exstitum, *v.* to emerge, appear

exstinguo, exstinguere, exstinxi, exstinctum, *v.* to put out, kill, destroy

extendo, extendere, extendi, extentum, *v.* to stretch out, spread, extend

exter/exterus, -a, -um, *adj.* on the outside

externus, -a, -um, *adj.* foreign

extinctus, -us, *n.* m. an extinguishing

extinguo, extinguere, extinxi, extinctum, *v.* to extinguish, put out

extispicium, -i, *n.* n. divination by entrails

exto, extare, *v.* to stand out, exist

extra, *prep.* (+ acc.) beyond

extraho, extrahere, extraxi, extractum, *v.* to draw forth, drag out

extremus, -a, -um, *adj.* furthermost, farthest, utmost

extruo, extruere, extruxi, extructum, *v.* to heap up, build

exuro, exurere, exussi, exustum, *v.* to burn up, burn out

exustio, -ionis, *n.* f. conflagration

exuviae, -arum, *n.* f. pl. spoils

fabricor (1), *v.* to form, fashion

fabulositas, -tatis, *n.* f. story-telling

fabulosus, -a, -um, *adj.* fabulous, in a fable

fax, facis, *n.* f. torch

facies, faciei, *n.* f. face

facilis, -is, -e, *adj.* easy

facio, facere, feci, factum, *v.* to do, make

factito (1), *v.* to do frequently, practice

facundia, -ae, *n.*, f. eloquence, fluency

Falisci, -orum, *n.* m. pl. the Faliscans

fallax, fallacis, *adj.* deceitful

fallo, fallere, fefelli, falsum, *v.* to deceive, cheat

fama, -ae, *n.* f. rumor, report, fame

fames, -is, *n.* f. famine, hunger

familia, -ae, *n.* f. family, household

fascis, fascis, *n.* m. a bundle of rods and an axe, carried by the lictors that attend a magistrate and symbolizing magisterial authority to have criminals beaten or executed.

fastidio, fastidire, fastidivi, fastiditum, *v.* to feel loathing, disgust, scorn

fastidium, -i, *n.* n. loathing, disgust, scorn

fateor, fateri, fassus, *v.* to confess, grant, admit

fatigo (1), *v.* to fatigue, vex, harass

faux, faucis, *n.* f. gullet, throat, jaw

faveo, favere, favi, fautum *v.* (+ dat.) to be favorable to, favor

febris, -is, *n.* f. fever

fecunditas, -tatis, *n.* f. fruitfulness

felicitas, -tatis, *n.* f. felicity, fruitfulness, happiness

felix, felicis, *adj.* lucky, happy

femina, -ae, *n.* f. woman, a female

femur, femoris/feminis, *n.* n. thigh, upper leg

fera, -ae, *n.* f. wild beast

fere, *adv.* almost, approximately, scarcely

feritas, -tatis, *n.* f. fierceness, wildness, savageness

ferme, *adv.* = *fere*

fero, ferre, tuli, latum, *v.* to bring, bear, relate

ferrarius, -a, -um, *adj.* pertaining to iron

ferreus, -a, -um, *adj.* made of iron

ferula, -ae, *n.* f. the giant fennel

ferus, -a, -um, *adj.* wild, untamed

ferveo, fervere, ferbui, also **fervo, fervere, fervi**, *v.* to boil, rage, seethe

fessus, -a, -um, *adj.* weary, tired

festino (1), *v.* to make haste

fetifer, fetifera, fetiferum, *adj.* fruit-bearing, causing fertility

ficus, -i, *n.* f. fig tree

fides, fidei, *n.* f. faith, good faith

fido, fidere, fisum, *v.* to trust, have confidence in

figlina, -ae, *n.* f. pottery

figo, figere, fixi, fixum, *v.* to fasten, affix

figura, -ae, *n.* f. figure, shape

filia, -ae, *n.* f. daughter

filius, -i, *n.* m. son

filum, -i, *n.* n. thread

fimbriae, -arum, *n.* f. pl. fringe

finis, -is, *n.* m. end, boundary

finitimus, -a, -um, *adj.* neighboring

fio, fieri, factus, *v.* to be made, to be produced, to be brought into being, become

firmus, -a, -um, *adj.* firm, strong

fiscus, -i, *n.* m. public treasury, fisc

fistula, -ae, *n.* f. pipe, tube, reed, ulcer

flamma, -ae, *n.* f. flame, fire

flatura, -ae, *n.* f. blowing, melting

fleo, flere, flevi, fletum, *v.* to weep, cry

floreo, florere, florui, *v.* to bloom, blossom

flos, floris, *n.* m. flower

fluito (1), *v.* to float, flow

flumen, fluminis, *n.* n. river

fluo, fluere, fluxi, fluxum, *v.* to flow

fluvius, -i, *n.* m. river

fodio, fodere, fodi, fossum, *v.* to dig, gouge

foedero (1), *v.* to make a treaty, ally

foedus, -a, -um, *n.* foul

foedus, foederis, *n.* pact, treaty

fons, fontis, *n.* m. fount, spring, source

for, fari, fatus, *v.* to speak, pronounce

foramen, -minis, *n.* n. an opening, hole

forceps, forcipis, *n.* m./f. tongs

foris, foris, *n.* f. door

forma, -ae, *n.* f. form, shape

formica, -ae, *n.* f. ant

formico (1), *v.* to creep, crawl, flutter

fortasse, *adv.* perhaps

fortis, -is, -e, *adj.* strong, brave

fortitudo, fortitudinis, *n.* f. strength
fortuitus, -a, -um, *adj.* casual, accidental, fortuitous
fortuna, -ae, *n.* f. fortune
forum, -i, *n.* n. forum, central marketplace
fossa, -ae, *n.* f. ditch, trench
fovea, -ae, *n.* f. small pit, snare
fragilis, -is, -e, *adj.* brittle, fragile, easily broken
fragilitas, -tatis, *n.* f. brittleness, fragility
frango, frangere, fregi, fractum, *v.* to break into pieces
frater, fratris, *n.* m. brother
fraus, fraudis, *n.* f. cheating, deceit, fraud
freni, -orum, *n.* m. pl. reins, bridle, bit
frequens, freqeuntis, *adj.* frequent, crowded
frequento (1), *v.* to frequent, to crowd, assemble
frigidus, -a, -um, *adj.* cold, chilly
frigus, frigoris, *n.* n. chill, cold
frivolus, -a, -um, *adj.* trifling, frivolous
frons, frondis, *n.* f. leaf, leafy branch
frons, frontis, *n.* m. forehead, face, brow
fructus, -us, *n.* m. fruit
frumentum, -i, *n.* n. grain
frux, frugis, *n.* f. fruit of the earth
fuga, -ae, *n.* f. flight, fleeing, retreat
fugio, fugere, fugi, fugitum, *v.* to flee, escape
fugo (1), *v.* to put to flight
fulgeo, fulgere, fulsi, *v.* to shine, gleam
fulgor, fulgoris, *n.* m. gleam, shine
fullonius, -a, -um, *adj.* pertaining to a fuller
fulmen, -minis, *n.* n. thunderbolt, lightning bolt
funarius, -a, -um, *adj.* pertaining to a baker
fundo, fundere, fudi, fusum, *v.* to pour, cause to rout
funebris, -is, -e, *adj.* funereal
fungor, fungi, functus, *v.* to perform, do a duty
funis, -is, *n.* m. rope
funus, funeris, *n.* n. death, funeral
furo, furere, furui, *v.* to rage, rave
furor, furoris, *n.* m. furor, madness
fustis, -is, *n.* m. club, cudgel

Gaetuli, -orum, *n.* m. pl. the people of Gaetulia, modern Morocco

Gaetulia, -ae, *n.* f. the land of the Gaetuli in north-western Africa

galea, -ae, *n.* f. helmet

Gallia, -ae, *n.* f. Gaul

Gallus, -i, *n.* m. a Gaul

gaudeo, gaudere, gavisum, *v. semi-deponent,* to rejoice

gaudium, -i, *n.* n. joy, gladness

geminus, -a, -um, *adj.* twin

gemitus, -us, *n.* m. groan, moan, complaint

gemma, -ae, *n.* f. gem

generatim, *adv.* by genus

generatio, -ionis, *n.* f. generation, begetting

genero (1), *v.* to beget, procreate

generus, -i, *n.* m. son-in-law

genitalis, -is, -e, *adj.* pertaining to birth

geno, genere, genui, genitum, *v.* to birth, give birth to

gens, gentis, *n.* f. people, tribe, race

genu, genus, *n.* n. knee

genus, generis, *n.* n. race, kind

geometricus, -a, -um, *adj.* pertaining to geometry, geometrician

Germania, -ae, *n.* f. the country of the Germans

germen, germins, *n.* n. seed

germino (1), *v.* to sprout

gero, gerere, gessi, gestus, *v.* to bear, carry, wage

Ges, genitive of *ge, ges, n.* f. earth.

gesto (1), *v.* to bear, carry, wield

gigno, gignere, genui, genitum, *v.* to beget, produce

gladiator, -oris, *n.* m. gladiator

gladiatorius, -a, -um, *adj.* pertaining to gladiators

gladius, -i, *n.* m. sword

glans, glandis, *n.* f. acorn

glaucus, -a, -um, *adj.* gray, green, the color of the sea

glomero (1), *v.* to form into a ball

gloria, -ae, *n.* f. glory, renown

glutinum, -i, *n.* n. glue

gradus, -us, *n.* m. step, pace, degree

graecus, -a, -um, *adj.* Greek

grammaticus, -a, -um, *adj.* grammatical; *n.* m. grammarian

grandis, -is, -e, *adj.* great, grand, strong, powerful
gratia, -ae, *n.* f. grace, influence
gratus, -a, -um, *adj.* pleasing, agreeable
gravidus, -a, -um, *adj.* pregnant
gravis, -is, -e, *adj.* grave, serious, heavy
gregatim, *adv.* in herds, swarms
gressus, -us, *n.* m. step
grex, gregis, *n.* m. flock, herd
grus, gruis, *n.* f. crane
grypus, -i, *n.* m. gryphon
guberno (1), *v.* to steer
gurges, gurgitis, *n.* m. whirlpool, abyss, waters
gusto (1), *v.* to taste, take a little
gymnasium, -i, *n.* n. gymnasium, school
gymnicus, -a, -um, *adj.* pertaining to the gymnasium, exercise
gymnosophistae, -arum, *n.* m. pl. a sect of Indian ascetics

habeo, habere, habui, habitum, *v.* to have, hold
habito (1), *v.* to inhabit, dwell
habitus, -us, *n.* m. condition, state, habit
halitus, -us, *n.* m. breath
harena, -ae, *n.* f. sand
harpago, harpagonis, *n.* m. grappling hook
harundo, harundinis, *n.* f. swallow
haruspex, haruspicis, *n.* m. a diviner
hasta, -ae, *n.* f. spear
haud, *adv.* scarcely, hardly
haurio, haurire, hausti, haustum, *v.* to drink, drain
haustus, -us, *n.* m. draught
hebes, hebetis, *adj.* dull
hebesco, hebescere, *v.* to grow dull
hebeto (1), *v.* to make dull
herba, -ae, *n.* f. grass, vegetation
herbarius, -a, -um, *adj.* pertaining to grass
Hercules, -is, *n.* m. Hercules
heres, heredis, *n.* m. heir
hermaphroditus, -i, *n.* m. hermaphrodite
heros, herois, *n.* m. hero

heu, *interj.* alas

Hiberia, -ae, *n.* f. Iberia, modern Georgia

hibernus, -a, -um, *adj.* pertaining to winter

hiems, hiemis, *n.* f. Winter

hilarus, -a, -um, *adj.* (variant of *hilaris*) cheerful

hinc, *adv.* from here

hippegus, -i, *n.* m. horse transport ship

hippocentaurus, -i, *n.* m. centaur

hirtus, -a, -um, *adj.* shaggy, hairy

hirudo, hirudinis, *n.* f. leech

Hispania, -ae, *n.* f. Spain

historia, -ae, *n.* f. history

histrio, histrionis *n.* m. actor

hodie, *adv.* today

homo, hominis, *n.* m. man, person

honos, honoris, *n.* m. honor, office

hora, -ae, *n.* f. hour

hordeum, -i, *n.* n. barley

horologium, -i, *n.* n. clock

horreo, horrere, horrui, *v.* to shudder, bristle

hortus, -i, *n.* m. garden

hostia, -ae, *n.* f. sacrificial victim

hostis, -is, *n.* m. enemy (in war)

humanus, -a, -um, *adj.* human

humilis, -is, -e, *adv.* humble, pertaining to the ground

humo (1), *v.* to bury, cover with earth

humus, -i, *n.* f. earth, soil

hydraulicus, -a, -um, *adj.* hydraulic, pertaining to water operated
   machinery

iaceo, iacere, iacui, iacitum, *v.* to lie, be flat

iacio, iacere, ieci, iactum, *v.* to throw, cast, send

iaculor (1), *v.* to throw a javelin, fight with a javelin

iaculum, -i, *n.* n. javelin

iam, *adv.* now, already

ianitor, -oris, *n.* m. doorkeeper

ianua, -ae, *n.* f. door, doorway

ibi, *adv.* there

ichthyocolla, -ae, *n.* f. isinglass
icio, icere, ici, ictus, *v.* to strike
ictus, -us, *n.* m. strike, blow
idem, eadem, idem, *pron.* the same person or thing
ideo, *adv.* for that reason, therefore
idus, iduum, *n.* f. the Ides
ieiunus, -a, -um, *adj.* fasting
igitur, *conj.* therefore
ignis, -is, *n.* m. fire
ignispicium, -i, *n.* divination by fire
ignobilis, -is, -e, *adj.* unknown, basely born
ignominia, -ae, *n.* f. disgrace, dishonor
ignoro (1), to be ignorant of, misunderstand
ignosco, ignoscere, ignovi, ignotum, *v.* to forgive, or excuse (someone, dat.)
ignotus, -a, -um, *adj.* unknown
Ilias, Iliadis, *n.* f. *Iliad*
ilico, *adv.* in that place
ille, illa, illud, *pron.* that, the former
Illyricum, -i, *n.* n. the country Illyria/Illyricum
imago, imaginis, *n.* f. image, likeness, copy
imitor, imitari, imitatus, *v.* to imitate, copy, resemble
immo, *adv.* nay rather, by all means
immolo (1), *v.* to immolate, sacrifice, sprinkle with sacrificial flour
impar, imparis, *adj.* uneaven, unequal
impedio, impedire, impedivi, impeditum, *v.* to hinder, entangle
imperator, -toris, *n.* m. emperor
imperium, -i, *n.* n. empire, rule, power, dominion
impero (1), *v.* to order, command
impetro (1), *v.* to obtain, procure
importo (1), *v.* to bring in, carry in
importunus, -a, -um, *adj.* inconvenient, troublesome, uncivil
inaequabilis, -is, -e, *adj.* uneven, unequal
inanimus, -a, -um, *adj.* lifeless, inanimate
inanis, -is, -e, *adj.* empty
inauratus, -a, -um, *adj.* not gilded
inauspicatus, -a, -um, *adj.* unlucky
inbecillitas, -tatis, *n.* f. weakness
incedo, incedere, incessi, incessum, *v.* to go forward

incendium, -i, *n.* n. blaze, conflagration
incertus, -a, -um, *adj.* uncertain, unsure
incessus, -us, *n.* m. going, walking, gait
incido, incidere, incidi, incasum, *v.* to fall into, fall upon
incido, incidere, incidi, incisum, *v.* to cut into, incise
incipio, incipere, incepi, inceptum, *v.* to begin
inclaresco, inclarescere, inclarui, *v.* to grow clear
inclino (1), *v.* to bend, incline, turn
includo, includere, inclusi, inclusum, *v.* to include
incoho, incohare, incohavi, inchoatum, *v.* to begin, commence
incolo, incolere, incolui, incultum, *v.* to cultivate, dwell in
incolumis, -is, -e, *adj.* unharmed
incommodus, -a, -um, *adj.* inconvenient, uncomfortable
incomparabilis, -is, -e, *adj.* incomparable
inconditus, -a, -um, *adj.* unburied, disordered, unmade
inconstantia, -ae, *n.* f. changeableness
incredibilis, -is, -e, *adj.* not believable
increpitus, -us, *n.* m. a rebuke
incresco, increscere, increvi, incretum, *v.* to grow in, increase
incus, incudis, *n.* f. anvil
incuso (1), *v.* to accuse, find fault with
inde, *adv.* from there, thence
index, indicis, *n.* m./f. a pointer, indicator
India, -ae, *n.* f. India
indicium, -i, *n.* n. notice, disclosure, indication
indico (1), *v.* to point out
Indicus, -a, -um, *adj.* Indian, pertaining to India
indignatio, -ionis, *n.* f. anger, indignation
indiscretus, -a, -um, *adj.* not divided
indo, indere, indidi, inditum, *v.* to put upon
indomitus, -a, -um, *adj.* untamed, unconquered
indubitatus, -a, -um, *adj.* undoubted
induco, inducere, induxi, inductum, *v.* to lead in, bring in, conduct to
indulgeo, indulgere, indulsi, indultum, *v.* to indulge, concede
induo, induere, indui, indutus, *v.* to put on, dress in
Indus, -a, -um, *adj.* Indian
indutiae, -arum, *n.* f. pl. armistice, truce
inebrio (1), *v.* to make drunk

inedia, -ae, *n.* f. fasting, starving
inenarrabilis, -is, -e, *adj.* indescribable
ineo, inire, inivi, initum, *v.* to go into, enter, begin
inermis, -is, -e, *adj.* without *arma*, defenseless, unarmed
infans, infantis, *adj.* incapable of speech
infaustus, -a, -um, *adj.* unlucky
infelix, infelicis, *adj.* unfortunate, miserable, calamitous
infero, inferre, intuli, inlatum, *v.* to carry in, bring in
inferus, -a, -um, *adj.* low, beneath
infesto (1), *v.* to trouble, attack, disturb
infestus, -a, -um, *adj.* unsafe, unquiet, molested
inficio, inficere, infeci, infectum, *v.* to stain, dye
infigo, infigere, infixi, infixum, *v.* to fix, thrust in
infinitus, -a, -um, *adj.* endless
infirmus, -a, -um, *adj.* feeble, weak
inflatio, -ionis, *n.* f. blowing up, swelling up
inflexibilis, -is, -e, *adj.* inflexible, unbendable
informis, -is, -e, *adj.* shapeless, ugly
ingeniosus, -a, -um, *adj.* talented, clever
ingenium, -i, *n.* n. skill, talent, genius
ingens, ingentis, *adj.* huge, vast, great
ingenuus, -a, -um, *adj.* native, noble, upright, characteristic of a free-born
   person
ingestabilis, -is, -e, *adj.* unbearable
ingredior, ingredi, ingressus, *v.* to go into, enter
ingressus, -us, *n.* m. entrance
ingruo, ingruere, ingrui, *v.* to rush into, attack
inguen, inguinis, *n.* n. groin, loin
inhaereo, inhaerere, inhaesi, inhaesum, *v.* to stick in, adhere to
inicio, inicere, inieci, iniectum, *v.* to throw onto
inimicus, -a, -um, *adj.* (personal) enemy
initium, -i, *n.* n. beginning
iniuria, -ae, *n.* f. injury, harm, injustice
inligo (1), *v.* to fasten, attach
inlustris, -is, -e, *adj.* bright, distinguished
inmensus, -a, -um, *adj.* immense, boundless
inmobilis, -is, -e, *adj.* motionless, immobile
inmorior, inmori, inmortuus, *v.* to die in or upon

inmortalitas, -tatis, *n*. immortality, deathlessness

innitor, inniti, innixus/innisus, *v*. to lean upon, rest upon

innumerabilis, -is, -e, *adj*. innumerable, uncountable

innumerus, -a, -um, *adj*. countless

inopia, -ae, *n*. f. scant, lack

inops, inopis, *adj*. without resources

inpatiens, inpatientis, *adj*. unable to endure, impatient

inpello, inpellere, inpuli, inpusum, *v*. to push, drive, strike against

inpingo, inpingere, inpegi, inpactum, *v*. to strike against, drive into, force upon

inpleo, inplere, inplevi, inpletum, *v*. to fill up, fill in

inpono, inponere, inposui, inpositum, *v*. to put on, apply

inprecor (1), *v*. to curse

inprimo, inprimere, inpressi, inpressum, *v*. to press into, impress, stamp

inproprius, -a, -um, *adj*. unsuitable, improper

inprudens, inprudentis, *adj*. not expecting, imprudent

inquit, *v*. he says, said (+ direct quotation)

insanabilis, -is, -e, *adj*. incurable

inscitia, -ae, *n*. f. ignorance, lack of skill

inscribo, inscribere, inscripsi, inscriptum, *v*. to inscribe, title

inscriptio, -tionis, *n*. f. inscription, titling

insculpo (1), *v*. to carve upon, engrave

insequor, insequi, insecutus, *v*. to follow after

insero, inserere, insevi, insitum, *v*. to implant, graft

insideo, insidere, insedi, insessum, *v*. to sit on

insidiae, -arum, *n*. f. pl. treachery

insidior, insidiari, insidiatus, *v*. to lie in ambush

insignis, -is, -e, *adj*. remarkable, notable, eminent

insisto, insistere, institi, *v*. to tread upon, step upon

instituo, instituere, institui, institutum, *v*. to set up, erect, fix, arrange

insto, instare, institi, instatum, *v*. to draw near, loom upon, threaten

instumentum, -i, *n*. n. implement, tool

insula, -ae, *n*. f. island

insum, inesse, infui, *v*. to be in, be upon

integer, integra, integrum, *adj*. whole, untouched

intego, integere, intexi, intectus, *v*. to cover over

intellectus, -us, *n*. m. intellect, understanding

intellego, intellegere, intellexi, intellectum, *v*. to understand

intendo, intendere, intendi, intentum/intensum, *v.* to bend, stretch, aim

inter, *prep.* (+ acc.), amongst, between

intercedo, intercedere, intercessi, intercessum, *v.* to intervene, come between

interdictum, -i, *n.* n. prohibition

interdiu, *adv.* by day, during the day

interdum, *adv.* occasionally, meanwhile

intereo, -ire, -ivi, -iturus, *v.* to perish

interemo, interemere, interemi, interemptum, *v.* to destroy, kill

interfector, -oris, *n.* m. killer

interficio, interficere, interfeci, interfectum, *v.* to kill, destroy

interim, *adv.* meanwhile

interimo = interemo

interlunium, -i, *n.* the new moon

intermitto, intermittere, intermisi, intermissum, *v.* to elapse, let space between

internicio, -ionis, *n.* f. destruction

internodium, -i, *n.* n. space between the knots on a reed

intero, interere, intrivi, intritum, *v.* to rub into, bruise, crush

interpres, intrepretis, *n.* m. translator

interpretatio, -ionis, *n.* f. explanation, interpretation

interpretor, interpretari, interpretatus, *v.* to interpret, explain

interrogatio, -ionis, *n.* f. questioning

intersum, interesse, interfui, interfuturum, *v.* to be different, be between or among; *impersonal:* it matters, interests, makes a difference

intolero (1), *v.* not to tolerate

intonsus, -a, -um, *adj.* unshorn

intorqueo, intorquere, intorsi, intortum, *v.* to twist around

intra, *adv.* and *prep.* (+ acc.) within, inside

intractio, -ionis, *n.* f. dragging

intremesco, intremescere, *v.* to tremble intensely

intro (1), *v.* to enter

intueor, intueri, intuitum, *v.* to regard, contemplate

inunguo, inunguere, inunxi, inunctum, *v.* to anoint

invalidus, -a, -um, *adj,* unwell, unhealthy, weak

invenio, invenire, inveni, inventum, *v.* to find, invent

inventor, -toris, *n.* m. inventor, discoverer, author

inventio, -ionis, *n.* f. invention, discovery

invictus, -a, -um, *adj.* unconquered

invidia, -ae, *n.* f. envy, jealousy, grudge
invito (1), *v.* to invite
invoco (1), *v.* to call upon, invoke
ipse, -a, -um, *pron.* himself, herself, itself, very
ira, -ae, *n.* f. wrath, anger
irascor, irasci, iratus, *v.* to be in a rage
is, ea, id, *pron.* this/that, he/she/it
ita, *adv*, so, thus
Italia, -ae, *n.* f. Italy
item, *adv.* likewise
iter, itineris, *n.* n. path, road
itero (1), *v.* to repeat, do again
iterum, *adv.* again
iubeo, iubere, iussi, iussum, *v.* to order, command
Iudaea, -ae, *n.* f. Judea
Iudaeus, -a, -um, *adj.* Judean; *n.* m. pl. the people of Judea
iudex, iudicis, *n.* m. judge
iudicium, -i, *n.* n. judgment, trial
iudico (1), *v.* to judge
iumentum, -i, *n.* n. a cart, draught-animals
iungo, iungere, iunxi, iunctum, *v.* to join
iusiurandum, iurisiurandi, *n.* n. an oath
iuro (1), *v.* to swear
ius, iuris, *n.* n. right, law, justice
iussus, -us, *n.* m. a command, order
iustitia, -ae, *n.* f. justice
iustus, -a, -um, *adj.* just, appropriate, fit
iuvenis, -is, -e, *adj.* youth, in the prime of life
iuventa, -ae, *n.* f. variant of *iuventus*, youth
iuventus, -tutis, *n.* f. the youth, the young people
iuxta, *adv.* and *prep.* (+ acc) next to

Kalendae, -arum, *n.* f. pl. Calends, first day of the month

labor/labos, laboris, *n.* m. labor, toil
labor, labi, lapsus, *v.* to slip, glide, slide
laboro (1), *v.* to work, labor
lac, lactis, *n.* m. milk

Lacedaemonius, -a, -um, *adj.* Lacedaemonian, Spartan

lacesso, lacessere, lacessivi, lacessitum, *v.* to provoke, challenge, stimulate

lacrima, -ae, *n.* f. tear

lacus, -us, *n.* m. basin, lake

laetitia, -ae, *n.* f. happiness

laevus, -a, -um, *adj.* left, lefthand, on the left side

lamentatio, -ionis, *n.* f. lamentation, weeping

lamina, -ae, *n.* f. laminate, thin wood or marble, veneer

lana, -ae, *n.* f. wool

lancea, -ae, *n.* f. light spear

lancino (1), *v.* to rend, destroy

languor, languoris, *n.* m. feebleness

lanificium, -i, *n.* n. weaving

lanugo, lanuginis, *n.* f. down

lanx, lancis, *n.* f. platter, dish

lapidicinae, -arum, *n.* f. pl. stone-quarry

lapis, lapidis, *n.* m. stone

lapsus, -us, *n.* m. slipping

largus, -a, -um, *adj.* abundant, plentiful

lascivio, lascivire, lascivii, lascivitum, *v.* to be wanton, frolic

lassesco, lassescere, *v.* to grow tired

latebra, -ae, *n.* f. hiding place, den

laterculus, -i, *n.* small brick, tile

latitudo, -tudinis, *n.* f. width, breadth

Latius, -a, -um, *adj.* pertaining to Latium; Latin

latratus, -us, *n.* m. a bark

laudatio, -ionis, *n.* f. a praising, speech of praise

laudo (1), *v.* to praise

laureus, -a, -um, *adj.* pertaining to a laurel

laus, laudis, *n.* f. praise

lautus, -a, -um, *adj.* elegant, costly, beautiful, fine (from *lavo*, to wash)

lectica, -ae, *n.* f. sedan-chair, litter

lectus, -i, *n.* m. bed, couch

legatio, -ionis, *n.* f. embassy

legatus, -i, *n.* legate, ambassador

lego, legere, legi, lectum, *v.* to read, choose

lembus, -i, *n.* m. a small, swift sailing vessel

leo, leonis, *n.* m. lion

letalis, -is, -e, *adj.* fatal

levis, -is, -e, *adj.* light, trifling

lēvis, -is, -e, *adj.* smooth

levo (1), *v.* to lighten, relieve, lift

lex, legis, *n.* f. law

libella, -ae, *n.* f. carpenter's level

Liber, Liberi, *n.* m. the Italian god of planting, identified with Dionysus

liber, libri. *n.* m. book

liberi, liberorum, *n.* m. pl. children

libero (1), *v.* to free, liberate

libertas, -tatis, *n.* f. freedom, liberty

libertus, -a, -um, *adj.* freed, freed-person

libet, libere, libui, libitum, *v.* to be pleasing

libido, libidinis, *n.* f. lust

libra, -ae, *n.* f. the pound, balance, scale

libro (1), *v.* to weigh, balance

liceo, licere, licui, licitum, *v.* to put on sale, (impersonal) to be allowed, (+ subjunctive = "although")

lictor, -oris, *n.* m. lictor, the attendant of a higher Roman magistrate

lienosus, -a, -um, *adj.* pertaining to the spleen

lignum, -i, *n.* n. wood

Lilybaeum, -i, *n.* n. a town and promontory in southern Sicily

limen, liminis, *n.* n. threshold

linea, -ae, *n.* f. line, thread

lingua, -ae, *n.* f. tongue, language

linum, -i, *n.* linen

lis, litis, *n.* f. litigation, quarrel

littera, -ae, *n.* f. letter, *pl*: epistle, literature, writing

litterarius, -a, -um, *adj.* pertaining to reading and writing

litus, litoris, *n.* n. shore

loco (1), *v.* to place, locate

loculus, -i, *n.* m. a small place, spot

locus, -i, *n.* m. place; in the plural: *loci, locorum* individual places; *loca, locorum*, connected places, region

locusta, -ae, *n.* f. locust

longinquitas, -tatis, *n.* f. length, distance

longinquus, -a, -um, *adj.* long, extensive, far off, removed

longitudo, -tudinis, *n.* f. length

longus, -a, -um, *adj.* far, remote, distant
loquor, loqui, locutus, *v.* to speak, converse, address
lorica, -ae, *n.* f. breastplate
loripes, loripedis, *adj.* bandy-legged
Luca bos, Lucae bovis, *n.* m. Lucanian cow = elephant
Lucanus, -a, -um, *adj.* Lucanian
lucerna, -ae, *adj.* oil-lamp
lucrum, -i, *n.* n. gain, profit
luctor, luctari, luctatus, *v.* to wrestle
luctus, -us, *n.* m. grief
ludibrium, -i, *n.* mockery, derision
ludus, -i, *n.* m. game, play, school
lumen, luminis, *n.* n. light
luna, -ae, *n.* f. moon
luo, luere, lui, *v.* to wash
lusorius, -a, -um, *adj.* sportive, playful
lustrum, -i, *n.* the five-year period between censuses
luteus, -a, -um, *adj.* muddy, made of clay
lutum, -i, *n.* mud, muck, clay
lux, lucis, *n.* f. light
luxuria, -ae, *n.* f. extravagance, excess

Macedonia, -ae, *n.* f. Macedonia, the land north of Greece
machina, -ae, *n.* f. war machine
machinalis, -is, -e, *adj.* pertaining to war machines
macula, -ae, *n.* f. spot, stain
Maeotae, -arum, *n.* m. the Scythians on lake Maeotis
maeror, maeroris, *n.* m. grief
magis, *adv.* more
magister, magistri, *n.* m. master, chief, leader
magisterium, -i, *n.* n. office of a magistrate
magnanimitas, -tatis, *n.* m. greatness of soul
magnificentia, -ae, *n.* f. magnificence
magnitudo, magnitudinis, *n.* f. magnitude, size, bigness
magnus, -a, -um, *adj.* great
maiestas, -tatis, *n.* f. greatness, grandeur, majesty
maleficium, -i, *n.* n. evil deed, offense, crime
malignus, -a, -um, *adj.* ill-disposed, evil

malo, malle, malui, *v.* to prefer (*magis + volo*)

mālus, -i, *n.* f. apple

mālus, -i, *n.* m. mast of a ship

malus, -a, -um, *adj.* wicked, evil, bad

mamma, -ae, *n.* f. breast

mancipium, -i, *n.* n. formal legal purchase

mando (1), *v.* to commit, charge

mando, mandere, mandi, mansum, *v.* to chew, masticate

maneo, manere, mansi, manum, *v.* to remain, stay

manes, manium, *n.* m. pl. the powerful spirits of the dead

mango, mangonis, *n.* m. slave dealer

manifestus, -a, -um, *adj.* clear, plain, evident

mantele, mantelis, *n.* n. napkin, hand-cloth

manubiae, -arum, *n.* f. money from the sale of war spoils

manumitto, manumittere, manumisi, manumissum, *v.* to free a slave, manumit

manus, -us, *n.* f. hand

mare, maris, *n.* n. sea

margarita, -ae, *n.* f. pearl

maritimus, -a, -um, *adj.* maritime, pertaining to the sea (inanimate things)

maritus, -i, *n.* m. husband

marmor, marmoris, *n.* n. marble

martulus, -i, *n.* m. small hammer

mas, maris, *n.* m. a male

mater, matris, *n.* f. mother

materia, -ae, *n.* f. material, matter

materiarius, -a, -um, *adj.* pertaining to lumber, timber

materies, -ei, *n.* f. = *materia, -ae*

matertera, -ae, *n.* f. maternal aunt

matrona, -ae, *n.* f. matron, married woman

matutinus, -a, -um, *adj.* at morning

Mauretania, -ae, *n.* f. the country of the Mauri in North Africa

maximus, -a, -um, *adj.* greatest, biggest

meatus, -us, *n.* m. passage, motion

medeor, mederi, *v.* to heal, remedy

medicamen, medicaminis, *n.* n. medication, drug

medicamentarius, -a, -um, *adj.* pertaining to drugs, poisons, medicines

medicina, -ae, *n.* f. medicine

medicus, -a, -um, *adj.* pertaining to healing

mediocris, -is, -e, *adj.* middling, average

meditor, meditari, meditatus, *v.* to reflect upon

medius, -a, -um, *adj.* middle

medulla, -ae, *n.* f. marrow

mel, mellis, *n.* n. honey

melicus, -a, -um, *adj.* lyric, lyrical; *n.* m. lyric poet

membrana, -ae, *n.* f. skin, parchment

membratim, *adv.* by species

membrum, -i, *n.* n. limb, arm, member

memor, memoris, *adj.* mindful

memorabilis, -is, -e, *adj.* remarkable, worthy to be remembered

memoria, -ae, *n.* f. memory, recollection

memoro (1), *v.* to mention, remind, tell of

mens, mentis, *n.* f. mind

mensis, -is, *n.* m. month

mensor, mensoris, *n.* measurer, surveyor

menstrualis, -is, -e, *adj.* monthly

mensura, -ae, *n.* f. measure

mentior, mentiri, mentitus, *v.* to lie, cheat, deceive

mercatura, -ae, *n.* f. commerce

merces, mercedis, *n.* f. wages, pay

mercor (1), *v.* to purchase

mereo, merere, merui, meritum / mereor, mereri, meritus, *v.* to merit, deserve

meretrix, meretricis, *n.* f. prostitute, call-girl, courtesan

mergo, mergere, mersi, mersum, *v.* to submerge, dip

meridianus, -a, -um, *adj.* pertaining to mid-day

meridies, meridiei, *n.* m. mid-day, noon

merito (1), *v.* to earn

metallum, -i, *n.* a mine, the metal from a mine

metior, metiri, mensus, *v.* to measure, mete out

metor (1), *v.* to measure, lay out

metus, -us, *n.* m. fear, dread

meus, -a, -um, *adj.* my, mine

miles, militis, *n.* m. soldier

Milesius, -a, -um, *v.* from Miletus

militaris, -is, -e, *adj.* pertaining to a soldier, to war

militia, -ae, *n.* f. soldiery, warfare

milito (1), *v.* to be a soldier

mille, *n.* n. thousand (plural declines: *milia, milium*)

mima, -ae, *n.* f. a female mime

mimus, -i, *n.* f. a male mime

minimus, -a, -um, *adj.* smallest, least

ministerium, -i, *n.* n. ministry, office, labor

minus, *adv.* less

mirabilis, -is, -e, *adj.* marvelous

miraculum, -i, *n.* n. miracle, wonder

mirificus, -a, -um, *adj.* wonderful, marvelous, causing wonder

miror, mirari, miratus, *v.* to marvel at

mirus, -a, -um, *adj.* marvelous

misceo, miscere, miscui, mixtum, *v.* to mix, stir

miser, misera, miserum, *adj,* miserable, wretched, pitiable

misereo, miserere, miserui, miseritum, *v.* to feel pity for

misereor, miserere, miseritus, *v.* to feel pity for

miseret, *v. impersonal* (+ acc. of person affected, gen. of cause), feel pity for

miseria, -ae, *n.* f. misery, wretchedness

misericordia, -ae, *n.* f. pity

mitifico (1), *v.* to make mild, ripen

mitto, mittere, misi, misum, *v.* to send, let go

modero (1), *v.* to moderate, regulate

modicus, -a, -um, *adj.* moderate

modulus, -i, *n.* measure, musical time, rhythm

modus, -i, *n.* m. mode, manner, way

moenia, moenium, *n.* n. pl. walls, fortification walls

mola, -ae, *n.* f. a mill, milled-grain, and therefore the cakes made from the grain

moles, molis, *n.* f. mass

mollio, mollire, mollivi, mollitum, *v.* to soften

mollis, -is, -e, *adj.* pliant, soft, delicate

molo, molere, molui, molitum, *v.* to grind in a mill

momentum, -i, *n.* n. motion, movement

monaulus, -i, *n.* m. a single pipe

monimentum, -i, *n.* n. a memorial, monument

mons, montis, *n.* m. mountain

monstrificus, -a, -um, *adj.* monstrous, strange

monstro (1), *v.* to show, point out

monstrum, -i, *n.* n. an omen, portent, monster

monumentum, -i, *n.* n. monument, memorial

morbus, -i, *n.* m. sickness, disease

mordeo, mordere, momordi, morsum, *v.* to bite

morior, mori, mortuus, *v.* to die

moror (1), *v.* to delay, tarry

mors, mortis, *n.* f. death

morsus, -us, *n.* m. bite, taste

mortalis, -is, -e, *adj.* mortal, liable to death

mortalitas, -tatis, *n.* f. mortality

mos, moris, *n.* m. manner, custom, fashion

motus, -us, *n.* m. motion

moveo, movere, movi, motum, *v.* to move

mox, *adv.* soon

mucro, mucronis, *n.* m. point, dagger, tooth

mulceo, mulcere, mulsi, mulsum/mulctum,
    v. to stroke, soothe, make pleasant

muliebris, -is, -e, *adj.* pertaining to a woman

mulier, mulieris, *n.* f. woman

mulio, mulionis, *n.* m. a mule driver

multiformis, -is, -e, *adj.* many-shaped, manifold

multitudo, multitudinis, *n.* f. great number, multitude

multus, -a, -um, *adj.* much, many

mulus, -i, *n.* m. mule

mundus, -i, *n.* m. world

munificentia, -ae, *n.* f. generosity

munus, muneris, *n.* n. duty, service, office, tribute

muralis, -is, -e, *adj.* pertaining to city walls

murmillo, -onis, *n.* m. a type of gladiator

mus, muris, *n.* m. mouse

musca, -ae, *n.* f. midge, mosquito

musicus, -a, -um, *adj.* musical, pertaining to music/poetry

mustum, -i, *n.* must, unfermented and unfiltered wine

mutatio, -ionis, *n.* f. change, alteration, mutation

mutilo (1), *v.* to lop off, mutilate

muto (1), *v.* to change

naevus, -i, *n.* m. mole, wart

nam, *conj.* (explanatory) for, because

naris, -is, *n.* f. nostril

narro (1), *v.* to narrate, dedicate

nascor, nasci, natus, *v.* to be born, produced, come into being

natalis, -is, -e, *adj.* pertaining to birth

natio, nationis, *n.* f. species, race, nation

natura, -ae, *n.* f. nature

naturalis, -is, -e, *adj.* natural, of nature

natus, -us, *n.* m. birth

naufragium, -i, *n.* n. shipwreck

navalis, -is, -e, *adj.* pertaining to ships, the navy

navigabilis, -is, -e, *adj.* navigable

navigo (1), *v.* to sail, set sail

navis, navis, *n.* f. ship

necessarius, -a, -um, *adj.* necessary, unavoidable

necesse, *adj.* n. necessary

neco (1), *v.* to kill, slay

nedum, *conj.* much less, to say nothing of

neglego, neglegere, neglexi, neglectum, *v.* to neglect

nego (1), *v.* to deny, to say . . . not

negotiator, -oris, *n.* m. banker, trader, wholesale dealer

nemo, neminis, *n.* m./f. no one

nempe, *conj.* to be sure

nepos, nepotis, *n.* m./f. grandchild, niece, nephew

neptis, -is, *n.* f. granddaughter

nequeo, nequire, nequivi, nequitum, *v.* to be unable

neque, *conj.* and not, nor

nequidem, *adv.* not even (often *ne . . . quidem* surrounding the word it negates)

nervus, -i, *n.* m. tendons, sinews, nerves, cords, strength

nescio, nescire, nescivi, nescitum, *v.* not to know, to be ignorant of

neuter, neutra, neutrum, *adj.* neither

nexus, -us, *n.* m. binding, tying

ni, *adv., conj.* except, unless (= *nisi*)

nidus, -i, *n.* m. nest

nigresco, nigrescere, nigrui, *v.* to grow black, darken

nihil, *n. indeclinable*, n. nothing

Nilus, -i, *n.* m. the Nile River

nimirum, *adv.* without doubt, truly

nimius, -a, -um, *adj.* excessive, very great

nisi, *conj.* except, unless

nitesco, nitescere, nitui, *v.* to begin to shine

nitor, niti, nisus/nixus, *v.* to strive, press forward, struggle

nitor, nitoris, *n.* m. brightness, sheen, luster

no (1), *v.* to swim, float

nobilis, -is, -e, *adj.* noble

nobilito (1), *v.* to make known, make famous

noceo, nocere, nocui, nocitum, *v.* (+ dat.) to harm, do harm to

noctu, *adv.* at night

nocturnus, -a, -um, *adj.* at night

nodus, -i, *n.* m. knot

nomen, -minis, *n.* n. name

nomino (1), *v.* to name, call by name

nonaginta, *n.* n. ninety

nonus, -a, -um, *adj.* ninth

norma, -ae, *n.* f. carpenter's square

nosco, noscere, novi, notum, *v.* to become acquainted with, recognize; in
   perfect: to know

noster, nostra, nostrum, *adj.* our

nota, -ae, *n.* f. mark, note

notabilis, -is, -e, *adj.* notable, noteworthy

nothus, -a, -um, *adj.* spurious, illegitimate, false

notitia, -ae, *n.* f. notice, knowledge, notion

noto (1), *v.* to note, mark, signify

notus, -a, -um, *adj.* known, well-known

novem, *n.* n. nine

noverca, -ae, *n.* f. stepmother

novitas, -tatis, *n.* f. novelty

novus, -a, -um, *adj.* new, recent

nox, noctis, *n.* f. night

noxius, -a, -um, *adj.* hurtful, harmful, noxious

nubilus, -a, -um, *adj.* cloudy, overcast

nubo, nubere, nupsi, nuptum, *v.* (+ dat.) to marry

nudus, -a, -um, *adj.* bare, nude

nullus, -a, -um, *adj.* no one, none

numen, -minis, *n.* n. divinity, divine will

numero (1), *v.* to count, number

numerosus, -a, -um, *adj.* numerous

numerus, -i, *n.* m. number

numquam, *adv.* never

nunc, *adv.* now

nuncupo (1), *v.* to call by name

nuntio (1), *v.* to announce

nuntius, -i, *n.* m. message, messenger

nuper, *adv.* just now, recently

nuptiae, -arum, *v.* f. pl. marriage

nurus, -us, *n.* f. daughter-in-law

nux, nucis, *n.* f. nut

ob, *prep.* (+ acc) on account of, in front of

obduco, obducere, obduxi, obductum, *v.* to cover

obedientia = oboedientia

obeo, obire, obivi, obitum, *v.* to go to meet, depart, perish

oberro (1), *v.* to wander about

obicio, obicere, obieci, obiectum, *v.* to throw against/towards, to offer, present

obliquus, -a, -um, *adj.* slanting, askew

oblivio, -ionis, *n.* f. forgetfulness

obliviscor, oblivisci, oblitus, *v.* to forget

obnitor, obniti, obnixus, *v.* to lean against, strive against

obnoxius, -a, -um, *adj.* guilty, subject to punishment, culpable, infirm

oboedentia, -ae, *n.* f. obedience

obruo, obruere, obrui, obrutum, *v.* to overwhelm

observatio, -ationis, *n.* f. observation, watching, duty

observo (1), *v.* to observe, watch

obsideo, obsidere, obsedi, obsessum, *v.* to sit at, besiege

obsidio, obsidionis, *n.* f. siege

obsidionalis, -is, -e, *adj.* pertaining to a siege

obsido, obsidere, *v.* to besiege

obstringo, obstringere, obstrinxi, obstrictum, *v.* to hamper

obtero, obterere, obtrivi, obtritum, *v.* to crush, bruise

obtineo, obtinere, obtinui, obtentum, *v.* to obtain, get

obvius, -a, -um, *adj.* in the way of, to meet

occasus, -us, *n.* m. setting, sunset, West

occido, occidere, occisi, occisum, *v.* to strike down, crush, kill

occido, occidere, occidi, occasum, *v.* to fall, fall down

occiduus, -a, -um, *adj.* setting, falling, sinking

occissime, *adv.* superlative of *ocior*

occultatio, -ionis, *n.* f. hiding

occumbo, occumbere, occubui, occubitum, *v.* to fall, die

occurro, occurrere, occurri, occursum, *v.* to run up to, meet, oppose

occursus, -us, *n.* m. meeting

oceanus, -i, *n.* m. ocean

ocior, ocior, ocius, *adj.* quicker

ocrea, -ae, *n.* f. greave

octavus, -a, -um, *adj.* eighth

octiens, *adv.* eight times

octo, *n.* n. eight

octogensimus, -a, -um, *adj.* eightieth

octoginta, *adj.* eighty

octoni, -ae, -a, *adj.* eight at a time

oculus, -i, *n.* m. eye

odi, odisse, *v.* to hate

odium, -i, *n.* n. hatred, grudge

odor, odoris, *n.* m. smell, scent

odoro (1), *v.* to emit a smell, perfume

offendo, offendere, offendi, offensum, *v.* to strike against

officium, -i, *n.* n. duty

oleum, -i, *n.* n. olive, olive oil, olive-tree

olfactus, -us, *n.* m. the sense of smell

olim, *adv.* once (in the past)

Olympia, -ae, *n.* f. the city Olympia, at which the Olympic games were held

Olympionices, ae, *n.* m, Olympian victor

omitto, omittere, omisi, omissum, *v.* to omit, let fall

omnis, omnis, omne, *adj.* all, each, every

oneraria, -ae, *n.* f. a transport ship

onus, oneris, *n.* n. burden

onustus, -a, -um, *adj.* burdened, laden

opera, -ae, *n.* f. work, effort

operarius, -a, -um, *adj.* pertaining to labor (*opus*)

operosus, -a, -um, *adj.* painstaking, laborious

opinio, -ionis, *n*. f. opinion, reputation

oppidum, -i, *n*. n. town

oppono, opponere, opposui, oppositum, *v*. to set opposite, oppose

opportunus, -a, -um, *adj*. opportune, advantageous, suitable

opprimo, opprimere, oppressi, oppressum, *v*. to suppress, crush, overwhelm

oppugnatio, -ionis, *n*. f. siege, attack

ops, opis, *n*. f. wealth, resource, power, influence, aid

opto (1), *v*. to choose, opt

opus, operis, *n*. n. work, labor (in any sense)

ora, -ae, *n*. f. shore

oraculum, -i, *n*. prophecy, oracle

oratio, -tionis, *n*. f. speech

orator, -oris, *n*. m. orator, speaker

orbis, orbis, *n*. m. orb, sphere, globe, circle

orbitas, -tatis, *n*. f. bereavement, orphanage

orbus, -a, -um, *adj*. deprived, bereft, orphaned

ordino (1), *v*. to set in order

ordo, ordinis, *n*. m. order, political class

organum, -i, *n*. n. instrument, engine

origo, originis, *n*. f. origin, beginning

orior, oriri, ortus, *v*. to rise

ornamentum, -i, *n*. n. furniture, trappings, ornament

oro (1), *v*. to pray, beg

ortus, -us, *n*. m. rising, sunrise, East

os, oris, *n*. n. face, mouth, speech

os, ossis, *n*. n. bone

oscitatio, -ionis, *n*. f. yawning

osseus, -a, -um, *adj*. boney, made of bone

ostendo, ostendere, ostendi, ostentum/ostensum, *v*. to show, present, proffer

ostentatio, -ionis, *n*. f. exhibition, display

ovis, ovis, *n*. m./f. sheep

pabulum, -i, *n*. n. fodder, nourishment

paene, *adv*. almost

paenitentia, -ae, *n*. f. repentance

pala, -ae, *n*. f. spade

palam, *adv., prep*. (+ abl.), openly, publicly

palma, -ae, *n*. f. palm

palmus, -i, *n*. m. palm, a measure of width

palpito (1), *v*. to throb

palus, paludis, *n*. f. swamp, marsh

pando, pandere, pandi, passum/pansum, *v*. to spread out, unfold

pango, pangere, panxi/pegi/pepigi, pactum, *v*. to make fast, determine, fix, contract

panis, panis, *n*. m. bread

Pannonicus, -a, -um, *adj*. pertaining to the region Pannonia

panthera, -ae, *n*. f. panther

pantomimus, -i, *n*. m. pantomime, dancer

Paphlagonia, -ae, *n*. f. a province on the Black Sea, now northern Turkey

papyrus, -i, *n*. m. papyrus, paper

par, paris, *adj*. equal

parco, parcere, peperci, parsum, *v*. (+ dat.) to spare

parcus, -a, -um, *adj*. sparing

parens, parentis, *n*. m/f. parent

pareo, parere, parui, paritum, *v*. to appear, be present, be obedient to

pario, parere, peperi, partum, *v*. to give birth to

pariter, *adv*. equally

paro (1), *v*. to prepare, ready

parricida, -ae, *n*. f. parricide, murder of a parent

pars, partis, *n*. f. part, region

Parthus, -a, -um, *adj*. Parthian

particulatim, *adv*. piecemeal, bit by bit

partus, -us, *n*. m. birth, birthing

parum, *adv*. too little

parvus, -a, -um, *adj*. small, puny, little

pasco, pascere, pavi, pastum, *v*. to feed, pasture

passim, *adv*. at random, in every direction

passus, -us, *n*. m. step, pace

pateo, patere, patui, *v*. to lay open

pater, patris, *n*. m. father

patientia, -ae, *n*. f. patience, endurance

patior, pati, passus, *v*. to suffer, endure, experience

patria, -ae, *n*. f. country, fatherland

patrius, -a, -um, *adj*. paternal, fatherly, pertaining to a father or country

pauci, -ae, -a, *adj*. few

paulus, -a, -um, *adj.* little, small

paululus, -a, -um, *adj.* very little, very small

paveo, pavere, pavi, *v.* to tremble in fear, feel panic

pavidus, -a, -um, *adj.* panicky, frightened

pavo, pavonis, *n.* m. peacock

pavor, pavoris, *n.* m. panic, anxiety, trembling

pax, pacis, *n.* f. peace

pectus, pectoris, *n.* n. chest

pecuarius, -a, -um, *adj.* pertaining to cattle

peculiaris, -is, -e, *adj.* extraordinary

pecus, pecoris, *n.* n. herd of cattle (cf. *pecus, pecudis, n.* n. single cow)

pecus, pecudis, *n.* f. one of a herd of cattle (cf. *pecus, pecoris, n.* n. herd of cattle)

Pelius, -i, *n.* m. (variant of Pelion, -i, n.) Mount Pelion in Thessaly

pellis, -is, *n.* f. skin, leather

pello, pellere, pepuli, pulsum, *v.* to strike, beat, beat back

penates, penatium, *n.* m. the gods of the household

pendeo, pendere, pependi, *v.* to hang

pendo, pendere, pependi, pensum, *v.* to weigh, weigh out

penetro (1), *v.* to penetrate, pierce, enter

pensito (1), *v.* to weigh out

penuria, -ae, *n.* f. poverty, penury (also *paenuria*)

per, *prep.* (+ acc.) through, via, by

perago, peragere, peregi, peractum, *v.* to carry out, complete, pierce

percenseo, percensere, percensui, *v.* to count up, survey

percussus, -us, *n.* m. striking

percutio, percutere, percussi, percussum, *v.* to strike through, pierce, slay

perdo, perdere, perdidi, perditum, *v.* to lose, destroy

perduellis, -is, *n.* m. enemy

pereo, perire, perivi, peritum, *v.* to perish

perfero, perferre, pertuli, perlatum, *v.* to endure, carry through to the end

perfundo, perfundere, perfudi, perfusum, *v.* to bedew, drench

perfungor, perfungi, perfunctum, *v.* (+ abl.) to discharge a duty

perhibeo, perhibere, perhibui, perhibitum, *v.* to hold out, extend, provide, bestow

periclitor (1), *v.* to be in danger, run a risk

periculum, -i, *n.* n. danger, hazard, risk

perinde, *adv.* just so

periplus, -i, *n.* m. a circumnavigation
permuto (1), *v.* to change around
pernicialis, -is, -e, *adj.* pernicious, destructive, deadly
pernicies, -ei, *n.* f. disaster, calamity
pernicitas, -tatis, *n.* f. swiftness, nimbleness
pernix, pernicis, *adj.* swift
perpendiculum, -i, *n.* n. a plumb line,
perpetuus, -a, -um, *adj.* uninterrupted, unbroken, constant, universal
perquam, *adv.* exceedingly
Persa, -ae, *n.* m. a Persian
perscribo, perscribere, perscripsi, perscriptum, *v.* to write in full,
     note down
persequor, persequi, persecutus, *v.* to follow after, persevere
persona, -ae, *n.* f. mask
persto, perstare, perstiti, perstatum, *v.* to stand firm, be constant
pertineo, pertinere, pertinui, *v.* to stretch out to, arrive at, pertain to
pertraho, pertrahere, pertraxi, pertractum, *v.* to be dragged
Perusinus, -a, -um, *adj.* pertaining to the city Perusia, modern Perugia
pervenio, pervenire, perveni, perventum, *v.* to arrive at
pervideo, pervidere, pervidi, pervisus, *v.* to see, survey, discern
pes, pedis, *n.* m. foot
pestifer, pestifera, pestiferum, *adj.* bringing destruction
pestilentia, -ae, *n.* f. pestilence, plague
petitio, -tionis, *n.* f. seeking, canvassing for office
peto, petere, petivi, petitum, *v.* to seek, attack
phalangae, -arum, *n.* f. pole, roller
phalerae, -arum, *n.* f. pl. boss, metal disc, decoration
Pharsalia, -ae, *n.* f. district in northern Greece
philosophus, -i, *n.* m. philosopher
phoenix, phoenicis, *adj.* Phoenician
phoenix, phoenicis, *n.* m. the Phoenix
piaculum, -i, *n.* an expiation
pictor, pictoris, *n.* m. painter
pictura, -ae, *n.* f. painting, picture
pietas, pietatis, *n.* f. piety, devotion
pila, -ae, *n.* f. ball
pilum, -i, *n.* n. heavy javelin
pilus, -i, *n.* m. a hair

pingo, pingere, pinxi, pictum, *v.* to paint, decorate

pinna, -ae, *n.* f. = *penna*, wing

pirata, -ae, *n.* m. pirate

piraticus, -a, -um, *adj.* pertaining to pirates

piscator, piscatoris, *n.* m. fisher

piscis, -is, *n.* m. fish

pituita, -ae, *n.* f. phlegm

pius, -a, -um, *adj,* pious, devoted

Placentia, -ae, *n.* f. the city Placentia, modern Piacenza

placeo, placere, placui, placitum, *v.* to please

placidus, -a, -um, *adj.* peaceful

planta, -ae, *n.* f. sole of the foot

plaudo, plaudere, plausi, plausum, *v.* to clap, strike, applaud

plebs, plebis, *n.* f. the people, common people also **plebes, plebei**

plenilunium, -i, *n.* n. full moon

plenus, -a, -um, *adj.* full

plerusque, pleraque, plerumque, *adj.* very great many, very great part

plicatura, -ae, *n.* f. folding

ploro (1), *v.* weep

pluma, -ae, *n.* f. feather, down

plumbeus, -a, -um, *adj.* made of lead, leaden

plumbum, -i, *n.* lead

plus, pluris, *adj.* more

pneumaticus, -a, -um, *adj.* pneumatic, pertaining to air

poema, poematis, *n.* n. poem

poena, -ae, *n.* f. penalty, punishment, recompense

Poenus, -a, -um, *adj.* Phoenician

poeta, -ae, *n.* m. poet

poeticus, -a, -um, *adj.* pertaining to poetry

polleo, pollere, *v.* to be powerful

pollex, pollicis, *n.* m. thumb, big toe

polliceor, polliceri, pollicitus, *v.* to promise

pollicitatio, -ionis, *n.* f. a promise

pompa, -ae, *n.* f. a procession

pondo, *adv.* by weight

pondus, ponderis, *n.* n. weight

pono, ponere, posui, positum or **postum**, *v.* to put, place

pons, pontis, *n.* m. bridge

pontifex, pontificis, *n.* m. priest

Pontus, -i, *n.* m. the Black Sea, Black Sea region

poples, poplitis, *n.* m. hamstring, back of the knee

popularis, -is, -e, *adj.* pertaining to the people

populus, -i, *n.* m. people, populace

porrigo, porrigere, porrexi, porrectum, *v.* to stretch out, spread out, extend

porta, -ae, *n.* f. door, gate

portendo, portendere, portendi, portentum, *v.* to presage, foretell

portio, -tionis, *n.* f. a share, portion, part

porto (1), *v.* to carry, convey, bear

portus, -us, *n.* m. port, harbor

posco, poscere, poposci, *v.* to request, demand

possessio, -ionis, *n.* f. possession, taking, seizing

possum, posse, potui, *v.* to be able

post *prep.* (+ acc.) after

postea, *adv.* afterwards

posterus, -a, -um, *adj.* later, afterwards; in plural: descendants

postis, postis, *n.* m. post, doorpost, door

postremo, *adv.* finally, at last

postulo (1), *v.* to demand, ask, require

poto (1), *v.* to drink

potentia, -ae, *n.* f. potency, power

potio, -ionis, *n.* f. a drink, a draught

potius, *adv.* rather

poto (1), *v.* to drink

potus, -us, *n.* m. a drink

praeacuo, praeacuere, praeacui, praeacutum, *v.* to sharpen at one end

praealtus, -a, -um, *adj.* exceedingly high

praebeo, praebere, praebui, praebitum, *v.* to hold forth, supply, furnish

praeceler, praeceleris, praecelere, *adj.* very swift

praecello, praecellere, *v.* to excel

praecipio, praecipere, praecepi, praeceptum, *v.* to instruct, teach, take in advance

praecipito (1), *v.* to throw headlong

praecipuus, -a, -um, *adj.* particular, special, principal

praeclarus, -a, -um, *adj.* very distinguished, very bright

praecludo, praecludere, praeclusi, praeclusum, *v.* to shut, close

praecox, praecocis, *adj.* hasty, premature

praeda, -ae, *n*. f. booty, loot, prey

praedico, praedicere, praedixi, praedictum, *v*. to proclaim, publish, predict

praedictio, -ionis, *n*. prediction, telling in advance

praedium, -i, *n*. n. an estate, manor

praedo, -onis, *n*. m. brigand, robber

praefatio, -tionis, *n*. f. preface, title

praefectura, -ae, *n*. f. the office of prefect

praefero, praeferre, praetuli, praelatum, *v*. (+ acc.) to prefer one thing, (+ dat.) to another

praefor, praefari, praefatus, *v*. to pronounce in advance

praegravis, -is, -e, *adj*. very heavy

praematurus, -a, -um, *adj*. early, untimely

praemitto, praemittere, praemisi, praemissum, *v*. to send in advance

praemorior, praemori, praemortuus, *v*. to die in advance

praepes, praepetis, *adj*. swift, headlong, flying

praeposterus, -a, -um, *adj*. reversed

praepilatus, -a, -um, *adj*. a blunted/ball tipped (of a spear)

praerodo, praerodere, [praerosi], praerosus, *v*. to gnaw off, esp. the tip

praerogativum, -i, *n*. n. a token, sign

praesagio, -ire, -ivi, -itum, *v*. to have foreknowledge, forebode, predict

praesagium, -i, *n*. n. foreboding, presage

praesens, praesentis, *adj*. present at hand

praesepium, -i, *n*. n. stable, pen

praeses, praesids, *n*. m. ruler

praesidium, -i, *n*. n. defense, bulwark, garrison

praesto, praestare, praestiti, praestitum, *v*. to stand out, be superior, show, offer

praestringo, praestringere, praestrinxi, praestrictum, *v*. to tie up, compress, weaken

praeter, *prep*. past, beyond

praeterea, *adv*. additionally

praetereo, praeterire, praeterivi, praeteritum, *v*. to pass over

praeterquam, *adv*. beyond, besides, except

praetor, praetoris, *n*. m. praetor

praetorium, i, *n*. n. the imperial bodyguard

praetorius, -a, -um, *adj*. pertaining to a praetor

praetura, -ae, *n*. f. praetorship

praevaleo, praevalere, praevalui, *v.* to be more powerful, to prevail

praeverto, praevertere, praeverti, praeversum, *v.* to turn one's attention to

prandeo, prandere, prandi, pransum, *v.* to have breakfast

pravus, -a, -um, *adj.* crooked, distorted

prehendo, prehendere, prehendi, prehensum, *v.* to catch, grab

pretiosus, -a, -um, *adj.* precious, valuable, expensive

pretium, -i, *n.* n. price, value

prex, precis, *n.* f. prayer, imprecation

pridem, *adv.* long ago

iam pridem, *adv.* long since

pridie, *adv.* on the day before

primarius, -a, -um, *adj.* first rate, chief

primatus, -us, *n.* m. the first place, primacy

primoris, -is, -e, *adj.* foremost, front rank

primus, -a, -um, *adj.* first

princeps, principis, *n.* m. first man, prince

principatus, -us, *n.* m. principate, first place

principium, -i, *n.* n. beginning, origin

prior, prior, prius, *adj.* prior, earlier

priscus, -a, -um, *adj.* ancient, antique

priusquam, *conj.* before

privatim, *adv.* separately, individually

privignus, -i, *n.* m. step-son

pro, *prep.* (+ abl.) on behalf of, due to, in lieu of, for

probitas, -tatis, *n.* f. uprightness, honesty

probo (1), *v.* to inspect, approve, deem fit

proboscis, -idis, *n.* f. trunk

probus, -a, -um, *adj.* proper, upright, honest

procer, proceris, *n.* m. chief, leading man

proceritas, proceritatis, *n.* f. height, growth

procerus, -a, -um, *adj.* tall

procido, procidere, procidi, *v.* to fall forward, fall out

proconsul, proconsulis, *n.* m. proconsul

procul, *adv.* from afar

procurator, procuratoris, *n.* m. bailiff, overseer

procuro (1), *v.* to care for, attend to

procurso (1), *v.* to attack, sally forth

prodigiosus, -a, -um, *adj.* unnatural, prodigious

prodigium, -i, *n.* n. a prodigy, portent, omen

proditio, -ionis, *n.* f. discovery, betrayal

prodo, prodere, prodidi, proditum, *v.* to produce, bring forth, publish

produco, producere, produxi, productum, *v.* to bring out, produce

proelior (1), *v.* to battle

proelium, -i, *n.* n. battle

profecto, *adv.* indeed, truly, aye

professio, -ionis, *n.* f. profession

professor, -oris, *n.* m. professor, teacher

proficio, proficere, profeci, profectum, *v.* to benefit

proflo (1), *v.* to blow forth, breathe out, melt

profluvium, -i, *n.* n. flow

profugio, profugere, profugi, profugitum, *v.* to flee in front of

profugus, -a, -um, *adj.* fugitive

progredior, progredi, progressus, *v.* to go forward, proceed

prohibeo, prohibere, prohibui, prohibitum, *v.* to prohibit, restrain

proinde, *adv.* in like manner, therefore

promitto, promittere, promisi, promissum, *v.* to promise

promoveo, promovere, promovi, promotum, *v.* to move forward, advance

promunturium, -i, *n.* n. a promontory, headland, highest point

pronepos, pronepotis, *n.* m. great-grandson

pronuntio (1), *v.* to proclaim, announce

pronus, -a, -um, *adj.* bent forward, face-down

propago (1), *v.* to propagate, extend, generate

prope, *adv.* and *prep.* (+ acc.), near, near to

propemodum, *adv.* nearly, almost

propere, *adv.* hastily

propinquus, -a, -um, *adj.* near, neighboring, related

proprius, -a, -um, *adj.* one's own, particular

propter, *prep.* (+ acc.), on account of

propugnator, -oris, *n.* m. defender

prora, -ae, *n.* f. prow

prosa, -ae, *n.* f. prose

proscribo, proscribere, proscripsi, proscriptum, *v.* to proscribe

proscriptio, -tionis, *n.* f. proscription

proscriptor, -oris, *n.* m. one who issues proscriptions

prosequor, prosequi, prosecutus, *v.* to follow, pursue, honor

prosperitas, -tatis, *n.* f. success, prosperity

prospicio, prospicere, prospexi, prospectum, *v.* to spy from a distance, look out toward

prosterno, prosternere, prostravi, prostratum, *v.* to strew in front of, throw down on the ground, prostrate

protego, protegere, protexi, protectum, *v.* to protect, cover

protero, proterere, protrivi, protritum, *v.* to drive away, trample

protinus, *adv.* straightaway, immediately

provenio, provenire, proveni, proventum, *v.* to come forth, arise

provincia, -ae, *n.* f. province

provocatio, -tionis, *n.* f. a summons, an appeal to a higher court, hand-to-hand combat

proximus, -a, -um, *adj.* nearest, next

prudentia, -ae, *n.* f. foresight, good sense

pubertas, -tatis, *n.* f. puberty

pubes, puberis, *adj.* pubescent, adult

publico (1), *v.* to make public, publish

publicus, -a, -um, *adj.* public

pudet, pudere, pudui, puditum, *v.* (+ acc. of person, + gen. of cause of shame) to feel shame

pudicitia, -ae, *n.* f. modesty, chastity

pudicus, -a, -um, *adj.* modest, chaste

pudor, -oris, *n.* m. shame, modesty

puer, pueri, *n.* m. boy

puerilis, -is, -e, *adj.* childish, boyish

pueritia, -ae, *n.* f. boyhood, childhood, youth

puerperium, -i, *n.* n. childbirth, infant

puerpera, -ae, *n.* f. a woman in childbirth

puerperus, -a, -um, *adj.* child-bearing, in labor

pugno (1), *v.* to fight

pullus, -i, *n.* m. chick

pultarius, -i, *n.* m. a cup for warm drinks

Punicus, -a, -um, *adj.* Punic, Carthaginian

pupilla, -ae, *n.* f. pupil

pupillaris, -is, -e, *adj.* pertaining to a ward

puppis, puppis, *n.* f. the stern of a ship, a ship

purifico (1), *v.* to purify, cleanse

putamen, -minis, *n.* n. shell

Puteoli, -orum, *n.* m. pl. the city Puteoli, modern Puzzuoli

puteus, -i, *n.* m. well

puto (1), *v.* to think, consider, reckon

pycta, -ae, *n.* f. boxer

Pyrenaeus, -a, -um, *adj.* pertaining to the Pyrenees Mountains

pyrriche, -es, *n.* f. (Greek declension) the Pyrrhic dance in armor

quadrageni, -ae, -a, *adj.* forty each

quadragensimus, -a, -um, *adj.* fortieth

quadragiens, *adv.* forty times

quadraginta, *n.* n. forty

quadriduum, -i, *n.* n. a period of four days

quadriennium, -i, *n.* n. period of four years

quadriga, -ae, *n.* f. a team of four horses, the chariot they pull

quadrini, -ae, -a, *adj.* four each

quadripertitus, -a, -um, *adj.* divided into four

quadripes, quadripedis, *adj.* having four feet

quadriremis, -is, -e, *adj.* with four banks of oars

quadruplus, -a, -um, *adj.* fourfold

quaero, quaerere, quaesivi, quaesitum, *v.* to seek, procure

quaestio, -ionis, *n.* f. question, inquiry, seeking

qualis, -is, -e, *pron. adj.* of what sort, what kind

qualiter, *adv.* in which way

quamquam, *conj.* although

quando, *adv.* and *conj.* since, when

quandoquidem, *adv.* since indeed

quantulus, -a, -um, *adj.* how little

quantus, -a, -um, *adj.* how much, how great

quapropter, *adv.* wherefore, why

quare, *adv.* how, why, wherefore

quartanus, -a, -um, *adj.* quartan, on the fourth day

quartus, -a, -um, *adj.* fourth

quater, *adv.* four times

quaterni, -ae, -a, *adv.* four by four, four at a time

quattuor, *n.* four

queo, quire, quivi, quitum, *v.* to be able

qui, quae, quod, *pron.* who, which

quia, *conj.* since, because

quicumque, quaecumque, quodcumque, *pron.* whoever, whatever

quidam, quaedam, quoddam, *pron.* a certain one

quidem, *adv.* indeed

quies, quietis, *n.* f. rest

quiesco, quiescere, quievi, quietus, *v.* to rest, be quiet

quilibet, quaelibet, quidlibet, *pron.* anyone at all

quin *conj.* (interrogative particle = *qui [abl] ne*) why not? (rel. particle = *qui [nom] ne*) but that, who . . . not . . .; that not, yea verily

quindecem, *adj.* fifteen

quindeciens, *adv.* fifteen times

quingenarius, -a, -um, *adj.* consisting of five hundred

quingentus, -i, *n.* m. five-hundred

quini, -ae, -a, *adj.* by fives

quinquageni, -ae, -a, *adj.* fifty by fifty, by fifties

quinquagensimus, -a, -um, *adj.* fiftieth

quinquagiens, *adv.* fifty times

quinquaginta, *adj.* fifty

quinque, *n. indecl.* five

quinquennis, -is, -e, *adj.* of five years

quinqueremis, -is, -e, *adj.* with five banks of oars

quini, -ae, -a, *adj.* five each

quippe, *adv.* to be sure, in fact

quis, quis, quid, *pron.* who? what?

quisquam, quaequam, quidquam or **quicquam,** *pron.* anyone, anything

quisque, quidque, *pron.* each one, each thing

quisquis, quaequae, quodquod, *pron.* whoever, whatever

quodammodo, *adv.* in a certain way

quoniam, *conj.* since

quoque, *conj.* also

quot, *adj.* how man

quotiens, *adv.* how many times, how often

rabidus, -a, -um, *adj.* rabid, furious, enraged

rabies, -ei, *n.* f. madness

radius, -i, *n.* m. ray

radix, radicis, *n.* f. root

rado, radere, rasi, rasum, *v.* to shave

ramus, -i, *n.* m. branch

rapio, rapere, rapui, raptum, *v.* to seize, snatch, grab, carry away

raritas, -tatis, *n*. f. looseness, distance

rarus, -a, -um, *adj*. rare, loose, thin, opposite of dense

ratio, rationis, *n*. f. reason, account

ratis, -is, *n*. f. raft

rebellio, -ionis, *n*. f. rebellion

rebello (1), *v*. to rebel

recens, recentis, *adj*. recent, fresh

recipio, recipere, recepi, receptum, *v*. to receive

recito (1), *v*. to recite, repeat from memory

recognosco, recognoscere, recognovi, recognitum, *v*. to recollect

recondo, recondere, recondidi, reconditum, *v*. to put back up, bury

recte, *adv*. upright

rector, rectoris, *n*. m. leader, guider, director

recupero (1), *v*. to recover

reddo, reddere, reddidi, redditum, *v*. to return, give back

redigo, redigere, redegi, redactum, *v*. to bring back

redimo, redimere, redemi, redemptum, *v*. to buy back, buy off, ransom, avert, compensate for

reditus, -us, *n*. m. return

reduco, reducere, reduxi, reductum, *v*. to bring back, return

redundatio, -ionis, *n*. f. abundance, overflowing

redux, reducis, *adj*. leading back

refello, refellere, refelli, *v*. to disprove

refero, referre, retuli, relatum, *v*. to bring back, carry back, relate

refert, *v. impersonal*. it matters, it makes a difference, it is important

refodio, refodere, refodi, refossum, *v*. to dig up, dig out

refuto (1), *v*. to refute, disprove

regenero (1), *v*. to reproduce

regimen, regiminis, *n*. n. guiding, direction, ruling

regio, regionis, *n*. f. region, area

regius, -a, -um, *adj*. royal, pertaining to the king

regno (1), *v*. to rule, reign as king

regnum, -i, *n*. n. kingdom

regredior, regredi, regressus, *v*. to go back, return

regulus, -i, *n*. m. kinglet, chieftain

relatio, -ionis, *n*. f. bringing back, narration

relegatio, -ionis, *n*. f. banishment, exile

relego (1), *v*. to send away, remove

religio, ionis, *n*. f. superstition, obligation, religion.

religo (1), *v*. to bind back, fasten up

relinquo, relinquere, reliqui, relictum, *v*. to leave behind

reliquus, -a, -um, *adj*. remaining

remaneo, remanere, remansi, *v*. to stay, remain behind

remeo (1), *v*. to go back, return

remitto, remittere, remisi, remissum, *v*. to let go, send back

remus, -i, *n*. m. oar

renuo, renuere, renui, *v*. to refuse, deny

reor, reri, ratus, *v*. to think, deem, reckon, suppose

repello, repellere, reppuli, repulsum, *v*. to reject, repel, drive back

repens, repentis, *adj*. sudden

repente, *adv*. suddenly

repentinus, -a, -um, *adj*. sudden, hasty

reperio, reperire, repperi, repertum, *v*. to find out, obtain, procure, discover, uncover

repeto, repetere, repetivi, repetitum, *v*. to attack again, revisit

repo, repere, repsi, reptum, *v*. to creep, crawl

repraesento (1), *v*. to represent, exhibit

repudio (1), *v*. to divorce, reject

repudium, -i, *n*. n. divorce, rejection

repulsa, -ae, *n*. f. repulse, defeat

reputation, -ionis, *n*. f. thinking over, reckoning

reputo (1), *v*. to think over, reckon

requiro, requirere, requisivi, requisitum, *v*. to look for again, inquire after

res, rei, *n*. f. matter, affair, business

resisto, resistere, restiti, *v*. to arise, stand back up, resist

resolvo, resolvere, resolvi, resolutum, *v*. to untie, unbind, release, relax

respiro (1), *v*. to exhale, breathe out, breathe

respondeo, respondere, respondi, responsum, *v*. to answer, reply

res publica, rei publicae, *n*. f. republic

respuo, respuere, respui, *v*. to spit back out, reject

restis, -is, *n*. f. rope, cord

restito (1), *v*. to loiter, tarry

restituo, restituere, restitui, restitutum, *v*. to restore, rebuild, set back up

resupinus, -a, -um, *adj*. bent backwards, on one's back

rete, retis, *n*. n. net, tapestry

retineo, retinere, retinui, retentus, *v*. to hold back, restrain, keep back

retro, *adv.* backwards, from behind
retroago, retroagere, retroegi, retroactum, *v.* to drive back, turn back
retrorus, *adv.* backwards, turned back
reveho, revehere, revexi, revectum, *v.* to carry back, convey back
reverto, revertere, reverti, reversum, *v.* to turn back, return
revivesco = revivisco, reviviscere, revixi, *v.* to come to life again
revoco (1), *v.* to call back
rex, regis, *n.* m. king
Rhodii, -orum, *n.* m. pl. the people of the city Rhodes
rideo, ridere, risi, risum, *v.* to laugh, smile
rigeo, rigere, *v.* to be stiff, numb
rigor, rigoris, *n.* m. stiffness, rigidity
ripa, -ae, *n.* f. river bank
ritus, -us, *n.* m. custom, mode, rite
robigo, robiginis, *n.* f. rust, mildew, mold
robur, roboris, *n.* n. hardwood, oak
robustus, -a, -um, *adj.* made of oak, strong
rogus, -i, *n.* m. funeral pyre
Roma, -ae, *n.* f. Rome
Romanus, -a, -um, *adj.* Roman
rostrum, -i, *n.* n. beak, snout
rota, -ae, *n.* f. wheel
ruber, rubra, rubrum, *adj.* red
ructo (1), *v.* to belch
rudimentum, -i, *n.* n. beginning, first attempt
ruga, -ae, *n.* f. wrinkle, crease
ruina, -ae, *n.* f. ruin, collapse
rumpo, rumpere, rupi, ruptum, *v.* to break burst
rupes, rupis, *n.* f. crag, cliff, rock
rursus, *adv.* again
russeus, -a, -um, *adj.* red, reddish

sacer, sacra, sacrum, *adj.* sacred, consecrated, accursed
sacrificium, -i, *n.* n. sacrifice
sacrifico (1), *v.* to make a sacrifice
saecularis, -is, -e, *adj.* pertaining to the secular games
saeculum, -i, *n.* n. century, age
saepe, *adv.* often

saepes, saepis, *n.* f. hedge, fence, enclosure

saeta, -ae, *n.* f. bristle

saevio, saevire, saevii, saevitum, *v.* to rage, be in a rage

saevitia, -ae, *n.* f. savagery

saevus, -a, -um, *adj.* savage

sagitta, -ae, *n.* f. arrow

saliva, -ae, *n.* f. saliva

salivo (1), *v.* to spit out, salivate

salsus, -a, -um, *adj.* salted

saltatio, -ionis, *n.* f. dancing

saltem, *adv.* at least, at any rate

salto (1), *v.* to dance, pantomime

saltus, -us, *n.* m. a grove, pasture

salubris, -is, -e, *adj.* healthful

salus, salutis, *n.* f. health, safety

saluto (1), *v.* to greet, (esp. the early morning greeting from a client to a patron)

salveo, salvere, salvui, *v.* to be healthy, hail (*imperative*: greetings)

salvus, -a, -um, *adj.* safe, healthy, whole

Samius, -a, -um, *adj.* from the island Samos

Samnites, Samnitium, *n.* m. pl. the Samnites, inhabitants of Samnium

sancio, sancire, sanxi, sanctum, *v.* to ratify, sanction, degree

sane, *adv.* to be sure, rightly, by all means

sanguis, sanguinis, *n.* m. blood

sanguisuga, -ae, *n.* f. blood-sucker

saniosus, -a, -um, *adj.* bloody

sapiens, sapientis, *adj.* wise

sapientia, -ae, *n.* f. wisdom

sapio, sapere, sapivi, *v.* to taste, be wise

sapor, saporis, *n.* m. taste, flavor

sarmentum, -i, *n.* n. brushwood, twigs

satis, *adv.* n. enough

satyrus, -i, *n.* m. satyr

scaena, -ae, *n.* f. stage of a theater

scala, ae, *n.* f. ladder, stairs

scalpo, scalpere, scalpsi, scalptum, *v.* to engrave, sculpt

scansilis, -is, -e, *adj.* climbable

scateo, scatere, *v.* to bubble up, teem

scelero (1), *v.* to defile, desecrate

scelus, sceleris, *n.* n. crime, wicked deed

scientia, -ae, *n.* f. knowledge, science

scio, scire, scivi, scitum, *v.* to know

scirpus, -i, *n.* m. rush

scirros, -i, *n.* m. tumor

scorpio, -ionis, *n.* m. scorpion, a type of catapult

scriba, -ae, *n.* m. scribe, clerk

scribo, scribere, scripsi, scriptum, *v.* to write

scrinium, -i, *n.* n. a chest, box for books

scutum, -i, *n.* shield

Scythia, -ae, *n.* f. the country Scythia, North and East of the Black Sea

secessus, us, *n.* departure, separation

seco, secare, secui, sectum, *v.* to cut, cut off

secundus, -a, -um, *adj.* second, favorable, following

securis, -is, *n.* f. axe

securitas, -tatis, *n.* f. security, lack of care, unconcern

secus, *adv.* otherwise; *non secus ac = non aliter ac*, not otherwise than

sed, *conj.* but

sedecim, *adj.* sixteen

sedeo, sedere, sedi, sessum, *v.* to sit

sedes, sedis, *n.* f. seat

seditio, -ionis, *n.* f. sedition, civil insurrection

sella, -ae, *n.* f. chair, seat

semel, *adj.* once

semen, seminis, *n.* n. seed

semianimus, -a, -um, *adj.* half-alive, half-dead

semifer, semifera, semiferum, *adj.* half-wild

semipes, semipedis, *n.* m. a half foot

semper, *adv.* always

senator, -oris, *n.* m. senator

senatus, -us, *n.* m. senate

senecta, -ae, *n.* f. variant of "senectus"

senectus, senectutis, *n.* f. old age

senesco, senescere, senui, *v.* to grow old

senex, senis, *n.* and *adj.* old, old man

senilis, -is, -e, *adj.* pertaining to the old

senium, -i, *n.* n. old age, decline, decay

sensus, -us, *n*. m. sense

sententia, -ae, *n*. f. opinion, judgment, thought

sentio, sentire, sensi, sensum, *v*. to feel, discern

separo (1), *v*. to disjoin, sever, separate

sepelio, sepelire, sepelivi, sepultum, *v*. to bury, inter

septem, *n*. seven

septeni, -ae, a, *adv*. seven at a time, seven by seven

septentrio, septentrionis, *n*. one of the seven stars forming the Great Bear

septimus, -a, -um, *adj*. seventh

sepulcrum, -i, *n*. tomb

sepultura, -ae, *n*. f. burial

sequax, sequacis, *adj*. following, pliant

sequor, sequi, secutus, *v*. to follow, pursue

serenus, -a, -um, *adj*. clear, bright, serene

Seres, Serum, *n*. pl. the Silk People

series, seriei, *n*. f. series, succession

sermo, sermonis, *n*. m. speech, discourse

serpo, serpere, serpsi, serptum, *v*. to creep, crawl

serra, -ae, *n*. f. saw

serus, -a, -um, *adj*. late

servitium, -i, *n*. n. slavery

servitus, servitutis, *n*. f. slavery

servo (1), *v*. to preserve, save

servus, -i, *n*. m. slave, servant

sesquipedalis, -is, -e, *adj*. a foot and a half long

sestertius, -i, *n*. m. sesterce

sex, *n. indecl*. six

sexageni, -ae, -a, *adj*. sixty each

sexage(n)simus, -a, -um, *adj*. sixtieth

sextus, -a, -um, *adj*. sixth

sexus, -us, *n*. m. a sex

Sibylla, -ae, *n*. f. a prophetess

sic, *adv*. thus, so

sicco (1), *v*. to dry

Sicilia, -ae, *n*. f. the island Sicily

Siculus, -a, -um, *adj*. pertaining to Sicily or to the native people of Sicily

sicut, *adv*. just as

sicuti, *adv*. see "sicut"

Sicyon, -onis, *n.* f. a town in the Peloponnese near the Isthmus

sideralis, -is, -e, *adj.* pertaining to the stars

sido, sidere, sidi, *v.* to sit, settle

sidus, sideris, *n.* n. star, constellation

significatio, -ionis, *n.* f. significance, indication

significo (1), *v.* to signify, indicate

signum, -i, *n.* n. sign, military standard, statue

silex, silicis, *n.* f. flint

silva, -ae, *n.* f. wood, forest

silvestris, -is, -e, *adj.* pertaining to a forest

similis, -is, -e, *adj.* similar, like

similitudo, -tudinis, *n.* f. likeness, resemblance

simplex, simplicis *adj.* simple, plain, unmixed

simul, *adv.* at the same time

simulacrum, -i, *n.* n. likeness, image

singuli, -ae, -a, *adj. pl.* individual, single

sinister, sinistra, sinistrum, *adj.* on the left

sino, sinere, sivi, situm, *v.* to allow, suffer, permit, place

sinus, -us, *n.* m. fold, bosom, bay

siquidem, *adv.* if indeed, since indeed

sisto, sistere, stiti, *v.* to stand, cause to stand

sitis, sitis, *n.* f. thirst

situs, -us, *n.* m. location, position, situation

sive, *conj.* or if, whether

soccus, -i, *n.* m. a slipper worn characteristically in comedies

socer, soceri, *n.* m. father-in-law

societas, -tatis, *n.* alliance

sol, solis, *n.* m. sun

solarium, -i, *n.* n. sundial

soleo, solere, solitus, *v.* to be accustomed to, used to

solidus, -a, -um, *adj.* firm, dense, solid

solitarius, -a, -um, *adj.* solitary, alone

solitudo, solitudinis, *n.* f. solitary, loneliness

solivagus, -a, -um, *adj.* wandering alone

sollemnis, -is, -e, *adj.* appointed, established, solemn, religiously fixed

sollertia, -ae, *n.* f. shrewdness, ingenuity

sollicitudo, -tudinis, *n.* f. anxiety, uneasiness

solum, -i, *n.* n. ground, soil

solus, -a, -um, *adj.* alone, sole, only

somnio (1), *v.* to dream

somnium, -i, *n.* n. dream

somnus, -i, *n.* m. sleep

sopio, sopire, sopivi, sopitum, *v.* to lull to sleep

sorbeo, sorbere, sorbui, *v.* to suck up, swallow, absorb

sordidus, -a, -um, *adj.* low, base, foul

soror, sororis, *n.* f. sister

sors, sortis, *n.* f. rank, share, order, lot

spado, spadonis, *n.* m. eunuch

spatium, -i, *n.* n. space

species, -ei, *n.* f. appearance

specillum, -i, *n.* n. probe, eye-dropper

specimen, -minis, *n.* n. proof, evidence, token, a thing seen

spectaculum, -i, *n.* n. spectacle

specto (1), *v.* to look at, gaze at

speculor, speculari, speculatus, *v.* to observe, spy

speculum, -i, *n.* n. mirror

specus, -us, *n.* m. cave

spelunca, -ae, *n.* f. cave

sperno, spernere, sprevi, spretum, *v.* to scorn, spurn

spes, spei, *n.* f. hope, expectation

sphaera, -ae, *n.* f. globe, sphere

spina, -ae, *n.* f. thorn, spine

spiritus, -us, *n.* m. breath, spirit

spiro (1), *v.* to breathe

spithama, -ae, *n.* f. *spithamos*, a span

spolium, -i, *n.* n. spoil, booty

sponsio, -ionis, *n.* f. promise

sponte, *n.* f. (ablative *sponte* and genitive *spontis* only) of free will

squama, -ae, *n.* f. scale

stabulum, -i, *n.* n. stable, standing place, dwelling

stadium, -i, *n.* n. a stade, length of a stadium (approximately 202 yards)

statim, *adv.* immediately

statuo, statuere, statui, statutum, *v.* to set upright, construct, appoint

stella, -ae, *n.* f. star, meteor

sterilesco, sterilescere, *v.* to grow sterile

sterilis, -is, e, *adj.* barren, unprofitable

sterno, sternere, stravi, stratum, *v.* to lay low, flatten

sternuo, sternuere, sternui, *v.* to sneeze

stipendium, -i, *n.* n. tribute, soldier's pay, tour of duty

stipes, stipitis, *n.* m. log, trunk, bole

stipo (1), *v.* to crowd together

stirps, stirpis, *n.* f. stalk, stock

sto, stare, steti, statum, *v.* to stand, stop

stomachus, -i, *n.* m. stomach, irritation, taste, liking

strages, -is, *n.* f. confusion, disordered mass, heap

stragulus, -a, -um, *adj.* covering, spread

strangulo (1), *v.* to strangle, choke, suffocate

stridor, stridoris, *n.* m. shrill sound, shriek

structura, -ae, *n.* f. structure, arrangement

strues, -is, *n.* f. pile

studium, -i, *n.* n. enthusiasm, study

suadeo, suadere, suasi, suasum, *v.* (+ dat. of person) to persuade, advise

suarius, -a, -um, *adj.* pertaining to swine

subeo, subire, subivi, subiturus, *adv.* to enter, approach, follow (esp. in secret)

subigo, subigere, subegi, subactum, *v.* to bring under, subjugate

subinde, *adv.* immediately, forthwith

sublimis, -is, -e, *adj.* sublime, uplifted

sublimitas, -tatis, *n.* f. loftiness

submitto = summitto

suboles, -is, *n.* f. offspring

subsisto, subsistere, substiti, *v.* to stand still, loiter, remain

subsolanus, -a, -um, *v.* eastern

subter, *prep.* (+ acc) under, beneath

subvenio, subvenire, subveni, subventum, *v.* to come to aid

succedo, succedere, successi, successum, *v.* to enter, submit, follow, succeed

successio, -ionis, *n.* f. succession

succurro, succurrere, succurri, succursum, *v.* to occur, meet, aid

sucus, -i, *n.* m. juice

sudor, sudoris, *n.* m. sweat

sufficio, sufficere, suffeci, suffectum, *v.* to supply, take the place of, be sufficient

suffodio, suffodere, suffodi, suffosum, *v.* to pierce, dig under, undermine

suffragium, -i, *n.* n. vote, the right to vote

suggillatio, -ionis, *n.* f. bruise, black-and-blue mark

summitto, summittere, summisi, summissum, *v.* to send under, submit
summus, -a, -um, *adj.* highest
sumo, sumere, sumpsi, sumptum, *v.* to take up, assume
super, *adv, prep.* (+ acc.) over, on top
superbia, -ae, *n.* f. pride, pridefulness, haughtiness
superbus, -a, -um, *adj.* proud, haughty, lofty
superfeto, superfetare, *v.* to conceive again while already pregnant
superiacio, superiacere, superieci, superjectum, *v.* to throw over, exaggerate
supernato (1), *v.* to swim over, float
supero (1), *v.* to overcome, surpass, survive
superstes, superstitis, *adj.* survivor, bystander
superstitio, -ionis, *n.* f. superstition
supersum, superesse, superfui, superfuturum, *v.* to remain, to be in abundance
supervacuus, -a, -um, *adj.* superfluous, useless, redundant
superventus, -us, *n.* m. arrival, going over
supinus, -a, -um, *adj.* lying on the back, bent back
supplex, supplicis, *adj.* beseeching, suppliant
supplicium, -i, *n.* n. supplication, torture
supplico (1), *v.* to kneel to (someone), beseech, beg
supra, *adv.* above, on top
suspecto (1), to look up at
suspicio, suspicere, suspexi, suspectum, *v.* to look up at, look up to, mistrust, suspect
sustineo, sustinere, sustinui, sustentum, *v.* to hold up, sustain
sutrinus, -a, -um, *adj.* pertaining to a shoemaker, cobbler
suus, -a, -um, *adj. reflexive.* his, her, its, their own
Sybaris, Syabaritis, *n.* f. a Greek town of southern Italy
Syracusanus, -a, -um, *adj.* pertaining to the city Syracuse
Syracusi, -orum, *n.* m. the people of Syracuse
Syria, -ae, *n.* f. Syria
Syrticus, -a, -um, *adj.* pertaining to Syrtis, the sand-bank on the northern coast of Africa

taberna, -ae, *n.* f. tavern
tabes, tabis, *n.* f. wasting, melting
tabificus, -a, -um, *adj.* melting, corroding, dissolving
tabula, -ae, *n.* f. tablet, table

taceo, tacere, tacui, tacitum, *v.* to be silent

tacitus, -a, -um, *adj.* silent

tactus, -us, *n.* m. touch

taedet, taedere, taeduit, taesum, *v.* (+ gen. of cause of emotion and + acc. of person affected) *impersonal,* it disgusts

taedium, -i, *n.* n. weariness, loathing, disgust

talentum, -i, *n.* n. a talent, a unit of weight used to measure large sums of money

talio, -ionis, *n.* f. punishment, retaliation

talis, -is, e, *adj.* such

tamen, *adv.* yet, however, nevertheless

tamquam, *adv.* as if

tango, tangere, tetigi, tactum, *v.* to touch

tantus, -a, -um, *adj.* so much, so great

Taprobane, -es, *n.* f. an island in the Indian Ocean, Sri Lanka

tardo (1), *v.* to slow, delay, hinder

tardus, -a, -um, *adj.* slow, sluggish

taurus, -i, *n.* m. bull

taxation, -ionis, *n.* f. appraisal, estimation

tectum, -i, *n.* n. roof

tegimentum, -i, *n.* = *tegumentum,* covering

tego, tegere, texi, tectum, *v.* to cover

tegulae, -arum, *n.* f. pl. roof-tiles

tellus, telluris, *n.* f. the earth

telum, -i, *n.* n. weapon, missile weapon

temperies, -iei, *n.* f. a mixture, tempering, temperature

tempero (1), *v.* to manage, temper, regulate

tempestas, -tatis, *n.* f. tempest, storm, time, weather

tempestivus, -a, -um, *adj.* timely, seasonable

templum, -i, *n.* n. temple

tempto (1), to try, attempt

tempus, temporis, *n.* n. time

tenebrae, -arum, *n.* f. pl. darkness, murk

teneo, tenere, tenui, tentus, *v.* to hold, grip

tenor, tenoris, *n.* m. a holding fast, career, tenor

tepesco, tepescere, tepui, *v.* to grow warm

ter, *adv.* three times

terebra, -ae, *n.* f. gimlet, augur

tergum, -i, *n.* n. back

tergus, -oris, *n.* n. = *tergum*

terminus, -i, *n.* m. end, boundary, limit

terni, -ae, -a, *adj.* three each

tero, terere, trivi, tritum, *v.* to wear, rub

terra, -ae, *n.* f. earth

terreo, terrere, terrui, territum, *v.* to terrify, frighten

terrestris, -is, -e, *adj.* pertaining to the earth

tertius, -a, -um, *adj.* third

tessera, -ae, *n.* f. token, watchword

testa, -ae, *n.* f. brick tile

testamentum, -i, *n.* testament, will

testimonium, -i, *n.* evidence, testimony

testis, -is, *n.* m. witness

testor, testari, testatus, *v.* to testify, bear witness to

testudo, testudinis, *n.* f. tortoise, tortoise-shell

tetartemorion, -i, *n.* one fourth of the Zodiac

textile, -is, *n.* n. cloth

textilis, -is, -e, *adj.* woven, texile

Thapsus, -i, *n.* m. a city in Africa

theatralis, -is, -e, *n.* pertaining to the theater

theatrum, -i, *n.* theater

Thebae, -arum, *n.* f. pl. the city Thebes in Boeotia

Thebani, -orum, *n.* m. pl. the people of Thebes

thorax, thoracis, *n.* m. chest, breastplate

tibia, -ae, *n.* f. pipe

Ticinus, -i, *n.* m. a river in Cisalpine Gaul, site of a battle with Hannibal in November, 218 BCE

tigris, tigris or **tigridis,** *n.* m/f. tiger, tigress

timeo, timere, timui, *v.* to fear

tirocinium, -i, *n.* n. a soldier's first tour of duty, such soldiers

titulus, -i, *n.* m. title, placard

toga, -ae, *n.* f. the toga

togatus, -a, -um, *adj.* wearing a toga

tolero (1), *v.* to tolerate, endure

tollo, tollere, sustuli, sublatum, *v.* lift up, take up, extol, destroy

tonsor, tonsoris, *n.* m. barber

tormentum, -i, *n.* n. any catapult-like siege weapon, torment

tornus, -i, *n.* lathe

torpeo, torpere, *v.* to be stiff, numb

torqueo, torquere, torsi, tortus, *v.* to torture, twist, whirl

torquis, torquis, *n.* m.f. a torque, twisted necklace, collar

torreo, torrere, torrui, tostum, *v.* to bake, roast, burn, parch

torvitas, torvitatis, *n.* f. wildness, savageness, severity, sternness

tot, *adv.* to so many

totidem, *adv.* the same number

totiens, *adv.* so many times

totus, -a, -um, *adj.* all, whole, entire

tracto (1), *v.* to treat, handle, manage

tractus, -us, *n.* m. tract, extent of space, dragging, drawing

trado, tradere, tradidi, traditum, *v.* to hand over, deliver, hand down

traduce, traducere, traduxi, traductum, *v.* to carry over, translate

trafero = *transfero*

tragicus, -a, -um, *adj.* pertaining to tragedy

traho, trahere, traxi, tractum, *v.* to drag, draw, haul

tralaticius, -a, -um, *adj.* handed down, hereditary

trans, *prep.* (+ acc.) across

transcendo, transcendere, transcendi, transcensum, *v.* to climb across

transeo, transire, transivi, transitum, *v.* to pass over, go across

transfero, transferre, transtuli, translatus/tralatus, *v.* to bring over, transport

transfiguratio, -ionis, *n.* f. change in shape

transgredior, transgredi, transgressus, *v.* to cross over, go over, climb over

transvolo (1), *v.* to fly across

trapeta, -ae, *n.* f. oil-mill

Trasimennus, -a, -um, *adj.* pertaining to Trasimene, a lake south of the Po, site of a battle with Hannibal in April 217 BCE

traveho = **transveho, transvehere, transvexi, transvectum,** *v.* to transport

traversus, -a, -um, *adj.* "transversus," orthogonal, cross-wise

trecenti, -ae, -a, *adj.* three hundred

tredecim, *adj.* thirteen

tres, tres, tria, *adj.* three

tribunatus, -us, *n.* m. tribuneship

tribunus, -i, *n.* m. tribune

tribuo, tribuere, tribui, tributum, *v.* to attribute, distribute

triceni, -ae, -a, *adj.* thirty, by thirties

triclinium, -i, *n.* n. dining-chamber, the couch therein

triduum, -i, *n.* n. three-day period

triennium, -i, *n.* n. a three-year period

triginta, *n.* n. thirty

trimatus, -us, *n.* f. three years of age

trimenstris, -is, -e, *adj.* of three months

trini, -ae, -a, *adj.* three each

triplico (1), *v.* to triple

triremis, -is, -e, *adj.* having three banks of oars

tristis, -is, -e, *adj.* grim, sad, sorrowful

triumphalis, -is, -e, *adj.* triumphal

triumpho (1), *v.* to triumph

triumphus, -i, *n.* m. triumph, triumphal procession

triumvir, -i, *n.* m. one of a board of three men

triumviratus, -us, *n.* m. triumvirate

Trogodytae, -arum, *n.* m. pl. Troglodytes, people of Ethiopia who dwell in caves

tropaeum, -i, *n.* n. a trophy, mark of victory

trucido (1), *v.* to cut to pieces, savage

truculentus, -a, -um, *adj.* savage, ferocious

truncus, -i, *n.* m. trunk, block

tuba, -ae, *n.* f. war-trumpet

tumeo, tumere, *v.* to swell

tumor, tumoris, *n.* m. swelling, state of being swollen, excitement

tumultuor, tumultuari, tumultuatus, *v.* to be in confusion, tumult

tumultus, -i, *n.* uproar, commotion

tunc, *adv.* then, at that time

turba, -ae, *n.* f. crowd, multitude

turbo (1), *v.* to disturb, confuse

turgidus, -a, -um, *adj.* swollen

turma, -ae, *n.* f. band (usually of cavalry)

turris, -is, *n.* f. tower, turret

turritus, -a, -um, *adj.* towered, turreted

tutor, tutari, tutatus, *v.* to watch over, guard

tutus, -a, -um, *adj.* safe

tyrannicida, -ae, *n.* m. a tyrannicide

tyrannus, -i, *n.* m. tyrant

Tyrius, -a, -um, *adj.* pertaining to the city Tyre, pertaining to the color purple (for which Tyre was famous)

uber, uberis, *n.* n. udder, teat
ubertas, -tatis, *n.* f. richness, abundance
ubi, *adv., conj.* where, when
ullus, -a, -um, *adj.* any, anyone, anything
ulterior, -ior, -ius, *adj.* further
ultimus, -a, -um, *adj.* furthest
ultra, *adv.* beyond, further beyond
umbra, -ae, *n.* f. shade, shadow
umerus, -i, *n.* m. shoulder
umor, umoris, *n.* m. liquid, fluid, moisture
umquam, *adv.* ever
uncia, -ae, *n.* f. one-twelfth, ounce, inch
unde, *adv,* from where, from which, whence
undecentum, *adj.* ninety-nine
undeciens, *adv.* eleven times
undecimus, -a, -um, *adj.* eleventh
undequadragiens, *adv.* thirty-nine times
unguentarius, -a, -um, *adj.* pertaining to perfume; *fem.*: a female perfumer
unguentum, -i, *n.* oil, perfume
unguiculus, -i, *n.* m. finger-nail
unguis, -is, *n.* m. nail, claw
unicus, -a, -um, *adj.* one, single, only
unitas, -tatis, *n.* f. oneness, unity
universitas, -tatis, *n.* f. the whole
universus, -a, -um, *adj.* whole, entire
unus, -a, -um, *adj.* one
urbs, urbis, *n.* f. city
urgeo, urgere, ursi *v.* = *urgueo*
urgueo, urguere, ursi, *v.* to drive, urge, impel
urna, -ae, *n.* f. urn, pot, jar
usquam, *adv.* anywhere
usque, *adv.* all the way
usurpo (1), *v.* to use, make use of, employ
usus, -us, *n.* m. use, experience, employ
uterlibet, utralibet, utrumlibet, *pron.* either of two, whichever you please
uterque, utraque, utrumque, *pron.* each of two
uterus, -i, *n.* m. womb
Uticensis, -is, -e, *adj.* pertaining to the city Utica in northern Africa

utinam, *adv.* would that (+ subjunctive)
utique, *adv.* in any case, at any rate
utor, uti, usus, *v.* (+ abl.) to use, employ
uva, -ae, *n.* f. grape
uxor, uxoris, *n.* f. wife

vacatio, -ionis, *n.* f. freedom, exemption
vacuus, -a, -um, *adj.* empty, free
vadimonium, -i, *n.* n. bail, security
vadum, -i, *n.* n. a shallow place, ford, body of water
vagina, -ae, *n.* f. sheath, scabbard
vagitus, -us, *n.* m. crying, wailing, squalling
vagor, vagari, vagatus, *v.* to stroll about
vagus, -a, -um, *adj.* wandering
valeo, valere, valui, *n.* to be healthy
validus, -a, -um, *adj.* strong, hale, healthy
valitudo, valitudinis, *n.* f. health
valles, vallis, *n.* f. hollow, vale, valley
vanitas, -tatis, *n.* f. emptiness
vanus, -a, -um, *adj.* empty
vapor, vaporis, *n.* m. steam, vapor
varietas, -tatis, *n.* f. variety, difference
vario (1), *v.* to vary, change, cause to change
varius, -a, -um, *adj.* varied, various
vas, vasis, *n.* n. vessel, utensil
vasarium, -i, *n.* n. record archive
vastitas, -tatis, *n.* f. emptiness, waste, desert
vaticinium, -i, *n.* prophecy
vaticinor (1), *v.* to prophesy
vatis, vatis, *n.* m. bard, priest, poet
vectis, -is, *n.* m. bar, spike, crowbar
vehiculum, -i, *n.* n. vehicle
veho, vehere, vexi, vectum, *v.* to carry, convey
vel, *conj.* or; *particle* indeed
velitaris, -is, -e, *adj.* pertaining to the vellites
vellus, velleris, *n.* n. fleece, pelt, hide
velo (1), *v.* to veil, cover
velocitas, -tatis, *n.* f. swiftness, speed

velox, velocis, *adj.* swift
velum, -i, *n.* n. sail
velut, *adv.* just as
veluti, *adv.* see "velut"
vena, -ae, *n.* f. vein
venabulum, -i, *n.* n. hunting spear
venatus, -us, *n.* m. hunting
venenum, -i, *n.* n. poison, venom
veneratio, -tione, *n.* f. respect, veneration
vendo, vendere, vendidi, venditum, *v.* to sell
venio, venire, veni, ventum, *v.* to come
venor (1), *v.* to hunt
venter, ventris, *n.* m. belly
ventus, -i, *n.* m. wind
Venus, Veneris, *n.* f. Venus, sexual intercourse
verbena, -ae, *n.* f. foliage, herbage
verber, verberis, *n.* n. whip, scourge
verbero (1), *v.* to lash, beat
verbum, -i, *n.* n. word
vere, *adv.* truly, not falsely
verecundia, -ae, *n.* f. shame, modesty
vereor, vereri, veritum, *v.* to fear
vergo, vergere, *v.* to verge, incline, bend, tend
veridicus, -a, -um, *adj.* truth-speaking
veritas, veritatis, *n.* f. truth
verno, vernare, *v.* to bloom, be green, be like spring
vero, *adv.* truly, in truth, indeed
versutus, -a, -um, *adj.* clever, shrewd
vertex, verticis, *n.* m. whirlpool, eddy, swirl
vertigo, vertiginis, *n.* f. spinning, dizziness
verto, vertere, verti, versum, *v.* to turn
verum, *adv.* truly, but
verus, -a, -um, *adj.* true
vesanus, -a, -um, *adj.* insane
vescor, vesci, *v.* to feed, eat
vescus, -a, -um, *adj.* small, thin, feeble
vespera, -ae, *n.* f. evening
vestigium, -i, *n.* trace, footprint

vestio, vestire, vestivi, vestitum, *v.* to dress, clothe

vestis, -is, *n.* f. clothes, garment

veto, vetare, vetui, vetitum, *v.* to forbid

vetus, veteris, *adj.* old, ancient

vetustus, -a, -um, *adj.* old, ancient

vexatio, -ionis, *n.* f. shaking, agitation

via, -ae, *n.* f. road, way

viator, -toris, *n.* m. traveler

viceni, -ae, -a, *adj.* twenty each

viciens, *adv.* twenty times

vicinus, -a, -um, *adj.* neighboring

vicis, vicis, *n.* f. change, alternation

victor, -oris, *n.* m. victor

victoria, -ae, *n.* f. victory

victrix, vitricis, *adj.* victorious, victor (female)

victus, -us, *n.* m. food, nourishment

vicus, -i, *n.* m. village, row of houses

video, videre, vidi, visum, *v.* to see (passive: seem)

vigilo (1), *v.* to keep watch, stay awake at night

vigilia, -ae, *n.* f. wakefulness

viginti, *n. indeclinable.* twenty

vigor, vigoris, *n.* m. force, vigor

vilis, -is, -e, *adj.* cheap, trifling

vilitas, -tatis, *n.* f. cheapness

villosus, -a, -um, *adj.* shaggy

villus, -i, *n.* m. shaggy hair

vinco, vincere, vici, victum, *v.* to conquer, win

vinculum, -i, *n.* n. fetter, chain

vindemio, vindemiare, *v.* to gather grapes

vinum, -i, *n.* n. wine

violentia, -ae, *n.* f. violence

violo (1), *v.* to injure, treat with violence

viperinus, -i, *n.* m. a snake

virga, -ae, *n.* f. rod, stick, wand

virgo, virginis, *n.* f. maiden

virilis, -is, -e, *adj.* pertaining to a man

virilitas, -tatis, *n.* f. manliness

virtus, -tutis, *n.* f. virtue, manliness

virus, -i, *n.* n. poison

vis, vis, pl. **vires, virium**, *n.* f. force, strength

viscus, visceris, *n.* n. internal organs

viso, visere, visi, visum, *v.* to look at, see, behold

visus, -us, *n.* m. vision, sight

vita, -ae, *n.* f. life

vitalis, -is, -e, *adj.* vital, pertaining to life

vitilis, -is, -e, *adj.* woven, made of wicker

vitium, -i, *n.* n. vice

vittatus, -a, -um, *adj.* dressed in fillets, beribboned

vitulus, -i, *n.* m. calf

vivax, vivacis, *adj.* long-lived, holding to life

vivo, vivere, vixi, victum, *v.* to live

vivus, -a, -um, *adj.* living, live, alive

vix, *adv.* scarcely

voco (1), *v.* to call

volo, velle, volui, *v.* to wish, want

volo (1), *v.* to fly

volucer, volucris, volucre, *adj.* swift, winged, flying

volumen, -minis, *n.* n. volume, roll

voluntas, -tatis, *n.* f. will, wish, desire

voluptas, -tatis, *n.* f. pleasure

volva, -ae, *n.* f. wrapping, covering, womb

volvo, volvere, volui, volutum, *v.* to turn, roll

vomica, -ae, *n.* f. an ulcer, boil, cyst

votivus, a, um, *adj.* pertaining to a vow

votum, -i, *n.* n. a vow

voveo, vovere, vovi, votum, *v.* to vow, promise

vox, vocis, *n.* f. voice, utterance

vulgaris, -is, -e, *adj.* pertaining to the common people

vulgo (1), *v.* to publish, make commonly known

vulgus, -i, *n.* n. the common people, the mob

vulnero (1), *v.* to wound

vulnus, vulneris, *n.* n. wound

vultus, -us, *n.* m. face, expression

Indices

Of the following indices, the General Index gives citations for people, places, and topics only where they have a non-trivial treatment. References to the Latin are given first and in bold, while references to the commentary are in plain text. The indices of proper names, places, and ethnonyms, in contrast, give every instance of the word as it occurs in the Latin text. To find commentary on these terms, simply turn to the corresponding section of the commentary or cross-reference with the General Index.

General Index

Index of Proper Names in Book VII

Curiatii 33
Curio, Manius 166
Curio senior *see* Scribonius Curio,
    Gaius
Curius Dentatus, Manius 68
Cyclops 10, 195, 197–8
Cymbri 86
Cyrni 27
Cyrus the Great 88, 205

Dactylus 197
Daedalus 198, 205, 209
Damastes 154, 207
Damon 17
Danaus 195, 206
Dando 155
Daphnis 128
Darius III 108
Delas 197
Delphus 203
Demetrius Poliorcetes 126
Democritus 189
Demosthenes 110
Diana 125, 127
Dinochares 125
Diodorus Siculus 180
Diogenes Cynicus 80
Dionysius II of Syracuse 110, 180
Domitius Ahenobarbus, Lucius 186
Domitius Corbulo, Gnaeus 39
Drusus *see* Claudius Drusus
    Germanicus, Decimus
Duris 30

Ennius, Quintus 101, 114
Ephorus 155
Epicharmus 192
Epigenes 160, 193
Epimenides 154, 175
Epius 202
Erichtonius 197, 202
Erythras 206
Euchir 205
Eudoxus 24
Eumolpus 199
Eupalamus 209
Euryalus 194
Euthymenes 76
Euthymys 152
Eutychis 34

Fabius 150
Fabius Ambustus, Marcus 133
Fabius Maximus, Quintus (cons. 121
    BC) 166
Fabius Maximus, Quintus (cons. 45
    BC) 181
Fabius Maximus Gurges, Quintus 133
Fabius Maximus Paulus 150
Fabius Maximus Rullianus, Quintus
    133
Fabius Maximus Verrucosus
    Cunctator, Quintus 156
Fabius Senator 44
Fabius Vestalis 213
Felix 186
Fidustius, Marcus 134
Flavius Vespasianus Caesar (I), Titus
    (emperor Vespasian) 162
Flavius Vespasianus Caesar (II), Titus
    (emperor Titus) 162
Fonteius Capito, Gaius 84
Fufius Salvius 83
Fullonius, Titus 159
Fulvius Curvus, Lucius 136
Fulvius Flaccus 120
Fulvius Flaccus, Quintus 157

Gabbara 74
Gabienus 178–9
Gaius princeps *see* Iulius Caesar
    Augustus Germanicus, Gaius
Galeria Copiola 158
Gallio Annaeanus *see* Iunius Gallio
    Annaeanus, Lucius
Ganges 25
Gellius, Gnaeus 192, 194, 197–8
Germanicus *see* Claudius Drusus
    Nero, Germanicus
Glitius Gallus, Publius 39
Gorgias Siculus 156
Gracchus, Gaius *see* Sempronius
    Gracchus, Gaius
Gracchus, Tiberius *see* Sempronius
    Gracchus, Tiberius
Gyges 151, 205
Gymnetae 28
Gymnosophists 22

Hannibal 35, 104
Harmodius 87

Index of Places and Ethnonyms in Book VII

Gaditanus 156
Gallia 76, 105
Galli 104
Germania 84
Ges Clithron / Γῆς Κλεῖθρον 10
Gnidius 127
Gnosius 125, 154, 175
Graecia 89, 119, 123, 192, 195, 205–6, 212
Graecostasis 212
Graecus 8, 107, 112, 119, 175, 210

Hellespontus 13, 206
Hiberia 98
Hispania 96

Idaeus 197
Illyri 16, 123
Illyricum 149
Imaus mons 11
India 21, 23–5, 28, 30
Indi 24–5, 27–8, 30
Iolcus 205
Ionis 210
Isara (flumen) 166
Isthmus 205
Italia 9, 15, 39, 113, 149, 152, 160, 164, 211
Iudaea 65
Iudaei 98

Lacedaemon 84
Lacedaemonius 84, 109, 119, 133, 200
Laestrygones 9
Latiaris 117
Latinus 210
Latium 136, 193
Lilybaeum 85
Locri 152
Lutmii 155
Lydius 204
Lydus 195, 197, 205

Macedonia 111
Macedonicus 142
Maeoti 97
Magnetes 126
Mare Rubrum 97, 206
Marsici 34
Massilia 186
Megarensis 196

Messenius 200
Milesius 203
Mysus 206

Nilus 33, 206

Oceanus Britannicus 206
Olympia 86, 119, 152, 205
Olympius 127
Ophiogenes 13
Ostia 33

Padus 162
Palatium 210
Panchaia 197
Pangaeus 197
Pannonicus 148
Paphlagonia 98
Parius 13
Parma 162–3
Parthi 135
Pelasgi 193
Peloponnesus 33
Persae 108
Perusinus 148
Pharsalia 94
Pheraeus 166
Philippensis 148
Phoenix 192, 195, 197, 201, 208–9
Phrygius 204
Phryx 197, 199, 202, 204
Pisae 181
Pisaurensis 128
Placentia 105, 163
Plataeae 209
Poeni 198
Pontus 98
Proconnesius 49
Proconnesus 174
Prusiensis 124
Psophidius 151
Punicus 85, 139, 212, 214
Pyrenaeus 96
Pythius 119, 205

Rhodius 110, 182, 208
Rhodos 126
Roma 19, 115, 120–1, 136, 140, 175, 181, 211–12
Rostra 212, 214

Index of Proper Names in Book VIII (1–34)

Index of Place Names and Ethnonyms in Book VIII (1–34)